the dark end of the street

A M E R I C A N   C U L T U R E

Cutting across traditional boundaries between the human and social sciences, volumes in the American Culture series study the multiplicity of cultural practices from theoretical, historical, and ethnographic perspectives by examining culture's production, circulation, and consumption.

Edited by Stanley Aronowitz, Nancy Fraser, and George Lipsitz

the dark end of the street

Maria Damon

American Culture 7

 University of Minnesota Press

Minneapolis

London

For copyright information see pages 304-5.

Published by the University of Minnesota Press
2037 University Avenue Southeast, Minneapolis, MN 55455
Printed in the United States of America on acid-free paper

Library of Congress Cataloging-in-Publication Data

Damon, Maria.
    The dark end of the street : margins in American vanguard poetry / Maria Damon.
        p.   cm. — (American culture ; 7)
    Includes bibliographical references and index.
    ISBN 0-8166-1986-7 (hc : alk. paper). — ISBN 0-8166-1987-5 (pbk. : alk. paper)
        1. American poetry — 20th century — History and criticism.   2. Literature and society — United States — History — 20th century.   3. Experimental poetry, American — History and criticism.   4. Avant-garde (Aesthetics) — United States. 5. Marginality, Social, in literature.   I. Title.   II. Series : American culture (Minneapolis, Minn.) ; 7.
PS325.D36   1993   92-21872
811'.509 — dc20   CIP

The University of Minnesota is an
equal-opportunity educator and employer.

Contents

Pre-Monitions: Definitions, Explanations, Acknowledgments

In this series of case studies, I argue that the American literary avant-garde comes out of the work of the socially marginalized. In the hands of deterritorialized writers, poetry, itself "antidiscursive" in the modern situation, cannot help but produce a level of vanguard experimentation, a shock of defamiliarization, a resonant disorientation that permits new consciousness. My purpose is not to claim that this or that avant-garde is empirically the true one in opposition to others, but rather that, used with a particular valence that both resonates with and alters more traditional uses of the term, the rubric "avant-garde" or "vanguard" has special and urgent meaning when applied to the work of social outsiders. The term "avant-garde" has several meanings on the continuum from specific to vague, from historicist to aestheticist, in current literary studies; I want to briefly review those meanings only to sketch in a rudimentary background and then, returning to the term's etymological derivation, I want to sharpen and bring into focus my own provisional definition in order to examine usefully the writings, lives, and subcultures of a range of twentieth-century American poets: Black/Jewish Beat surrealist Bob Kaufman, Robert Lowell and three unknown teenage women writing in a South Boston Housing Project educational program, gay poets Robert Duncan and Jack Spicer, and last but first, Gertrude Stein, the Jewish lesbian godmother of exciting American writing.

The most commonly used specific historical meaning of "avant-garde" refers to European developments of the early twentieth century, particularly Dadaism, Surrealism, Fauvism. This specificity with regard to Europe's literary history, however, is absent from the modern American scene; there is no clearly defined historical avant-garde. Most of the "high modernists," whose literary styles might make them appropriate for such an epithet, and who were writing at the same time as the Eastern and Western European vanguards, were either apolitical or conservative, and as such so sharply distinguishable from the European avant-garde movements as to forfeit association with them altogether (with the exception, perhaps, of Ezra Pound's brief Vorticist days, and Gertrude Stein, who, as I shall argue at some length, belongs more properly in the category of social outcast-writer than in the company of her coeval male modernists).

Different American literary movements have laid claim to or had attributed to them the honorary status of avant-garde: the bohemian leftist intellectual circles of Greenwich Village and the *Partisan Review*; the Beats' San Francisco incarnation, which latter has been termed the only "indigenous" American avant-garde; the postmodern male fiction writers such as Donald Barthelme, John Hawkes, or Gil Sorrentino, whose works flirt with sur- and antirealism and stretch conventional writing to absurdity; the contemporary language poets who challenge the tyranny of commonsensical referentiality in the service of liberating language into new phenomenological possibilities.[1] In these cases, especially the first two, the term "avant-garde" describes an ideological position vis-à-vis art-and-society rather than a historically specific artistic movement linked to its European counterparts. In the latter instances especially, the term continues to operate as a formalist category if not as a historical one; the *form* of the work challenges received conventions of literary art as reflected in either popular or academic literary models, but breaks new ground that will in turn eventually become overtilled by more timid or less imaginative imitators. This kind of formalist argument, however, reinscribes itself in a conservative aesthetic meritocracy: you can tell it's avant-garde because it is ("probably") destined to survive on the strength of its transcendent artistic merit, to be recognized by posterity in the sense of "[inspiring] future . . . endeavors."[2] In the face of this confusion between the avant-garde as transhistorical formalist orientation and as specific historical category, most literary historians who write about the avant-garde, even the most perceptive and discerning, trace it, if not as a continuous tradition, then as a roster of "great names" and/or movements (as in Charles Russell's excellent *Poets, Prophets, and Revolutionaries: The Literary Avant-Garde from*

Rimbaud through Postmodernism).[3] There seems to be consensus, though, that the term obtains in instances in which socially critical "attitude" and experimental aesthetic praxis are consciously and necessarily linked and foregrounded. Another underlying and some-times explicit criterion of avant-gardism is its vehement and princi-pled opposition to mass and popular culture.

Peter Bürger's *Theory of the Avant-Garde*, by focusing on art as a social institution rather than as an ahistorical category that opposes the social (à la Kostelanetz), offers a salutary analysis that breaks the impasse separating the formalist avant-gardists from the politicos.[4] Departing from the high modernists' exclusively aestheticist orienta-tion, the dadaists, surrealists, and futurists challenged the separation of art from the material sphere. The collage technique especially, in that it incorporated fragments of the material and discursively nor-mative world in contemporaneous juxtaposition, challenges the autonomy of the work of art from the material or social, and also challenges the anti-mass/pop culture stance that is often axiomatic in more naïve definitions of the avant-garde. While the French and Ger-man avant-gardes Bürger chooses to examine are explicitly and pro-grammatically political, I believe it is possible to posit this materialist orientation—this consummate worldliness—as well as a lived cri-tique of social norms in imaginative work that is less programmatic, less easily subsumable under the sheltering label of one "movement."

Given the leeway for difference in this spectrum of approaches, my use of the term "avant-garde" differs but derives from denota-tions of a formal tradition, a historical moment, and a series of names. I want to argue for the avant-garde as writing that pushes at the limits of experience as well as at the limits of conventional form. While each instance of avant-garde writing occurs in a historical con-text, there is not necessarily a continuous historical development linking these instances in a seamless teleological narrative. To bor-row from Phillipe Sollers (whose title *Writing and the Experience of Limits* I consistently misremember, in an echo of David Antin's *talk-ing at the boundaries*, as *Writing at the Limits of Experience*) the "dis-continuity" of the historical field (of writing) breaks with the "pseudo-continuity of all 'literary history' " and, in so breaking, re-veals its strategic points, its "borders ... designated by the words: 'mysticism,' 'eroticism,' 'madness,' 'literature' (this latter taken solely in the sense that entails rupture). Normality of discourse is conceived [in Sollers' "Program"] of as need for a defense (ideology) vis-à-vis these points"[5] While this pronouncement reveals a frankly romantic and subjectivist orientation, it offers an important way to historicize and legitimate antidiscursive modes—"madness," "eroticism," poetic language—and by extension social outsiderhood. Who is better equipped to push literature and sensibility to its limits than the dispossessed, those whose material and social resources are themselves constantly strained to or beyond their limits? In a telling and moving anecdote linking poetry and madness, the confessional poet and chronic mental patient Anne Sexton described with the same words her excitement at encountering her spiritual community first in other "sick" people during a hospitalization and then in other poets in John Holmes's workshop: "These are my people" because like her they "talked Language."[6] It is in this elision of poetry and madness that I want to locate the embodiedness of poetry; the poets and texts written about in this study embody *living critiques* of inhumane social conditions not through their separation from but through their immersion in those conditions.

Under the looser rubric of avant-garde as an (op)position one can occupy at any time and whose contours are contextually determined, it becomes possible to claim that the artistic vanguard in America comes from the social margins. Moreover, if we attend to the meaning of "avant-garde" in its original military capacity, it becomes poignantly clear that the vanguard party, sent out ahead of the main forces, ran the greatest dangers of death or captivity—as front-line forayers, they were also, imminently, cannon fodder. The major empires of Europe were known to send their least esteemed denizens ("citizens" would be a misnomer) into the fray first; the Russians sent the Jews—military service lasted twenty years, and the entire shtetl would say Kaddish for a boy immediately upon his conscription; the British sent their colonials: Sudanese, Australians, and New Zealanders; the French similarly used the Senegalese; during the Viet Nam war and into the present, "minorities" and working-class boys comprise the bulk of active-duty American armed forces. I don't mean to overemphasize a relationship between poetic and military activity (modern gender ideology has more often dictated the opposite) although the poets under discussion in the present study could be said to adopt the roles of guerrilla verbalists in their struggle for survival. However, the military sense of "avant-garde" makes possible an insight central to my thesis: the marginalized, ostensibly most expendable members of the American socius have produced its truly vanguard literature. Their often neglected work becomes canon-fodder in the construction of a respectable façade of American letters that would erase the indigence and illegitimacy of its vital sources. Thus the avant-garde can include mass and popular cultural texts or can at the very least enjoy a productive rather than hostile relationship to them, and it can include work that may not be formally experimental but breaks social taboos and formalist rules in its attempt to create a new consciousness borne of heretofore inexpressible experience.

Although the commonsensical precepts of Newtonian physics are in question today, we know from Foucault and from experience that, in the cultural and political realm of life at least, for every instance of oppression there is a comparable *up*-pression—even if the form this resistance takes is not always readily recognizable as such. The history of the provisional title of this work, from "Poetics and Resistance" to " . . . and Marginality" to " . . . and Minority" to " . . . and Oppression" to, finally, *The Dark End of the Street: Margins in American Vanguard Poetry* illustrates some of the ideas and images I've had to entertain and reject or at least amend to fit a particular vision of cultural and social life in the twentieth-century United States. The term "resistance," while appealing precisely because of its Foucauldian pervasiveness, had to cede before strong evidence that many writers who fit into categories of "oppressed" or "marginal" people do not overtly appear to be engaged in any active political resistance. Bob Kaufman, for example, while he embodied a Beatnik-style resistance to convention, was not actively involved in the Black Arts Movement. Though he constantly acknowledged his debt and connection to jazz and other Black art forms, and while Langston Hughes and others expressed concern about him,[7] his immediate community, both artistic and domestic, consisted of the San Francisco Beat scene rather than any circle of Black writers. "Resistance" implies organization and some degree of intentionality, unity, and unanimity.[8]

The word "oppression" suggested itself because, among other things, it lifts the euphemistic veil from words like "marginal" and "minority," and because it implies verticality rather than lateral dispersion: certain aspects of American life are submerged, perhaps (though this aspect is not apprehensible or admissible to some) in a conceptual hierarchy. (In the same sense in which psychologists speak of re-pression or sup-pression, as a self-destructive containment/ denial of certain truths about one's experience, so op-pression works by forcing down.) The trope of verticality provides an image consistent with the Great Chain of Being, a metaphor that, I argue, underlies most Western poetic texts up through the modernist mode, and begins to recede with the advent of postmodernism's return to the lateral and cofoundational. Thus "oppression" describes a social and textual relationship that is part of the history of this discussion, and certainly continues to color it, but does not currently evoke the most useful or accurate set of metaphoric relations for talking about vanguard poetry. Somewhat akin to "resistance," the word conveys a monolithic sense that each poet is responding to the same repressive conditions in the same way—an absurdity for a book that treats both Robert Lowell and Bob Kaufman, for example—and implies a degree of conscious strategizing to counter these conditions. Both of these words could be associated with a misleading teleological agenda, on my part and also on the part of the writers examined here. These particular words, moreover, have a history and a set of associations that to some extent seem incompatible with the styles and sensibilities of the writers under discussion. While Stein could be said to "resist" easy accessibility, Lowell could be "resisting" parental influence in his confessional verse; the wreckage of Kaufman's and Spicer's lives and work issues partially from their status as "oppressed" persons; and when the South Boston poets write of "oppressive" conditions, the words connote a realism and a representational flavor wholly uncharacteristic of most of these writers.

"Minority" seems appropriate in that one chapter treats children and teenagers, and the word is often used to describe people of color and other groups traditionally underrepresented in official political process. Nonetheless, there is a troublesome, patronizing ring to the word underscoring the myth that we are powerless, isolated, less-than. Furthermore, although in recent literary studies there has been a redefinition of the term "minor literature" to denote literature produced by "minorities," the connotation of "second-rate" lingers. Theorists and critics who thus address the issue of "minority" in literature unintentionally contribute to an implicit split between "excellence" and "mediocrity" even while they attempt to foreground and privilege the "minor." Louis Renza's work on Sarah Orne Jewett, for example, raises the possibility that Jewett willingly embraced the designation of "regional" writer—that is, minor in the conventional sense of mediocre, unambitious, safe.[9] The conventional sense of the word and the emergent celebratory and subversive sense in which it is used in, for example, Gilles Deleuze and Félix Guattari's study of Kafka, come to imply and involve each other in ways as suspect as they are interesting—suspect especially because these champions of "minor literature" are not members of the "minority" groups their respective writers represent.[10] While the final chapter here, the Stein essay, draws heavily on Deleuze and Guattari's terminology, it does not do so uncritically, and I have adopted their concept of a "minority discourse" with several caveats.

Some writers, such as lesbian poet Judy Grahn, who plant themselves firmly outside of the mainstream, nonetheless caution against the term "marginality," because it contributes to a false notion that there is a "center," a central stronghold of straight white upwardly mobile maledom or of an ideology and culture supporting such a group, surrounded by different groups of outsiders attacking this center from some vague outfield, outback, or periphery, or parasitically clinging to its edges.[11] Again, the image is of isolation, alienation, and, in a sense, superfluity. No image could be more misleading. Not only are so-called marginal people actually central in terms of their economic position as the under- or unpaid workers on which capitalism depends, but they are culturally central as well.[12] H. Bruce Franklin, for instance, points out that jazz, blues, gospel, and the rock and roll derived from these Black musical styles are generally acknowledged to be America's unique contribution to world music; he goes on to make a parallel case for slave narratives and prison literature in the literary world.[13] Moreover, as Grahn points out, "we are not marginal to ourselves," implying that one's point of reference should not be the mainstream but one's own fellow and sister outsiders.[14] Marginality, to Grahn, implies cultural outsiderhood in a culture that is so internally heterodox and heterogeneous that, while it may make sense to speak of a "dominant" culture and its relation to subcultures, the image cannot be one of mutual exclusivity or periphery/centrality. These subcultures function inside and beside dominant cultures, challenging more often than subscribing to them, borrowing from, rewriting and replenishing, always interacting with them.

Nonetheless, unlike "minority," "oppression," and the like, the term's etymological origin implies no devaluation or comparative worth. The "border" or "edge" (Latin *margo*) of a riverbank is not "less than" the river; it forms the necessary condition for the river's being a river. The border of a fabric keeps it from unraveling, often decoratively calling attention to itself through extra ornamentation. Moreover, its meaning in the context of writing affords a rich set of associations appropriate here. A margin is the "unofficial" space around a printed text, where handwriting either shapes the text (as in a teacher's amendments and corrections) or responds deferentially to it (as in a student's annotations to him- or herself on a "master-text"). It is a space for response, immediacy, and fragmentation (as opposed to the finished critique or analysis, for example, that will comprise the student's "official" and public response). It is also, however, the frame that fetishizes the finishedness of a literary product, that announces it as finished. Known also as "white space," it comes to signify absence and silence, a holy aura surrounding the printed text. ("What does all this white space mean?" is a question commonly asked students in an Introduction to Literature class: silence, the unspeakable, the autonomy of the aesthetic moment.) With the advent of open verse, concrete poetry, and experimentation with the printed page, however, the margin talks back; it is not always so easily definable as negative space with secondary value. Most significant for this study, the margin/border marks a discontinuity, setting up images of contemporaneous disunity that lateralize the last vertical vestiges of the Chain of Being inhering in modernism, undoing the hierarchy and anteriority characteristic of mainstream work. It replaces the Chain with the Street, which functions both as border of exclusion and of access, as a trope of circulation and as a dividing line. As an image of potential pluralism, it also works against an easy equation of different kinds of exclusion. However, the Street as image of dynamic pluralism and contemporaneity should not once again euphemize behind a rhetorical veil of Pollyannaish pseudo-democracy the harsh exigencies of a border life: the Street itself continues to be a devalued image, as in "street people" for the poor and homeless; "street smarts" for untrained but intuitive survival skills; "streetwalker" for prostitute; "street Arabs" (!) for neglected children. Hence, because I have wanted to valorize the devalued, the final title: *The* Dark *End of the Street.*

Furthermore, to be marginal means to be on the cutting edge. The term captures the fragmentation of style and identity that characterizes many of my subjects and their work. The marginal is the avant-garde; as Bob Kaufman writes, "Way out people know the way out."[15] I would argue that this case could be made even for writers whose work does not correspond to conventional understandings of "avant-garde"—that is, tending toward the nonrepresentational, the disruptive, the inaccessible. For instance, the South Boston poems, though they conform to very clear, arguably outdated, precepts of what poetry is, are avant-garde, marginal, experimental, both in their challenge of middle-class readers' assumptions about who gets to write what about whom, and in their deconstruction and reassemblage of other dominant discourses, a practice currently labeled "postmodern," but observable in any culture that has relations with other cultures. All writing is experimental, especially for people whose status as writers has traditionally been challenged: women, children, people of color, and members of the working classes. While the radicalism of Julia Kristeva's conclusions—that all language is "poetic," is "revolutionary"—has been criticized as ultimately reactionary, undermining the possibility of an effective revolution based on a shift in demographic power, the claim that everyone has access to the tools for transformation is profoundly democratic.[16]

Standing on the threshold of double vision, of the dualities that mark modern culture, the poets whose work I discuss here do, for the most part, play on the borderline of assimilation and difference through stylistic experimentation. Even the "straightest" of the writers, Robert Lowell, who has never been considered part of an avant-garde canon, broke into new terrain when *For the Union Dead* and *Life Studies* inaugurated the confessional mode and its accompanying relaxation of formal structure. This move was experimental *for him,* and brought him closer to the edge of his own split psyche. Robert Duncan's "poetics of process" play out and represent the constitution of a poetic community within the gay subculture of the 1950s and 1960s. The work of both Duncan and Jack Spicer mediated the problems of community and isolation, physicality and spirituality, democracy and the self-protective elitism of a cultural ghetto—this last pair politically analagous to the binary accessibility/hermeticism that faced the classic avant-garde movement, Surrealism. Duncan and Spicer, members of both Berkeley and San Francisco "Renaissances," explicitly associated gay identity with open serial form, a precursor to contemporary postmodern language poetry. Spicer compares single, discrete poems to "one-night stands filled ... with their own emotions, but not going any where, as meaningless as sex in a Turkish bath," and argues in favor of communities of poems: "They cannot live alone any more than we can."[17] Paradoxically, his violently agonistic version of Keats's negative capability demands that the poet deny himself the comfort of companionship—indeed, of personality—in order to channel poetic messages from otherworldly realms. This aesthetic conviction bridges the seemingly vast abyss separating T. S. Eliot the traditionalist from experimentalists in poetic language, through its joining of a radically nihilistic "objective correlative" to the currently prevalent devalorizing of the author, the speaking subject. Spicer's hermetic, self-lacerating verse complements Duncan's Whitmanesque delight in inclusion and eclecticism. The polyvocality of Duncan's serials and the erotic mysticism he attributes to poetic language celebrate a process of creative self-acceptance, indicating a congruence between the experiments of his life and work.

Bob Kaufman's work combines the popular aesthetics of his time—the Beat sensibility, the imported and Americanized version of existentialism, the new acceptance of jazz as a "serious" art form—with a harrowing embodiment of modernist and postmodernist possibilities. His poetry is an experimental collage of popular and high-art influences; similarly, he lived his life "under the influence" of street drugs, of "Poetry" as an extreme and exacting ethos of self-denial and self-indulgence, and of the resulting psychic deracination—experimentation with no controls. If way-out people know the way out, way-out people also fall apart, and, as in the case of Jack Spicer and Bob Kaufman (and Lenny Bruce, who comes up briefly in the final chapter), it seems disingenuous to celebrate unequivocally a destruction (as opposed to a deconstruction) of personality when this "dérèglement des sens" has its roots in the self-centeredness of obsession rather than in the release of heavy-handed insistence on a one-to-one correspondence of event to meaning, of signifier to referent. In a true deconstructive mode, the sense of loss accompanying such detachment does not become the governing emotional tone, as it does for Spicer and Kaufman; instead, one would experience primarily an exhilaration of conscientious "detach[ment] of [language/body/]movement from story framework."[18] I have tried not to veil despair with the glamor of the doomed *maudit*, even while acknowledging the charisma of these martyr-figures, and finding much that is useful in their aesthetics of despair. Their resolute refusal of comfort rescues this project from unqualified affirmation of life on the margins.

Gertrude Stein's compositional experiments scarcely require explanation or defense in the context of a modernist tradition, or, more accurately, a proto-postmodernism. Compared to her literary colleagues Henry Miller, Ernest Hemingway, Anaïs Nin, and Sherwood Anderson, she is incontestably miles ahead in terms of formal and thematic daring. While the others have their places in American literary history (of her American contemporaries, perhaps only Djuna Barnes, another lesbian in exile, can boast a comparable importance), the vanguardism of Stein's work instantiates Sollers's denouncement of "pseudo-literary histories" in favor of a different *order* of historicity. She could be said to define the terms "avant-garde" and "experimental." Until recently, most Stein criticism has confined itself to treating Stein as an avant-gardist in the modernist movement, overlooking or downplaying for the most part the possible relevance of her multiple marginality as a Jew, a woman, a lesbian. However, new work on Stein has focused on demonstrating how aesthetic experimentation is rooted in her experience as a marginalized person. An emergent body of feminist criticism explicitly treats the links between these aesthetic experiments and her status as a woman and/or as a lesbian.[19] I have tried to carry this paradigm of inquiry into a discussion of Stein's Jewishness, attempting to explore the relationship between this particular ethnicity and her radical defamiliarizing of everyday language.

A final note on "quality," choice, and canonicity: This endeavor has not been an exercise in alternative canon-formation (at least not primarily). Only the chapter on Bob Kaufman is structured as an introduction to a hitherto under-studied poet's oeuvre. While I hope it affords readers pleasure in acquainting them with Kaufman, this agenda has been secondary to my concern to explore the *dynamics* of neglect at the level of majority culture, and the concomitant dynamics of legend-building at the level of minority subculture. What cultural work is done and what needs are met by both sets of dynamics at both cultural registers, and additionally by my choosing to inquire into them? This study has not concerned itself with the question of "good" or "bad" poetry (Robert Duncan has claimed that there is no such thing as good or bad poetry),[20] but with what is aesthetically compelling—thrilling—about certain verbal structures, and how this thrill itself is intrinsic to poetry as social practice. This thrill can be as minimal and specific as what happens dynamically between two words: Stein's "Yet Dish," for example; or as general as the blinding quality of agony that pours from Lowell's reconstructions of childhood in the discursive "91 Revere Street"; or as startling as the initial sight of the South Boston poems handwritten in Cheryl's notebook. A number of colleagues have suggested that, for instance, Lowell's presence in the project was a burdensome concession to canonical credibility: "It must have been dreadful for you to have to include Lowell," or, using the same logic but different values, "What a smart self-marketing device" designed to prove that I could write about "real poetry." Or that the South Boston poets appear here because of my missionary desire to "give them a voice": "It's noble for you to want to dignify these poems by analysis, but aren't you straining a bit?" These poets already have a voice, an audience, and a sense of themselves as writers; academics tend to exaggerate our importance by imagining that MLA talks and book publications substantially change lives other than our own. This observation is not intended critically: changing our own lives is a radical undertaking. My work on all of these poets has been, like most criticism of most literature, an attempt to bring myself into communication with someone else's language—to involve myself parasitically with their aesthetic aura by problematizing it. In this way the entire project has been appropriately egoistic and as pleasurable as one of this nature can be.

The number of people, institutions, and powers to whom I am grateful and to whom I owe thanks exceeds the bounds of the decorum governing these pleasant exercises. Here are some of them:

David Halliburton, Sandra Drake, and Diane Middlebrook oversaw the earliest developments of this manuscript. Mary Pratt, Renato

Rosaldo, Albert Gelpi, and Simone di Piero read, commented on, and supported various aspects of the project.

In friendly and/or professional capacities George Lipsitz, Stanley Aronowitz, Ed Cohen, Janaki Bakhle, and an anonymous reader read the manuscript in its entirety: my thanks to them for their seemingly limitless carefulness, patience, and enthusiasm. George Lipsitz deserves special thanks in this area, and also as a scholar whose commitment to "telling truth to power" has been an inspiration. Likewise, Biodun Iginla at the University of Minnesota Press offered his editorial skills with humor and verve.

Betsy Franco and Solomon Deressa gave unqualified moral, spiritual and emotional support which I can only hope to repay in kind; friendships with Mary Wood, Julee Raiskin, Ira Livingston, Riv-Ellen Prell, Carol Roos, Lorraine Bates-Noyes, and Mary Ann Brown have also significantly affected the development of this book, as has the support of colleagues and friends in the departments of English, American studies, humanities, comparative literature and women's studies at the University of Minnesota. Again, the list is exhaustive; special thanks to Marty and Martha Roth, Joanna O'Connell, Helen Hoy, Nancy Armstrong, Paula Rabinowitz, Ed Griffin, Charles Sugnet, Richard Leppert, and Rey Chow.

A Mrs. Giles Whiting Dissertation Fellowship at Stanford University facilitated the project's initial development; a Recent Recipient of the Ph.D. Fellowship from the American Council of Learned Societies enabled its completion. In addition, the University of Minnesota provided me with a single quarter leave, a faculty summer research stipend, and three absolutely fabulous research assistants. Rachel Buff, Carolyn Krasnow, and Frieda Knobloch have been of greater assistance than they probably know; the latter especially deserves acknowledgment for seeing me through the last stages of manuscript completion. I hope someday you all will have assistants as great as you, if such a thing is possible.

I want to thank the graduate and undergraduate students who have participated in what feels like a years-long, open-ended serial course entitled "Poetry as Cultural Critique." From them, and from the example of my undergraduate advisor Louise Brown Kennedy, I have learned and continue to learn how to teach.

Cheryl Mellen, Charlotte Osborne, Susan Johnson, and Barbara Machtinger, all formerly of City Roots GED Program in South Boston, have been extraordinarily welcoming and helpful after years of no contact. My profound thanks and wishes for the fulfillment of all your aspirations. Thanks also to Jan Egleson for sending me a hard-to-get copy of his movie *The Dark End of the Street*. An earlier version of "Tell Them About Us" appeared in *Cultural Critique*, and parts of it were presented at an MLA conference panel organized by Paul Lauter as well as conferences at Cornell University, Stanford University, and the MidHudson MLA.

Bob Kaufman's career continues its hold over my imagination thanks to many people who provided artifacts, anecdotes, and encouragement. Among them are David Henderson and Vic Bedoian of radio station KPFA, George Kaufman, Eileen Kaufman, Marlene Blackwell, Alix Geluardi, Father Alberto Huerta, Kush, Paul Landry, Lasana Taylor, George Tsongas, Al Young, Jay Fliegelman and Arthur Stockett, Tony Seymour, Michelle Maria Boleyn, Ethelbert Miller, the late Charles Nilon, Houston Baker, Wahneema Lubiano and Raphael Allen, and the staff of the Bancroft Library at the University of California-Berkeley. Thanks also to Frank Lentricchia and Stanley Fish of the *South Atlantic Quarterly*, in which an earlier version of the Kaufman chapter appeared.

Joseph Conte and again the Bancroft Library were valuable sources of camaraderie and information respectively for research on Jack Spicer and Robert Duncan. A brief part of this chapter was presented at an MLA panel on Duncan organized by Michael Lynch, and another brief passage on Spicer's "Car Song" appeared in different form in *Studies in American Humor*. Also, sections of the Stein chapter were presented at the conferences "Feminism and Representation" at the University of Rhode Island and "Women in America: Legacies of Race and Ethnicity" at Georgetown University; my special thanks to Caren Kaplan with regard to the latter. Rebecca Mark, Stacey Vallas, and Riv-Ellen Prell commented perceptively on this section; and Marjorie Perloff and Bob Strand initiated the dual strands of its trajectory by (respectively) engaging me on the subject of Stein as "dog"/"dyke," and giving me a copy of Arthur Naiman's *Every Goy's Guide to Common Jewish Expressions*.

For support of all kinds and karmic lessons that just won't quit, I want to acknowledge my family crucible: Selma Thomsen Damon, Kristina Damon, Elsa Damon, Bessie Damon (now in her 103d year), Gladys Damon, Laurel Reiner-Goldin and Julie Reiner, Jonathan Goldin, and Linda Hillyer. The memory of my father, Albert Damon, has informed this book as it has every aspect of my life. To him, who feared his otherness, and to Jean Genet, who exalted his, this book is dedicated, as well as to the golden urn with the pink silk scarf wrapped around its slender neck.

1

Introductions and Interdictions

The Dark End of the Street: Passion, Commitment, and Subversion in Modern American Poetry

Soul Hit: No There There

In 1967, James Carr, who was to sink into the obscurity of poverty, drugs, and mental illness, recorded the greatest version of the "greatest cheating song in soul history," entitled "The Dark End of the Street."[1] The mournfully triumphant ballad of a clandestine love doomed to perish upon discovery has been covered many, many times, by (among others) Aretha Franklin, Ry Cooder and his backup team Terry Evans and Al King, and most recently by the "black" Irish "saviours of soul" in the movie *The Commitments*. Invoking all the power of a gospel hymn, the lover exhorts his love to walk past him unrecognizing, unweeping, if they should chance to meet "downtown" during the day. The lyrics and melody recreate the agony of a deep passion that flourishes in the shadows, that feeds on its own shame, that can't be acknowledged in the world of normative discourse indicated by the alliterative "daylight"/"downtown." Despite and because of their hiddenness and illegitimacy, the few nocturnal moments stolen away to meet "at the dark end of the street" frame the lovers' lives, give those lives meaning, fuel the spiritual resources they need to withstand the pressure of conscience and convention. The power of the passion itself justifies a subversive commitment to it, turns "wrong" into "strong," abjection into transcendence, the dark end of the street / wrong side of the tracks into the golden path of glory.

1

The song allegorizes the predicament of poetry, of social outcasts, of outsiders who are poets, who live in dark corners of social lacunae, in the psychic and physical slums of the marginal imagination. Jacques Derrida has pointed out that the dark end of the street can't be a dwelling place; transgression is characterized by its necessarily transient nature, defined by and dependent upon the norm it violates. No one can live in the perpetual and unqualified "outside," not only because it is difficult enough to strain ordinary human resources beyond their limits but because such a "place" does not even exist.[2] As the adult Gertrude Stein remarked on revisiting the Oakland of her childhood, "there is no there there." But the poets of this study attempt just that: to live perpetually in the nonplace, the constant currency, of language. The avant-gardes they comprise occupy the razor's edge, the margin of constant error that permits no mistake but failure, which is not a mistake but inevitable and not unexpected. "Street" life conducts its commerce on the thin margin of sidewalk that defines discrete neighborhoods, language usages, cultures; and puts these in uncontrollable circulation, simultaneously permeating the core of American culture and defining its margin. The margin is not a habitat but an event, a state of becoming and devolving in constant flux. The transgressive gesture is motile, embodied in the mental patient and the sailor, the hustler and the housing-project tenants, the Jews and the juveniles whose poetry makes up the matter of this book—whose vanguard persistence in public life has nominalized the adjective. And the transgressive gesture is embodied as well in the hoboes, the homeless, the voyagers they write about. The dark end of the street is not a geopolitical locale but a condition of subversive passion: the lovers of Carr's soul hit create the dark end of the street in every passionate utterance, in every instance of transgressive intersubjectivity, in every attempt to force their eyes not to meet during chance encounters "downtown."

Teen Movie: There

The title of the soul hit also served as the title of a full-length feature film made in 1981 by working-class teenage students at the Group School, an experimental high school in Cambridge, Massachusetts, a city (as part of "greater Boston") characterized by a racial and ethnic factionalism which not infrequently erupts into violence. Having grown up in Newton, Boston's "golden ghetto," I was struck each time I returned for brief vacations by the regularity with which tales of racial, class, or gender brutality occupied the *Globe*'s headlines, be it police shootings of unarmed Black or Hispanic youth, the rape/murders of prostitutes, or, as in the case that made national headlines several years ago, the accusation by a middle-class white man that his wife had been shot by a Black man, an accusation that prompted police harassment of Black neighborhoods and the random round-up of Black men until it was discovered that the husband himself was the murderer. Based on these kinds of incidents, and the violent anti-desegregation busing riots of the 1970s, Boston is seen, and sees itself, as violently self-contradictory: genteel / vicious, heterogeneous / intolerant, liberal / profoundly reactionary, intellectually enlightened / educationally backward—a city embodying ideological and temperamental dichotomies that can only be held together by violent authority. Different ethnic groups, each with its particular class and ideological affiliations, struggle with and for this authority.

The teen movie *The Dark End of the Street*, however, tells a different story, one of the cruel effects of this civic self-misperception on the lives of the young, the poor, those disenfranchised by the social value assigned to skin-color (a relatively immanent trace of that Platonic chimera called "race"), income, and gender. The film is at least partially a collectively produced work of art (with a professional director and scriptwriter), a stunning instance of working-class youth art, written and acted by the teenage students of a progressive high school that services primarily the urban working-class. In the story, a party in the housing projects ends in a drunken argument in which a young Black man falls off one of the project roofs. The only witnesses, a young white couple, are too afraid to tell the police. Although all participants in the altercation are friends, the media assumes the accident to be an instance of racial conflict, and this assumption comes to determine the teens' relations with each other, especially endangering the friendship between the young white woman and the Black girlfriend of the victim of the accident. The final episode takes place in the project home of one of the two girls; against the background of an a capella jazz female-voice version of "The Dark End of the Street," they resolve the conflicts with which the party incident has disrupted their lives. The star-crossed, illicit love of James Carr's 1967 hit is not, in this context, the romance of adulterous passion, but the cross-racial friendship between two poor teenage women who are no longer naïve about the social transgression their friendship represents.

In one of the most telling, breathtakingly complex scenes of the movie, a television reporter shows up at the projects to interview its denizens for a human-interest spot on the local news. Her self-presentation, that of the professional middle-class woman, contrasts sharply with that of the poorly dressed and angry teenagers who drive her away with taunts of what they know she wants to hear: racial tensions in the unusual (for Boston) integrated project boiling over, the inevitable violence Bostonians presume follows upon too intimate a multicultural proximity, the hopelessness of converting the barbarian poor to an enlightened liberal "tolerance" of others—when this barbarism is a middle-class media projection. The teens know how they will be constructed for the consumption of the middle-class, and they resist that process to the extent that they can. Within the fiction of the movie, for the fictional would-be TV viewers whose emissary they thwart, the teens' anger reinscribes them in the role of savage youth, though that is what they are protesting. For the nonfictional Bostonian viewers of *The Dark End of the Street* (the movie was not widely distributed), the fictional teens' passionate efforts to counter any commodification of their experience subverts easy ascription of clichéd meaning to the scene.

In examining my own relation to the subject matters at hand, I'm aware of how easily I risk assuming the role of the power-dressing lady from the media, full of good intentions and misinformation she is only too happy to replicate in a way that promotes her in the hierarchy of her profession; after all, as a female, she too faces the now-proverbial glass ceiling, and better she should rise by doing pieces sympathetic to the masses from which she must distinguish herself. The heat is on: what does it mean, my telling the story of the dark end of the street of poetic exile—*in order to* move into the power bloc of academia? Stories get mistold by people in power (who, of course, never experience themselves as powerful because, as Genet says, everyone is somebody's chicken) and, within the institution in which I have found a home, I'm aware that I'm somewhere near the bottom of the top. As I draft this introduction on a Saturday afternoon in November, my more professionally advanced colleagues are reviewing my performance and deciding whether it merits my continued "probation." I had assumed that I'd be tempted, under such pressure, to tell the story in a way that would enhance my standing in the eyes of these colleagues. However—and I hope this is a formula I can share with others in my predicament, that is, those who dwell in a perpetually liminal stage in a vocational context that is itself liminal, both powerful and pitiful, both grandiose and abject—I find that, like the kids in *The Dark End of the Street*, being in the position of being judged, however benevolently, simply makes it more imperative that I tell—*a* "truth." Telling the dark end of the street is a compulsion; if I get it "wrong," which I will, somebody else can come along and correct me, and make it "strong." This is how we can generate discourse about the nondiscursive, about the un-discourse-able, and at least legitimate it as a (non)place to try to go or imagine.

Stories get told differently by people in power, by the disenfranchised, and by people who occupy mutable and fluid relations to both of these polar groups; I tell the story differently from, on the one hand, my senior white male colleagues, and on the other, from the subjects I write about (for example, I'm writing expository prose; they write imaginative poetry), and, again, differently from how I would have told it in the past. The form of the story as well as its content is necessarily changed when the underdog takes back the means of verbal production, the means of performance. In the dynamic interplay of these different stories, the "countermemory"— the story told by those in exile from the power bloc—serves as the dark end of the street. It is not inaccessible from Main Street, from "downtown," but may look radically foreign, unrecognizable to those who have never been there at night. And it has a different "feel" to it: the familiar defamiliarization of the déja vu, the guerrilla attack of the dream-fragment that revisits during the day. The poeticity of countermemory is not so much the pure defamiliarization the Russian formalists claimed for literary language but the uncanny: the disorienting (deterritorializing) effect of a collision of known and unknown, the familiar with a dissociative twist.[3]

The material conditions of thereness, the physical impact of location, profoundly affect the writers who would break out of them. This study examines the work and lives of Black/Jewish street-surrealist Bob Kaufman, Berkeley Renaissance gay poets Robert Duncan and

Jack Spicer, Jewish-American lesbian-in-exile Gertrude Stein, Boston Brahmin Robert Lowell, and three unpublished poets, teenage women from a South Boston housing project: Charlotte Osborne, Cheryl Mellen, and Susan Johnson. The metaphysics and utter physicality of place and placelessness are key issues in each poet's oeuvre, though the *way* in which this is so is exquisitely peculiar and unique for each poet. I am not concerned with a poetics of space per se, much less with regionalism, except to note that space and place are imbued with social meaning, and heavily inflect what we call culture: the social location (a metaphysical and physical place) out of which each poet writes. Thus most of the housing-project poetry notes the unlivability of the place—"the D"—the girls describe; Robert Lowell's work relies on our geosocial knowledge of polite society to understand the import of cues like "91 Revere Street" and "hardly passionate Marlborough Street"; Kaufman's genealogical indeterminacy is underscored by his New Orleans origins, and his stature in the poetic pantheon of the 1960s rests partially on his San Francisco Beatstreet milieu; Spicer and Duncan were groundbreakers in establishing the gay scene of California's Bay Area; and Gertrude Stein is legendary for the ways in which her expatriate status facilitated the literary blossoming of American high modernism. In not being "there," or in inhabiting an untenable "there" or an anachronistic one that, like Lowell's Boston, is decaying behind a façade of respectability, these writers enact biographically the ways in which their poetic language disorients their readers. Their deterritorialization, then, is geopolitically literal as well as formally literary. Our attentiveness to the confluences and dissonances of particular subcultures, biographies, and poetic texts make for rich, thick descriptions of the value of poetry in deterritorialized survival.[4] Poets are real people with life stories that may not be richer than others' life stories, but are certainly no less so: the interpenetration of social locations and emotional sensibilities enacted in their work becomes allegorical of those of others. Thus in my elaboration of each poet and his or her oeuvre as an experiential moment of social contradictions and resonances, I hope to suggest some general structures and metaphorics—the physics and metaphysics—of oppression and resistance. These individual instances can be read as allegorical of other or larger such struggles not specifically addressed in this study.

For these reasons my choice of poets has been governed not so much by each one's canonical or noncanonical relation to American modernism or even to the avant-garde as understood in historical categories or formalist theories. Rather, these poets share an existential and phenomenological opposition to dominant cultures (even when, like Lowell, or like Stein living on the stipend made possible by her brother Michael, who inherited their father Daniel's Western-expansionist San Francisco trolley business, they appear to be prime beneficiaries thereof). I want to demonstrate, in each case, how this complex of oppositions is lived and stylistically manifested primarily in the genre of lyrical poetry. As poets and social deviants these subjects are not being good aristocrats, good Jews, good Blacks, good girls, good citizens; even the ambiguity of gay masculinity that would presumably make poetry an acceptable vocation for a gay man (as it was decidedly *not* for Lowell) does not read out for Spicer and Duncan: the former excoriated his gay community for the meaninglessness of its sexual connections, and the latter, after all, had his poems returned to him by John Crowe Ransom at the *Kenyon Review* after and because he came out in an essay in *Politics*. Rather, their orientation toward poetry associates them with the social exile to which Plato relegated poetry, and where it has wandered ever since.

This latter statement is an arguably romantic and subjectivist claim that requires some elucidation.

Elucidating the Dark: The Chain, the Street, and the Text

Exile on Main Street

> *Then I really felt in exile, and my nervousness was going to make*
> *me permeable to what—for want of other words—I shall call poetry.*
> Jean Genet[5]

Poetry as a form of discourse has been marginalized—specifically feminized and exiled—by the founders of the philosophical system that dominates the West.[6] We can see the way this feminization and exile operates even today, with, for example, the dismissal of poetry for being either too low a form of low culture—as in street rhymes, kitchen talk, and song lyrics, or too high a form of high culture—as in what gets taught in underpopulated English department courses, derided as effete or obscure. A range of theorists participating in Western philosophy and aesthetics, from Plato to Trinh T. Minh-ha, have separated poetry from discourses of mastery, which include the abstractions of philosophy or government and the putatively unambiguous speech of justice as well as the empiricism of positivist science.[7] The uses to which this separation has been put, however, have varied hugely; most recently, subaltern theorists claim that poetry coming out of groups not represented in the mainstream of public power subverts this mainstream. My project shares this claim, and aims to demonstrate its validity by examining specific American writers who fall outside traditional power centers. Alongside the development of the master trope of the Great Chain of Being—a philosophy based on domination and subjection—the subversive radical subjectivity of poetry has emerged with particular relevance for nondominant groups, those who experience what I call marginality: disenfranchisement, ostracism or, quite simply, oppression, but which W. E. B. Du Bois refers to as the experience of "twoness,"[8] or of "being a problem."[9]

Of the several dominant schools of twentieth-century American poetry, some have struggled more directly than others with the "problem" of the Other—with their role, as members of a dominant social group, in both questioning and possibly sustaining the "problematicness" of the people who work for them, who are not their social and political equals. In particular, the Americanist (Crane-Williams-Olson-Ginsberg, etc.) school of American modernist poetry (as distinct from, but not necessarily opposed to, Pound's and Eliot's European orientation) implicitly domesticated and aestheticized a primeval Other, valorizing organicity and primitivism, turning away from high culture for subject matter and language, and embracing in its field theory all manner of subjects with both emancipatory and imperialist undertones. Even these relatively renegade (to Eliot, the Agrarians, and the New Critics) efforts on the part of mainstream American modernists to break with the tradition of academic poetry and examine their relationship to the social and natural world reenact certain questionable conventions about who gets to speak for and about whom—conventions which, along with the Chain, have characterized Western imperial discourse. Likewise, contemporary attempts to write about this poetry as sociocultural rather than strictly aesthetic artifact tend likewise to replay the desire to subsume all, to designate and account for all "foreignness" it declares to be within its scope. The perceptive analysis of Williams's poem "Elsie" with which James Clifford inaugurates his book of ethnographic essays on "the predicament of culture," for instance, foregrounds Williams's attempt to understand (in two senses: to master and to empathize with) the situation of a young working-class woman who does housework for his wife.[10] In this gem of an essay on poetry as cultural critique, Clifford's tone of bemused power and ambivalent excitement/anxiety about his impending loss of control over the means of discourse res-onates with what he so accurately targets in Williams's tone: a desire and reluctance to gracefully relinquish the reins of power and let oneself be taken by the forces of modern (in Clifford's case, post-modern) chaos. For both Williams the modernist and Clifford the postmodernist, the Other is an object whose subjectivity they strug-gle to acknowledge, against the grain of their Anglo-American mas-culinist training. However, within the imperial domain of American post/modernism, Others inside the walls of the city reappropriate lit-erary conventions to represent their own experience as contraband subjects — "miners" rather than "minors," in that they undermine dominant discourses, unearthing precious materials from the hidden worlds under and within the metropolis, their bodies ravaged with signs of their Orphic enterprise. These contraband subjects are the focuses of my study. My goal is to let their work speak through my text rather than the reverse; for instance, I place the young women's poetry before my analysis of it rather than as appendix, and I engage in those close readings that, in our legitimation of wider cultural con-cerns, we nowadays tend to relegate to the dustbin of past misguided text-fetishizing aesthetic practice, or to dismiss as a patronizingly an-titheoretical "information-retrieval" approach to hitherto neglected work.[11]

Recent scholarship on the lyric, notably by Hans Robert Jauss, has demonstrated its role in transmitting rather than countering socially normative values.[12] Likewise, Robert von Hallberg's work on Ameri-can poetry and culture has done much to show the "centrism" — that is, the congruence of the poetry of a given period with the general national values and intellectual trends of that era — of postwar Amer-ican poetry, and the role of poetry in the development of empire. His work deals primarily with writers who are rather unambiguously headed for literary canonization, however, and with those aspects of their opus that conform to the centrist view.[13] Some of the same writers von Hallberg examines—Merrill and Lowell—come up for discussion in my project as well, but from a different vantage point and with an emphasis on the silenced or marginalized parts of their experience. While such work as Jauss's and Von Hallberg's provides a necessary and valuable counterweight to claims that poetry always and exclusively serves either as rarified entertainment for the effete or as outlet for the disaffected lower fringes, it underemphasizes the *differences* between poetry and other forms of cultural or institutional discourse, and particularly its difference from both the positivistic and the abstract speculative modes of Western philosophical expression.

Without engaging too crudely the "romance of oppositionality" per se, the present study focuses on the ways in which poetry can undermine the philosophic and social systems that have declared it and its disenfranchised writers Other.[14] My bias presumes the inevitable failure of a philosophy that splits the world into hierarchic dichotomies; having said that, I find most interesting the dark side of the street, the counterhegemonic elements in poetry that articulate an admittedly complex relationship bweeen less powerful and more powerful strata of American culture. I propose that poetry takes on an anti-"humanist" role, insofar as Western humanism bases its principles on Platonic and Aristotelean concepts of order, and I will explore those aspects of these poets' work that either have their origin in an altogether different cultural tradition (as in the "African" aspects of African-American poetry), or which actively, if not intentionally, reverse, equalize, or dissolve entirely the terms of Western philosophical order and the neat dualisms that have informed the Western value system.

Also, this study for the most part confines itself to writing that falls under a fairly conventional and academic definition of the word "poetry"—that is, lyric or experimental poems by individual "poets" who self-consciously consider themselves so. Gertrude Stein's uncategorizable experiments and the heretofore unpublished poems by my former students in South Boston are somewhat less lyrical and more balladic, street-aphoristic, or even journalistic in their diction and form than the poems of Robert Lowell, Bob Kaufman, Robert Duncan, or the other nationally acknowledged poets under discussion. However, the former poems share with the latter the self-conscious poeticity of the language and the form; they are fully intended as "poems" or art-writing. Besides, the use of the works is similar; the writers engage a verbal aesthetic to counter an oppressive social situation, and in doing so, to paraphrase Genet, they turn an otherwise painful experience to good account.[15] Street-rhymes, toasts and dozens, popular music lyrics, letters and stream-of-consciousness therapy journals all share some of these characteristics and are worthy of study along comparable lines, and they clearly constitute cultural riches from which these poets have borrowed heavily, but they are not my focus here. A comprehensive definition of poetry would have to expand to fit Owen Barfield's guideline that a "felt change of consciousness" on the part of the recipient or listener determines the poeticity of a verbal construct,[16] or to fit even a Kristevan extreme of the poetic and revolutionary potential of all utterance (so that, for example, Lowell's prose piece is his most poetic, because most revolutionary, moment, not only for the poet but for the reader who encounters it after having become accustomed to Lowell's highly wrought verse)—but within such comprehensive definitions, I have limited my scope to writers who use and challenge specific modernist conventions.

Furthermore, just as it is impossible to take on "poetry" in its unbounded significance, it has not proven especially useful to attempt to represent writers from a comprehensive catalogue of marginalized American cultures. Most of the writers here are marginal in more than one sense; I have not addressed exclusive categories of marginality. For example, I do not treat categories of gender or of class as isolated from other aspects of marginality, although these are issues for many of the writers under discussion: Lowell is obsessed with the curse of his patrician origins; the South Boston poems are permeated with as much working/unemployed class consciousness as they are with the pain of being female and young; in fact, these three aspects of oppression are of a piece, indivisible in the poems. Moreover, most children of the world are economically dependent, including those with wealthy parents; women and children comprise most of the world's poor, as indicated by one of the several meanings of the media phrase "the feminization of poverty." Kaufman's bare subsistence treads a shaky tightrope between a *maudit* exotic-ascetic renunciation ("I would die for Poetry"—which he did on the same day I first drafted this paragraph) and an all-too-everyday urban African-American experience of addiction and poverty. Even though the specific areas of sensibility, the particular sense of powerlessness or empowerment, may resonate with different symbols, youth oppression and class oppression are comparable in the sense that these are quite obviously mobile—youth, in fact, is so by definition. But ageism and other forms of injustice are linked and possibly—to use a loaded word—universal, since all adults were children once and as such were indoctrinated into the mores and conventions of social oppression.

The obvious mobility of age and class should not, however, blind us to the constructedness and even the arbitrariness of many other current classifications of categories of oppression, and the mutability of these categories over time and space. As Henry Louis Gates, Jr., has pointed out, it is the arbitrariness of the designation of "race" that makes it the ultimate signifier of difference in American social discourse.[17] Using the trope of performance, Judith Butler and others are making similar points in the realm of gender and sex. This is not in any way to deny that culturally constructed markers of difference are real, in the sense that they have real consequences in the lives of real people. But the very notion of category participates in the limited and limiting language of fixity and objectification that imprisons consciousness and identity. That is one reason I have not tried to cover all the bases in my attention to oppressed Americans: there is no Native American chapter, no Nuyorican or Chicana/o poet featured here, although some of the paradigms I use could be profitably applied to poetry by writers who have these identifications. In the Stein chapter I argue for a conception of identity, ethnic or otherwise, which reflects a mélange of cultural elements in any self-identification by the enunciating subject. There can be no "final" self-identification; we understand ourselves differently every day. Deleuze and Guattari's useful prefix "becoming-" evokes such a nonstatic notion of identity, as does Michael Fischer's term "the reinvention of ethnicity."

ChainChainChain: The Discourse of Verticality

Most philosophers and historians of ideas point to Plato and his protégé Aristotle as the men who first articulated the images and concepts that have developed into the "Western metaphysical system": a conceptual hierarchy underlying the justification of a social order dependent on category, ranking wealthy men of European descent above women of the same origins, and these in turn above the poor of comparable background, and these in turn above people of color of both genders, and all of these above animals, plants, and earth in descending order—the Great Chain of Being. It is against and after this construct, its persistence and evolution from classical Greece to the twentieth century, and its refinements and variations within contemporary Western metaphysics, that the argument of this work unfolds, and it is against the background and recent memory of this construct that the modern poets addressed here develop their own poetics and a corresponding metaphysics. For instance, in 1933 (ten years after Williams published "Elsie," which in turn appeared less than a decade after American women could vote legally), Arthur Lovejoy delivered the William James Lecture Series at Harvard University on the Great Chain of Being; one could speculate that Lovejoy's choice to devote so much analysis to this ancient trope was a reaction to the latter political development, and to Williams's attempt to imagine social breakdown as positive. Both these moments represented challenges to the construct Lovejoy legitimates as the underpinnings of Western civilization. The lecture series and the tome it resulted in refer to the entire development of Western philosophy, with particular reference to the Great Chain of Being, as "footnotes to Plato."[18] Plato is commonly credited with introducing the notion of an Ideal reality (a reality of Ideas) both split off from and more "real" than immanent, apprehensible, physical phenomena, which were seen to be imperfect approximations of this Ideal, invisible and abstract; this Ideal realm was assigned a higher value than its polar-opposite partner. The form of this idea has been duplicated in the proliferation of other binarisms—good versus bad, culture versus nature, mind versus body, truth versus appearance, depth versus superficiality, individual versus community, permanence versus flux, and so on—in which one member of the pair is clearly coded as superior to the other.[19]

Aristotle, according to Lovejoy, both modified and reinforced this concept with the notion of categories and gradation; the plenitude of life forms could be organized into an order ranging from the lowest and most primitive natural organisms to the highest and most perfect abstractions. This hierarchy both bridged and underscored the distance between the humble Immanent and the lofty and complex Ideal.[20] Aristotle's preoccupation in the *Poetics* with good as opposed to bad, noble as opposed to base human beings and the respective art forms corresponding to each—tragic and comic drama—and the questions of relative merit that organize the poetic forms he chooses to address into a hierarchy ("Which is the higher form, Epic Poetry or Tragedy?"),[21] reflect a more general predisposition toward order in terms of differential value. While these hierarchically organized dichotomies have sustained explicit challenges from within the Western philosophical and political traditions in the last hundred years, such that it would be inappropriate to assume that they still reign unquestioned in the realm of ideas, they are firmly entrenched in many of the assumptions that govern political and social life; they had their genesis, after all, in the everyday social life of the Greek men who formulated them.

While Lovejoy's work, the major modern treatise on Western hierarchic philosophy, is by no means an unqualified apologetic for the Great Chain and its influence on Western social and cultural life, the location of Harvard University as intellectual power center of a United States that is the political and military power center of the world overdetermines the ideological thrust of the project, implicating it in the system it describes with qualified approval. In a sense, however, this enormous labor of love, this concern to outline the philosophical cornerstone of the West, represents an elegiac moment. In documenting a metaphysics already disqualified by the turn of the century, *The Great Chain of Being* articulates the last gasp of the modernist allegiance to traditional hierarchy. In 1933 the United States, already imbued with the imperial consciousness of its European former colonists and present allies, was making its bid as "leader of the free world," reaching for global domination and foreign exploitation to buttress its internal democracy. Even as the nation stood on the threshold of achieving this aim, however, its philosophical underpinnings were collapsing. Nietzsche, in the *Genealogy of Morals*, had already revealed the socially constructed basis of an epistemology based on gradation and valuation. Using his etymological imagination, he points out that the classical Greek words that Plato and Aristotle used to describe good and bad, noble and base, had specifically classbound meanings: words for "good" actually meant "aristocratic, highborn," and so on, and the words for "bad" meant "illborn." He demonstrates this in Latin as well, linking *malus*/"bad" with *melas*/"dark," which certainly speaks to social life in the contemporary world.[22] (The evolution of the word "shiftless" points toward the same pattern in English: what begins as a description of poverty—too poor to own the most basic undergarment—becomes a moral judgment: too lazy to work.)

Economic and political privilege are not only associated with virtue, they are associated with truth itself:

> They call themselves, for instance, "the truthful"; this is so above all of the Greek nobility, whose mouthpiece is the Megarian poet Theognis. The root of the word coined for this, *esthlos*, signifies one who *is*, who possesses reality, who is actual, who is true; then, with a subjective turn, the true as the truthful: in this phase of conceptual transformation it becomes a slogan and watchword of the nobility and passes over entirely into the sense of "noble," as distinct from the *lying* common man.[23]

Gerald Else's work on Aristotle's *Poetics* documents this syntactic conflation of heroes with aristocrats, moral degenerates with the poor or common, and asserts simply that the Greeks, "obsessed" with the dichotomy between good and bad, considered these terms to be "quite as much social, political, and economic as they are moral. ... The dichotomy is absolute and exclusive for a simple reason: it began as the aristocrats' view of society and reflects their idea of the gulf between themselves and the 'others.' "[24]

Furthermore, the figure of the philosopher himself merged with that of the aristocrat, since truth was the highest metaphysical construct in the world (the top of the Chain, simultaneously the most abstract and the most "real"), and philosophy the highest of callings.[25] Thus, the search for truth, the ability to abstract, was connected to political power. The implications of this merging have cut both ways throughout the centuries: free (upper-class or propertied) adult male humans have been attributed (by themselves) reasoning powers far exceeding those of other beings; and skill in analytic, discursive logic has itself become associated with various forms of material and social prestige. Societies that permit upward mobility generally look for evidence of this particular form of intelligence as a major criterion in determining whether a given individual or group merits recognition and reward; by corollary logic, as I shall argue in the essay on Gertrude Stein's "Jewish" language use, a lesser value is assigned to associative, affective, and especially tactile and kinetic modes of expression, and to the people who are perceived by the power bloc to engage in these modes.

In arguing for a postmodern vanguard poetry that supersedes while growing out of the modern concern with valuation and community, I do not want to posit the Platonic era as a point of origin. Nor do I want, by offering a contending myth of origin, to argue that the current possibilities of a poetics of marginality hearken back to a more authentic pre-Chain, pre-Platonic mode, though some developments in contemporary poetics, particularly ethnopoetics, contain an element of nostalgia in precisely this vein. Nonetheless, in claiming a shift from the modern to the postmodern, from the verticality of the Chain to the laterality of the street, I want to acknowledge a precedent for lateralism. In a work whose polemical project is similar to this one, but concerns itself with Greece in the fourth century B.C.E., Page Dubois documents the prehistory and rise of the Great Chain of Being in terms of those subordinated in its hierarchy, placing Plato's and Aristotle's writings in historical context. The shift in the basic sociopolitical unit, in Greek political thought and deed, from polis to empire, from a contained democracy to a potentially limitless imperial domain, was accompanied by other related changes. A shift in worldview took place, from one in which the Greek male citizen saw himself as a center surrounded by powerful mythological Others (women as Amazons, animals as Satyrs and Centaurs), to one in which he saw himself at the top of a ladder of beings, qualitatively superior to women, noncitizens (slaves and foreigners, who were potential slaves), and beasts, who in turn were above fish, plants, and earth, in descending order.[26] In social terms, this change meant that the dangerous Other was now contained *within* the boundaries of the empire (or could be, through expansionist activity), and this volatile containment had to be defused with images of superiority legitimated by a rational philosophy. (The difference in imagery is similar to that between the terms "marginal" and "oppressed" described in my preface.)

Accompanying this shift in polity was a change in the primary form of discourse from a "celebratory ritual art" coming out of a "mythic, literary, poetic [I would add the word "lyrical"] consciousness to one which examines problems in terms of logos, reason": discursive, an alytic, linear philosophy.[27] This latter philosophy itself incorporates first a tremendous split between the ideal and the immanent (the overwhelming and troublesome legacy with which progressive philosophers have since struggled), and then a series of gradations and categories separating and ordering the denizens of the immanent realm. Dubois argues persuasively that this philosophy's governing image is that of domination and subordination — of slavery, which, ultimately, was the institution it was developed to defend.[28] Again, as with the conflation of the figures of philosopher and aristocrat, the legitimation works both ways: philosophic discourse offers a rationale for slavery, imperialism, and the subordination of women, children, and animals; and the historical fact of empire makes the philosophy look like an objective description of a "natural order."

Pre-Platonic Poetry, Post-Platonic Poetics

To an Army Wife, in Sardis:

Some say a cavalry corps,
some infantry, some, again,
will maintain that the swift oars

of our fleet are the finest
sight on dark earth; but I say
that whatever one loves, is.

This is easily proved: did
not Helen — she who had scanned
the flower of the world's manhood —

choose as first among men one
who laid Troy's honor in ruin?
warped to his will, forgetting

love due her own blood, her own
child, she wandered far with him.
So Anactoria, although you

being far away forget us,
the dear sound of your footstep
and light glancing in your eyes

would move me more than glitter
of Lydian horse or armored
tread of mainland infantry.

Sappho[29]

*The question finally suggests itself: Which is the higher form of art,
Epic Poetry or Tragedy? Those who favor the Epic may argue thus:
The less vulgar form is the higher; and that which addresses the better
audience is always the less vulgar. . . . The reply to this argument is
twofold . . . it is clear that Tragedy, since it attains the poetic end
more effectively than the Epic, is the higher form of the two.*
Aristotle[30]

The terms of the "old quarrel between poetry and philosophy,"[31] at
least as formulated by those (philosophers) who posited the quarrel,
is thrown into sharp relief when we consider that the Western lyric
tradition is generally acknowledged to begin with Sappho. If we contrast her work with that of Aristotle, the most obvious difference is
the one mentioned by Page Dubois: namely, that Sappho writes
poetry—celebratory, ritualistic—while Aristotle writes analytic prose
about poetry. The contrast between Sappho's and Aristotle's discursive practices can help foreground, in a wider sense and with more
contemporary application, those aspects of poetry which, though
they may have been attributed to "her" by a patriarchal philosophic
system, may provide the terms for the subversion of that system.

In reviewing some of the recent literature on the nature of poetry,
we find a great deal of attention centered on the "radical subjectivity"
of the lyric. Theorists engage the familiar language of dichotomies to
distinguish the lyric's tendency toward the subject rather than the object, both of which are held to be elements in any utterance. The lyric
is designated the most subject-oriented of all verbal statements even
more so than other forms of poetry and literature. This subject, represented by the trope of the "lyric I," stands in a peculiar relation to
other subjects, as the lyric occupies a peculiar position vis-à-vis other
discursive practices. According to Karlheinz Stierle, who draws on
Foucault and Jakobson for his lyric theories, all other forms of discourse are institutionally governed and generated, and all of the subjects posited through these institutional forms of discourse are soci-
etally prescribed "roles"—the graduate student with her dissertation,
the mother with her newsy letters to sons and daughters away from
home, the boss with his communiqués and memos to employees.[32]
Only the "lyric I" constitutes true, unmediated subjectivity sans role,
and only the lyric is not institutionally circumscribed: "La poésie lyrique est essentiellement anti-discours."[33] Its position is on the out-
skirts, marginally abutting these other normative public discursive

practices. The imagery is familiarly Platonic: poetry as exiled (female) Other—in this case, because it valorizes "subjective" experience, or, as Plato describes it, strong emotions which are inappropriate (unmanly) for public display.

Poignantly enough, however, Plato's writing is itself so "poetic" and parabolic that his suggestion for the exile of poetry must be read with some indulgent suspicion, and one can imagine that, as Stierle suggests, "she" has been exiled only with the understanding that she maintain some kind of permanent relationship to the center from which she has been banished—that she somehow continue to carry the responsibility for its constant replenishment; Plato coyly undermines his own argument by insisting that "she" have the right to "return, if she can make her defence in lyric or other metre."[34] She can be the Other against which civic discourse can define and know itself. A liminal genre, she represents access to the beyond. Cast out of the *res publica*, public matter, poetry turns both to the inner limit—to private subjectivity where matters inappropriate for public expression can come to light and find articulation in lyric—and to the "far-out"—the expressive medium for social "outsiders," as well as the outer limits of experience and language use implicit in "experimental" writing that claims to go beyond the "merely personal," in, for instance, contemporary language poetry or aleatory exercises. If banishment is a harsh rejection, it is also implicit permission to go wild in the wilderness, to try anything. Just report back to us, Poetry, so that we can write institutional discourse about you ("we should give her defenders, men who aren't poets but who love poetry, a chance of defending her in prose and proving that she doesn't only give pleasure but brings a lasting benefit to human life and human society").[35]

In turning to Sappho's lyrics vis-à-vis Aristotle's expository arguments as exemplary of these principles, we easily find what we're looking for, even beyond the clear split along gender lines, which conform with almost embarrassing literalness to Plato's figurative tropes. The lyric clearly valorizes "concrete" over the philosophical "abstract" here (even though we can be irritated as hell at the dogmatism of the creative writing teacher's "show don't tell" and the modern worship of the objective correlative, it must be granted that these hobbyhorses of "good writing" challenge the dominant discourse's predilection for generalization and abstraction). Moreover,

Sappho's division of island from mainland underscores the sense of exile, though Sappho reverses the hierachy of mainland/island by intimating that Anactoria has betrayed the women's community on the island Lesbos by following her military husband and that this can only lead to devastation. But we find that what is "radical" is perhaps not so much subjectivity itself as the special domain of this lyric, but its frank thematic acknowledgment as such. By comparison, Aristotle proposes his hierarchy of genres as rationally derived, and hence objective. The etymologies traced earlier do indeed point toward the formulation of values — good versus bad — deriving from the subjective experience of privileged Athenians, but this origin is cloaked in the assertion of universality. Sappho, writing about three hundred years before Plato's famous student, uses a similar attention to superlatives in this translation ("the finest / sight on dark earth") ("the highest form of poetry"), but here it is to acknowledge the plurality of subjects and of pleasing things, and to directly challenge the idea of an absolute standard, or a philosophical war between absolute standards:

> Some say a cavalry corps,
> some infantry, some, again,
> will maintain that the swift oars
>
> of our fleet are the finest
> sight on dark earth; but I say
> that whatever one loves, is.

Here, Sappho equates the assertion of an objective absolute with militarism and nationalism, with the heroism that Plato sets up as superior to, and in direct opposition to, the (feminine) values inhering in poetry. Perhaps the major discrepancy between the two subjectivities under discussion is precisely that the philosopher's claims to be absolute, uniformly applicable to an entire empire/state's cultural system, and the poet's celebrates the plurality of subjects, difference itself, and it is an emotion — "love," unmanly and unseemly — which allows for that difference.[36]

However, according to these theories, poetry still serves a social function, even as it provides the only ground for a non-socially prescribed identity. This function is homeopathic; the fact of its coexistence with institutional forms of utterance, even while it transgresses their rules, means that there is a space where these prescribed forms can be not only healthily violated, but healthily recombined and rejuvenated. It would thus appear to actually strengthen, rather than to threaten in any serious way, normative discourse. In political terms, we could translate this to mean that the possible expression of oppressed groups' subjective experience through poetry simply strengthens the hegemonic system that keeps them down, by appearing to "give them a voice" in as rarified and "safe" a venue as poetry. Publishing an anthology of homeless kids' poetry every few years satisfies (humanist) liberal human-interest sensibilities, and costs less than employment and housing programs. But writers such as Stierle and Eric Gans, who specifically claim this ultimately socializing function for the seemingly "individualistic" lyric, compare Sappho's lyrics with Anacreon's ribald verses or Rilke's poetry, and find that her poetry, which we read as the starting point of the lyric tradition, falls short of this redemptive imperative, and thus fails. Sappho's "I," apparently, remains an "I," unassimilated into any greater social network.[37]

How can the alleged founder of a tradition not live up to that tradition? These theorists take for their point of departure a split between public and private, community and individual, even while they aim to show how poetry can bridge that split. Unsurprisingly, just as the rebels within Plato's tradition are considered "nihilists" or "prophets of extremity," so the Others who write are considered outsiders, and their writings shots in the dark. Multiple communities and multiple subjects all involve each other in elaborate interplay. Sappho's poetry is not asocial; she writes from a community of women. Writing that expresses a philosophy different from that of the dominant one does not come out of a void, but rather from a nondominant culture with a complicated relation to the whole, which is itself not a centralized, coherent entity, but a series of relationships between cultures.

Another aspect of poetry, however, complements these. Poetry had its origins in healing rituals, invocations to the powers that govern material (epidemiological, meteorological, nutritional, anatomical) conditions and was intimately connected to the bodily and spiritual life of communities. Recent work in ethnopoetics and anthropology has raised both the possibilities of kinship between traditional forms of ritual utterance and modern Western poetry, and the dangers of a presumptuous and too hasty equivalence of the two, born perhaps of a romantic desire to see poetry as a means toward global unmediated consciousness, a bridge between "modern" and "primitive" that can serve as a way out of the alienation of industrialized society.[38] Despite the dangers of ahistoricity, it is worth considering that the needs served by contemporary Western poetry may bear a family resemblance to those served by other forms of ritual utterance elsewhere and at other times.

To reiterate the two aspects of poetry elaborated on here: poetry as *subjective activity* allows the poet or reader to validate her or his own experience in relation to a normative myth of experience; poetry as *communal activity* gives this subjective expression a sympathetic context—a constantly mobile "tradition"—whether or not the poet or reader is in actual contact with like-minded souls. Judy Grahn brings together the communal aspect of poetry with affirmation of nonnormative experience, and simultaneously touches on the idea of poetry by "marginals" as indigenous:

> Poetry helps the language stay open, and language is what you think with. We lead history. . . . Almost all women write poetry, and they write it in very real ways. They write love poetry when they are adolescents, and they write protest poetry too. When I was eleven, I wrote a long ballad about not wanting to do the dishes and my Girl Scout troupe put it on as a matter of course. That's indigenous art. It doesn't necessarily get on television, but that isn't our function.[39]

In spite of their (sometimes unconscious) relationship to community, the significant loneliness of many of the writers studied here contributes to the singularity of vision to which the lyric lends itself, because it speaks to the subjective suffering so often overlooked in studies of oppression.[40]

While a discussion of Sapphic antidiscourse in conflict with Platonic discourse is not wholly irrelevant in a study of contemporary American poets, and while we have by no means confidently left behind the modern adaptations of the hierarchic tropes and structures of the latter (ladder) mode, the postmodern (anti)discursive scene reflects no such neat dichotomy as the one I have outlined between poetry and philosophy, or between the lateral and the vertical. The poetry is not neatly contained in a respectable, closed lyric: even the fragmentation of modern poetry—unlike the literal fragments of Sappho's extant work that have been pieced together variously by different scholars, poets and translators to most closely resemble postulated anterior "whole" lyrics—was conceived fragmentedly. Its "wholeness" a priori violated, it is already a collage of contemporaneous, mutually jostling discourses—including what was once philosophy.

Taking It To The Street

I Speak in an Illusion

I speak but only in an illusion
For I see and I don't

It's me and it's not
I hear and I don't

These illusions belong to me
I stole them from another

Care to spend a day in my House of Death?
Look at my Garden ... are U amazed?
No trees, no flowers, no grass ... no gardens ...

I love and I don't
I Hate and I don't
I Sing and I don't
I live and I don't

For I'm in a room of clouded smoke
And a perfumed odor

Nowhere can I go and break these bonds
Which have me in an illusion

But the bonds are real

#21918[41]

Theory as non-theory leaves the field open. For, it is in the space of such voiding that theory can be said to come closest to poetry, making possible analytical discourses that take into account crises of meaning, subject, and structure by reflecting and acknowledging within their own fabric that these crises are inherent to the signifying function. ... [Poetry] is ... "the major voice of poor, working class, and Colored women" ... Hence, it is also a political tool to question multiple forms of repression and dominance, including the linear use of language as an instrument or a vehicle to support a praxis rather than constituting one. Poetic language communicates and works with meaning, but being only one of its limits, meaning can

never exhaust the poetic activity. . . . Working with subject-ivity is an
ongoing practice that [does not concern] inserting a "me" into
language, but [creates] an opening where the "me" disappears while
"I" endlessly come and go . . .
Trihn T. Minh-ha[42]

With Nietzsche and the late nineteenth century came challenges to
the hegemonic imagery of the Chain, even as imperial efforts in Western Europe strove to manage popular support by promulgating
myths of difference and superiority. Globally expansionist activities
brought Anglo-Europeans into close contact with "other" cultures,
and once again the vertical images of hierarchy had to cede to those
of a lateral, panoramic acknowledgment of difference. Contemporaneous juxtaposition has come to replace narrative structures based
on (implicitly hierarchic) anteriority and causality. The language of
center and margin, rather than top and bottom, reenters the tropic
imagination. Even though difference continues to be rhetorically cast
as "bad," "less than," and worthy of rule by the "better," the breakdown is underway; the proliferation of discourse about "Others" allows cracks and fissures in the ideological edifice it was intended to
buttress. From Romantic critiques of positivism to contemporary
poststructuralist attacks on "logocentrism," with Nietzsche's evolution from *The Birth of Tragedy* to *Beyond Good and Evil* serving to
instantiate a microcosmic fulcrum of transition, these challenges are
especially poignant and relevant here for several reasons. Primarily,
these philosophers, from Nietzsche through Heidegger to Foucault
and Derrida, embody their antipositivism in a highly "poetic" poetics
of discontinuity rather than a heretofore traditionally linear argu-
mentation; one commentator refers to their "aestheticist" orientation.[43] Nietzsche used stinging, self-referential aphorisms and an ex-
travagantly vigorous tempo as weapons to attack traditional Western
metaphysics, a project central to his entire opus.[44] These stylistic
characteristics resonate with some of the trends in modern poetics
that have started to unravel the lyric mode—MacLeish's highly con-
testable "a poem should not mean but be" and the Williams-Creely
continuum: "No ideas but in things," "no things but in words," which
moves from an objectivist stance to a deconstructive, proto-"language" position. Heidegger's stylistic and intellectual preoccupation
with the open-ended process of the "poetics of being" makes his
work appealing to admirers of experimental, and marginalized, mod-

ernists such as Woolf and Proust. Derrida's challenge to the notion of language as primarily referential and mediating a fixed reality, and the consequent difficulty of his style, has obvious resonances in the language poets' impatience with the rigid referentiality of the traditional lyric or (as they often put it) "workshop" poem. Foucault's similarly radical historiographic undertakings are made manifest in the shimmering, elusive quality of his prose.[45] These writers poeticize philosophy, lateralize hierarchy, and complicate heretofore unambiguous narratives about empire, language, and difference. This lateralization turns the Chain into a street. It is impossible to return to the pre-Platonic state and prediscursive utterances Page Dubois describes; the simultaneity and circulatory possibilities of the street bear the scars of hierarchy, exploitation, and ongoing cruelty. The poetic utterances of this condition echo but differ sharply from Sappho's self-confident separation of island and mainland, her assertion of her right to subjectivity ("but *I* say . . . "), her ability to name absolutely the woman who has betrayed and abandoned her, and the institutions that that woman has preferred to Sappho's.

As I have suggested, the breakdown of positivist discourse finds an analogous breakdown in traditional lyric poetry. Walter Benjamin's essay on Baudelaire declares the lyric to be in crisis; Baudelaire (publication of whose *Les Fleurs du Mal* in 1857 is commonly credited, along with that of Flaubert's *Madame Bovary* in the same year, with inaugurating European literary modernism) serves as the first antilyrical lyricist; in other words, no sooner does the lyric become the dominant mode of poetic expression than it is in crisis, about to be superseded by a form reflecting a consciousness that sees through the elegiac yearning for the autonomous subject made evident by the lyric's popularity.[46] To the extent that the traditional lyric still exists in the modern American scene, this crisis is in full evidence in the works I examine. While a fully developed discussion of modernism and postmodernism would skew this project digressively, I would claim that, in the current transition from the modern to the postmodern, modern (twentieth-century) poetry is "modernist" to the extent to which it adheres to lyrical principles, "postmodernist" to the extent to which those principles are obviously inadequate to the most urgent contemporary utterances: those emanating from the subcultures, the margins, the "outside."

Gilles Deleuze and Félix Guattari define texts of "minor" literature in terms of three major criteria: these texts always "take on a collective value," everything contained therein is always "political," and their language is always "affected by a high coefficient of deterritorialization."[47] Deleuze and Guattari reject the hierarchic model in favor of a spatial, lateral one in which poetic or minor discourse is variously "inside" or "outside" of the dominant discursive modes of the majority culture. Though the model they use (Kafka as the paradigmatic minor writer) is certainly Eurocentric, it is useful here because the writers I focus on are writing from within a world power; their being is both subversive and central to it. Nonetheless, while Deleuze and Guattari's categories are provocative and produce useful analyses of texts that might not otherwise be considered political or collective (such as Kafka's, which are often decontextualized to the point of being considered merely mythic rather than historically constructed), there are severe limitations to the reasoning whereby Deleuze and Guattari arrive at these critical categories. Specifically, they overlap and conflate two of the senses of "minor" — "second-rate" and "minority (oppressed population)" — in a way that not only insults the imaginative capabilities of the less privileged but in doing so adopts an evaluative, condescending tone that simply reinscribes the power relations one would assume that they want to challenge. For example, in accounting for the criterion of "collectivity," they assert that, since there is so little talent in "minor" literature, what little talent there is necessarily becomes representative and enunciates a collectivity.[48] They exemplify privileged fellow-travelers who arrive at brilliant and useful pronouncements through tainted reasoning.

Both the epigraphs that head this subsection enact the poeticity of postmodern "minority discourse." Judy Lucero was a "tecata" (female junkie) and a prisoner who died in 1973 at the age of twenty-eight (reports vary as to whether the cause of death was an overdose or a brain hemorrhage caused by a beating); like many prison writers, she signed her creations, which appeared in various Raza publications in California and elsewhere, with her prisoner number. The poem corresponds to informed but informal expectations of lyric: the subjective mode ("lyric I"); the short, highly metaphoric lines; the hermetic, closed feeling; the "punchline" ending; the rarefied, haunted, solitary feeling it evokes. Nonetheless, knowledge of the material conditions of Lucero's life are critical to understanding that the poem describes far more than a metaphysical or existential impasse; it represents the way the philosophical problem of subjectivity and agency ("It's me and it's not") is inseparable from—inherent in—her imprisonment and addiction. The disorientation of the "I" and the way Lucero recreates it in the reader indicates not only the psychic deterritorialization that is part of Lucero's personal history but also the different kinds of deterritorialization—geopolitical, physical, emotional, sexual—that inflect Mexican-American history, working-class history, women's history. The unplaceability of the "lyric I" in this poem undermines the convention of the "I" as focal point (the "eye," as the well-worn pun has it) which filters all information. This "I" is unreliable and cannot even claim itself; as both pure subjectivity and pure object, its abjection obscures the tremendous power of its own self-creation. The seeming capitulation of the final line ("But the bonds are real") to enchainment as the speaker's ur-reality dissolves as we realize that it is the speaker herself as subjective agency who determines the reality of the bonds. As agent, she can play hostess to the dismayed reader even as she is hostage to her "House of Death." "Are U amazed?" she asks, punning us readers into the maze of her un/reality, undoing our confidence in ourselves as second-person interlocutor by calling us not "you" but the street-version "U," which both capitalizes us and truncates us into a symbolic letter: we find ourselves reified as authority figures who are nonetheless disadvantaged by our privileged naïveté, and who can't reach our subject. When I recently asked a colleague in Chicano studies if Judy Lucero's work was widely taught, he replied that it used to appear fairly often in literary syllabi until "better" Chicana poets, sophisticated, "real" poets came along. If this means that there are poets whose work looks more like modernist lyric, with more "original" or "concrete" metaphors, tighter "control," and a more self-conscious appeal to literary traditions, I want to argue that the elusive, "unfinished," decentered tendencies of her work are exactly what I prize as negating a closure (typical of lyric poetry) that would put the reader safely outside of the intersubjective process of meaning-making. If it means that her poetry is too depressing for students who need positive role models and uplifting PC messages, I can only appeal to contact with the dark side of the street as an equally empowering field of knowledge.

Like Judy Lucero, Vietnamese filmmaker Trinh Minh-ha employs multiple layers of knowingness in her films and her written theory. Though it deploys the Latinate abstraction of "high theory," the passage presented here eschews the scientism of many subjectivist theorists such as Kristeva and Sollers; it refuses footnotes, it is a collage of quoted poetry, aphoristic half-sentences, and more conventionally discursive critiques of linear thought and the objectification of perceived Others in (post)colonialist ethnography. In rejecting a stable "me"-object in favor of an infinitely protean "I"-subject, her text describes its own paradoxicality as well as that of the Lucero poem: "It's me and it's not . . . "/ "subject-ivity is an ongoing practice," not a fixed condition. That a postcolonial woman refugee chooses to speak in all tongues at once marks a significant shift from a condition in which only the dominant can speak, or in which the subcultural, like Sappho, can take an unambiguously self-assertive oppositional stance not from underneath but from outside. The montagelike nature of Trihn's (written and cinematic) speech enunciates a layered "reality" similar to the nonreality of Lucero's "illusion," which she both masters and suffers. Both of these writers articulate a poetics of philosophy and a philosophics of poetry. Both of these writers are able to sustain—must sustain—multiple "lyric I"s, multiply performative subject-personae. Must sustain: in order to survive, and one of them didn't.

It is not my purpose, however, to celebrate naïvely the vanguard poet's psycho-emotional tap dance for survival as an unqualified affirmation or unambiguous declaration of position. Nor is it useful, though it may be inevitable, that my fellow academics (who will, I assume, comprise the bulk of this book's readership) receive this study as an impassioned humanistic plea for the recognition of the poetic impulse as making "Others" "just like us"—whoever "we" may be. In a perceptive article on the worker-poetry vogue in nineteenth-century France, Jacques Rancière points out that, from the point of view of their bourgeois sponsors and to some degree from their own experiential standpoints, worker poets could be poets to the extent that they were *not* workers, to the extent that they saw themselves as alienated from their own class culture and drawn toward "higher things," particularly imaginative language use.[49] They could make the emotive argument to the bourgeois reading public that they too aspired to the same ethereal dreams (smoke rings:

28

"ronds de fumée" evocative of Lucero's "room of clouded smoke": reading this phrase as a reference to poetic activity as well as to pharmaceutical euphoria complicates the scenario productively) and they too loved the finer things of the spirit as much as any leisured person did. Their poets' souls were trapped inside the bodies of workers just as these workers' bodies were themselves trapped inside the temporal, spatial, and cultural constraints of workshops and factories. Nonetheless, they were not leisured or middle-class people, and derived their poignant *cachet* precisely from the perceived distance between their poetic aspirations and their class circumstances. If they were not "really" workers, they certainly had no place in the bourgeoisie or aristocracy either; they were as estranged from the latter class cultures of privilege as from their own.

As a potential "bourgeois sponsor" writing to others who want their course offerings and scholarly methods to reflect the cultural heterogeneity of contemporary American life, I want to acknowledge the necessity of teaching the economic and political power differentials that operate in multicultural relations, and the need to understand individual poets and texts as nonautonomous, interdependent with and implicated in vast and specific social matrices. At the same time it is important to avoid Deleuze and Guattari's maneuver in the direction of a logic of representation, their rationale for collectivity whereby a single "gifted" poet is permitted to speak for others presumably less articulate. As Rancière points out, this is reductive in that it ignores the poet's subjective relations to both her or his subculture and to the mainstream culture. None of the poets studied here, except possibly Lowell the aristocrat, saw themselves as representative, and even he risked social and familial censure when he committed himself to poetry (especially when it entailed abandoning Harvard for the relatively modest Kenyon College); their calling as poets does make them different, often unacceptable to their class cohort even as their class/caste standing removes them from the possibilities of easy assimilation into privileged recognition (except, of course, for Lowell, who continually struggled with precisely this privilege). In a sense, however, this estrangement on both ends of the spectrum of privilege puts the poet at advantage: "inside inside, outside outside,"[50] the poet has to reinvent him- or herself in language. Paradoxically, through representing their experiences of exile and self-invention these writers become "representative" and their texts "collective." Thus, if a collectivity voices its aspirations through these texts, it may be aside from any intention or felt experience on the part of the writer; as Deleuze and Guattari point out, it is precisely the outsiderhood of these writers, their marginality vis-à-vis the mainstream as well as their own "fragile community" that enables "minor(ity)" writers to "express another possible community and to forge the means for another consciousness and another sensibility."[51]

W. E. B. Du Bois speaks of the African-American aspiration toward equality or freedom as a longing to "be a co-worker in the kingdom of culture, to escape both death and isolation, to husband and use his best powers and his latent genius,"[52] and reiterates these central issues of "work, culture, and freedom,"[53] in the opening essay of *The Souls of Black Folk*, his attempt to explain the consciousness of his particular subculture to the people of the dominant culture. The same essay, published in 1903, remains one of the best and most succinct elucidations of the simultaneous dilemma and blessing of the marginalized consciousness.

> The Negro is a sort of seventh son, born with a veil, and gifted with second-sight in this American world,—a world which yields him no true self-consciousness, but only lets him see himself through the revelation of the other world. It is a peculiar sensation, this double-consciousness, this sense of always looking at one's self through the eyes of others, of measuring one's soul by the tape of a world that looks on in amused contempt and pity. One ever feels his twoness—an American, a Negro; two souls, two thoughts, two unreconciled strivings.[54]

Here, Du Bois outlines not the false dichotomies we have been discussing, but the related situation of *internalized* duality, in which members of the abased part of a classical social dualism—white/black, man/woman, adult/child—live an (at least) double life-of-the-mind of one kind or another: either having to maintain the appearance of second-classness while not fully believing it, or maintaining fluency in two sometimes contradictory cultural systems, or having simply to believe in one's right to exist, to participate in general and individual undertakings in the areas of "work, culture, and freedom" in the face of strong dominant-cultural messages to the contrary. In a sense this is an internalized reproduction of the dualism that has enchained one—a belief that one is equally worthy of life and its opportunities and responsibilities and deserving of the love requisite for survival (otherwise, object relations psychologists tell us, the subject would literally not survive and these cultures would not exist), coupled with a socially mandated sense of inferiority and circumscribed potential. Books by members of these nondominant cultures that explore the social and psychological consequences of this dual life have titles like *Woman's Consciousness, Man's World* and *Black Skin, White Masks*, and young people's poems include lines like "a tortured [torched] mind behind a smile," which not only hint at internal and external schisms, but also allude to the *dis*simulation that perforce accompanies the 'attempt to *as*similate, an attempt sometimes perceived as necessary for survival.[55] The component of internalized duality, which Du Bois the modernist (appealing to what at that time he still believed to be the humanist largesse of post-Enlightenment white America) understood as a destructive and debilitating erosion of identity and power, can be reconceptualized as a powerful, almost magical gift of "second-sightedness," or, more appropriately in the postmodern era, multiple-sightedness. Second/plural sight means double vision, living on the Janus-edge, the marginal vanguard. Not only are marginalized writers already "co-workers in the kingdom of culture," they are its founders and replenishers.

Now to collect our Orphic tools—passion, commitment, subversive intents, and, yes, that embarrassing hermeneutical training; to be led in—intro-duced—and to go "there": into the particular underworlds of antidiscourse. Now, in other words, to get our hands dirty with our fellow miners of the kingdom of culture.

2

"Unmeaning Jargon" / Uncanonized Beatitude
Bob Kaufman, Poet

*If reality is taken only as it is given in the immediate impression, if it
is regarded as sufficiently certified by the power it exerts on the
perceptive, affective, and active life, then a dead man indeed still "is,"
even though his outward form may have changed, even though his
sensory-material existence may have been replaced by a disembodied
shadow existence.*
                                        Ernst Cassirer

. . . the myths themselves are persons.
                                        Robert Duncan

*These men are metaphors. Whatever they originally were or did as
actual persons has long since been dissolved into an image of what
[is regarded] to be true spirituality.*
                                        Clifford Geertz

*You must mention Bob's eidetic memory capacity. It was
extraordinary. Also his amazing influence on all who met, heard or
read him thru the years. They speak of "spheres of influence": Bob's
were/are spirals!*
                                        Eileen Kaufman's comments on this chapter

The Myths

Surrealist poet Bob Kaufman died in January of 1986. Prolific and
flamboyant during the late fifties and early sixties, and again briefly
productive in the seventies, he had drifted into silent obscurity by the
time of his death, and died poverty-stricken and physically debili-
tated. He has remained, however, a revered cult figure within the

somewhat circumscribed San Francisco street poetry orbit. Through-out and despite his silence, this "prince of street poetry" continued to represent Beat values: nonconformism as an all-encompassing "poetic" way of life, antiestablishment anger, scorn for material wealth and comfort, and copious drug use in the search for ecstatic vision.[1]

The vivid legends that coalesced around the "hidden master of the Beats" during his lifetime contributed to this mystique. His hagiog-raphy is comprised of compelling details set forth in tags like: "Grew up in New Orleans, German Orthodox Jewish father and Martiniquan Roman Catholic voodoo mother." (Although Kaufman himself en-couraged this version of his genealogy, his brother George says that their paternal grandfather was [part] Jewish, and their schoolteacher mother came from an old, well-known Black New Orleans family, the Vignes. Kaufman's father was a Pullman porter, and many of the po-et's siblings have occupied notable positions in electoral politics, charitable organizations, and culture: his youngest sister, for exam-ple, married Little Richard's and Sam Cooke's manager Bumps Black-well, another sister worked in the Reagan administration under George Schultz, and yet another headed the League of Women Voters in her community; when I tried to contact a fourth sister, her hus-band was being honored by a New Orleans diocese for a distin-guished record of community service. Neither voodoo nor Martinique were involved in their early background, and the Kaufmans, all raised as Black American Catholics, could not be said to be Jewish in any meaningful sense — "not in New Orleans," at any rate.) "Joined the merchant marine at thirteen, circled the globe nine times, was introduced to literature by a first mate." (He was, in fact, eighteen when his brother signed him up. What has been less publicly known is his activism in the National Maritime Union. An impassioned grass-roots orator banned from shipping out under the McCarthy era be-cause of his union affiliation, he became a communist labor orga-nizer in the South.) "Coined the term 'beatnik.'" (In fact, although Kaufman founded the seminal *Beatitude* magazine, it was *San Fran-cisco Chronicle* columnist Herb Caen who coined the pejorative "beatnik" in writing about Kaufman.) "Took a ten- (or twelve-)year Buddhist vow of silence, from JFK's assassination to the end of the Vietnam war." (The joke among his North Beach friends is that, though he did withdraw from public writing and speaking, he frequently uttered the words: "Got any speed?") "Known in France as the 'Black American Rimbaud'." "Invented poems extemporaneously; only started writing them down at wife's insistence." "Knew all the jazz greats; Mingus loved him; the quintessential jazz poet." These phrases have worked their way from his immediate circle into dictionaries of literary biography, recent eulogies, brief biographical sketches in anthologies, and editor's prefaces: the legend has become the official story.[2]

One question that warrants further speculation is what purpose the legend has served. There are possible answers for the tenacious longevity of specific pieces of mis/information: the easy visual misreading of 18 for 13, for example, as the poet's age when he became a merchant seaman, as well as the romantic appeal of the unschooled autodidact. (In fact, according to the same interview with George Kaufman, the poet's mother was a schoolteacher who loved literature and whose living room walls were lined with bookshelves she would fill by buying entire libraries at estate sales; although he claims that Bob was the only sibling with literary interests, George Kaufman also mentions that the Kaufman children had extemporaneous limerick contests on the front porch, and that the whole family were bibliophiles, passing Proust, James, Flaubert, from the older siblings on down.) The power of the half-Black and half-Jewish myth may have arisen, in the war years and afterward, from a sense of solidarity with suffering and the desire to appropriate a doubly marginal status, which might have appealed to a Beat sensibility, as would the idea of a powerful but unorthodox and variegated spiritual heritage. The myth's persistence in contemporary times reflects the utopian dream of a union between two groups whom the media now depict as mutually and violently estranged in American political life.

Moreover, the tenacity of the legend, with all its contradictions, exacerbates the instability of the category of biographical truth and calls dramatic attention to the importance of myth and grandeur in everyday life: as Aimé Césaire has said, "Only myth satisfies man completely; his heart, his reason, his taste for detail and wholeness, his taste for the false and for the true, since myth is all that at once."[3] The power of the Kaufman legend among his surviving North Beach coterie holds together a scene that is struggling to survive the external assaults of gentrification in San Francisco, Reaganomics and its legacy, and changes in national literary taste on the one hand; and on the other, the internal strains of aging, poverty, and the everyday physical and emotional ruin brought about by substance abuse and alcoholism. The myths provide existential nourishment and raisons d'être for a community whose heyday is past and whose material privation—once a defiant gesture of worldly renunciation in the face of national economic prosperity—has become involuntary and inescapable suffering. Tales of Kaufman, its mendicant prophet in all his brilliant decrepitude, comprise a large part of the mythology whereby this community constitutes itself as living and eulogizes itself as dying; almost every local poetry reading since his death has featured several elegies that draw direct parallels between the poet's demise and the waning of San Francisco's bohemian culture.[4] These self-consciously larger-than-life stories, an integral part of the street poetry culture in San Francisco, help the remaining "skeleton crew" (to quote Paul Landry, one of the survivors) to withstand increasing hardship. David Henderson's radio tribute to Kaufman, for example, features elaborately metaphysical descriptions of the poet's room in a transient hotel ("we'd sit in silence for hours, and when the wind would move the blue plastic curtain, we'd know we were there"), several anecdotes about "the time Bob pissed on a cop," and many, many interpretations of the poet's years of silence.

In spite of this rich legend telegraphed in dramatic catchphrases, Kaufman's name has remained obscure in mainstream cultural circles. Similarly, although his work is published by the respectable New Directions and a few pieces have been widely anthologized, his corpus is virtually unknown beyond his immediate milieu and has suffered serious critical neglect. Even if his name is familiar to African-Americanists, most academics, even specialists in modern poetry, have barely heard of him. The only article on the subject, in twenty years of MLA listings, is Barbara Christian's appropriately titled "Whatever Happened to Bob Kaufman?"(1972). While the personality-cultish, local-legend pieces on Kaufman serve a crucial function, because of, as well as in spite of, their relentless marshaling of dramatic and contradictory facts, it is also important to redress the critical lacuna and to acknowledge Kaufman's contributions to the body of modern American poetry.[5]

Furthermore, Kaufman's case illustrates the role and position of a writer in certain social and historical circumstances: his biographical status as stereotyped Beat legend and overlooked Black poet com-

plements, even as it can obscure, the problematics of a marginal writer's relationship to modernism. His work exemplifies a mélange of
many of the cultural trends of the American 1950s and 1960s: the "individualism versus groupism" model for understanding social
dynamics prevalent in the era of McCarthy and the Beats; the popu-
larizing of European modernist developments such as surrealism
and existential philosophy; and the blending of these European
influences with African-American themes and structures. A quintessential subcultural poet, Kaufman is at once multiply marginal and
properly paradigmatic; embodying the mainstream trends and stereotypes of his era, his work is at once high-cultural and streetwise.
For example, as Charles Nilon has pointed out, although Kaufman
writes in Standard English laden with allusions to Camus, Picasso,
and Miro, he also employs street language, Black American verbal
structures (rapping, running it down, and signifying) and jazz modal-
ities in his verse.[6] The following chapter is a twofold attempt: to introduce the reader to Kaufman and his work in general, and through
thematic discussion to explore that work as a meeting place of cultural influences. Because, in this particular case, the status of biographical truth is so wonderfully tenuous, my analysis is frankly
dependent on the contested and contradictory features of his life as
set forth in the legend: his ethnicity, for example, his addictions and
commitment to street life, his life as a sailor, his status as a "jazz
poet," and the historical periods (extending from the McCarthy/
Eisenhower and Kennedy eras into the last decade) across which he
wrote and lived. Thus this study primarily documents, and reenacts
through that documentation, a crisis in representation in which each
possible observation that could be made (that I could make) about
Kaufman participates in an implicit or explicit social project—be it
canon-building, canon-challenging, subject-forming or -deforming,
the academic gentrification of the Beat movement or of street poetry,
or the community-building thereof—that goes far beyond (but is always implicit in) the ostensible limits of the "monograph study" or a
"special case" plea for inclusion in the pantheon of American letters.

Anonymity: The Black Beatnik

The editor's preface to Kaufman's last book, *The Ancient Rain: Poems
1956-1978*, quotes the poet: "I want to be anonymous. I don't know

how you get involved with uninvolvement, but I don't want to be involved. My ambition is to be completely forgotten." Although many
of the biographical facts to which I have alluded seem to support
such a claim, the paradoxes in the words themselves—ambition juxtaposed against anonymity, involvement against uninvolvement—as
well as their placement in a published volume, indicate a deliberate
antirationalism even as they seem to convey an absolute and un-
equivocal commitment to a particular stance. As in a Nietzschean
aphorism, the tension between the words themselves breaks the sentences apart. This is not surprising, since Kaufman lived out the com-
binations and conflicts of several different cultural traditions—Euro-
American, Judeo-Christian, African-American, African-Caribbean,
even African, since his maternal grandmother (or great-grandmother), with whom he was very close, came over on a slave ship.[7]
While it is clear that some of these traditions have been violently dis-
torted in the interests of others, and hence have been the locus of
much suffering, Kaufman reworks this pain, turning it, as Jean Genet
says saints do, to good account.[8] The seeming paradox of Kaufman's
claims to anonymity constitutes a rich, if sometimes conflicting, plurality of themes throughout his life and work that radically undermines the hierarchic logic of dominant Euro-American metaphysics
and its attendant political and aesthetic organizing principles. His
statement, in other words, as well as his use of surrealist techniques,
challenge what Jacques Derrida has criticized as the "logocentrism"
of Western poetic and philosophical discourse. His corpus riddled
with contradictions and illness, his language rich and heteroglossic
(literally: he was fluent in non-English Louisiana patois), he instantiates the Derridean challenge to live—as well as write and speak—by
riddles, antilogocentrically.

The concept of anonymity provides a signal opportunity for examining the conventions of naming, which is an integral strategy in
Kaufman's work and life. The Beats spurned material goods and fame
in favor of "voluntary poverty" and artistic obscurity; this ethos of
self-effacement and downward mobility paradoxically appealed to
many whose parents had just started to inch out of the working class
into middle-class semiprofessional jobs or skilled labor, or who, like
Jack Kerouac, were first-generation college kids.[9] Nonetheless, in
Kaufman's case, namelessness is not simply or unequivocally a matter of choice. Unnaming, naming, and renaming, as acts of violence,

have been crucial in the history of Blacks and Jews in the West. Africans, when imported as merchandise to the New World, were renamed as the property of the men who purchased them as slaves: their new surnames were their masters', often with the genetive marker "s" added to underscore their status as owned things (for example, a slave belonging to Mr. Lee would be Anne Lees). Their new first names were often either infantile, reflecting the theory that slaves were childlike and happy in their servitude, or, especially for men, faintly exotic and regal (names of Roman statesmen, for example), as one might name fine animals. Jews were renamed first in Europe with names that spoke of degradation (Eckstein, for example—curbstone, where dogs urinate), or that alternatively evoked mercenary stereotypes—words for precious metals and jewels. "Kaufman" itself means "merchant," though it could also be a version of "*Yakov*man." Sometimes these names changed once again in transit through various ports of entry into the States, and still once again in an attempt to hide one's Jewishness—the evolution, for example, of (?) to Diamant to Diamond to Damon, or more dramatically, from (?) to Goldberg to Mont D'Or. The subject who has undergone such a series of transformations is surely, in one sense, anonymous. The "original name," having lost its context, loses its meaning as well—not to mention that its retrieval is virtually impossible and not necessarily desirable. In this context, the new name testifies to the oppression it seeks to vitiate. Thus *un*titling, or unnaming, as Kimberly Benston has pointed out, becomes an act of *en*titlement, as in the case of Malcolm X, who, rather than taking on another designator of oppression as did some ex-slaves after the Civil War, adopted the anonymous X to convey not only the destruction of his African history but his fraternity with all others similarly violated.[10] By taking himself outside of the conventional taxonomy of masters and slaves, he not only commented on it but established an entirely new relationship to it. Another critic speaks of Césaire's poetry as his "most intimate way to conciliate . . . his sense of his own blackness with his yearning for an anonymous and universal presence in the future fraternal world."[11] Positively associating anonymity with a diffuse metaphysical consciousness (consonant with Kaufman's Beat Buddhist leanings) and also with social community suggests that in the play between unnaming and renaming, marginal poets create themselves in language.

One's given name is thus simply the top layer of a palimpsest, a series of historical masks that reveal as they conceal. Namelessness implies a multiplicity of names. Since names cannot be removed, one can only add another name to the chain, enriching the linguistic texture of one's sojourn through history. It is the evolution from Malcolm Little to Malik El-Shabazz and Malcolm X, or from Joe Gardner Junior to James Joe Junior Brown to JAMES BROWN that gives the final name its power.[12] Those who are invisible become masters of performance and disguise, and poetry is that mastery. Kaufman plays on versions of his own and others' names chopped up, rearranged, and punned upon. The "Abomunist Manifesto, by Bomkauf" satirically deconstructs what Barbara Christian has referred to as "isms": contrived attempts to regiment thought into systems, "last words" which claim authority as the only words, and which thus become implicated in such final solutions as the atomic bomb. The Manifesto issues behavioral imperatives in descriptive form:

ABOMUNISTS DO NOT FEEL PAIN, NO MATTER HOW MUCH IT HURTS.

. . .

ABOMUNISTS DO NOT WRITE FOR MONEY; THEY WRITE THE MONEY ITSELF.

. . .

ABOMUNIST POETS [ARE] CONFIDENT THAT THE NEW LITERARY FORM "FOOTPRINTISM" HAS FREED THE ARTIST OF OUTMODED RESTRICTIONS, SUCH AS: THE ABILITY TO READ AND WRITE, OR THE DESIRE TO COMMUNICATE. . . . [13]

"Further Notes (taken from 'Abomunismus und Religion')" are attributed to "Tom Man," whose name, a hybrid of Thomas Mann and Tom Paine (the aesthetic and the political), picks up the crucial syllable the poet left out of "Bomkauf." "Excerpts from the Lexicon Abomunon," we are told, have been compiled by "Bimgo" (Bill Margolis, another founding editor of *Beatitude*). A section of surrealist couplets is captioned "Boms." In the "Abomunist Rational Anthem" language completely disintegrates; Tom Man becomes Shakespeare's Mad Tom, a sane man in disguise to save his life:

> Derrat slegelations, flo goof babereo
> Sorash sho dubies, wago, wailo, wailo.

Though it is possible to decode this poem to some degree ("derrat" is "tarred" backwards; "slegelations" elides "sludge" and "legislations," indicating Kaufman's assessment of United States justice; "flow," "goof," "dubies," and "wailo" evoke jazz/Beat/drug culture, etc.), the point is not to do so, but to experience the disorientation of babble. This type of linguistic play recalls Langston Hughes's "Syllabic Poem," a songlike arrangement of nonsense syllables with which he intended to deflate the pretentiousness typical of poetry readings; he wrote to Countee Cullen, who was to perform it in his absence, that "the poetry of sound . . . marks the beginning of a new era . . . of revolt against the trite and outworn language of the understandable." He suggests that it would lead the literati to "discuss the old question as to whether . . . poets are ever sane. I doubt if we are."[14] Though Hughes calls the whole notion "amusing," another African-diaspora poet foregrounds the militant purposiveness of such nonsense poetry: Césaire explicitly articulates the project of "breaking the oppressor's language" by using it to, and beyond, capacity.[15] This deconstructive syllabification is also reminiscent of scat singing, the improvised nonsense syllables invented and used for sonic pleasure by jazz vocalists with names like King Pleasure, who influenced Kaufman. Ishmael Reed chose the "Rational Anthem" under another title, "Crootey Songo," as the epigraph for the first volume of the *Yardbird Reader.*[16]

These outbursts of fragmented language joining sorrow, defiance, and (king) pleasure suggest the immediacy of the body and its expulsive processes. In the out-of-print broadside *Does the Secret Mind Whisper?* "clouds of coughed sorrow" echo the opening line of Kaufman's first book: "I have folded my sorrows into the mantle of summer night"; ("I Have Folded My Sorrows," SCL 3); likewise the weakest personality of the five in the poem "Cincophrenicpoet" "cough[s] poetry in revenge." (SCL 49) The poet is a "cough-man" whose poetry, as a bodily function, bursts from his innards as if involuntarily, evoking the sharp and rhythmic out-breaths punctuating the work songs of Southern chain gangs. The identification of sorrow and poetry as literal "gut reactions" to oppression resonates with W. E. B. Du Bois's discussion of the spiritual "sorrow songs" as the almost instinctive and visceral expression of a tyrannized culture (see especially his transcription of the song, of unknown language, his "grandmother's grandmother" passed down to him, and note its kinship to Hughes's poem); and with Frederick Douglass's impassioned assertion that "[slaves singing] . . . words which to many would seem unmeaning jargon, but which, nevertheless, were full of meaning to themselves ... breathed the prayer and complaint of souls boiling over with the bitterest anguish. Every tone was a ... prayer to God for deliverance from chains." Kaufman's unmeaning jargon differs sharply from meaninglessness. His unmeaning—as in unnaming— aims to destroy actively the comfort of meaning, to burst its chains in service of the furious, spasmodic play of jazz energy. His jargon is both the special code of initiated hipsters (the underground cultural counterpart to an elite of educated expertise) and the original "jargon": etymologically, the babble of (yard)birds, gurgling—the bubbling up and over of untamable sound. Julia Kristeva has used Artaud's term "expectoration" (kauf-ing) to describe this boiling over, a pulsating gush of poetic language as so much bodily excess that " 'creates' [and] ... reinvents the real" through the physical contortions of expulsion and release. However, the ascetic and fragmented ecstasies of Kaufman's unmeaning jargon partake of a tradition inflected as much by social and physical suffering as by presymbolic *jouissance*. Perhaps James Brown's signature *ex tempore* ejaculations best epitomize this ambiguous pleasure-pain, especially during the militant "Say It Loud, I'm Black and I'm Proud," which he pierces with "ooee—baby—you're killing me," a cry usually of sexual delight turned in context to social outrage.[17]

Like "Abomunist Manifesto," the long poem "Carl Chessman Interviews the PTA (from his swank gas chamber)" joins social protest and physical fracturing through linguistic play. In the second section of this satiric poem, which opens *Golden Sardine*, Kaufman manipulates Caryl Chessman's name to place him in a heroic pantheon ("Charlie Chaplin," "Caryl Melville," "Carl Darrow," "F. Scott Chessman"), to draw attention to the international dimensions of the case ("Carlos," "carlito," "Carl" as well as "Caryl" Chessman, "Call Chez-Main": appeals for clemency for Chessman came from Brazil, Uruguay, the Vatican, Britain, Denmark, etc.), and to make the name itself physical ("Caul," "Chest-man"). Chessman, the victim of one of the most notorious and protracted capital punishment cases in the twentieth-century United States, becomes mythified through the fragmentation and dispersal of his name; and, as in any instance of wrongful death at the hands of the powerful, the analogy to Jesus' crucifixion offers itself, crossing over from the dominant culture to serve as a charged subtext.[18] In "Benediction," the poet announces:

America, I forgive you . . .
Nailing Black Jesus to an imported cross
Every six weeks in Dawson, Georgia.
(SCL 9)

The poet's role itself is Christlike, oral poetry streaming from the sacred bodily wounds which become alternate mouths: he "sings the
nail-in-the-foot song, drinking cool beatitudes" ("Afterwards, They
Shall Dance," SCL 6). And Jesus himself was a hip cat who wrote jazz
poetry, as the satire on the Dead Sea Scrolls in the "Abomunist Manifesto" implies:

> Had a ball this morning, eighty-sixed some square bankers from the
> Temple, read long poem on revolt. Noticed cats taking notes, maybe
> they are publishers' agents, hope so, it would be crazy to publish
> with one of those big Roman firms.[19]

Kaufman's circle has not been slow to associate the Christic attribute of humility, of giving up one's physical integrity and personal
claim to sacredness to die in obscurity, with Kaufman's withdrawal
and decline; one of the elegies that appeared after his death was A. D.
Winans's "Black Jesus of the Fifties." Accordingly, Kaufman's preoccupation with anonymity and silence come, in his life story, to indicate
strength and choice even as they continue to evoke their traditional
negative association with the silencing of the dispossessed. The vow
of silence carries with it the force of the powerful—the users of
words—assuming the powerlessness of those whose voices are ig-
nored. Like Gandhi, whose assumption of asceticism enhanced his
position of leadership, or more appropriately like Genet, who goes
the authorities one better by embracing with enthusiasm the deprav-
ity projected on him by the straight bourgeois world, Kaufman, one
of the politically marginal and silenced, turns the tables on authority
by *choosing*, as an iconic poet-shaman, the silence of religious withdrawal and political disillusionment rather than *submitting* to the silence socially enforced on him as a Black person. The distinction,
though, becomes ambiguous. His withdrawal from the world helps
to fuel the Kaufman legend among a handful of people; it also as-
sures his ongoing obscurity, contributing to his continued exile from
the American canon. The self-mythologizing and powerful aspects of
Kaufman's silence are counterweighted by his actual critical neglect,
a fate suffered involuntarily by many Black American artists. For ex-

ample, some years ago a French television camera crew arrived in North Beach with the intention of making a television special on Kaufman. For two weeks the poet managed to elude them completely and they returned to Europe with no footage. This kind of anecdote serves both to explain the poet's own role in maintaining his obscurity (millions of French viewers remained unexposed to him) and to heighten the mystery and mystique of his authenticity (in itself it remains a wonderful anecdote treasured by his North Beach *confrères*).[20]

The Poetics of the Body; or, Knight-Errant of the Living Dead: The Shaman

If anonymity has to do with presence or absence in history, one's relation to one's body has to do with spatial presence or absence. A noteworthy aspect of Kaufman's career has been his in/visibility as a street person and his experiences with alcohol and drugs, imprisonment and poverty; the poet's body as well as his literary output bears the traces of the Black American condition. His poetic pantheon prominently features Hart Crane, Coleridge, Rimbaud, Poe, and Lorca, all of whom represent some form of physical destruction or self-destruction in the name of an all-encompassing, implacably demanding poetic vision. But at the same time, Kaufman's commitment to an oral immediacy over graphological mediation indicates that his poetics intimately connects physical being and presence. Moreover, the inclusion of political martyrs such as Crispus Attucks and Caryl Chessman (and, of course, Lorca) in this roster of heroes demonstrates a conviction that physical sacrifice is noble, and necessary to achieve political as well as aesthetic fulfillment—that in fact the two are indivisible. While it seems a contradiction to predicate wholeness on the body's devastation, it is possible to approach this phenomenon in a number of ways that make sense.

The cliché of grandiose and conscious self-immolation enhances an artist's mystique, à la Werther. The idea of the artist as a being made superior through suffering cannot be entirely dismissed in Kaufman's case, though his social status precludes at least the more cynical aspects of this interpretive possibility. Kaufman doesn't have to invent drama to aggrandize or even convey his alienation. Rather than either acquiescing to a failure seemingly predestined by social circumstances or opting full tilt for willfully narcissistic self-destruction, Kaufman makes an aesthetic choice based on exigency. The statement "I would die for Poetry" (" 'Michelangelo' the Elder," GS 34) does not swear allegiance to an abstraction; instead, poetry constitutes a way of life as well as a state of mind, both a means and an end coextensive and cofoundational with freedom, transformation, "true" life itself. Death, then, also becomes a means to these ends. According to many who knew him in his North Beach years, Kaufman does not call so much on the relatively modern Western spiritual and literary tradition's notions of mortifying the flesh to feed the spirit, as he does on the older and more inclusive tradition of the poet as shaman, who mediates the spirit world through body as well as through mind, and who often undergoes a near-fatal illness as part of her or his initiation into shamanism. Kaufman filters this tradition through his Western modernist influences to arrive at his own Beat aesthetic. Furthermore, the verbal aspect of shamanism is oral rather than written; the healing chant derives its power in the ritual speaking or singing of it, as jazz and jazz poetry derive their power — in fact exist — in the improvised moment.[21]

Though the term has specific roots in non-Christian Siberian traditions, "shaman" is an overused word in the poetry world and the current spiritual counterculture, a catchall referent for anyone who has access to nonquotidian states of consciousness; any charismatic who "speaks truth to power" based on an authority other than political fervor; who "heals" with ritual, especially ritual in which words play a crucial role; who assumes priestly powers in unorthodox, guerrilla contexts. Though the word derives from Sanskrit (from a root meaning "to exhaust, fatigue," much as the word itself has become), controversies around irresponsible appropriation of the concept have been publicized primarily by Native Americans, who find their spiritual practices invaded and consumed by spiritually starved white folks.[22] Kaufman clearly is not one of these desperately well-intentioned marauders, and according to some of his supporters, would never have applied the term to himself.[23] Nonetheless, it is one of the tropes that fits him well: he is a figure of exhaustion, excess, and dedication to an unworldly calling. Lynne Wildey, Kaufman's self-described "full-time consort" during his last five years, is one of his cohort who has attributed shamanistic characteristics to him, describing how he "charged the night with rare magic."[24] Others have mentioned his prophetic acumen. Kush, the unofficial video-archivist for the North Beach poetry scene and professor of anthropology at New College, tells of Kaufman announcing to him cryptically that "Nazis will come in pyramids from outer space to take over North Beach"; shortly thereafter, Kush received notice that the building he lived in was to be put on the market by Pyramid Realty, whose agent was a Mr. Goebbels. Kaufman's utterance, easily dismissable as delusional street-babble, brilliantly connected the bureaucratic gentility of urban gentrification programs to the sci-fi unthinkable horrors of Nazi Germany's gentile-ification pogroms.[25] Others attribute his prophetic abilities to a New Orleans childhood steeped in alternative, diasporic ways of knowing; before he lost the battle to shock treatments, alcohol, speed, and poverty, he had "the touch."[26]

A specifically African-American or African-Caribbean experience — particularly in the crescent crucible of New Orleans — can put a particular spin on an Orphic or shamanistic creative death. Susan Willis has pointed out the relationship, in the literature of slavery, between forms of mutilation and spiritual as well as physical freedom. Amiri Baraka writes in *Blues People*, with perhaps some rhetorically affected enthusiasm, of junkies as the ultimate rebels, the nonconformists par excellence. Thus, while acknowledging the self-destructive drive in substance addiction and subsistence living, we can also see its integral role in Kaufman's poetics. Moreover, if we look at the African-Caribbean influence on the poet, the African belief that life and death are interchangeable and reversible states, and the Caribbean version of this belief — the zombi myth — physical death becomes another form of life. To die for poetry is to transform oneself for and through poetry; in short, to live for poetry. In this sense, the poet's or political martyr's way of life — death — is simply her or his way, one among many, of achieving freedom. In "The Night that Lorca Comes," Lorca's posthumous advent heralds a Black American movement:

> . . . IT SHALL BE THE TIME WHEN NEGROES LEAVE THE SOUTH
>   FOREVER . . .
> CRISPUS ATTUCKS SHALL ARRIVE WITH THE BOSTON
> COMMONS . . .

(AR 60)

In "Oregon," the poet, transformed into a bird, flies "the Hart Crane trip" (suicide in the Gulf of Mexico) to Heaven where the "florid Black [is] found"(AR 58).[27]

There are different kinds of living dead in Kaufman's poetry: there are those who appear to be dead but live, the lucid minds in impaired bodies who have given their lives to poetry and freedom— and there are those who appear to be alive but are in fact soulless (zombis deadened by exploitation, masters deadened by exploiting). In "The Poet," a work clearly indebted to Langston Hughes's "Wise Men," wherein the speaker wishes to have dead and fishlike eyes like all the wise men he has seen, Kaufman sets forth this opposition as well as the simultaneity of life and death, of the womb and the grave, the embryo and the martyr:[28]

FROM A PIT OF BONES
THE HANDS OF CREATION
FORM THE MIND, AND SHAPE
THE BODY IN LESS THAN A SECOND.
   A FISH WITH FROG'S
    EYES,
    CREATION IS PERFECT.
THE POET NAILED TO THE
BONE OF THE WORLD
COMES IN THROUGH A DOOR
TO LIVE UNTIL
HE DIES,
WHATEVER HAPPENS IN BETWEEN,
IN THE NIGHT OF THE LIVING
DEAD, THE POET REMAINS ALIVE,
   A FISH WITH FROG'S
    EYES,
    CREATION IS PERFECT.
THE POET WALKS ON THE EARTH
AND OBSERVES THE SILENT
SPHINX UPON THE NILE.
THE POET KNOWS HE MUST
WRITE THE TRUTH,
EVEN IF HE IS
KILLED FOR IT, FOR THE
SPHINX CANNOT BE DENIED.
WHENEVER A MAN DENIES IT,

A MAN DIES.
THE POET LIVES IN THE
MIDST OF DEATH. . . .

(AR 68)[29]

Again Kaufman asserts a connection between truth, or freedom, and mutilation, by associating the poet with the Oedipus who sacrificed his standing in the community and his physical integrity for the truth. The implacable Sphinx plays muse to the poet's Oedipus. Access to "truth," rather than one's biological status, determines whether one is living or dead. Kaufman distinguishes sharply between the soulless living dead and the poet who, though alive, is "born to die," and walks wrapped in a cloak of death:

THE BLOOD OF THE POET
MUST FLOW IN HIS POEM
SO MUCH SO THAT OTHERS
WILL DEMAND AN EXPLANATION.
THE POET ANSWERS THAT THE
POEM IS NOT TO BE
EXPLAINED. IT IS WHAT IT
IS, THE REALITY OF THE POEM
CANNOT BE DENIED,
   A FISH WITH FROG'S
   EYES,
   CREATION IS PERFECT.
. . . .
WHEN THE POET PROTESTS THE
DEATH HE SEES AROUND
HIM,
THE DEAD WANT HIM SILENCED.
YET LORCA SURVIVES IN HIS
POEM, WOVEN INTO THE DEEPS
OF LIFE. THE POET SHOCKS THOSE
AROUND HIM. HE SPEAKS OPENLY
OF WHAT AUTHORITY HAS DEEMED
UNSPEAKABLE, HE BECOMES THE
ENEMY OF AUTHORITY. WHILE THE
POET LIVES, AUTHORITY
DIES. HIS POEM IS
FOREVER . . .

The poet's physical sacrifice not only serves as proof that he is alive, but incites others to participate in the poetic/communal project by making them ask questions that can't be answered; the poem becomes ritual and public, even though the poet himself is isolated. And Kaufman neatly juxtaposes poetry with authority, the poet who mediates versus the author who dictates. Poetry is an absolute, a state of grace. Note that the poet refers to "Lorca's poem" in the singular: Lorca's poem is his life, which in turn mingles inextricably with the universal "deeps of life."

The mention of Lorca implicates another poet whose influence, though unacknowledged, Kaufman certainly felt. The mystical paradoxes and oxymorons of Lorca's poetic ancestor, Saint John of the Cross, find Beat American expression in Kaufman's dark night of the living/dead soul. Living/dead, engaged/alienated, isolated/public, transcendent/plunged in the most vivid physical and psychic suffering, "less than a second"/ "forever": all resonate with the ecstatic suffering of (the also apocryphally Jewish) St. John, whose rapturous poems were composed under torture. The word "beat" is itself a paradox of joy and suffering: in the 1950s and 1960s, to the people who adopted a Beat life, the term meant beatific, wasted, and, especially in Kaufman's case, steeped in the soulfully erotic tradition of jazz. John of the Cross, along with Lorca, had a tremendous surge of popularity in the 1950s and 1960s. The first year that the poems were published in English separately from the rest of the mystic's work was 1951; interest in him spilled over from the religious domain into the secular, with Pantheon publishing Roy Campbell's translations at the same time as Burns, Oates of London put out E. Allison Peer's translations. By the end of the decade, the Beats and the American literary avant-garde had adopted St. John as one of them, having found in St. John's poetry the *ekstasis* they felt to be their trademark. Grove Press in New York, one of the few commercially successful venues for avant-garde writing, published yet another translation of the *Poems* in 1959. New Directions still publishes this translation. Since Kaufman lived in New York from 1960 to 1963 and moved in the same circles as these publishers, he could not have escaped St. John's influence.[30]

In "All Hallows, Jack O'Lantern Weather, North of Time," which invokes the holiday of the living dead, Kaufman presents a negative version of the possibilities of living death. Although extremely dissimilar in style and sensibility, "All Hallows" shows some thematic influence of Eliot's *Wasteland* and the title, taken from the first poem in (another

New Orleans writer) Tennessee Williams's *In the Winter of Cities,* resonates sonically with "The Hollow Men." The refrain in Williams's "In
Jack-O'-Lantern's Weather" echoes the clause that Eliot's "Love Song
of J. Alfred Prufrock" forever associated with alienated, depersonal-
ized longing: "I have seen them . . . " (Kaufman committed to memory and rap/recited the works of both Williams and Eliot, but especially the latter: the poet broke his vow of silence by reciting Becket's
opening speech from *Murder in the Cathedral* and then his own "All
Those Ships That Never Sailed.")[31] Kaufman shares Eliot's and
Williams's sense of detachment, disembodiment, disorientation; his
poem is peopled with "loudly walked bruises, thick string unbeings
pouring themselves into each other, filling themselves with each other's emptiness, shouting silences across screaming rooms." Oppres-
sors and oppressed participate in a symbiotic sickness in which emptiness and silence are the exchange currency. But, departing from
Eliot's global pessimism and unreconciled alienation, in a move
closer to Williams's privileged though closeted erotic gaze on "marvelous" schoolboys, Kaufman asserts that the marginal poet, though
he suffers intense loneliness, occupies a privileged position of access:

> . . . I KNOW OF A PLACE IN BETWEEN BETWEEN, BEHIND BEHIND, IN FRONT OF FRONT,
> BELOW BELOW, ABOVE ABOVE, INSIDE INSIDE, OUTSIDE OUTSIDE, CLOSE TO CLOSE, FAR
> FROM FAR, MUCH FARTHER THAN FAR, MUCH CLOSER THAN CLOSE, ANOTHER SIDE OF AN
> OTHER SIDE . . . IT LIES OUT ON THE FAR SIDE OF MUSIC. . . . THAT DARKING PLANE OF
> LIGHT ON THE OTHER SIDE OF TIME. . . . IT BEGINS AT THE BITTER ENDS.
>
> (AR 48)

The outsider-poet is both excruciatingly close, intimate with the
world, and cast out of it. The consequence of not being allowed to
take up space is that one knows the ins and outs of spatiality, and the
consequence of being a poet is that one can use that knowledge to
advantage.[32]

Space and time, history and geography meet in the poet's body:
that is, a Black and Jewish male body takes up space in the United
States between 1925 and 1986, survives World War II, the McCarthy
era, the sixties and seventies and most of the Reagan years. The history of this body is marked by its subjection to multiple addictions
and brutality at the hands of others. (At thirteen, for example,
Kaufman was hung by his thumbs in an icehouse all night by a lynch
mob, an event he alludes to in "Unhistorical Events" and "Blue

Slanted Into Blueness" [GS 30-31, 35]; in his active Beat days he was arrested thirty-five times in one-and-a-half years; in 1963 he was arrested for walking on the grass in Washington Square Park, given between 50 and 100 shock treatments, and threatened with a lobotomy. Some of his North Beach friends speculate on a connection between those treatments and his vow of silence.) And like his name, that other conventional index of identity, Kaufman's body, and the concepts of space and time themselves, appear in his work in characteristic double guise. Like language, they function as arenas of oppression and, to borrow again from Césaire, as "miraculous weapons."[33]

It is not useful, however, to underestimate, glamorize, or pass over in silence the painful aspects of substance addiction and the way the addict experiences his or her body. Kaufman's poetry describes a process in which the subject experiences a separation of mind and body, so that the latter becomes other and foreign. Depersonalization has been noted as a survival technique for, among others, sexual abuse survivors and the concentration camp inmates of World War II; we might want to consider adding to the list social outsiders whose bodies bear the marks of their exclusion. Elaine Scarry has commented on the role of physical pain in undoing a coherent worldview and with it, coherent utterance governed by the will of the speaking subject.[34] To the extent that Kaufman's poetry reflects his experience with the physical pain of police brutality and drug addiction in tandem with the psychic pain of social outsiderhood, its language is made up of fragments, deconstructing back into presymbolic scraps of sound ex-pressed through outbursts of protest and play ("Crootey Songo"); the body is presented alternately as disintegrating, devolving back into nature, separating from the "I" of the poem, or rigidly alien. Like the "unbeings" who pour themselves into each other's emptiness, the poet's body is a hollow space he inhabits, or a set of discrete body parts:

> I wish whoever it is inside of me,
> would stop all that moving around
> go to sleep, another sleepless year
> like the last one will drive me sane,
>
> I refuse to have any more retired burglars
> picking the locks on my skull, crawling in
> through my open windows, i'll stay out forever
> ("I Wish," GS 66)

> Sometimes in extravagant moments of shock of unrehearsed
> curiosity, I crawl outside of myself, sneaking out through the eyes,
> one blasé, one surprised, until I begin to feel my own strangeness;
> shyly I give up the ghost and go back in until next time.
>
> ("Unanimity Has Been Achieved, Not a Dot
> Less for Its Accidentalness," AR 16)

> My body is a torn mattress,
> Dishevelled throbbing place
> For the comings and goings
> Of loveless transients.
> The whole of me
> Is an unfurnished room
> Filled with dank breath
> Escaping in gasps to nowhere.
>
> . . .
>
> I have walked on walls each night
> Through strange landscapes in my head.
>
> . . .
>
> My face is covered with maps of dead nations;
>
> . . .
>
> I can't go out anymore
> I shall sit on my ceiling.
> Would you wear my eyes?
>
> ("Would You Wear My Eyes?" SCL 40)

These poems demonstrate an acute alienation of body and consciousness; a soul, present or absent, rattles around in and out of a
gutted tenement of a body. The reader experiences the poet's objectified body from the inside and simultaneously sees it, in its various
forms of decrepitude, from the outside. The "strange landscapes"
and the "maps of dead nations" on the body's surface both point toward the involuntary dissociation from native landscapes and traditions that underlies African-American history, and serve as ties with
the past; his history is inscribed in his body.

Sometimes, however, in the tradition of the waking of the living
dead, despair turns. In "All Those Ships That Never Sailed," the recital
of which poem broke the ten years of silence, Kaufman sums up his
body's history in terms of political and romantic betrayal and resur-
rects it, re-membering it through love:

My body once covered with beauty
Is now a museum of betrayal.
This part remembered because of that one's touch
This part remembered through that one's kiss—
Today I bring it back
And let you live forever.

(AR 55)

This poem asserts a universal body; the resurrection of "my" body allows "you" to live forever in the moment that the poet once again joins words and physical presence. In "Dolorous Echo":

The holey little holes
In my skin,
Millions of little
Secret graves,
Filled with dead
Feelings
That won't stay
Dead.

The hairy little hairs
On my head,
Millions of little
Secret trees,
Filled with dead
Birds,
That won't stay
Dead.

When I die,
I won't stay
Dead.

(SCL 30)

Here the body and its parts are presented as wasted, used up from years of exploitation, though on hand for resurrection. At the same time, though, the body is part of nature, a collage of despoliation, dessication and rampant fertility:

My hair is littered with drying ragweed.
Bitter raisins drip haphazardly from my nostrils
While schools of glowing minnows swim from my mouth.
The nipples of my breasts are sun-browned cockleburrs;

52

Long-forgotten Indian tribes fight battles on my chest
Unaware of the sunken ships rotting in my stomach.
My legs are charred remains of burned cypress trees;
My feet are covered with moss from bayous, flowing
      across my floor.

                    (SCL 40)

My face feels like a living emotional relief map, forever wet.
My hair is curling in anticipation of my own wild gardening.
         ("Afterwards They Shall Dance," SCL 6)

My hair is overrun with crabgrass, parts of my anatomy are still
unexplored.
             ("Blues for Hal Waters," AR 28)

Kaufman rewrites the "Song of Songs" *blason* in narcissistic, night-
marish terms. Beside the noticeable influence of Whitman in these
pieces, indicating the landscape as the United States, the ironic use of
travel-section or geography-book cliché suggests his body as a "dark
continent." Elsewhere it is "Oregon."

You are with me Oregon,
Day and night, I feel you, Oregon.
I am Negro. I am Oregon.
Oregon is me, the planet
Oregon, the State Oregon, Oregon.
In the night, you come with bicycle wheels,
Oregon you come
With stars of fire. You come green.
Green eyes, hair, arms,
Head, face, legs, feet, toes
Green, nose green, your
Breast green, your cross
Green, your blood green.
Oregon winds blow around
Oregon. I am green, Oregon.
You are mine, Oregon. I am yours,
Oregon. I live in Oregon.
Oregon lives in me,
Oregon, you come and make
Me into a bird and fly me
To secret places day and night.
The secret places in Oregon,

> I am standing on the steps
> Of the holy church of Crispus
> Attucks St. John the Baptist,
> The holy brother of Christ,
> I am talking to Lorca. We
> Decide the Hart Crane trip, home to Oregon
> Heaven flight from the Gulf of
> Mexico, the bridge is
> Crossed, and the florid black found.
>
> ("Oregon" AR 58)

Written on the occasion of a trip to Ken Kesey's Oregon farm for the "First Poetry Hoo-Haw," the poem presents two seemingly contradictory principles. Kaufman presents "Negro-ness" as an arbitrary designation: a "Negro" may be distinguished as well by the color green as any other—indeed, many different colors are termed "Negro" or Black, because anyone of any African ancestry is referred to as Black in this country. (As Henry Gates has pointed out, "race is the ultimate trope of difference because it is so very arbitrary in its application.")[35] Arbitrarily yoking "green," "Oregon," and "Negro" draws attention to one aspect of African-American history: one is arbitrarily and cruelly thrust into a landscape with a preexisting historical meaning and expected to accommodate and conform. But as in so many other instances, Kaufman simultaneously undermines the arbitrary violence he posits. The poem samples Lorca's "Somnambule Ballad" with its haunting refrain:

> Green how much I want you green.
> Green wind. Green branches.
>
> . . .
>
> Green flesh, hair of green . . .

Lorca's poem is charged both with romance and with hints of a dangerous, possibly fatal political situation, involving the drunken civil guards knocking on the door in the moonlight. (Lorca was himself executed by Franco's troops and his body thrown into an unmarked grave reminiscent of Kaufman's "pit of bones.")

For Lorca, green, like moonlight, may have signified death as well as rebirth, and in the context of the poem, desire. Robert Duncan, another San Franciscan reading Lorca at the same time, discusses the

"Romance Sonambule" in a gay context, bearing out this possibility of desire. His Spanish dictionary yields sexual meanings for "verde":

> Verde, we find, means not only "green" with all that sense of freshness and entranced forthrightness ... but it also means "off-color," "indecent"—the lewd green of hot leaves—even as, in English, getting "fresh" can mean going too far. Is there ... a magic sense in which the quickening power of being a man, the quickening of a man, and the greening are identical? Is there a greenness to verity, an almost indecent freshness in being aware of what is at issue?[36]

Green, in other words, suggests wildness, potency, and possible insurrection—the rampant fertility of a "living emotional relief map." But Kaufman borrows from this European poet/martyr's work for his own purposes. Here again, Kaufman juggles meanings and countermeanings–he "unmeans." The color symbolism of green resonates multiculturally. Associating Black consciousness with green in a suggestion of fertility and growth, and with landscapes as human ("green eyes, hair") asserts an identification with nature not based on domination; in the African-Caribbean literary tradition, moreover, green often signals magical events or supernatural transitions. Furthermore, Kaufman himself uses green in this way elsewhere, especially in the broadside *Second April* (1959), which interweaves an "autobiographical journey" with "such events as Christ's April crucifixion, death and resurrection by A-bomb, and the author's own birth" (Kaufman was born on April 18). This poem, comprised of a series of paragraph "sessions," juxtaposes assertions of "thingness" ("pants, that's a thing ... mattress, a thing, that's a thing ... future, that's a thing ... ") against the refrain "look out for green"—the static known of material fixity versus the unbounded energy of life/death and constant change. The poem ends in fiery green apocalypse:

> We watch them going on watching us going on going, wrapped in pink barley leaves, almost, the time is not near, but, nearer we are to time, and time nearer to ticks. Burning in torch surrender to auto-fantasy, we illuminate the hidden December, seen, flamelit in the on core of the second April, come for the skeleton of time.

> Kissed at wintertide, alone in a lemming world,
> Green bitches, harlequin men, shadowed babes,
> Dumped on the galvez greens, burned with grass.[37]

Through sheer fracturing of language and imagery, Kaufman abstracts Negroness, the "florid black," and greenness out of existence, deconstructing their literal significance. Against the arbitrariness of racism Kaufman juxtaposes the arbitrariness of play; if oppression happens in language it can be undone there. "Oregon," as well as "green," are anagrams for "Negro." Not only is the referent, "blackness," linguistically and imagistically arbitrary (as well as crucially significant in Kaufman's case), but the syllables of the signifier are too, and the poet scrambles the word to both overdetermine and undermine the notion of Negroness. But as in "North of Time," in which the poet's marginal status carries with it certain esoteric privileges, the state (condition) of Oregon, of being a Negro, permits certain poetic and political changes. Like "Poetry," prophetic and all-encompassing, it is a physical, metaphysical, and absolute state, it belongs to the poet and the poet belongs to it. Kaufman takes the last two lines of "Oregon" almost verbatim from "Los Negros" in Ben Belitt's translation of Lorca's *Poet in New York*, in which the Spanish poet links Black Americans' oppression to their creative vitality, which he finds the only humanly redeeming aspect of the megalopolis:

> Yes: the bridge must be crossed
> and the florid black found
> if the perfume we bear in our lungs
> is to strike, in its guises of peppery pine,
> on our temples.

Through the mediation of Oregon, the poet can be a Black American Revolutionary martyr like Crispus Attucks, who here associated with John the Baptist plays the derelict prophet central to Kaufman's aesthetics (and both of them come to us, like Kaufman, with apocryphal genealogy).[38] The poet can be conversant with Lorca and Crane, and can become a nonhuman animal. (L-orca is a dolphin-whale, Hart Crane is a deer sea-bird.) As a bird he can fly to Heaven the Hart Crane way—jumping overboard in the Gulf of Mexico, as many Africans did, preferring death to slavery. By overturning the Chain of Being, which holds humans higher than animals, he can transcend the limits of human time/space, going to "secret places" (beyond beyond) where the "florid Black [is] found." When Crane's bridge is crossed, on the other side of death green gives birth to Black, the flowering of consciousness. On the other side of the United States from Northwestern Oregon is Southeastern Florida reaching down toward the Caribbean and Africa itself. The movement rejects associations of progress with upward and westward directions, reversing once again the imagery implicit in the dominant worldview.[39]

The poem on the right-hand page of the volume facing "Oregon" serves to explicate it: it *embodies* the florid black, asserting a Black cosmos, but with an all-encompassing sense that tends, by its very absoluteness, toward its own deconstruction:

THE SUN IS A NEGRO.
THE MOTHER OF THE SUN IS A NEGRO
THE DISCIPLES OF THE
SUN ARE NEGRO.
THE SAINTS OF THE
SUN ARE NEGRO.
HEAVEN IS NEGRO.

("Untitled," AR 59)

In "Oregon," Kaufman signals the arbitrariness of referentiality by fragmenting and rearranging letters and syllables; here he effects an incipient return to meaninglessness through hypnotic repetition. Signifying function "unmeans" itself, becoming more sonic than intellectual. However, this unraveling of "meaning" does not simply fall into insubstantial assertion, which sometimes marks surrealist work: images here are not violently forced together or apart. Rather, the poem's antirationalism lies in the intuitive access we are allowed when the repeated words become transformative Words. The imagery, black on black on black, echoes, symmetrically opposes and overturns the hierarchy implicit in the greatest Heaven poem of the Western canon, the *Paradiso*, in which Dante similarly deconstructs visual rationality by asserting heaven as white on white on white—the white pearl on the white forehead. In other words, though both Kaufman's and Dante's poems constitute deconstructive attempts to undermine rationality, they privilege as the central focus of each work the material content they choose to deconstruct: blackness and whiteness respectively; this content is so charged with hierarchic assumptions that hierarchy itself becomes foregrounded within the deconstructive project. Dante implicitly upholds the hierarchy; Kaufman explicitly challenges it. Dante points up the Chain to an abstract God—his antirationalism serves a traditional faith that surpasses understanding; Kaufman points toward nature (the sun), and privileges those considered less than human in the Chain's logic.[40] As in "Oregon," though, "Untitled" has its unifying aspect; the pun on sun points toward the coextension of the order of human communal ties with celestial order, and reunifies the family shattered by slavery in the image of a Holy Family extending to saints and disciples. "Creation is perfect" in its Negroness.[41]

"O Minstrel Galleons of Carib Fire": The Voyager

The sea and images of passage have been crucial tropes in the literature of Black slavery in the West as long as there has been such a literature, and have continued in the postslavery era as charged symbols around which entire narratives turn. The centrality of the river Jordan and images of crossing over water to freedom in the African-American oral religious tradition points not only, as some have suggested, to veiled references to passage from the Southern to the "free" Northern states, or, as used to be argued, to evidence that desperate slaves bought the Christian line and all its imagery at face value, believing the crossing to be a passage into a Christian afterlife. Such images also rewrite and redirect the Middle Passage, in which Africa becomes a spiritual ideal, an Eden to return to (similar to the idea of "Nature" in Anglo poetry). Even when Africa as a geographical entity does not enter into the text, water-crossings or nautical themes in general continue to resonate through African-American literature and history. Some ethnomusicological research even suggests a link between sea shanties and slave work songs in American folk music.[42]

Kaufman, in another instance of living out on a literal level what in other instances may be a literary or historical image, became a sailor, working for years in the merchant marine and actively participating as an impassioned orator for the more radical factions of the National Maritime Union.[43] As Olaudah Equiano, who wrote the first known slave narrative, eventually reversed his slave status by becoming a competent seaman, taking power in the same element in which he had first encountered bondage, so Kaufman was able to bring new significance to his history as an African-American and a Jew by, for example, smuggling European Jews into Palestine during World War II, in a reversal of the trajectory of the Middle Passage, which moves from the First World to the Third. Frederick Douglass writes of look-

ing out over the Chesapeake Bay weeping with longing for the freedom of the white-sailed ships; and, within paragraphs, makes his
famous statement of reversal: "You have seen how a man was made a
slave; you shall see how a slave was made a man." And while the
narrative leaves his actual means of escape to freedom a secret,
Douglass's first escape attempt involves "the water route," and his
stepping stone to freedom is a paid job building ships. Langston
Hughes, like Kaufman a merchant seaman, titled the first volume of
his autobiography *The Big Sea*, and its first chapter opens with a declaration of independence: at twenty-one, he throws his library of
summer reading overboard (except for *Leaves of Grass*) and heads
for Africa on the *S.S. Malone*. Similarly, though Marcus Garvey's ultimate plan to return to Africa was foiled, the purchase of the *Black
Star* ocean liner by African-Americans and its pleasure-cruise from
New York to the Caribbean constituted a symbolic triumph over and
"rewriting" of the slave trade on the surface of the sea.[44]

The sea, however, is not only a metaphor for emancipation; aside
from the ultimate horror of the Middle Passage for its captives and
their descendants, working conditions for sailors and other maritime
laborers were notoriously oppressive, a type of modern serfdom. The
overlap between slavery and maritime employment indicates official
and popular disregard for sailors and nautical subculture. Bruce Nelson
points out that "until 1915, federal law officially defined [sailors] as
wards and the equivalent of orphans." An 1896 Congressional hearing
and the 1897 Supreme Court's finding on the case of the *Arago* af-
firmed that "seamen, . . . deficient in that full and intelligent responsibility for their acts which is accredited to ordinary adults," remain
unprotected by the Thirteenth Amendment and other legal prohibi-
tions of involuntary servitude, and constituted the "most vicious" and
"most unruly" elements of society, the flotsam and jetsam of the native countries they were perceived to have abandoned (and with
these native countries, any claim to respectable propertied subjectivity). Significantly, this case became known among maritime workers
as the "second Dred Scott decision."[45] Possibly, the confused Boston
Massacre Trial testimony on the origins of Kaufman's hero Crispus
Attucks stemmed not only from his nonwhiteness, but from his nautical trade. He was a "crewman off a Nantucket whaler," who, in the
words of John Adams's defense, led a "motley rabble of saucy boys,
negroes and molattoes, Irish teagues and outlandish jack tarrs" up

the hill to confront the British soldiery.[46] Adams's dismissive categories rhetorically indicate these folks as the lowest of the low, generic troublemakers undeserving of attention as specific individuals: Why should anyone care about the particulars of such human detritus: adolescents, Blacks and other people of color, Irish, and sailors? The term "outlandish" here means not only funny-looking and strange, but foreign, nonnational, and perhaps most important for this founding father of what was to become the first bourgeois nationalist revolution, unpropertied, not "landed." As literal "floating" subjects, sailors of the colonial period and afterwards threatened the social order even though their labor—transporting New World resources to Europe, transporting unpaid African laborers to the New World—was central to its establishment and maintenance.

While seamen, because of their necessary exposure to other parts of the world, tended toward a more critical internationalist perspective than the average American worker (particularly, Black American seamen had the opportunity to experience nonracist environments and hence apprehend how very context-specific and local American racism is), the atomized and mythic individual loneliness of the seafarer's life worked against any easy sense of stable community. Thus the twentieth-century unionizing project had great periods of dangerous fragmentation as well as exhilarating solidarity. Though Kaufman joined up in 1943 at the age of eighteen, the very year the War Labor Board (under pressure from the NMU) officially vowed to break the color line among seamen and several years after the violent period of labor-versus-employer and AFL-versus-CIO showdowns of the 1930s, union activity was still turbulent and conditions still difficult, particularly during the war years when nonmilitary American ships were routinely blown up by the Nazis.[47] As in his later adoption of the vow of silence and his stance of life-in-death, Kaufman, like Hughes (and like his fellow Beats Kerouac and Ginsberg, who also "shipped out"—but after graduating from Columbia), entered adulthood by renouncing its conventional terms: assuming the persona of the outcast nomadic sailor, he rewrote his "surfdom" in emancipatory terms, first in his political affiliations and then in his poetry.

According to legend, Kaufman's acquaintance with the sea began when as a child his "voodoo" grandmother (or great-grandmother) the ex-slave took him for walks by the docks and in the bayous of his native Louisiana, in which his father drowned when he was nine (according to legend; according to George Kaufman, the senior Kaufman died of a heart attack), and by which he experienced his early love encounters. The sea in its many forms is Word/song, mother, lover:

WE WALKED A RIVER'S FLOOR. A BIRD I HEARD SING IN A TREE IN THE GULF OF MEXICO . . . BIRD OF LOVELY SALT, A LOVE SONG.

("The Celebrated White-Cap Spelling Bee," AR 44)

A father. Whose, mine?
Floating on seaweed rugs.
To that pearl tomb, shining
Beneath my bayou's floor.

Dead, and dead,
And you dead too.

. . .

Later in hot arms, hers,
Between sweaty lovemakings.
Crying will [wild?] wet moss swamps,
Hidden beneath her arms.

("Early Loves," GS 36)

The sea dissolves boundaries; on a metaphysical as well as an internationalist geopolitical plane, a sailor who "circled the globe nine times" knows that the earth is one unit, and the seven oceans one sea:

WHEN OCEANS MEET, OCEANS BELOW, REUNION OF SHIPS, SAILORS, GULLS,
    BLACK-HAIRED GIRLS.
THE SEA BATHES IN RAIN WATER, MORNING, MOON & LIGHT, THE CLEAN SEA.
GREAT FARMS ON THE OCEAN FLOOR, GREEN CROPS OF SUNKEN HULLS
    GROWING SHELLS.   . . .
THE LAND IS A GREAT, SAD FACE. THE SEA IS A HUGE TEAR, COMPASSION'S
    TWINS. . . .
THE SEA, DILUTED CONTINENTS LOVING FALLEN SKIES, TIME BEFORE TIME,
    TIME PAST, TIME COMING INTO TIME. TIME NOW, TIME TO COME, TIMELESS,
    FLOWING INTO TIME.
EVERYTHING IS THE SEA. THE SEA IS EVERYTHING, ALWAYS . . .
    ETERNALLY, I SWEAR.

("Spelling Bee," AR 44)

DEEP ROLLING GALILEE, ETERNAL SEVEN OCEAN NAMED SEA ENDLESSLY FLOWING HOLY SEA, . . . SEA NEVER STILLED, ALL FLOWING SEA, SEA DESTROYER OF BAAL AND MAMMON . . .

SWEET GREEN WET BLUE SALTLESS SEA: BELOVED GALILEE, THE GREEN WALKING, BLUE
WALKING JESUS CHRIST, SEA.
("Rondeau of the One Sea," AR 49)

The circularity of the "rondeau" form (*rond d'eau, eau ronde*)
chants a round that echoes the spherical form of the green-blue
planet, with Christ as the sailor who is his own ship; and the "Spelling Bee" ends as a prayer, an incantatory "spell," with its envoi—*in
secula seculorum*—to eternity.

For Kaufman, "voyaging" implies not only political freedom, risk-
taking and possible martyrdom, but spiritual and visionary freedom
as well. In "Plea" and the almost identical "Night Sung Sailor's
Prayer," written during the heyday of space-age technological optimism (when sea travel was actually being phased out, and the seafarer's skills in less demand), the sailor is a star-voyager, an astronaut
with a global perspective that is political as well as organic; as in the
much later "Untitled [THE SUN IS A NEGRO]," black is the privileged color
of discovery and spiritual enlightenment:

> Voyager, wanderer of star worlds,
> Off to
>   a million tomorrows, black, black,
> Seek and find Hiroshima's children,
>   Send them back, send them back.
> Tear open concrete-sealed cathedrals, spiritually locked . . .
>
> Voyager now,
>   Off to a million midnights, black, black . . .
> ("Plea" SCL 22)

In "All Those Ships that Never Sailed," the newly revived poet rein-
vests once-impotent ships with power:

> All those ships that never sailed
> The ones with their seacocks open
> That were scuttled in their stalls . . .
> Today I bring them back
> Huge and intransitory
> And let them sail
> Forever.

The image of powerlessness is transformed to exhilarating hugeness
by the soul-power of the sailor/poet. When body and soul, words and

presence are sundered, nothing is possible; their union unleashes tremendous energy—even resulting in a neologism, "intransitory," echoing the ambiguities of Crane's "irrefragibly" in "Voyages IV." Language changes when the silent poet chooses to speak again. One of the more horrific images from the Middle Passage also comes to mind with this stanza: when a ship illegally trafficking slaves would reach sight of land and be approached by an official vessel, the crew would "scuttle"—sink—the ship, drowning its human contraband, and make their own escape. In this context, Kaufman's poem declares a resurrection, and sailing, as for Douglass and Hughes, becomes emblematic of freedom.

Typically, though, Kaufman's voyagers are not only visionaries but, of course, beatniks and beautiful "born losers" ("Night Sung Sailor's Prayer," GS 69): losers in a socioeconomic sense (as sailors often were) as well as those who feel that they have lost their identities, or who purposefully have cut loose from convention, seekers in a more mundane, existential vein.

> Black leather angels of
> Pop-bopping stallions searching . . .
> Creeping away into highway dark
> To find spark-born oblivion . . .
> Twice-maimed shrews, ailing
> In elongated slots
> Of pubic splendor . . .
> Hopelessly hoping hopefully
> To find love
> Of a dead moon
> Or a poem.
>
> ("Voyagers," SCL 36-39)

The influence of French existentialism, a popular import after World War II, on the Beats and other intellectuals coming of age in the fifties is evident in this and other poems, such as "Camus: I Want to Know" (SCL 46). In "Voyagers," for example, one senses the presence of Camus's *The Stranger*, translated into English in 1946. The poem also resonates thematically with *The Stranger*'s comic/pathetic adolescent American counterpart, J. D. Salinger's *The Catcher in the Rye* (1951), and with Chandler Brossard's proto-Beat *Who Walk in Darkness* (1952), in which the drama revolves around the villain's alleged Blackness ("It was rumored that Henry Porter was a 'passed Negro' " becomes "It was rumored that Henry Porter was illegitimate" in the censored version),[48] and even with Bette Davis's 1942 lachrymose film of psychological "adjustment," *Now Voyager*, in which a psychiatrist writes out a line of Walt Whitman ("Now, voyager, sail thou forth to seek and find . . . ") for Davis, the client, urging her to go on a sea cruise. The final line of the movie, "Don't let's ask for the moon. We have the stars," which advises compromise with the discontents of civilization, finds resonance in the final lines of "Voyagers" ("hopelessly hoping" . . .). Hardly lachrymose, however, the "coolness" here, the flippancy tinged with pathos, is Kaufman's trademark.

Henry Louis Gates has pointed out that every African-American text has both white and Black antecedents; Hughes's and Douglass's autobiographical prose and Hughes's sea poetry (see especially "Long Trip") comprise part of the latter; white poetic antecedents likewise leap readily to mind.[49] Whitman's "Sea-Drift" cycle, with the bird-song of "Out of the Cradle Endlessly Rocking," the shoreline musings of "As I Ebb'd With the Ocean of Life," the salty "compassion's twin" of "then the unloosened ocean, / of tears! tears! tears!" anticipate Kaufman's sea poetry. In particular, "Aboard at a Ship's Helm" affirms the union of body and soul in spiritual and literal voyage.

> But O the ship, the immortal ship! O ship aboard the ship!
> Ship of the body, ship of the soul, voyaging, voyaging, voyaging.

This is union in terms similar to "All Those Ships that Never Sailed," with the important difference that the latter poem also acknowledges a crisis survived. Whitman's "The World Beneath the Brine" offers a catalogue similar to "Blues for Hal Waters":

> Forests at the bottom of the sea, the branches and leaves,
> Sea-lettuce, vast lichens, strange flowers and seeds . . . pink turf
>
> . . .
>
> Passions there, wars, pursuits, tribes, sight in those ocean-depths . . .

And "On the Beach at Night Alone" chants the same global unity as "Rondeau of the One Sea":

> As I watch the bright stars shining, I think a thought of the clef
> of the universes and of the future.

A vast similitude interlocks all,
All spheres, grown, ungrown, . . .
All distances of place however wide,
All distances of time, all inanimate forms,
All souls, all living bodies though they be ever so different . . .
This vast similitude spans them, and always has spann'd,
And shall forever span them and compactly hold and enclose
  them.[50]

And perhaps even more compellingly than Whitman, Hart Crane, who "devoted a tormented life to the perfection and then the exhaustion of an extraordinary talent, and bequeathed to his successors a body of brilliantly visionary poetry along with an image of tragic failure," serves as a model and antecedent for Kaufman's life and poetry.[51] "At Melville's Tomb" is Crane's reading of the ocean ("a scattered chapter, livid hieroglyph, / The portent wound in corridors of shells"), a meditation on human wreckage and death that, like "All Those Ships," holds the Word as one aspect of the sea's and the sailor's power.[52] And above all, the thread that winds from Whitman's ship of the body/soul voyaging to Kaufman's glamorous and self-destructive black leather "voyagers" passes through "Voyages," Crane's love poem to Emil Opffer, his merchant seaman lover. The significance Kaufman invests in Crane's poetic martyrdom in the sea is made explicit not only in "Oregon," but in "The Celebrated White-Cap Spelling Bee":

If there is a god beneath the sea, he is drunk and telling fantastic lies.
When the moon is drinking, the sea staggers like a drunken sailor.
Poets who drown at sea, themselves, become beautiful wet songs,
  Crane.[53]

Here again, as in his father's "pearl tomb" in "Early Loves," instead of seeing Crane's suicide in conventionally tragic terms, Kaufman evokes an evolutionary sea-change, an apotheosis in which Crane becomes poetry itself, a god "telling fantastic lies," making things up. (The word "poet" stems from the Greek *poietes*, one who makes, from *poiein*, to make.) The trope of the drowned poet also suggests not only Shelley's death but Milton's "Lycidas," in which, as in Kaufman's elegies to lost souls of the hip subculture, the poem itself becomes a cenotaph for one whose body has disappeared into an anonymous bone-pit even as his creative spirit is liberated into posterity. "So Lycidas, sunk low, but mounted high ... " could as well describe Kaufman as any others in the drowned poets' society.[54]

Herein lies the significance of Kaufman's kinship with and difference from his gay white predecessors: Whitman and Crane dwell on the inhumanness of the sea, speaking of it as a foreign but compelling element to which they feel drawn as they feel drawn toward death. For them, the frightening aspect of the sea is redeemed through the beautiful person of the sailor, the lover, the "precious wealth" of the ship, the "young steersman" who "speeds away gayly and safe," and into whose hands the landlubber poet is permitted voyage. Until the moment of Crane's suicide, both his and Whitman's contact with the sea is mediated by the figure of the beloved sailor, whose beauty gives the sea what little safety it has:

> Take this Sea, whose diapason knells
> On scrolls of silver snowy sentences,
> The sceptred terror of whose sessions rends
> As her demeanors notion well or ill,
> All but the pieties of lovers' hands.
>
> ("Voyages II")

Furthermore, the attractiveness of the sailor and the excitement of the marine underworld on land—that is, the "sailortowns" in port cities, which offered extreme alternatives, both sordid and exhilarating, to conventional amusements—were as potentially dangerous for gay men as they were glamorous. Despite the proximity between gay and nautical subcultures (instantiated in the development of San Francisco, New York, and Provincetown as major gay centers, and intuited in recent gay-studies attention to Herman Melville's work),[55] the coextension of homosociality and homosexuality was here, as elsewhere, complex and volatile; not that nautical society was more or less homophobic than others, but given the social overlap of these two male outcast groups, violence and attraction were manifest in certain forms. The ambivalence of land-bound poets such as Crane and Whitman was not purely metaphysical, and extended to the physical roughness of nautical culture as well as to the sublime void of the sea itself. Crane and Opffer, for instance, were more than once robbed and beaten when cruising the waterfronts, sometimes to near-unconsciousness; and both Peggy Baird and Malcolm Cowley at-

tribute Crane's suicide, for Kaufman the ultimate in poetic martyrdom, to a recent beating by sailors whom he had solicited on board
the ship bringing him home from Mexico.[56] Though Crane's lyricism
transformed nautical violence, poetry, and drunkenness into the romantic exuberance of "minstrel galleons of Carib fire,"[57] he was also
their victim. Furthermore, if we read "galleons" as punning, intentionally or not, on "gallions," a jazz argot term for slave quarters,
Crane's ambivalent identification with sailors extends to a similar
perceived connection to African-Americans as romantic Others, a
connection whose fallaciousness Crane himself criticizes in glossing
his "Black Tambourine," attributing to "the popular mind" the "[sen-
timental or brutal 'placement']" of the Negro in the "midkingdom
[between man and beast]."[58]

Kaufman the African-American seaman poet, on the other hand,
commemorates other seamen by name, pointing out the ways in
which they are both tricksters and victims: in "Unhistorical Events," a
poem about countermemory using Guillaume Apollinaire as its foil,
the poet notes for posterity Rock Gut Charlie, for giving fifty cents to
a policeman, and Riff Raff Rolfe, who had to flee his home state "because he was queer." These men are not nameless, apotheosized am-
bassadors from outlandish and exotic realms. Although their names
play on stereotypical representations of sailors and thus keep them
anonymous in the Beat way that Kaufman values (rotgut for drunkenness; rock-gut for the "cast-iron stomach" of fighters, and of eaters
who can't afford to indulge a discriminating palate; riffraff for the
lumpenproletariat), their human situations thus recorded move
them beyond aesthetic socialism, out of ethereal distances or sor-
didly incandescent *courts de miracles* into the territory of familiar
reminiscence.

Kaufman had firsthand maritime experience through his choice of
livelihood, which choice constitutes a redemptive response to the
Middle Passage. Although the Middle Passage provides one of the
bleaker scenarios available in modern history, the sea, through this
very cultural familiarity, is not a strange and forbidding element.
While Whitman's "World Beneath the Brine" haunts because of its
nonhuman strangeness, and for Crane "the bottom of the sea is
cruel," the "oceans below" of Kaufman's "Spelling Bee" reunites
"ships, sailors, gulls, Black-haired girls." It is the tear of compassion-
ate suffering on the face of the land. "As I Ebb'd With the Ocean of

Life" has its echo in Crane's "At Melville's Tomb"; both are medita-
tions on death. Kaufman's sea-poetry represents the all-encompassing hugeness of the sea as reassuring and righteous, and sailing
becomes not a triumph over the sea but an act of physical harmony
with it. The intimate anger of "Early Loves" ("Dead, and dead. / And
you dead too") differs from the metaphoric speculations of Whitman
and Crane on alien death, and from the fear underlying their attraction to its immanent emissaries. In "All Those Ships," moreover, the
tragedy is not one of natural shipwreck (although Kaufman himself
survived four shipwrecks, one of which cost him 40 percent of his
hearing), but that the unsailed ships have been scuttled through implied human agency.[59]

Whitman's and Crane's sea-poetry derives its power, in part, from
the play of oppositional tension between the human and the elemen-
tal, and from the threat of personal danger; Kaufman's from a sense
of integration, harmony, and familiar expansiveness. The sea itself
was never an enemy; it was the slave merchants and shipowners who
misused it. Kaufman submitted himself to the destructive element;
like Crane, ultimately it was not the sea but social institutions that he
could not survive.

"Death is a Drum / Beating Forever": The Griot

Finally, Kaufman's work places itself unambiguously within an African-American artistic tradition in its direct connection to music, par-
ticularly jazz, blues, and the African talking drum. A partial survey of
his titles yields the following: "Bagel Shop Jazz," (nominated for the
Guinness Poetry Prize in 1963), "Tequila Jazz," "Walking Parker
Home," "Bird with Painted Wings," "Blues Note" (for Ray Charles's
birthday), "Session Tongues," "Mingus," "San Francisco Beat,"
"Round About Midnight," "Jazz Chick," "His Horn," "Night on Bop
Mountain," "O-Jazz-O War Memoir: Jazz, Don't Listen to It at Your
Own Risk." Virtually every African-American poet, essayist, and critic,
from Du Bois to Hughes to Baraka to Stephen Henderson to Ntozake
Shange to Houston Baker, has discussed the close ties between music
and the rest of Black culture.[60] The strong kinship Black American
poets feel with Black American music restores the lyric to its original
status as song, words written to accompany music and dance rituals.
The trendy phrase "performance art" is thus already a redundancy

where Jayne Cortez's chants, Ntozake Shange's choreopoems, and Bob Kaufman's extemporaneous deliveries are concerned.

The musical form most associated with Kaufman is bebop, the jazz style of the forties and fifties whose stars were Dizzy Gillespie, Thelonius Monk, Miles Davis, and Charlie "Bird" Parker. Kaufman, one of whose epithets is "the original bebop man," refers to Parker in a number of veiled and explicit ways, including the bird imagery in poems cited earlier; clearly he felt an affinity for Parker's breathlessly manic music and the flamboyant, addictive, and visionary personal style of the "sweet bird of sabotage." The rise of bebop as the first self-consciously artistic and intellectual jazz style (with the musicians, according to Baraka in *Blues People*, seeing themselves as "artists" rather than "entertainers"), the emphasis on disaffection and nonconformism in the social world of "bop," and the sophisticated sartorial campiness of the beboppers all indicate them as precursors of the beatniks; and Kaufman was, of course, the original beatnik.[61]

Furthermore, Kaufman's work reflects bebop's phrasing. The musical trademark of bebop is its fragmentary, atonal treatment of melody and its complex rhythms, both of which shattered the conventions of earlier jazz. The bebop musician breaks up, reverses, inverts, distorts, and repeats musical phrases in improvised play. Paradoxically, bebop initiated jazz into the category of "serious" music precisely because it so outraged conventional sensibilities that it had to be discussed or attacked *as music*. Baraka describes the enormous impact of the bebop musicians on the young Black intelligensia of the fifties, characterizing them as voyagers into new realms of consciousness and visual image as well as sound:

> The sound itself. The staccato rhythm and jagged lines. The breakneck speed and "outside" quality ... "Outside." Strange. Weird ... That word I read and heard. Weird. Thelonius. That's a weird name. What did it mean? Why were they sounding like this? They even looked ... weird. ... As we got more conscious of Bop we got more conscious of wanting to be *cool* ... Cool, for us, was to be there without being into nothing dumb. Like, the whole thing. The society—right? ... My father had asked me one day, ... "Why do you want to be a Bopper?" Who knows what I said. I couldn't have explained it then. But BeBop suggested *another* mode of being. Another way of living. Another way of perceiving reality—connected

to the one I'd had—blue/Black and brown but also pushing past that to something else. Strangeness. Weirdness. The unknown![62]

Kaufman's work is permeated with the sense of being present yet gone-beyond, with both the coolness of distance or dissociation and the manic speed of engagement, with an intimate (closer than close) sense of his blue/Black and brown reality but also straining toward and breaking the boundaries of identity itself—farther than far, on the other side of music. Blue/Black and brown . . . "crackling blueness," a phrase of Lorca's that becomes talismanic in Kaufman's work, not only captures that lightninglike, overcharged energy of heightened vision and aesthetic ecstasy that links Kaufman with high-flyers Diz and Bird. It also refers, of course, to the blues: Nathaniel Mackey observes that Lorca's primary appeal for Kaufman was the former's attraction to Black Americans, and the obvious connection between Andalusian and West African cultures.[63] I would also suggest that "crackling blueness" has a more sinister connotation in Kaufman's particular biography: the electroshock treatments to which he was subjected in 1963. Including this latter as a possible meaning overlapping with the others enables the metaphoric connection between perceived madness, social punishment and social death, and the acceptance of the poetic mode that Kaufman articulates in "THE POET."

The rhythmic and melodic fragmentation of bebop finds its verbal counterpart in Kaufman's surrealist imagery, alternately jarring and synthetic; in the breakup of language itself, as in "Oregon" and the "Abomunist Rational Anthem" / "Crootey Songo" (GS 54); and in his thematic preoccupation with bebop's inherently subversive nature. Bebop culture prided itself on language play, either through onomatopoeic nonsense syllables, self-reflexive rhyme, or the adoption of pseudo-French or other European languages: for example, Gillespie's "Oo-Bop-Sh'bam," "Bah-Dee-Daht," "Birks Works," "Oo-Pop-A-Da," and "Guarachi Guaro," Charlie Parker's "Auprivave" and "Scrapple from the Apple," Thelonious Monk's "Epistrophy," Charles Mingus's "Mingus Fingers," Miles Davis's "Miles Smiles," and so on. Gillespie makes explicit the connection between music, words, and the Black vernacular: "We didn't have to try [to adopt a distinct and improvised speech] . . . as black people we just naturally spoke that way. As we played with musical notes, bending them into new and different meanings that constantly changed, we played with words."[64]

Reading Kaufman's poetry aloud can highlight these connections, especially in one formally atypical instance. *Does the Secret Mind Whisper?* is a ten-page tract justified at both margins, whose only punctuation is an initial capital letter and a final period. This is unusual for Kaufman, who uses line-breaks, commas, elipses, and fairly traditional sentence structure to inflect his work; even his other broadsides, *Abomunist Manifesto by Bomkauf* and *Second April* (SCL 65), are comprised of smaller units—sections, stanzas, or paragraphs. The reader-aloud of *Secret Mind* faces a task even more challenging than the reader of the final pages of *Ulysses*, which, though unpunctuated, fall fairly easily into a traditional reading (as if Joyce had initially written in the punctuation and then erased it from the text). *Secret Mind*, lacking any cues from the writer, demands split-second decisions about phrasing, inflection, emphasis—the same kinds of extemporaneous decisions the jazz improviser has to make, and that Kaufman made as he recited his poetry.

But though superbly theoretical, bebop was not only a high-flying intellectual adventure, a dizzying cerebral deconstruction of accepted musical convention. It was intensely physical. In counterpoint to Baraka's emphasis on bebop's way-out speed, its going-beyond the limits of ordinary consciousness, Miles Davis talks about feeling the music "all up in my body."[65] Bebop got down, into the rhythm of the organs and the blood, making the body conscious of its internal movement and the eruptions, eliminations and ejaculations by which it expresses itself and shatters decorum: Oo-Pop-A-Da!—orgasm, defecation, flatulation, oral exclamation, and belch.[66] One of the supreme achievements of bebop was its perfect union of theory and praxis: it gave to theory an inexorably physical and emotional embodiment, and its experiments with the nature of time/space infused a formal, sensuous popular medium with metaphysical sophistication.

The Old World antecedent for a music both intellectual and sensuous, both "verbal" and "musical," is the West African talking drum. The importance of rhythm in Kaufman's work also draws on the tradition of the talking drum, arguably a "verbal" rather than "musical" instrument (to the extent that these descriptors exclude each other), since it imitates speech.[67] "A drum beats behind my ribs," he writes in "The Celebrated White-Cap Spelling Bee." The drum with its "heartbeat," its urgent summons and its hollow echo-chamber body, provided not only Kaufman but many other Black poets with a supersaturated cultural trope for the importance of their own craft to the human enterprise; the subtitle of this section, for example, cites Hughes's "Drum."[68]

According to an Anglo-European balladic trope, the body parts of a dead person are crafted into musical instruments which, when played upon, tell the tale of the oppression and murder of the dead one. Often in this tradition, a jealous woman drowns her sister or a man rapes and murders his beloved; the talking flute or harp made of the dead woman's bones and hair incriminate her murderer when played. The art with its origins in unjust suffering stands witness to the injustice. Beside this folk-aesthetic version of the reliquary emblems of sexism, there are grisly and recent real-life examples of the conversion of body parts into serviceable items. Kaufman began writing only fifteen years after the architects of the Third Reich ordered that Jews be made into soap and lampshades, products now on display in the Holocaust Museum in Israel. The ongoing use of the physical labor and bodily ravaging of ex-slaves, colonial and postcolonial subjects—the living dead—likewise constitutes a dismemberment brought about through political power relations. Their art, in global currency now, stands in complex relation to the market that exploits them.

Kaufman plays on all these aspects of the subject, but especially turns pain to good account by adapting the first trope to Black American imagery. Where a Euro-Romantic tradition would have the poet as Aeolian harp, and where the Euro-folk tradition would have the poet as the bones and hair of a wronged girl, Kaufman becomes a blues guitar, an African drum, a jazz wind instrument:

> My head, my secret cranial guitar, strung with myths . . .
> ("Blues for Hal Waters")

MY BODY A SINEWED HURT FOR ALL THE NOTHING THAT I AM, THE NOTHING THAT IS ALL MY MINGLES OF AFRICAN HAIR SPEAK FOR ME . . . I DREAMED I DREAMED AN AFRICAN DREAM. MY HEAD WAS A BONY GUITAR, STRUNG WITH TONGUES . . . DRUMMING HUMAN BEATS FROM THE HEART OF AN EBONY GODDESS . . .
> ("Darkwalking Endlessly," AR 22)

> Who crouches there in my
> Heart?
> Some wounded bird,

> Hidden in the tall grass
> That surrounds my heart.
>
> Unseen wings of jazz . . .
> Carry me off, carry me off
> . . .
> My secret heart,
> Beating with unheard jazz.
> Thin melody ropes
> Entwine my neck,
> Hanging with
> Tequila smiles,
> Hanging, Man,
> Hanging.
> ("Tequila Jazz," GS 40)

> That silent beat makes the drumbeat, it makes the drum, it makes the
> beat. Without it there is no drum, no beat . . . the silent beat is beaten
> by who is not beating the drum, his silent beat drowns out all the
> noise, it comes before and after every beat, you can hear it in
> beatween, its sound is
> Bob Kaufman, Poet
> ("Oct. 5, 1963," GS 80)

This latter poem, which is a letter to the *San Francisco Chronicle*,
announces outrage over his civic treatment on returning from New
York and links it to racial matters:

> Arriving back in San Francisco to be greeted by a blacklist and
> eviction, I am writing these lines to the responsible non-people.
> One thing is certain I am not white. Thank God for that. It makes
> everything else bearable.

The topicality and socially conscious overtones here suggest another
dimension of Kaufman's place in the African-diaspora musical tradition. The West African caste of *griots* is comprised of poet-musicians
who act as repositories of local history and commentators on the
contemporary political scene. Their New World cousins, Caribbean
calypso singers like King Swallow, Lord Melody, and the Mighty Sparrow, likewise serve up sharp social wit as urbane and accomplished
musical entertainment. Known both for their prodigious memories,
which hold at least seven generations of social information, genealogies, and other matters of importance for the community records,
and for their abilities to extemporize upon and aestheticize (in the

sense of delivering up in formally developed song and jest) any contemporary social event, griots are nonetheless something of an outsider caste even though their skills are highly valued; they are traditionally buried in hollow baobab trunks far from community burial grounds and certain conventions prohibit them from participating in everyday community life.[69] Furthermore, the principles of the griots' music, if not the sound, bear a strong family resemblance to bebop: "[griots who play the *kora* (21-stringed harp-lute)] combine melodic inventivenesss with subtle and constantly moving rhythms. . . . Or they may play a ground bass and play intricate patterns over it while singing in a third layer a praise song, or improvised marketplace satire."[70] Kaufman's stinging social commentary, in "Carl Chessman" or "Benediction," for example; his reputation for extraordinarily virtuoso feats of improvisation and memorization; and his conscious stance as Beat outsider (Beat poet as a caste) and simultaneously qualified inside commentator on every "scene" he observes; and the intricacy with which he manipulates different registers of vernacular and standard English, clichés ("another sleepless year / Like the last one will drive me sane . . . "), street idiom, and formal poetic principles all place Kaufman in a tradition in which the artist is at once poet and musician, outside the social mainstream but eminently integrated into and crucial to it, mystic and comedian, otherworldly and absolutely materially present and accounted for. However, the poet is not only inventor but instrument. His head as "cranial guitar" resonates with, amplifies, alters, and retransmits what it receives. Think of Paul Oliver's description of the *halam*, a plucked African instrument, in light of Kaufman's poetic and tortured self-descriptions: "A hollowed wood *body* has *hide* stretched over it to form a resonator and the strings are fixed by leather tuning thongs to the rounded *neck* and stretched over a bridge on the resonator" (my emphasis).[71] Elsewhere in the passage the words "arm," "skin," "moaned and wailing notes," further anthropomorphize plucked and bowed instruments in chiasmatic counterpoint to the way Kaufman reifies his body into a musical instrument; his head as "cranial guitar" refers (as in "being out of one's gourd") to the calabash or gourd body of the African guitar. Kofi Awoonor writes about Ewe poets in West Africa similarly: "the poet . . . is only an instrument in God's hands," and at the same time, the poet is a master of the drum and participates in a drumming group. Likewise in Kaufman's work, the poet mediates; he is played upon as an instrument, and at the same time, he creates, playing upon creation.

> Sometimes when the wind is blowing in my hair,
> I cry, because its coolness is too beautiful.
>
> ("Image of Wind," SCL 62)

The "silent beat" of "Oct. 5, 1963" that comes "before and after every beat" describes the "beat inside" that a jazz drummer uses to protect the rhythm, to keep from dropping the time:

> The way you protect the groove is to have a beat in between a beat. Like "bang, bang, sha-bang, sha-bang." The "sha" in between the "bang" is the beat in between the beat. ... When a drummer can't do that, the groove is off and there ain't nothing worse in the world than to have a drummer in that no groove thing. Man, that shit is like death.[72]

However, as the final sentence of Miles Davis's explanation suggests, the "in beatween" beat whose absence spells death is not only a technical device, but represents the ongoing pulse of creation, the heartbeat of the Beat poet (the understated "lub" of the "lub-*dub*" we learn about as children from our pediatricians) as he is beaten. Jazz, breath, life-blood, poetic inspiration, compassion, all become coexistent, cofoundational, and they transform pain into beauty.[73]

There are dangers attendant on any argument that "unmeaning" — the dissolution of personal identity, bodily integrity, and artistic convention — must be subcultural self-assertion. I don't mean to suggest, simplistically, that Kaufman's art legitimates the conditions under which it was produced. Nor is Kaufman simplistic: "Thin melody ropes / Entwine my neck." If there is unity in this fragmentation, it is dynamic, comprised of insoluble paradoxes that won't stand still, won't stay / dead. No complacent resting place or safe position on the margin can be arrived at any more than one can find a comfortable bench on which to spend the night in Golden Gate Park. One can say that for Kaufman the Silent Beat, any change that occurs occurs in the body, soul, and intellect of the poet: holism, in other words, occurs in the poet's being and it is harrowing. Kaufman never returned from his Orphic journey, or he has gone straight for Orpheus's dismemberment and return to nature, his decapitated head singing as it floats down the river with Hart Crane and Emmett Till. Or he is the shaman who never recovered from his initiatory illness, the griot whose putrefying body cries out from the baobab trunk. Maybe this is why the founder of *Beatitude*, written off as a *maudit* or a beatnik burnout, has yet to be canonized. His body is the world's body, scarred and mediating the Word of creation.

3

The Child Who Writes / The Child Who Died

The melodious child dead in me long before the ax chops off my head . . .

Jean-Paul Sartre quoting Jean Genet[1]

Mixing Unmixables

In his essay "Mass Culture as Woman: Modernism's Other," Andreas Huyssen outlines and criticizes the division readily apprehensible from his title, familiar at this point to conscientious critics of mass culture and high art alike. In this scheme, mass-cultural consumption plays the passive, undifferentiated, exploitable, and conservative woman to the masculinist production of high art by sharply individuated and individual, iconoclastic, free-thinking men. In a myth of self-parthenogenesis, the modernist canon would define itself in clear outline against the swampy, womblike backdrop of mass-cultural anonymity.[2]

Any essay that proposes to treat both Robert Lowell and three unknown teenage women writing from the D Street Housing Projects of South Boston must account for itself somehow—must acknowledge the disparity between the two bodies of work it addresses. The attempt here to "mix unmixables" must be more than simply an elucidation of all-too-apparent differences in intent, self-understanding and aesthetic execution on the writers' parts. The task falls too neatly into Huyssen's delineations; it is tempting to stop, for instance, at an exploration of the two radically different Bostons the works portray: the girls' everyday experience with urban poverty and violence, Lowell's frustrated and decaying "hardly passionate" Marlborough Street aristocracy.

Foucault's useful question "What is an author?" can serve as a lever to dislodge these two loci of artistic endeavor and set them in orbit around each other, for each to illuminate and shade the other. Along with its necessary corollaries, "What is a self?" or "What is a subject?," the question underlies my teasing out the similarities and differences among them. Clearly Lowell's sense of his own authorship is heavy with the weight of historical responsiblity; as an American aristocrat who chose poetry as a vocation he saw his task as mediating and witnessing history in the form of critical events: the crisis of World War II, the crisis of Vietnam. Accompanying these were his personal crises: mental illness intermittently challenged and cruelly interrupted any intact sense of historical selfhood; marital strife called into question the possibility of intimate union. All of these events become, in his work, public matter: the drive toward aesthetic self-disclosure puts a performative spin on an impulse to shed the rigid casing of individualism of the writing, authorial self. The poetry both challenges and reifies the atomized self as public personality.

For the girls, any sense of subjectivity must be inextricably bound up with economic and sexual subjection. Though recognition is not unimportant to them, the selves that write these poems do not write with an eye toward publication or publicity in the same sense that Lowell does. The heavy rhymes and conservative meter, the formulaic language and relative absence of "intimate" detail and personal address point the girls' poems away from the lyric, high culture's favored poetic mode since the early nineteenth century, and toward the generic, mass-produced poetry of rock lyrics and newspaper verse. Shocking as the subject matter may be to the middle-class reader, it captures, in formulaic language, a set of standard pictures of urban poverty through the filter of female teen experience. Far from drawing attention to the subjectivity of the individual writer, most of their poems confirm for us the tableaux of project life that we have already constructed from media images. We know, for example, that not all of the poems are autobiographical, for the simple reason that in some, the protagonist, who speaks in the first person, dies. Since the lyric "I" is not generally considered a transparent reference to the author's person, this alone does not disqualify the poems from the lyric's purview; but given modernist lyric's conventions of free

verse and heightened subjectivity, whether expressed in the first person or projected atmospherically onto landscapes or objects, these
poems, with several notable exceptions, seem only remotely kin to
Lowell's.

The two subjects of this chapter offer a perfectly neat contrast, apparently, for engendering mass culture / high art differences. Couplets such as:

> Now I'm in a home for unwed mothers
> But why should you care you have all the others?

underscore the resentment bred by this engendered and internalized hierarchy. "I—female" am relegated to an anachronistic, mythological place for "people like me," the "home for unwed mothers,"
while "you—male" get to "have all the others—female." You get to
play, a single, differentiated male, against a backdrop of indistinguish-
able "others"—with all the connotations of that word in contemporary theoretical terms. You and your art ("the baby") will live—"I"
will die unrecognized. The resentment itself, mediated by the stock
rhyme "mothers/others," is formulaic. "You—male" could be Lowell,
in his capacity as representative of the high-cultural privilege of identity and free expression.

Moreover, the burden of my titular and epigraphic "dead child" is
always necessarily doubled for the girls. For them, the dead child is
not only, as for Lowell and Genet, the "inner child" of current psychotherapy: the innocent whose experience is as yet unmarred by
censorious adult expectations or insidiously self-destructive social
conditioning. In addition to the dead weight of their own thwarted
creative possibilities, which the "child within" metaphorically represents, a literal meaning of the term weighs them down as well. As
women (potential childbearers) and as members of housing-project
culture, Charlotte, Cheryl, and Susan forever risk remurdering their
own dead children externalized, immanently realized, through the
scenarios described in their poetry: abortions, manslaughter by child
abuse, and simply introducing real babies into the exigencies of ex-
tenuating conditions.

I am unwilling, however, to simply use the canonical poet's endeavor as a foil for that of the others—for instance, to criticize Lowell's
strident sense of authorial responsibility by discussing the girls'
problematic appropriation and subversion of the right to say "I" in

their work, their practice of group composition, and their works' mediation of a multiplicity of popularly available, mass-cultural verbal genres. Recent critical tendency has fostered a healthy mistrust of neat dichotomies, especially those arranged in hierarchy. One might call into question one of the most profoundly rooted of these divisions—that is, the easy demarcation of privileged and oppressed, of perpetrator and victim. Useful as Lowell may be to set off against a valorization of mass and popular art, or as an example of the reified "author" whose hegemonic control over the representation of Bostonian culture is intermittently threatened or broken through by outbursts from the undifferentiated female (or feminized) masses on the other side of town, this division would obscure some of the more interesting questions about the poetry. Both bodies of work pulsate with the anger of violated expectations, both bear witness to the devastations attendant upon a life within the claustrophobic strictures of a rigid cultural conditioning. Albeit with radically different intent and effect, the wounded child cries out in Lowell's work as the violated girl does in the South Boston poems. Lowell's anomalous prose piece about his childhood, "91 Revere Street," functions as his poetic "adolescence," cutting him loose from both of his constraining "families," a literary patriarchy and a reproductive and ostensible matriarchy: the former was the conservative Southern Agrarian poets under whose tutelage he came of age as a poet; the latter his biological parents, whose recent deaths made the self-disclosures of "91 Revere Street" possible. The prose piece appears in the center of *Life Studies*, a volume of verse, as a liminal formlessness that temporarily breaks and permanently changes the conventions of Lowell's verse. For the women, on the other hand, the structure of poetry creates a safe arena in which their anger can be aesthetically framed.

Herewith follows that poetry:

PORTRAIT OF A DROP-OUT

BY: Anonymous student from South Boston City Roots

He stood on the street corner. He had blonde hair. He had black hair.
He looked like me. He looked like you.
He would get into fights because he knew something was wrong, but he didn't know what.
One day while walking along the street he saw a sign.
It said "City Roots".
So, he went up to see what it meant.
He found out it was a school. He decided to sign up and try it out.
So, he went to school and finally found something that was right.

The Epitome of Courage

Courage is to smile when no one smiles,
to be able to laugh when no one laughs,
and even to cry when no one cries.
Courage is to listen to the music,
and not be deafened by it,
to run with it, and to sing with it,
and live by it's meaning, -
for this is the epitome of courage.
****

D Street

The brick buildings without any
hope.
The kids on the corner smoking dope.
The old ladies quiver with fear.
Of all the kids drinking beer.
        Just buzzing around in a stolen
car.
The cops are no help, but there not
very far.
        Vandelizm, robbers, B & E's look-
out for the rapers in the D.
        Everybody on a team basketball,
baseball are the reason.
But don't forget soon it will be
hockey season.
        Murders, rapers and thieves there
are.
So my aavice to you is stay very
far.
If you value your life, carry a knife
If you don't care I still say get
the fuck out of there!

                        Charlotte

1st Benches

Sitting on the Benches
Staring at the Fences
The Church Bells are Ringing
I feel like singing
All is quite
I wish there was a Riot
it Looks Like an institution
is there any solutions

Who will cut the grass
~~the we~~ we need some one to sweep the
glass
Dogs Always shitting
These old benches aren't made for sittin

By Charlotte

A Night in the Hallway.

Standing in the hall,
trying not to fall.
Hoping there's a way,
to get some money for a jay.

People always cutting through,
even the fucking cops to.
Telling some silly jokes,
anybody got any smokes?

We've got to be quite,
so we can't start no riots.
Ranking each other out with little
digs,
Oh Shit! I think someone called the pigs.

Oops sorry false alarm.
no-one that can do us any harm.
We've just did our last birdy
Oh Shit! Its 12:30.

Charlotte
"1979"

A Tortured Mind

An adult mind trapped in a body
years younger.
A place of soul, & mind for which I
hunger.
Being torn apart by a family I can't
please.
When will this tortured mind be at
ease.

Needed by many, and loved by none
The weight I bare is more than a ton.
A ~~force~~ tortured mind that wants to be
free.
Always wondering if others can see.

For around my friends I try to hide
Those haunting words "I wish I died!"
But to die by my own hand would be a
sin.
Because there's alway the thought of
what could have been.

I act as if I'm happy to be me.
Only because I don't want people to see
I've been this way for quit awhile
A tortured mind behind a smile   Charlotte

Remember Me.

Remember the fun we had, the trouble
we got into for being bad.
Remember our summer sunshine day
when we want horse back riding and
kissed by the bay.
Remember when we broke up we couldn't
stand it so we made up.
Remember the kisses we used to share
those were the times you really cared
Remember the night we went all the way
now I'm the one who has to pay.
I'm in a home for unwed mothers,
but why should you care you have all
the others.
Today I'm fighting the pain. I'm
keeping the baby she needs a name.
The doctor came in a few hours ago.
He said theres trouble but he didn't
know.
I found out later it wasn't a lie
The nurse had to tell me I was
gonna die. The baby, she said would
be alright. But I'd probley go sometime
tonight. Before I go theres one last
thing. I loved you and that was
a good thing.   Charlotte
                          12/17/ 79

I never could Stand It When They Cry.

It all started out as a normal day.
Until I sent the kids out to play.
Then the phone started ~~r~~ ringing
Would the radio ever stop singing?

I felt my head start to pound
my ears were filled with the sound.
The pot started to boil over,
someone had to let out rover.

My five year old daughter came in the door.
eating a cookie and crying for more.
I told her no and she started to fuss,
I yelled at her and started to cuss.

Without a warning I gave her a whack
I saw her fall and heard a Crack.
I never could stand it when they ~~cried~~ cry.
I couldn't stand the fear in her eye.

Her hair looked like mud
that's until I noticed it was blood.
I walked over, and got on my knees
She squeezed in the corner, "Don't hurt
me mommy, please!"
                                        our

I turned in discust and grabbed the
broom.
My son began to cry from his room
Its written in books on every page
I ran to the ~~chair~~ room in an uncontrolable
rage.

I feed him, I changed him It didn't
help the little bastard began to yelp.
I picked him up and shook him around
Then suddenly I dropped him to the ground.

Oh lord what have I done.
Yes, it's true I killed my baby son.
I don't remember the rest of the day.
I knew it was bad, because they took
the kids away.

They say there's no hope for me.
For everyday with them I plea.
Bring my daughter even though I'm
a mess.
I only want to ask for forgiveness.
                                    Charlotte

In Heaven at Quarter past 7

He acted as if it were a game, going
all the way I should have known
I was the one who'a have to pay.
It was the first time I saw him and
the last time too. He doesn't even know
about the baby. Oh what am I to do.

Abortion was the only route, because
you see there was no other way out.
The Clinic, "they'll tell on you." My
friends made jokes. So of course
I thought they'd tell my folks.

My friend had a pimp, she said he
could do it quick. But to pay him I'd
have to turn a trick. He brought me
into a room with a bright light. Then
I saw the coat hanger I got a fright.

My mind began to race. Especially
after I seen the look on his face.
At first it wasn't really so bad. So I
started to think about his dad.

89

Suddenly the pain became so fierce
I had to cry. Little did I know I was
going to die. I finally did, at quarter
past seven. I'm not sure what time
it was when I got to heaven.

When I got to the gate, I was
told to wait. I knew there was
something wrong I shook with fear.
"Let me see my child," I yelled. "Is
he here. If I could let you see him
I would my dear.

But for what you've done you'll have
to pay. I'm afraid your going the
other way. "No!" I started to yell.
When I stopped crying and opened my
eyes. I was standing at the gates of
Hell!

By Charlotte
"1980"

FRiENdSh.p   2-2-81
We are best of FRIENdS
hope it Never ends
When i'll down'
You Always come around

Our FRiendship is one of A kind
That you don't often Find.
We tell seCRets of all kinds
And leave bad memories behind

We've had our Fights
But Thay turned out all Right
When i Think of you At Night
I know every thing will be alRight

I like when your around.
Because No one can bring
me down
Because you will Act Like
a nut
And pick me Right up

By
Cheryl M.

Tell Them About Us

*Being a working-class woman with a working-class voice—speaking
out of the experiences of ordinary people and not a literary tradition
[has] kept me out of plenty of libraries. But other channels open up.
We're not dependent on our censors. My life has always been outside
of "the standard," and it will always be. We have tons of worlds that
stay volatile and alive by finding their own way.*
            Judy Grahn[3]

*When I took off for California, Susan teased me about my retreat
back into academia, then conceded, "At least you'll be teaching." Yes,
but it's different. Stanford's a private college. "Oh. Rich kids. Well
listen, if they give you any trouble just tell them about us."*

The poems presented here were written by three young women students at City Roots, a GED (General Equivalency Diploma) program
in the D Street Projects in South Boston, where I taught English and
mathematics for six months before entering graduate school. Some
of them appear here as they did in the notebook from which I first
copied them in the summer of 1981: startling, scrawled in ballpoint
pen. Others, notably Charlotte's, have been rewritten for the publication. I brought them with me to Stanford for sentimental reasons,
assuming that the texts I would be writing about would not resemble
these. In the intervening years, however, in spite of my geographic
and social distance from the D Street Projects, I continued to experience the poems in the context of my new studies, trying to find a
critical language for them in an academic context. Studying the poems has been a self-reflexive as well as a critical enterprise; and thus
personal narrative seems the most appropriate way to initiate an
analysis of them.[4]

   Almost two decades ago South Boston was the scene of intense racial violence stemming from the busing crisis that followed judicial
attempts to integrate the Boston school system. South Boston has a
history of standoffishness toward the rest of Boston. As a peninsula, it
is geographically and socially isolated, and as long ago as 1847, its
officials complained of Boston's taxation of South Boston, claiming
that "South Boston has no natural connection with, much less any
necessary dependence upon the City of Boston."[5] The rest of Boston,
in turn, shows "Southie" the full range of treatment accorded an outsider in their midst, from violent disgust to a certain patronizing ad-

miration, an arm's-length tolerance that contributes to the myth of Southie's truculent autonomy. The following passage from a book on recent Boston politics epitomizes the latter condescending attitude.

> Southie has a bad name, partly of its own choosing, as a rough and strident place where the natives would prefer to give a stranger a fat lip instead of the right time of day. . . . It has a certain mucker's insouciant charm, a grinning bravado, which asserts that anyone who comes from Southie is superior to anyone who comes from any other place, simply by reason of that geographical accident, the strut and the defiant braggadocio that are adopted to console the swaggerer who doesn't have a damned thing in the world except his youth and strength, both of which are dwindling before his very eyes.[6]

In the busing days of the 1970s, Southie's continued undercurrent of irritation erupted into violent resistance as its citizens collectively perceived that their community was being colonized and "made an example of" by remote Boston officials. The title of the organization formed to rally the opposition—R.O.A.R. (Restore Our Alienated Rights)—spoke both to the outrage of South Boston residents and to their assumption of the role of animalistic "Other" in relation to "Boston proper."[7] Since that time, Southie has been a fiercely all-white neighborhood, composed of Irish Catholics and Italians with a sprinkling of Poles and Ukranians. But sociologists have argued that South Boston has constituted its own ethnic identity—the Southie community.[8] "Southie identity" draws most heavily on its own rein-vented version of Irishness: in Boston the use of the shamrock, instead of the initials KKK or the swastika, as the white power symbol originated in South Boston. In fact, a rumor on the left arose in 1980 (suggested by David Duke's visiting Boston) that Southie's vigilante group, the South Boston Marshalls, had entered into discusssion with the Klan about a possible alliance and the relocation in South Boston of the Ku Klux Klan's headquarters. At the same time, support for the IRA ran strong and fierce in South Boston; several City Roots students wore Bobby Sands t-shirts during his hunger strike and after his death. Although each ethnic group—Ukranian, Polish, and so on—has its own social club, there is one social club for each Irish county. A further crucial factor in the South Boston identity is the Catholic church, which plays such a major part in everyday life that until re-cently, when Southie residents met even outside of Southie, they identified themselves to each other by parish, which, again, divided up in accordance with the rural Irish parish system: "Where are you from?" "Saint Monica's, Saint Augustine's."[9] Although the church's influence diminished markedly when it took a stand in favor of busing and integration in the 1970s, a strong Catholic influence permeates some of the poems. Boston being the parochial, classbound, and ethnically divided city that it is, I had never been to South Boston before my interview for the job at City Roots, although I'd lived my whole life in the Boston area. Familiar only with Southie's recent but legendary violence, I expected armed checkpoints at the borders and barbed-wire fences to let me know I was really there. I felt that I was going into a war zone in which I would be personally unsafe—a feeling that turned out to be well-founded when I was assaulted one morning by a woman waiting to see her drug counselor, who worked in the same building that housed the school.

Some of the students in the GED program had been casualties of the turbulent period in the mid-seventies—either their parents had pulled them out of school because of racism or fear for their safety, or they had simply gotten lost in the chaos and had quietly dropped out. Now, years later, they wanted to come back and get their high-school equivalency certificates and the part-time state-subsidized jobs made available through the program. This was a courageous step. Some would speak of mothers pressuring them to get full-time work or else to help at home with younger siblings. Their own embarrassment at being seventeen or eighteen years old and unable to read or multiply or divide, and the constant subliminal encouragement to despair about their abilities and opportunities made it more difficult for them to be in school. Unfortunately their sense of the tight and discriminatory job market was fairly realistic. However, for these students, the appeal of the alternatives—which included "selling drugs to little kids," sitting around smoking, drinking, doing Valium, Quaaludes, or angel dust, or playing basketball all day—had eventually worn thin.

However, other students, such as Charlotte, had had excellent schooling elsewhere and needed only to graduate. Some had come to City Roots when other alternative state- or city-funded schools had been closed down for economic or other civic reasons. Many (again, Charlotte among these) had no first-hand experience of harder drugs, though they were a part of everyday life in that time and place.[10] The range of worldliness, academic preparation and personal circumstances blended well into a highly motivated group of students who were determined to get their degrees and, for the most part, succeeded in doing so.

Just as Southie perceived and identified itself as separate from Boston proper, the projects were an insular world within Southie. Charlotte recently wrote, "I never lived in D Street projects. When I first started to go down to D Street I was treated like an outsider even though I was a life-long resident of South Boston."[11] While the school itself was clean, light and pleasant on the interior—as were many individual apartment units in the projects—the overall exterior impression of the projects was not.

They were marked by fire-gutted buildings, broken glass, broken everything. During the summer, one of the toilets in the school, which was housed in a converted apartment unit in one of the buildings, stopped flushing; at the same time the hot water faucet of the bathtub couldn't be turned off, so there was a urinary steambath effect at school for about a month. Project life was marked by paranoia and poverty, depression, violence, illness, and premature death. Teaching the Great Depression was a delicate proposition at City Roots: how can you cite a 35 percent national unemployment rate for dramatic effect when that's the norm for the D? When I taught John Lennon's "Working-Class Hero," I asked the class what a working-class hero was; someone answered, "That's easy. If you're working, you've got a lot of class, so you're a hero." In Charlotte's "A Night in the Hallway," the lighthearted tone barely conceals anxiety and tension: one night of partying stretches into a lifetime of stagnant unemployment and paranoia; likewise in her "D Street," the baseball, basketball, and hockey teams organized by various youth services and sponsored by local businesses stand as attempts to prevent, and function as daytime analogues to, murders, rapes, and B & E (breaking and entering). In both poems, the police constitute a ubiquitous but menacing presence: they harass, rather than protect. I constantly heard, and heard talk of, firearms, though I never saw any—during morning classes I'd hear explosions of target practice in the abandoned building next door. Spraying bullets with aerosol cans to make them explode was a popular pastime that spring. However, one can't control the trajectory of the bullet: one of my students had almost blown his thumb off. Fires in dumpsters were an almost daily event. By the time I taught there, D Street had been surpassed by the Charlestown projects as the worst white projects in terms of poverty, internal violence, and racial violence. But a friend who'd grown up there pointed out the distinct advantages of project life: the rent is cheap, utilities included, and if you just keep flushing the toilet when you want to take a bath, you'll never run out of hot water.

Style Wars, a hip-hop era television movie about New York subway artists, made much of the fact that these artists refer to themselves as "writers" because they write their names. They play on what the word generally means in the straight world: a prestigious claim to individual literary creativity with all the attendant safeguards for that individual endeavor—a mystique around authorship and authority protected by copyright laws that assure ownership and recognition. The graffiti writers' appropriation of the term both underscores the literal "self-expression" of elaborating on one's name in a public arena, and undercuts the glory of individual ownership of the finished artifact, which is often collectively conceived and executed, mobile and vulnerable to defacement. Studies of disenfranchised youth subcultures by primarily British cultural critics have shown how these subcultures appropriate and reshape for their own use certain commodities and art forms of the dominant culture. Until recently, most of this work focused on boys and young men and created analytic paradigms that tended to equate "youth culture" with "street culture" with male culture; Angela McRobbie's early work on girls, while it redressed a glaring absence, tended to compensate for the male (sociologists and their subjects) monopoly of the public sphere (publications and street life) by examining girls specifically as inhabitants of the domestic sphere; her work on fan clubs and consumption of records and "fanzines" located girls' culture in the bedroom and the kitchen. McRobbie's later studies as well as those of Valerie Walker, Barbara Hudson, Mica Nava and Leslie Roman have acknowledged women as active participants in public dance scenes and interactions at school, continuing to emphasize how institutions such as family, school, and the social work system construct these girls as gendered beings.[12] I want to add to the discussion of working-class girls' culture by showing how the girls themselves generate meaning not only by participating in institutional constructions of their subjectivities but by self-consciously creating artifacts that are subversive through their very imaginativeness and through their active engagement with the public — writing — realm. For although the modern activity of writing typically takes place in solitude, this is not entirely the case with these poems, indicating both pre-and postmodern elements in their process. Furthermore, writing is a public act of self-empowerment, especially when that writing articulates the process of social construction.

The writers of these South Boston poems are writers in several senses: they composed the poems individually and with each other, they wrote their own and each other's poems in their notebooks; these notebooks also contained poems out of teen magazines and other high schools' anthologies. Some of the poems I saw in Cheryl's notebook are wholly original, some anonymous, some (not included here) falsely attributed, some appeared to be pastiches of copied-out clichés and original lines. All of this indicates a participation in the full range of activities offered by poetic production, without the self-interested anxiety of influence, ownership, or recognition. They appropriate and redefine poetry and the creative process in the context of their own community.

With the exception of Susan's two poems, photocopied out of the City Roots newsletter where they, along with Charlotte's "Tortured Mind," had been anonymously printed, these poems were selectively copied out of Cheryl's notebook with her consent. According to my interests at the time, I copied out poems that I believed to be original, omitting those obviously copied from elsewhere (from magazines or newspapers), or those that didn't excite me aesthetically. At the time, I gathered from remarks made by the head teacher that Charlotte, Cheryl and Susan (or at least the former two) spent afternoons together writing poetry, inventing it together or separately and copying it into each other's notebooks; more recently, Charlotte has told me that her compositions were produced individually and then copied by Cheryl into Cheryl's notebook. Charlotte writes of the process: "some of the poems were written for the benefit of my friends who at the time thought it was cool. Because I could take a pencil and a gum wrapper and write a poem."[13] The collaborative and public nature of this activity recalls the lyric's origins: Sappho and her girls on their island, conducting community rituals in which different arts — music and dance, poetry and friendship — necessarily implied and involved each other. In generating their poetry, these high-school women recreate poetry as it first appeared—as a verbal healing art. I must also point out that the girls did not write these for a class, mine or any other teacher's; they composed the poems on their own time, unsolicited, for their own purposes. I did not have any special rapport with these particular students, which would make access to the poems a privileged and rare entry into their world. Likewise, the following descriptions of the writers are limited and impressionistic, and should be understood as incomplete profiles.

All three women were older students—Charlotte, the author of "Tortured Mind," "D Street," "A Night in the Hallway," "Remember Me," and the two longer ballads, was nineteen years old, unemployed, separated from her siblings on the death of her mother and reared by her grandmother.[14] Having gone through the eleventh grade in Catholic school, she had more formal education than many of the other students, scored highest on the GED test and reluctantly became the graduation speaker. She'd been to Blaine Hairdressing School and often cut people's hair at school after hours, but felt uncomfortable taking money for it. She insisted that "Tortured Mind" be printed anonymously in the City Roots newsletter; consequently many students thought it was written by Susan, who was more overtly "different." When I encountered the poem in Cheryl's handwriting, one telling slip in her spelling of Charlotte's title ("Torched" for "tortured") indicated a phonetically accurate rendering, caused by a Boston accent, with its tendency to make a separate syllable of the "ed" at the end of a word (i.e., "tawched," as in "wretched").[15] But it has further significance as well, pointing toward the economic context of the speaker's psychic suffering. One of the sources of income for young people in the projects, especially the boys, was to be commissioned to "torch" a car for its owner, who wanted to collect insurance on it. Thus "torched" stands in metonymically for everyday strategies for material survival, even as it illuminates the speaker's psychic suffering. In a sense, although Charlotte did not live in the projects and has had no direct experience of drugs or of dependency on government assistance, her position as an insider/outsider gives her a perceptive edge in her poetic descriptions of project life. This is evident in "D Street," "D Street Benches," and "A Night in the Hallway," as well as in the brilliantly deft revision of "tortured" to "torched" by Cheryl, who did live in the projects. Charlotte also wrote in free verse and nonrhyming poetry, but I did not have access to these poems.

Susan, author of "Portrait of a Dropout" and "The Epitome of Courage," shared Charlotte's aversion to publicity, but was a conscious nonconformist, as her dress and her intellectual tastes reflected. She was actively fascinated rather than frightened by "the sixties," "liberals," and antiauthoritarian ideas. Her experience in the army had given her a relatively wider view of the world than the average project dweller. In 1988, when I first contacted the women for permission to publish their poems, Cheryl referred to her as a "free spirit" (no one had seen her for several years). Susan was frustrated by the parochial and paranoid atmosphere of the projects, and was aware of the vicious cycle of oppression and reactive defensiveness that kept people from getting out. She also realized that she was a victim of that phenomenon. One of three students who enrolled in the University of Massachusetts basic skills program, she expressed some fears that she might be "trying to be better than she really was." Her English teacher there responded to a long and exhilaratingly sophisticated paper she wrote about the projects for an assignment to "describe a place you know": "Susan, this isn't just a paper, this is *art*." He wanted to talk to her, help her revise it, "do something" with it, and as a result she nearly dropped out to hitch to Florida. Several years later, the piece won a community-wide writing award; significantly, it was submitted not by Susan, but by Barbara Machtinger, then City Roots's director. Susan's poem, "Portrait of a Dropout," contains unusual lines for a South Boston project resident, because they assert a commonality that threatens the tight, oppositional ethnicity that is such a potent issue in South Boston: "He had blond hair. He had black hair. / He looked like me. He looked like you." That is, the subtext might read something like: "He had white skin. He had black skin. / He looked like me. He looked like you." Her style is also familiar to us as modernist poetry: that is, free verse, with abstract words like "epitome" and "courage," concrete metaphoric and metonymic details, and philosophical implications that self-consciously go beyond the words on the page.

Cheryl, the third woman, had graduated earlier. She earned money primarily through babysitting. Her family has been a mainstay in the D Street community for many years, playing a leading role in tenant organizations and other activities on behalf of communal wellbeing. She was the archivist I relied on, borrowing her notebook to copy the poems. The most open of the three about sharing her writing, she is the author of the friendship poem, which is characteristically generous in sentiment.

If I read a book [and] it makes my whole body so cold no fire ever can warm me I know that is poetry. If I feel physically as if the top of my head were taken off, I know that is poetry. These are the only way I know it. Is there any other way.
                          Thomas Higginson quoting Emily Dickinson

For love—I would
split open your head and put
a candle in
behind the eyes.

Love is dead in us
if we forget
the virtues of an amulet
and quick surprise.

                          Robert Creeley, "The Warning"

In his work on British biker boys and hippies of the 1970s, Paul Willis offers a spirited rationale for the study of popular cultures as a tonic to an enervated, scholarly "humanism":

The sheer surprise of a living culture is a slap to reverie. Real, bustling, startling cultures move. They exist. They are something in the world. They suddenly leave behind—empty, exposed, ugly—*ideas* of poverty, deprivation, existence and culture. Real events can save us much philosophy.[16]

What comes as a surprise in the South Boston poems is the terrifying, vital, compelling way in which the girls create their own worlds out of the artistic forms of language use available to them—street aphorisms, ballads, tabloid journalese, teen-magazine verse. Surprise, in the face of any creative burst of spirit and liveliness, is what Emily Dickinson calls "feeling physically as if the top of my head were taken off"—her visceral index, her only index, for gauging "poetry." Art is imperative in the projects, and surprise is our charged receptivity to it. As William Burroughs is fond of pointing out, "All warm-blooded animals have to dream. If they can't dream they die. It's a logical extension to suppose that without art, people can't exist."[17] These poems become warnings—amulets against the deadening possibilities of life at the bottom of the hierarchies of class, age, and gender.

However, these artifacts do not transcend their context, like fragments of free-floating human spirit or lyrical trees growing in Brooklyn, independent from either mass culture or the history of deprivation that has shaped these girls' experience. The power of the poems lies in their understanding, acknowledgment, and retelling of this history. The poems of love gone wrong, "I Never Could Stand it When They Cry," "In Heaven at Quarter Past Seven," and "Remember Me," exemplify most pointedly this borrowing and subversion of mass-, popular-, and high-cultural genres in the interest of telling their own stories of psychic suffering. Here, "telling their own stories" does not mean autobiography, but rather virtual history: "It didn't happen, but could have, and it feels like it did." The poems' structure and tone participate in that anonymous popular art form, the ballad, with deadpan, affectless narrative style, straight description of dramatic event involving a minimum of subjective commentary, awareness of community judgment, and rigorous adherence to rhyme and couplets. The two longer poems, especially, focus on events that have civic and religious repercussions, and articulate the writers' entrenchment in those institutional values that so deeply inform the "Southie identity." And they recall the tabloid journalism one can read in the *Boston Herald Tribune*, the newspaper which the girls are most likely to have read. ("I Never Could Stand It . . . ," for instance, is reminiscent of a story that made headlines when I was a teenager, about the single mother who went to the grocery store: while she was gone, her starving German Shepherd ate her starving baby.)

The opening lines of the poems often resonate with the cloying rhymes of mass-produced verse for teenagers, recalling Gertrude Stein's extended plays on her favorite piece of popular sentimentality, "When this you see, remember me." "Remember Me," in fact, has the flavor of a pastiche, in which Charlotte makes use of commercial and mass-cultural sources to undermine the ideology of blissful first love. For instance, parts of the poem make no sense in the context of the whole: "Today I'm fighting the pain. / I'm keeping the baby she needs a name" — when we know that in the end of the poem, which is otherwise written in the past tense, the narrator is about to die. The opening verses appear to derive from one of these mass-produced sources. They pin every romantic cliché into place, down to horseback riding by the "bay" (Boston Harbor? Not likely). But then the poem reverts into the familiar, hard-driving D-Street Blues: "The nurse had to tell me I was going to die." In Cheryl's notebook, even the handwriting changes as the teenaged version of the American dream disintegrates and reforms into another, more painful, virtual truth of urban life. Although the phrase "homes for unwed mothers" strikes us as anachronistic and hence almost amusing, and death in childbirth even less likely, the fatalistic message that you can't win, as well as a consistent affinity for the worst-case scenario, indicate this bleak version of youthful romance as possibly more true to the poets' own experience than the familiar scenario promised in the saccharine opening lines.

In "Remember Me," the writer enjoins us to remember her as her social and material conditions dismember her, while she herself dis-members an inauthentic, prefabricated version of her experience — the teen-magazine poem — and with it, a conventional notion of au-thorship. She re-members, by piecing together shreds of these other versions, her own horrific understanding of these mythic experi-ences. In these rememberings, in turn, the dismemberment of the protagonists' bodies represents the violence of their fear: the poems' narrators die in childbirth, or, as in "In Heaven at Quarter Past Seven," in a botched abortion.

Paradoxically, a characteristic usually associated with high culture becomes a disruptive and riveting aspect of the poems: the use of the first-person pronoun, one of the trademarks of the modern lyric, cuts across and counters the impersonal discourse that has traditionally objectified and imprisoned these women. When the object says "*I*" — "*I* am the woman that died in childbirth," "*I*'m that woman you read about in the paper, who killed her baby," "*I*'m the woman who died from a coathanger abortion" — she collapses the distance between reader and writer. Although these poems show the protagonist in all the positions most thrown in the faces of working-class teenage women — abusive, unfit mothers; tawdry, sexually irresponsible delinquents — we can't maintain the comfortable, voyeuristic detach-ment offered us by journalism, or the case histories of sociology or psychology. The first person singular makes judgment inappropriate — the reader becomes "her."

Just as "Remember Me" sets up and then destroys the myths of teenage romance offered us by the media, the first stanza of "I Never Could Stand It . . . " parodies our media-constructed expectation of

middle-class family life, as all the accoutrements of modern suburban life, complete with Rover the dog, mutiny into an equally parodic
tale of child abuse, manslaughter, and loss of custody. The amusing,
sitcom chaos of a middle-class mother's unmanageable day flips into
its underside—the nightmare of poverty-stricken, raggedy-nerved
single-parenthood conducted under the steady gaze of the Welfare
Department and the criminal-justice system. This conscious address
of the gaze of authority casts further light on the first-person strategy.
John Berger has pointed out that women internalize the sense of always being watched as objects of desire,[18] and Tania Modleski has
demonstrated how this plays into mass-cultural narrative strategy in,
for instance, Harlequin romances, a genre for and about women, in
which the third-person narrative nonetheless takes the heroine's
point of view. First-person cannot be used because at key points the
protagonist must be presented as an object: "she had no idea how
lovely she looked," etc.[19] These poems, however, unsettlingly combine the effects of third-and first-person narrative to describe
heartrendingly pathetic scenes of humiliation and despair with an almost schizoid flatness, heightened and rendered ironic by the sing-
song regularity of the long-line couplets. Along with Arthur Rimbaud,
the quintessential teenage poet, the writers say, "Je est un[e]
autre." The effect of this elision is that there is no background or
foreground—the gaze as well as the subject's drama becomes foreground. The girls' use of "I" to close distance and unsettle the reader
has the effect of filling in, with faces and features we think we know,
perhaps with our own, the sprawling outlines of the victims of urban
violence spray-painted on sidewalks. The moment of shock when we
apprehend this familiarity sends us into the realm of "antidiscourse,"
which has been designated as the pure subjectivity of the lyric. The moment of defamiliarization depends upon the moment of recognition.

Interestingly, the two poems that do address the subjects' "looks"
(that is, what they look like to others), "Tortured Mind" and "Portrait
of a Dropout" most approximate, in different ways, what we consider
the modern lyric, with its emphasis on interiority and private intra-
personal communication. And both do so with an emphasis on the
"otherness" of their looks:

> Always wondering if others can see
> For around my friends I try to hide

Those haunting words "I wish I died" . . .

I act as if I'm happy to be me
Only because I don't want people to see
That I've been this way for quite a while
A tortured mind behind a smile.

And very differently, Susan describes a distanced third-person sub-ject, the delinquent everyboy, identified through metonymic hair color, in modernist free verse to assert a commonality through dif-ference, an underlyingly common experience of overt alienation. Here, the third-person subject is brought close by other intimate techniques: the conversational free verse, the sympathetic and sim-ple tone, the straightforward, autobiographical details. (Susan, in fact, had dark hair bleached blond.)

I am not trying to domesticate these poems; I don't mean to imply that using the first person saves these poems from consignment to some putative mass-or popular-cultural damnation, or that this strategy expresses an essential "truth" obscured by the other discourses. The po-ems interweave all these forms, strategically playing them off against each other. Each discourse interrupts another: the stark tabloid scenar-ios undermine the saccharine opening verses they follow; they in turn are deconstructed by the use of the subjective "I," which in turn associ-ates itself inextricably with the discourses it disturbs. The ahierarchic or-ganization of discourses within the poems again reminds us that the lyric had its origins in communal activity that blended artistic modes.

However, the parodic element in these poems deserves further ex-ploration, because it partially accounts for the odd sense of distance, as well as the pastiche of styles and sensibilities at work in the texts. The poems should not be accepted at their shock-effective face value as transparent documents of lives of the young female poor—to do so would overlook their complexity. Some terms from contemporary critical theory can clarify the parody and pastiche of these poems, tentatively positing a relationship between this oeuvre's unsettling tone and youth culture in general.

In an essay on Baudelaire, Fredric Jameson articulates the differ-ence between modernist and postmodernist poetry and then goes on to claim Baudelaire's place under both rubrics.[20] The distinction Jameson draws concerns the disappearance, in postmodernism, of any emotional referent or pathos—modernism's objective correlative correlates to nothing as easily apprehensible as feeling. The postmodern becomes a kind of "camp," in which surface is everything, and meaning is created not syntagmatically by reaching back or "beneath" the text, behind an objective correlative to the veiled but crucially foundational feeling it "expresses"; but synchronically, by the juxtaposition of different elements of surface, all of which could have referential echoes; which in turn are constantly undermined, denied, played with, canceled out.

In discussions of poetry, the terms "modernism" and "postmodernism" are typically invoked in high-art contexts to refer to different historical avant-gardes. Charlotte's, Susan's, and Cheryl's poems are far removed from the "language poems" often used as examples of literary postmodernism, and it may strike the reader as ludicrous to apply such unabashedly academic terms to poems whose initial appeal seems to be their raw "naturalism," their startling, palpable sense of outrage. But these poems are not so straightforward; they are not crude and naïve artifacts of a more "natural" Other. Exploration of the poems' affect or lack thereof, if not an explicit attempt to fix them on a modernist/postmodernist continuum, can prove useful as a way of beginning to talk about the iconic roles of youth and poverty to the middle-class culture.

If teenagerdom, especially as constituted by the creation of a postwar "youth culture,"[21] is a point at which both assimilation and resistance are stretched to their extreme points and articulated at extreme pitch, one way out of the impasse represented by these two incompatible imperatives is to leap into another level of apperception, into the giddiness of artifice that simultaneously has the depth of emotional engagement. Teenage culture in general is self-parodic and simultaneously tremendously moving—as if the only way to survive the horror of contemporary adolescent experience is through removal into the hyperreality of self-dramatization or "terminal uniqueness." The poems show both defiance of and adaptation to the gender and class roles assigned their authors. In "D Street," for example, the drastic portrait of a violent housing project is letter-perfect. The girls describe the "lumpen" scene accurately, but also with deliberate sensationalism: "look out for all the rapers in the D." The author's outrage about this situation takes an aesthetic leap into the hyperreal as she addresses an imaginary and internalized (remember, the poems were copied out of a private notebook) middle-class observer: "We know this is how you talk about us in your media—and we can give it right back to you, with a twist; *we're* the scary kids drinking beer—and we're scared too. We're watching ourselves watching you watching us; we look at ourselves *through* you." The literate middle-class yearns after this presumably raw material, which takes on the aura of authenticity associated with being "less than": kids say the darndest things, the experiences of the poor are "more real" than those of the well-off, women are "more intuitive," Black music is "more emotional."

Whatever motivates the combination of fascinated indignation and wistful nostalgia that accompany reminders that the poor are always with us, reportage on the poor—and especially on the young poor—is a genre well-entrenched in American letters and media. The D Street writers had not read Ken Auletta's series on the "underclass," which appeared in the *New Yorker* several months after I left Boston; and they were probably unaware of Janet Cooke's Pulitzer Prize-winning "Jimmy's World," an exposé of a heroin-addicted child, or the scandal that ensued when that piece, published in the *Washington Post*, was itself exposed as imaginative fiction rather than investigative exposé; nor, probably, *Maggie: A Girl of the Streets*, or any other canonical classics of muckraking journalism or naturalistic fiction.[22] But the poets do watch television, and their self-reportage eerily echoes the tough and poignant human-interest tales of local poverty and injustice, in which the talking head's voice thrills with indignation, but in which the object of indignation is not quite clear. Is it the nerve of those people for being poor? the viewers who watch television when they could be "doing something" to help? "the system"? fate? Since these stories are rarely accompanied by analysis, functioning as avenues for emotional discharge rather than as exemplary local cases of the same political dynamics at work in other news stories, these broadcasts serve as occasions for experiencing unproblematic and depoliticized pathos felt as reaction to *others'* pain and authenticity.

Although the poems lack explicit analysis and partake of the fatalism inextricable from pathos, the D Street poets are aware of the middle class's need to see them in objectified terms, and they parody these terms even as they expose, more authentically than these media or literary events (because they are the speaking subjects as well as the objects of inquiry), the extent and the reality of their own impoverishment. The writers' real-life contexts constantly deconstruct naturalistic drama. The girls' own narratives deconstruct Crane's *Maggie* and other discursive events that would represent the young poor. Their outrage is organic rather than reactive, and the lack of affect that Jameson calls "postmodern" indicates how bad things really are: since we all live in the shadow of the bomb, we all live in a world where it may be impossible to have an unproblematical emotional referent behind our utterances. This is especially true for teenage women in a housing project, for whom every possible self-description is always already mediated by demeaning, objectifying institutional discourse. If it is true that the historical circumstances and physical events of poverty dislocate the drama, the converse is true as well—the theatricality of available discourse deconstructs a priori the real-life scenario. In the teen center next to the classrooms of the school, one girl broke off a conversation with friends to challenge me (obviously not a local) as I walked through: "I'm on welfare, I'm not ashamed to say it; what do you think of that?" There was a kind of giddiness and defiant exhilaration in her voice, and her friends were embarrassed for her.

Defiance and assimilation are inextricable in D Street. "We are exactly what you say we are—and worse," the poets say, like Genet living up to and surpassing the picture "respectable" people form of the experience of violence and poverty. At the same time, they protest that picture: "It's an outrage that we should have to live this way, and that you see us this way." Once I assigned a class to describe a familiar setting in a written paragraph. One girl described a view of the projects from her bedroom window, and ended with a single sentence set off from the rest: "Would you like to live hear?" The final couplet of "D Street," "If you value your life carry a knife and if you don't care get the fuck out of there," has the ring of a well-worn street aphorism (like "if you can't do the time, don't do the crime," which also reveals this defiance/assimilation complex: the saying ignores the many motivations people might have for various criminal activities, whereby other needs could outweigh considerations of imprisonment, and is most often used by those who have themselves committed petty crimes). Read "straight," the lines make no sense if one assumes that the object of "care" is "your life"—that is, if you care about your life, carry a knife, and if you don't care about your life, leave. Why would one leave if one didn't regard one's life highly?

In a community whose primary identity consists of a sense of place, whose legitimacy rests on the geopolitics of civic and neighborhood borders, to leave *is* to die, so if you don't care, you get the fuck out of there.[23] The imperative in the primary clause, though, is emphatic enough to suggest a third alternative reading of Charlotte's couplet for the outsider/reader to take to heart: "If you don't care about this situation, you have no business reading this. Don't come in here just to gawk at the project, at our poems, or at us."

Whence the dizziness of the middle-class reader reading these poems? After all, it was I, and not the young girl in the teen center, who identified her challenge as "dizzy and exhilarated"; what *did* I think of her for being on welfare? Is it the histrionic indignation of the anchorwoman aiming her story at well-off Americans, unmindful (that is, unaware and unconcerned) that the objects of the story may be watching as well? Susan Stewart, in *On Longing*, speaks of the exotic artifact as reflecting the imperialist collector/tourist's desire to be perceived as worldly and exotic: What does a literary critic stand to gain by presenting herself as impresario, as curator of these poems, as the mediator between the world of the D and her own world?[24] Wary of domesticating the poems for safe consumption, the cultural critic turns to self-reflexivity, possibly to affirm a wishful status as a "different kind of critic." The exhilaration of reading these poems is both what Emily Dickinson would approve as a right response to authentic poetry (or the same idea in Jamesonian language: "the sense of some new, unnameable, ungeneralizable private bodily sensation — something that must necessarily resist all language but which language lives by designating")[25] and the emotionally deprived "high" Jameson attributes to the self-battering and jaded postmodern aesthetic. Is the former (the Dickinsonian response) "authentic" and the other metaphysically impoverished? If so, how is it possible to experience both in response to the same stimulus? Jean-François Lyotard offers a helpful explanation of the mechanics whereby apprehension of the sublime intersects with its simulacrum, the postmodern high: aesthetic response to the sublime becomes suspect through its very overwhelmingness, through the inadequacy of conventional aesthetic and emotional terms to contain it.[26] Jameson also tries to articulate this problem through a discussion of the sublime and Edmund Burke's attempt to find some explanation—not for our aesthetic pleasure in the pleasurable, in "beauty," . . . but rather for our aesthetic delight in spectacles which would seem symbolically to crush human life and to dramatize everything which reduces the individual human being and the individual subject to powerlessness and nothingness. Burke's solution was to detect, within this peculiar aesthetic experience . . . astonishment, stupor, terror.[27]

The giddiness and "aesthetic delight" is not simply shallowness but an acknowledgement that standard interpretative or appreciative attempts to assess this art fall short of the mark. However, a Platonic analysis (that, unable to fully apprehend or express our "authentic"— ideal—responses, we fall perforce into a derivative, superficial— immanent—mode) solves nothing. The complex of "astonishment, stupor, terror" that these poems elicit is appropriate response to the murderous conditions the poems enumerate; this response attests also to the thrill of acknowledging the self-expressive energy embedded in these enumerations. The experience of reading these poems, the conjunction of pleasure and pain they elicit, forces one to a new level of reception, but one made up of tatters and remnants of feelings and interpretations that look familiar, just as the poems are patchwork pastiches of different discourses that are not only familiar, but impoverished clichés in themselves. The poems are a trick mirror of what we think we know.

If the postmodern high is also the high of trying simultaneously to hold together and to resist the contradictions of modern culture, then youth is the postmodern age par excellence, in which, according to cliché, thrill is everything, experience is felt at an elevated pitch, and experimentation in extreme expressions of style and emotion is unmatched in other stages of life. To face these straining contradictions under conditions that in effect impose a continued youth[28]—that is, continued oppression as poor women, without social dignity or power—puts these writers in a position, vis-à-vis their everyday oppression, analogous to the one Jameson describes for the artist living in the shadow of the bomb and other contemporary tyrannies: subject to "force[s] which, enormous and systematized, [reduce] the individual to helplessness or to that ontological marginalization which structuralism and poststructuralism have described as a 'decentering' where the ego becomes little more than an 'effect of structure.' "[29] The art that results from this decentering is camp, or, in Susan Sontag's words, permeated with the "hysterical sublime."[30] Being a teenager is this dizziness, this self-parody. It is a dumping ground for excess, for the exaggeration of the roles into which young people have to grow. And adults remember our youth with nostalgia and horror—we were more "real" then but we'd never want to go through it again—like newscasters with their bracing scenes of the lives of the poor.

"91 Revere Street" and the Case of Robert Lowell

Always inside me is the child who died
Always inside me is his will to die—
                    Robert Lowell, *"Night Sweat"*

The conditioning of both groups, the target group and the non-target group of any given oppression, takes place through a specific form of oppression, the oppression of young people. In a society in which there is oppression, all young people will be the targets of this systematic mistreatment.
                    Ricky Sherover-Marcuse

Nostalgia

The word "nostalgia" has continually resurfaced in this complex of ideas: modernism/postmodernism, youth and youth culture (the nostalgia behind adults' impetus to name and study youth subcultures), emotion, aesthetics, empathy. From all accounts nostalgia has passed in meaning from a term coined specifically for the symptoms of homesickness evinced by mercenary combatants in seventeenth-century Europe, to a sense of spurious and deluded bathos, an inauthentic longing for something that never existed: an unproblematic love affair; a vacation isle or exotic continent purged not only of the "modernity" of everyday Western life but also of its own indigenous and independent past; or, of primary concern in this essay on Robert Lowell's confessional prose, a happy childhood. The original medical term—from *nostos* (return) and *algia* (pain)—referred to a disease: the pathological longing to return home—of which longing the *Odyssey* has become the literary embodiment.

But the ambiguous etymological juncture of "return" and "pain" lends itself equally to intimations of painful returns: the pain of knowing return is impossible (viz. Thomas Wolfe's titles), the pain of knowing the idyll is a lie anyway, the pain of holding desire and the knowledge of its futility in equilibrium. Blake's *Songs of Innocence and Experience*, for example, sets up and deconstructs myths of the child and the golden state of childhood; the songs stand in juxtaposition to Wordsworth's less ambiguous deification of "the child" and "his" blessed, prophetic realm. In some of the contemporary analyses of nostalgia, one can find the same range and combination of critical and sympathetic responses. Richard Louv joins "home" and "pain" in examining the integral role of nostalgia in the modern American life condition of transience and uncertainty—nostalgia for a TV-fabricated "simpler way of life" that the longers have actually never experienced;[31] and Renato Rosaldo points out the deplorable and psychologically necessary role of "imperialist nostalgia" in maintaining the denial system of dominant cultures—that is, participants in the colonial or imperialist project mourn the passage of the indigenous culture and reinvoke it in movies about the decline of empire: *Gandhi, A Passage to India, The Jewel in the Crown.*[32]

Some feminists have associated nostalgia with the backlash against the women's movement, while it seems clear that nostalgia for a whiter shade of male is fueling the current agitation to return to or maintain a cor(ps)e curriculum of predominantly white-male--authored, tautologically determined "classics."[33] James Hougan, on the other hand, writing with early-1970s optimism and a now dated enthusiasm for a strategically deployed fiction of authenticity, points to the possibility of an activist "radical nostalgia" in the service of recuperating and empowering endangered cultures; Native American occupations of Wounded Knee and Alcatraz furnish his primary examples.[34] Susan Stewart posits nostalgia as a product of industrial and consumerist capitalism, in which objects (consumer fetishes, tourist art, postcards) mediate between the subject's experience and the *desired* experience; alienation necessarily becomes a term in this discussion.[35]

If one wanted to pursue the idea that members of marginal subcultures or sociologically disempowered groups experience alienation from a dominant culture, one could point to elements of what seem to be nostalgia in their work—the consistent presence, for example, of "nature," powerful goddess-figures, or Africa, as distant if not wholly lost ideals recuperable through some kind of spiritual or social revolution, or to the possibility of a realm of disembodied spirithood where bodies could not be targets of abuse. Emphasizing the alienation of nondominant groups, however, presupposes a rigid binarism of dominant/nondominant that enables "majority" members to impute to subcultural members an envious desire to emulate them (that is, "they all want to be like 'us.' " One recent student paper on Henry Louis Gates, Jr.'s, *The Signifying Monkey* expressed—by attributing to Gates—the opinion that it would be a shame if all black children had to grow up as little Eshus, having to straddle two cultures; the writer completely missed the affirmative tone of Gates's book and the reality of multiculturalism as a fact of *everybody's* everyday contemporary life). Stressing alienation contributes to the construction of a putative mentality of *ressentiment* among subcultural members. Without underestimating the pain of cultural abuse suffered by the socially dispossessed, I want to reject an ethnocentric analysis that foregrounds the "lack" of subcultures and that presumes an impoverishment on all levels of cultural participation, in favor of a far more interpermeable model that acknowledges and affirms the metaphoricity of these apparently nostalgic tropes—the homeland, outer space, goddess culture—as contingent and tactical performances.

I would argue that outsider groups do not long for a gilded past; and that the evocations of nature, goddess-imagery, animal figures, and mythic homelands of which the writer has had no direct experience constitute *presences* rather than absences; these are not lost Edenic states to be mourned and romanticized but are consciously constructed as ongoing, informing sources of strength and creativity. As George Yeats told her husband through her automatic writing, "We bring you metaphors for poetry," not metaphysical, empirical, or imperial truths. Understood as tools rather than as master narratives, "retro-tropes" can be recuperated for a politics of liberation not based on essentialism but on guerrilla aesthetics, or, at the most, on "strategic essentialism." Africa, in the poems of Audre Lorde, for example, becomes the Africa within, which permeates everyday life ("125th Street and Abomey," "For Assata," "Sahara," and so on).[36] I would not call this nostalgia; it is making use of a tradition—renewing it—by remaking it in the present. (This is particularly true for immigrant or ethnic subcultural literature—Cynthia Ozick's and Maxine Hong Kingston's fiction come to mind as examples.)[37] If this is nostalgia at all, it would seem to fall into the category of Hougan's "radical, activist nostalgia": a proactive creation of collective experience, rather than a nostalgia in Rosaldo's or Stewart's sense, in which a foggy mystique attached to derivative artifacts helps to deny and stave off the experience of real pain and loss.

To return to the *Odyssey* and its current cultural significance, the more probable site of nostalgia lies with those who "lack the lack" — that is, with those who are presumed to "have" privilege and dominance, those who not only long for the chimerical place of grace assumed by the world to be their birthright but suffer the double pain of suspecting their own longings to be unfounded or nothing more than the guilt of privilege. Their literature forms the acknowledged cornerstone of canonical Western culture. The Western literary canon is delicately structured around the protection of a lie. Neo-Freudians formulate this idea around the concept of the Phallus, the illusory conferrer of real social power, which is control over Logos, the impossible appropriation of which allows the subject participation in the socially ordering discourses of public authority — access to what Audre Lorde calls "the master's house."[38] As much as this phallic order of mastery and authority is a lie, so is the other side of the dichotomy: the golden idyll of a graced childhood, a youth still touched by traces of presymbolic bounty and unbounded freedom. Nobody knows better than the emperors that they are tremulously naked, but nobody has more at stake than they in believing in the illusion of the golden cloth. This double pain of belief and denial, of obsession and horror, is most poignantly articulated by those who inhabit what might be considered a place of privilege. The lie is the lie of privilege — the lie that some of us actually have, at the expense of others, access to a state of grace and fearlessness. (Those of us who have not had this access contribute to the lie by believing that "their" imagined access is responsible for "our" imagined alienation.)

The nostalgia of the communally written epic *Odyssey* evolved, in high poetry's development in Western Europe, into Romantic, lyric nostalgia, for homeland (in the case of Novalis), or for private experience of childhood and nature (in the case of Wordsworth). This development paralleled the rise of individualism and that of the middle class, which preceded and reached its full flower in the era of industrial capitalism. The lyric, with its insistent focus on the subject and articulation of personal experience, came into favor once again after a period of obscurity, to give voice to the private experience now deemed worthy of public expression.[39] However, even as individualism became the nominally privileged ideology of the modern industrial West, the variety of human experience continued to be codified, organized along official institutional norms for behavior and expression; religious, philosophical, medical, legal, and economic discourses determined what could be considered appropriate self-presentation. And accordingly, even as the lyric continued to be nominally overvalued to such an extent that it is now practically synonymous with poetry in contemporary Western culture, it has become both a privileged/trivialized poetic genre and a forum for representing what continues to be inadmissible in public discourse — "private experience" that defies the norms it was created in conjunction with and named as Other to. While emphasis on privatized nuclear family relations and the "developmental years" spent in character formation found celebratory expression chiefly in the prose of the *bildungsroman*, they appeared also in Romantic poetry, particularly Wordsworth's, whose deification of childhood and assertion of its strong intrinsic identification with and love of nature verge on the hyperbolic:

> Thou, whose exterior semblance doth belie
>   Thy soul's immensity;
> Thou best philosopher . . .
>   Mighty Prophet! Seer Blest!
>   On whom those truths do rest,
> Which we are toiling all our lives to find,
> In darkness lost . . .
> Thou little Child, yet glorious in the might
> of heaven-born freedom on thy being's height . . .
> Delight and liberty, the simple creed
> Of Childhood . . . [40]

However, behind the creation, the standardization, and the celebration of innocent and untroubled childhood lay not only the actual harshness of child-labor practices introduced by industrialism (which Blake protested in his *Songs of Experience*, and which Wordsworth also implicitly criticizes here) but also the varieties of felt experiences of children in families.[41] As the tyranny of child labor was tamed by reform and the role of childhood reconstrued as a period of happy, idle exploration of natural and personal resources, a different kind of tyranny came into play, with which we are all somewhat familiar—that is, the tyranny of having one's experience defined a priori as happy, idle, loving, innocent. Wordsworth's and Blake's prescriptions have been culturally rewritten as descriptions, silencing expression of experience contrary to the happy idyll. And as this picture of exuberant bliss has increasingly become the norm for contemporary childhood, the lyric, because of its acknowledged creation and articulation of private and inadmissible experience, has paradoxically become the form most able to explore and challenge this myth. Most recently, Eve Kosofsky Sedgwick has posited a connection between the shamefulness of a fat girlhood, female anal eroticism via spanking as familial punishment, and the disciplining of the lyrical subject.[42] The privileged site of a golden childhood is also a treasure chest of shame and self-consciousness—the "family crucible"; the lyric is a vessel of containment and artistic display of family secrets. She associates the dramatic epic, by contrast, with breaking those secrets hitherto kept in check by the corseting formalism of lyric.

The Marginalization of Childhood

Against the blurry, yearning mystification of nostalgia for childhood, classical psychoanalysis, a pragmatic social philosophy, and the contemporary pop-psychotherapeutic recovery movement propose to remind us of the pain of powerlessness and humiliation we actually suffered as children (granted, as we know from Philippe Ariès and others, "childhood" and "adolescence" are not fixed categories but change according to historical developments).[43] I will address youth as a marginal state in the industrial and postindustrial West, with its mystification and subjection of the child. Much has been written about this phenomenon of mystification/subjection with respect to women and "nature," and it is easy to see the same pattern vis-à-vis children. The various approaches that inform my perspective—those of Alice Miller, Ricky Sherover-Marcuse, Jean-Paul Sartre, and Louis Althusser—point to the subtle and overt tyranny of adults over children in the family life of the modern West.

Alice Miller comes out of a classical Freudianist perspective, but believes (along with Jeffrey Masson and others) that when threatened with unbearable professional and personal consequences, Freud ceded his seduction theory (the seduction or sexual assault of children by their parents) for the safer concept of "wish fulfillment" (the child as desiring seducer / agent of sexual fulfillment with the parent) and thereby abandoned countless victims of child sexual abuse to further victimization. Much of the sense of urgent revelation in Miller's project comes from the belief that childhood *should* be the untroubled idyll of Wordsworth's "Ode"—or was, before the parents' violations—and the outrage that this is rarely, if ever, anyone's actual experience:

1. Every child comes into the world in order to grow, to develop himself, to live, to love and to articulate his needs and his feeling for self-preservation.
2. In order to be able to develop themselves, children need the help of adults who are aware of their needs, who protect them, respect them, take them seriously, love them, and honestly help them to orientate themselves.[44]

More often than not, however, "these vital needs of the child are frustrated and the child ... is abused for the needs of the adult." This abuse can take any number of subtle or crude forms, from physical abuse to ridicule or denial of emotional expression. Ironically, though, the child depends entirely and without recourse upon her or his parents, and must deny her or his resulting anger, repressing even the memory of pain, and "idealiz[ing] her or his aggressor." The negative feelings, suppressed, become "disconnected from their original cause," and result in "destructive actions against others (criminal behavior or mass murder) or against oneself (drug addiction, prostitution, psychic disorders, and suicide)."[45] The victim chooses the easiest target for destructive outlet—namely, her or his own children—perpetuating the cycle of psychic violence.

One problem with Alice Miller's theories is her insistence on the term "the child's true feelings" to refer to the pain of subordination and humiliation, which cannot be expressed for fear of losing the parent's approval and hence one's life, and which consequently become repressed or forgotten. Suppression of painful memories does not make these memories any more real than others that do not threaten parental hegemony—except that these repressed feelings and memories are determinant in the child's life into adulthood. Just as the socially "less than" are cast as more authentic, the invisible power of silenced feelings makes them seem "more real" when "discovered." Much of this analysis has passed into popular psychology: the concept of the "inner child" has become reified into a "thing," a fixed reference point around which a narrative is developed. The adult therapy client "discovers" this thing / child / static reference point "inside" her- or himself; once discovered, this inner child must be taken care of by, for example, buying teddy bears, "journaling" and reading daily affirmations, reentering the world of childhood pleasures and exorcising the world of childhood shame. I wonder, however, if the flurry of activity around this recently discovered inner child isn't analogous to Columbus' discovery of "unclaimed," "virgin" land (albeit already populated by flourishing cultures) or to the late nineteenth-century (re)"discovery" of sexuality. The silence surrounding the prediscovery stage, as Foucault has pointed out about the latter phenomenon of sexuality, is not silence at all; it is a thundering obsession, manifest in an overproliferation of controlling and defining devices which evince not unawareness but hyperawareness.

My use of Miller and Sherover-Marcuse focuses attention on the micropractices of oppressive family dynamics inflected by, but not of lesser subject-formative influence than, the apparently larger social situations of economics, ethnicity, and gender. With its historical roots inextricably entwined with economic, ethnic, and masculinist fear, traditional Freudianism, the only broad theoretical system to address the injustices of age difference and the familial institution, has provided an inadequate model for my exploration of the child (and the subsequent metaphoric "child within") as outsider. So although I am sympathetic to critiques of the level of generality and the prose-lytizing tone of the two pragmatists I cite extensively, their analyses—to some extent *because* of their flat-footed and partisan simplicity—have engendered an extremely useful and compelling reading of Lowell's oeuvre, one that goes against the grain of the profiles created for it both by partisans of the confessional school and by their more formally oriented opponents.

Without Miller's strategically prescriptive tendency toward psychic essentialism, Ricky Sherover-Marcuse's formulations politicize the former's psychoanalytic findings in short, declarative assertions:

> People hurt others because they themselves have been hurt. In this society we have all experienced systematic mistreatment as young people—often through physical violence, but also through the

invalidation of our intelligence, the disregard of our feelings, the discounting of our abilities. All of us are oppressed as children, through the inevitably harmful pedagogical practices characteristic of oppressive societies. As a result of these experiences, we tend both to internalize this mistreatment by accepting it as "the way things are," and to externalize it by mistreating others. Part of the process of unlearning (oppression) involves becoming aware of how this cycle of mistreatment is perpetuated in day to day encounters and interactions.[46]

Children's social and familial induction into prejudicial thinking violates them as much as, if more subtly than, physical and emotional abuse, neglect, or humiliation. It hurts those indoctrinated into privilege as much as those assimilated into lives of deprivation or subordination. To use Althusserian vocabulary, all children are interpellated into the socius via the ideological state apparatus of the family. Moreover, according to Sherover-Marcuse,

> people who are the *non-targets* (as well as targets) of any particular oppression have *resisted* and *attempted to resist* their socialization into the oppressive role. The fact that this resistance is not generally recognized is also a feature of the oppression. (emphasis is Sherover-Marcuse's)[47]

However,

> all people come from traditions which have a history of resistance to injustice, and every person has their own individual history of resistance to [oppressive] conditioning. This history deserves to be recalled and celebrated. Reclaiming one's own history of resistance is central to the project of acquiring an accurate account of one's own heritage. When people act from a sense of informed pride in themselves and their own traditions they will be effective in all struggles for justice.[48]

Both Miller and Sherover-Marcuse help to illuminate the lie behind the golden myth, and offer evidence for why children, even though some of them grow up to be straight white wealthy men, could be included in the lower ranks of the infamous Chain of Being. This point needs explicit articulation, because many ex-children, parents and nonparents alike, object to this aspect of my project, defending their own childhoods ("the happiest, least alienated period of my life") or their current treatment of their own children. I do not propose to deny the validity of happy memories, or to make struggling parents even more self-conscious. "Blame" is not at issue here. The problem is structural and societal.

Perhaps most persuasive on the subject of self-destructive socialization and the liberating possibilities offered by its recognition and appropriation is Sartre, whose masterpieces, arguably, were not the early philosophical tracts but his later psychobiographical portraits of Genet and Flaubert.[49] Sartre's exhaustive attention to the child's visceral experience of interpellation locates that moment as inexorably and incomparably formative: in Genet's case, the "dizzying word thief" came to define his subjectivity in all its various relations to the world; in Flaubert's case, the name of "family idiot" (because he was late in learning his alphabet) relegated him, in his own estimation, to the realm of the subhuman. Like the child in Countee Cullen's poem, who from an entire summer spent in Baltimore remembers only the word "nigger" coming at him from the mouth of another child,[50] Sartre's subjects, though one is the ultrabourgeois "father of modernism" and the other an icon of countercultural subversion, are both initiated into the social world by adults' withering circumscription of their potential.[51]

Sherover-Marcuse points out that shared oppression of children gives us a common experience on which to form emancipatory alliances: if we have suffered belittlement, then we can better understand and accept each other's need for freedom. Since even the privileged share the common, though unlegitimated, pain of childhood, they can participate in emancipatory activity; everyone stands to gain by each other's freedom. For the socially privileged, childhood thus becomes a charged concept, a site for the attempt to break through not only the feeling of deadness and isolation of adulthood, but the social alienation that often accompanies privilege, a condition so palpably obvious to the less privileged. Again, we have only to look at the work of Wordsworth, the grandfather, through Emerson, of American Romantic and post-Romantic poetry, for evidence of the power of the concept of youth, surfacing again in the work of the twentieth-century confessional poets and in that of others such as Dylan Thomas (whose influence in America was enormous) and Theodore Roethke, who claimed his greatest influences to be Freud and Mother Goose. Childhood experiences become larger than life; they throb with mystical potency and inchoate potential. This privileging of childhood, through psychoanalytic interest in early formation of subjectivity through language acquisition, continues to permeate contemporary continental poetry and poetics. The comprehensive poetic theories of Julia Kristeva, for example, draw on myths of an idyllic, pre-Oedipal and presymbolic state of consciousness characterized by nonlinear, playful, anarchic use of language.[52]

In this literature, then, childhood becomes the locus of relationship and harmony, a time when all was possible. Since we share with others the experience of childhood oppression, memories of youth can indeed be a powerful basis on which to connect with them. But concentration on and deification of a condition called youth does not inevitably elicit the feeling of fellowship and commonality with others to which Sherover-Marcuse points. On the contrary, it can lock one into isolation and mistrust, solipsistic resentment and suspicion that others have wrested away the lost Eden. The catch, according to Miller,[53] Sherover-Marcuse, and standard psychoanalytic folk wisdom, is that the subject must remember and acknowledge the pain of childhood through a willing act of consciousness-raising before such fertile alliance and fulfillment can take place. Experience must be brought not only to personal consciousness, but to *social* consciousness; "*only* experience confirmed and corroborated through discussion and coped with as *collective* experience can be said to be truly experienced."[54] The pain of childhood, however, is often so acute that, repressed, it is transformed into nostalgia, which makes this social processing difficult; so difficult, in fact, that in spite of repeated theoretical and pragmatic attempts to bridge the perceived gap, commitment to psychotherapy (micropraxis) and to radical social activism (macropraxis) continue to be crudely cast as incompatible.

Childhood's pain, prior to a willing commitment to recognize it, is experienced as nostalgia for childhood (the pain *of* return — of inescapability, in fact — disguised as the desire *to* return). The development of socially repressed pain and resistance parallels the rise of the "individual" subject within the nuclear family, as it has been articulated by capitalism. (With respect to imperialist nostalgia, we keep ourselves enslaved by repressing the unpleasant memories of our own internal colonization, of the conditioning by which we were assimilated into the hierarchy of our culture, just as we repress, in acts and artifacts of imperialist nostalgia, the painful destruction of indig-

enous cultures in the history of colonialism.) This relationship between the articulation of the subject and the memory of pain (the
creation of nostalgia) could intimate, as Kosofsky Sedgwick suggests,
that Romantic and post-Romantic lyric poetry depends in some sense
on intimacy, repression, shame, and the keeping of family and social
secrets—it is the genre of familial discipline and punishment.[55] The
lyric attempts to speak the forbidden, the variety of human experience outside the norm, in diminutive, distanced, and acceptable formulas, as disciplined and self-protective as the subject who produces
it. Just as the novel domesticates secrets by compulsively blabbing
them in overblown kitsch form, the modern lyric domesticates secrets through compulsively oblique and controlled utterance, dramatic because of its "compression," its anal virtue. Like the tourist-art
version of a sacredly charged fetish, it disarms and wards off, but also
expresses, unnameable experience through distance and miniatur-
ism.[56] Unlike and like the South Boston poems, whose amulet qualities, as in Creeley's "The Warning," slash through everyday inertia
with vibrant and violent color, high art's modernist, tightly controlled
and "beautifully articulated" poems are homeopathic amulets against
their own explosive subject matter, warding off their own consequences by the intensity of highly wrought artistry.

For the New Critics at least, the tension of the famous and questionable form/content dialectic, the element of threat "mastered"
through skill, gave a poem credibility. Especially in the era of the objective correlative, springing as it did from Eliot's self-denial and "abnormal reticence,"[57] poetry had to do with sitting on a secret, with
maintaining a harrowing balance between self-disclosure and self-
protection. The poets and critics most influenced by Eliot's closeted
and unnameable desire became, in turn, the most academically influential school of the twentieth century.[58] It was this group, the
Southern Agrarians and the New Critics, under whose tutelage Robert Lowell came of age as a poet.

Robert Lowell perhaps most strikingly exemplifies modern American post-Romantic subjectivity at its crudest and most accessible—
the tormented self, history's favorite son and history's victim. Scion of
an illustrious literary and historical Boston family (Amy Lowell and
James Russell Lowell were his literary ancestors), Lowell was the
"leading national poet" from the postwar 1940s until his death in
1977. Powerful academic critics as well as fellow poets acknowl-

edged his stature; every major university press has a "life and art" book on him.[59] He became the most respected member of the alcoholic, psychiatrically preoccupied confessional school (a term coined in a review of *Life Studies*), which included Ginsberg (a crossover figure in multiple arenas) Berryman, and Lowell's own students Plath, Sexton, and Snodgrass, among others.[60] What interests me in the context of this study is Lowell's nostalgia—the pain of return, the repetition compulsion of his themes of backward trajectory (family life, childhood, ancestral New England history)—which writes a Boston at once radically other than but analogous to that of Charlotte, Susan, and Cheryl, his unfamiliars in almost every respect. Also Bostonian, their contemporary but not their coeval, Lowell writes a patrician but no less oppressive city. Like theirs, his nostalgia is the outrage of violated expectations. His honesty in looking head-on at that violation, intertwined with the unbearable longing to alter that complex of disappointments, is akin to theirs. But there is nothing remotely postmodern about Lowell's opus. His work is drenched in personal emotion at the same time as it is highly wrought, aspiring consciously to take its place among the best that has been written, said, and done. Lowell does not engage a sense of play, distance himself, or radically question selfhood and authority. Any questioning of Robert Lowell as an author must be supplied by the reader.

I have not avoided, nor wanted altogether to avoid, the "life and art" template from which so much work on Lowell has been written. It is not a useless enterprise to include biographical information as part of the conditions of production; Lowell's confessional thrust (all connotations herein included) almost demands some detailed biographical attention. I have been more circumspect about the girls' biographies not because they are still living, but because the difference in power held by my subjects compels discretion and respect (this awareness begs the question "Why is Lowell's biography more important than those of the girls?"). In a book whose primary audience I assume to be academic humanists, revelations about Lowell provide the poignant anecdotes of teaching-anthology headnotes; analogous revelations about the girls, on the other hand, unless specifically authorized by them, may luridly reinscribe them as stereotypical objects. Empathetic as my reading of Lowell may be on a personal level, I hope to emphasize his poetry and personal conduct *as social practice*—privileged white male poet(ry) in crisis, as it were. Supremely privileged, preeminently public, and insistent on self-disclosure, Lowell serves as a powerful case study of the pathos of failed liberalism.

The titles of the collections from the period on which this essay focuses—*Life Studies, For the Union Dead, Imitations*[61]—echo Lowell's identification with official textbook history and the personalizing of institutional discourse. *Life Studies* plays on the delicate sense of life in death and death of life: biography as still life, or even as "death studies" of both the child "always inside" longing to die and of the decaying Boston aristocracy to which Lowell was heir; the "union dead" are not only the Northern soldiers who died in the Civil War, but the death of national unity as well as of union/marriage/intimacy/ wholeness, and also the shattering of a dignified and controllable "unified self" into mental illness; the translated *Imitations* reverberate with alienation and struggle for authenticity under the shadow of oppressive family history; the insistence on and simultaneous despair of autonomy ("selfhood") and difference. But Lowell seems to have experienced this flickering between various understandings of his poetic project and of his "self" in the light of psychiatrically and poetically inspired self-exploration and confession (influenced particularly by Snodgrass's *Heart's Needle*),[62] rather than as a challenge to the idea of selfhood. Lowell's poetry is a long and painful meditation on the awareness that "Robert Lowell" embodies a set of historically determined relationships—and the desire that "he" be more beyond that. The poetry enacts a desperate faith in Ego—if one could only get to it—in the face of experience that countermands that faith. It is as if Lowell, suffering a mental illness whose diagnosis tears his experience into dichotomous halves, tries to get it right by *willing* a unified self into being through a belief in history and intimate human relationships, rather than questioning the very idea of a unified self. He enacts the violent disjunction between Robert Lowell, historical personage with all the obligations of American aristocracy to engage publicly the national politics, and Robert Lowell, fragmented and free-floating subjectivity set awash in various mental institutions ranging from the patrician McLean's ("Waking in the Blue") to Boston Psychopathic, where he was once interned after refusing commitment unless it were to a public facility.[63] My essay examines one or two works from each of the three volumes of this period, which I formulate as Lowell's poetic "adolescence"—that is, the period in which his work attempts to constitute an identity both other than and continuous with his former familial and poetic histories. This era reflects a sharp change in his style, represented especially in the prose piece "91 Revere Street"; indeed, Marjorie Perloff has referred to the publication of *Life Studies* not only as "Lowell's central achievement"[64] but as a "turning point in the history of twentieth-century poetry,"[65] with specific reference to the fusion, in "91 Revere Street," of the "romantic 'poetry of experience' " with the innovations of nineteenth-century realist prose.[66] I discuss the transition indicated by that particular prose piece in its environment of original poems and translations—in particular, the Rimbaud translations in *Imitations* and "The Neo-Classical Urn" from *For the Union Dead*.

For Lowell, individual poems became salutary mirrors in which he could experience and represent himself as unified; even his writings about his manic-depressive episodes and periods of extreme psychic fragmentation became unified aesthetic objects. Lowell's work is in fact as fragmented, behind its apparent coherence, as that of the girls, although theirs seems to have the unity of essentialism, and his the unity of the highly wrought, autonomous work of art. The artistry of the girls' poetry shatters myths of mass-cultural passivity as much as the relatively unstructured prose of "91 Revere Street" shatters myths of lyrical autonomy. (Granted, Lowell chose, as his model for prose writing, Flaubert, the protomodern *styliste par excellence* who both invented and gave the lie to modernist "realism"; questions about the factuality of Lowell's confessions arise in the "realistic" "91 Revere Street.") Although "91 Revere Street" can't be taken as unmediated diaristic recollection or unselfconscious prose, the choice to write this material in prose rather than verse indicates an association of personal disclosure with relaxing boundaries formally as well as thematically. In that the poems' formal unity allow Lowell to say "I," the prose represents a step toward allowing fluidity into the concept of "I," even as the subject of his prose is autobiographical pain and psychic suffocation. After "91 Revere Street," the prose continues to be highly stylized and the verse relaxes, as Lowell finds a way to write about his psychic disorders in which any sense of unity cracks apart. The subject *becomes* division, the object absence: the dead parents, the dying child inside him, whose efforts at emergence are manifest and reified in writing.

Lowell Imitates Rimbaud

Lowell translated Rimbaud the adolescent, who tried to shatter the lyric and whose subject matter often involved orphaned children. Lowell initiates the Rimbaud translations in *Imitations*, with "Mémoire," which Lowell translates as "Nostalgia" and to which he appends a note telling the reader that the poem is autobiographical:

> *(An autobiographical poem: Rimbaud remembers the small boy in a rowboat under the old walls of Charleville. His mother and sisters are on the bank. His father has just deserted them.)* ("Nostalgia," 174; the italics are Lowell's)

In it, a young boy escapes his family, comprising his arch-rigid mother (Rimbaud's epithet for his mother was "la bouche d'ombre") and sisters (their alcoholic father has deserted them), and daydreams in a moored boat on the river. In a later, more famous poem, the one with which Rimbaud made his entry into Paris and the favors of the homosocial and homosexual Parnassian patriarchy,[67] the boy himself becomes "le bateau ivre," tearing loose from his moorings, bursting through the strictures of traditional lyric as he bathes himself in the tempestuous "Poème de la mer."[68]

Lowell identifies—perhaps overidentifies—with the more oppressive aspects of Rimbaud's childhood, although he takes liberties and wide leeway in translation, appropriating the adolescent symbolist's memories of childhood as his own. Significantly, however, his translation of "Le Bateau Ivre" loudly omits the poetically self-reflexive phrase "je me suis baigné dans le Poème / De la Mer . . . "[69] (Lowell's poetry does not engage, for the most part, the question of writing itself apart from the agency of a writing personality.) In his own words, the point of the *Imitations* was to "do what my authors might have done if they were writing their poems now and in America"[70]— that is, what they might have done had they been Robert Lowell. "Les Poètes de Sept Ans," which Lowell renders in the singular, becomes his own self-portrait—the child-poet matches Lowell's autobiographical sketches in *Life Studies* and *For the Union Dead*. Compare the following portraits:

> his lumpy forehead knotted
> with turmoil, his soul returned to its vomit.

> All day he would sweat obedience.

He was very intelligent, but wrung,
and every now and then a sudden jerk
showed dark hypocrisies at work.
. . . As for compassion,
the only children he could speak to
were creepy abstracted boys . . .
. . . His Mother was terrified,
she thought they were losing caste. This
    was good—
she had the true blue look that lied.
("The Poet at Seven," I 77)

I rub my head and find a turtle shell
stuck on a pole,
each hair electrical
with charges, and the juice alive
with ferment. Bubbles drive
the motor, always purposeful . . .
Poor head!
("The Neo-Classical Urn," FUD 47)

my mind always blanked and seemed to fill with a clammy
hollowness when Mother asked prying questions. Like other tongue-
tied, difficult children, I dreamed I was a master of cool, stoical repartée.
("91 Revere Street" LS 20)

and the final lines of "Child's Song":

Help, saw me in two,
put me on the shelf!
Sometimes the little muddler
can't stand itself!
(FUD, 22)

These unflattering self-portraits dwell on physical discomfort and
awkwardness. In direct contrast to Wordsworthian harmony, Lowell's
child "muddler" is disproportioned—head overlarge, a gooey, seeth-
ing ooze encased in hard bulkiness. The turtle in its shell imagistically governs "The Neo-Classical Urn"; the subject "I" of the poem
tortured turtles as a child, and is a turtle, captured and claustrophobic in his own self-protection. After the opening just cited, this poem
savagely twists the Wordsworthian code of blissful boyhood. It shows
a boy, ostensibly blissful, or at the very least, boyishly energetic.

> I sprinted down the colonnade
> of bleaching pines . . .
> . . . Rest!
> I could not rest. At full run on the curve,
> I left the caste stone statue of a nymph . . .

It then undermines our assumptions about that poetic code: far from expressing a natural joie de vivre, the boy is frantically torturing animals, cramming an ornamental garden urn with painted turtles, who inevitably die.

> the turtles rose,
> and popped up dead on the stale scummed
> surface—limp wrinkled heads and legs withdrawn
> in pain. What pain? A turtle's nothing. No
> grace, no cerebration, less free will
> than the mosquito I must kill—
> nothings! Turtles! I rub my skull,
> that turtle shell, and breathe their dying smell,
> still watch their crippled last survivors pass,
> and hobble humpbacked through the grizzled grass.

The boyish energy turns out to be self-hate compulsively turned on other small creatures. As the poem's title indicates, Wordsworth is not the only Romantic poet whom Lowell takes on here. He likewise savages the Keatsian strain of his Romantic heritage, and through oblique reference to the New Critical manifesto *The Well-Wrought Urn*, he defies the idea of aesthetic self-containment represented by the well-wrought urn. Rather than on a lover trapped in mid-passion on the outside of an urn, rather than on an autonomous work of art transcending personality and history, Lowell focuses on the all-too-historically specific "I" trapped inside the urn of his own body and consciousness, and trapped as well in the constraints of conventional lyric production. The masturbatory opening images, in which the head/mind is the only sex organ, indicate that he can relate to no one but himself. The subjectivity of lyric becomes obsessive self-hatred. The stasis of solipsism reproduces a split, cerebral self that mocks Keats's vision of beauty and art by showing us one of its possible endpoints: the history of Romantic lyric as a family history terminating in degenerative, inbred deformity of consciousness.

The poet's psyche breaks against the rigidity of neat dichotomies—

hard/soft, inside/outside—and then blurs in the confusion of subject/object, self/other: the boy tormenting the turtles is himself a tormented turtle. Like them, he is sluggish and vulnerable, hard and ungainly and inaccessible, loath to acknowledge the depths of his pain. The grown poet's pain in the opening and closing passages is not, as Marjorie Perloff suggests,[71] remorse at acts impulsively and unconsciously committed in a carefree youth, and sudden and mature recognition of creaturely kinship. Rather, it reflects pain continued from childhood and now brought to articulate consciousness. The opening lines suggest that science and psychiatry have mutilated the speaker/poet through electroshock treatment, as the wanton child mutilated the turtles. But beyond that, he acknowledges that even in childhood, this sense of victimization underwrote all activity. Although there are no adults in the poem and no explicit mention of oppressive authorities, the ordered, suffocating claustrophobia of the parental garden with its ominous

> caste stone statue of a nymph
> her soaring armpit and her one bare breast
> gray from the rain and graying in the shade

and the "two seins of moss" the boy "swerves" between, suggest that the boy is trapped inside his parents', especially his mother's, body, just as later the man feels trapped inside his own head/mind and the poet inside generic constrictions. The landscape, the projected world of his parents' passions in which the boy feels "drenched" ("91 Revere Street," LS 19), is both wet and sterile, oppressively sensuous and infertile, like an incestuous or otherwise inappropriately undifferentiated affective relationship; and the boy imprisons the turtles as he feels imprisoned—only violence can break him out of himself ("Help, saw me in two . . . "). He cannot understand relationship except in terms of domination and possession.

Here the monolithic and static female figure parallels neatly "la bouche d'ombre" as she is described in "Nostalgia," though Lowell does not grant the softness of grief and abandonment to *his* female overseer. Lowell outdoes even Rimbaud in his refusal of a golden childhood. Rimbaud, whose popularity was growing in the United States in the wake of several lurid, pathos-drenched biographies and the popularity (especially among the Beats of the fifties and sixties) of vagabonding pretensions and the *maudit* tradition in literary production, wrote some stunning poems in the golden vein—"Ma Bohème," for example, or many of the pieces in *Illuminations*. The substitution, in "The Poet at Seven," of "naked, red / Hawaiian girls dancing"—for "des Espagnoles . . . et des Italiennes" further Americanizes, updates, and Lowellizes Rimbaud's lines. The other Rimbaud poems Lowell includes are also typically Lowellian, or rendered thus, in subject matter: childhood, in "Les Poètes de sept ans" and "Les Chercheuses de poux"; and the historical interest of his series "Eighteen Seventy," which includes "L'Eclatante victoire," "Rages de Cesars"—which Lowell entitles "Napoleon After Sedan"—and so on.

In identifying with Rimbaud, in creating through translation a family of poets, as he did through early apprenticeship to the distinctly anti-Bostonian but equally patrician (in aspiration if not in literal genealogy) and even more conservative Agrarians and New Critics, who often explicitly functioned "in loco parentis,"[72] Lowell is both replicating and repudiating the (for him) unbearable sociohistorical visibility of his biological family and its decline. When Lowell first committed himself to being a poet, and demonstrated that commitment by leaving Harvard for Kenyon College to study under John Crowe Ransom, a patriarchy of high art, of poesy, replaced the oppressive matriarchy of the Winslow-Lowell heritage embodied by his overbearingly caste-conscious ("stone caste") mother. However, the new family had much in common with his nuclear family, especially through the linking character of Merrill Moore, Agrarian sonneteer and both Charlotte Lowell's and her son Robert's psychiatrist—and possibly Mrs. Lowell's lover.[73] The work produced during Lowell's early Tate/Ransom-influenced years, while it constituted a breakaway from his family in that writing poetry was itself a heretical activity for the son of a naval lineage, did not especially embody values in conflict with the conservative and genteel tenets of American aristocracy—especially in a family that ambivalently boasted James Russell Lowell and Amy Lowell as members. Lowell simply exchanged Northern for Southern aristocratic values, and his poetry followed the ethics and aesthetics of the latter.

If *Imitations* represented Lowell's attempt to place himself in a transnational and transhistorical poetic family extending beyond both biological and New Critical families, *Life Studies* and *For the Union Dead* represent a stylistic and thematic breakthrough. By common consensus, *Life Studies* constitutes the turning point in Lowell's career, in which the "cooked" aspect of his style — its highly wrought, "difficult," self-conscious poeticity — and the grandeur and public historical interest of his subject matter, gives way to the influence of the "raw":[74] the spontaneity and unmetrical influence of the Beats; the relaxation, following his mother's death in 1954, of strictures against close scrutiny and public utterance of his own family secrets — most notably his suffering as a child; the aftermath of devastating manic attacks, the most recent of which had led to a three-month internment in McLean's, Boston's famous private and exclusive psychiatric hospital. *Life Studies* is Lowell's descent, after bouts of "enthusiasm" for Catholicism and manic madness, for various "girls" (his manic episodes were usually signaled by obsessive attachments to clearly inappropriate women: young women he barely knew, the lesbian Elizabeth Bishop, Delmore Schwartz's wife, the widowed Jackie Kennedy, et al.), into simple family history, both public and private. Lowell studies his own life through that of his family, which he takes, through its social prominence and decline, as a kind of representative family. But he is not, like Whitman, the Poet as Emerson's Representative Man, though the poetic establishment worked hard to accord him premier status. He does not contain multitudes; unlike Whitman's self-proclaimed heir, his contemporary Beat complement Allen Ginsberg, his reach is not gargantuanly democratic. His focus is him-Self, which atomic unit becomes as mythically large as he felt dominated by it; and his democracy consists not in claiming everyman's voice as his own, but in giving a voice to his own most oppressed self, his stifled and stifling patrician childhood. As representatives, Whitman is diffusion; Lowell, distillation and then violent, rending explosion.

And within *Life Studies*, "91 Revere Street" is the explosive piece of the collection. Dismissed by some of Lowell's former mentors as distasteful and inappropriate for public readership, heralded by other critics as a welcome turn in the poet's development, it is a series of autobiographical vignettes from Lowell's childhood.[75] Here, Lowell introduces themes of his own boyhood that become crucial in subsequent work. Though this was the only prose piece he ever published in a book of verse, the break that it creates in the flow of his opus allows the raw pain of childhood to be reexposed and articulated as a recuperative process (though this latter claim can be challenged by evidence of Lowell's continued mental and emotional difficulties). It is not a question of glorifying a childhood "essence" or of identifying a monolithic, if unstable, subject through psychobiography. The social creates the subject through cruelty and indoctrination. Lowell, whose parents married in order to join together two illustrious Boston names, not two people with affinities and inclinations or disinclinations, indoctrinated him into Winslow- and Lowelldom. This meant that, no less than for the South Boston poets trapped in D Street, Lowell's self-imagining was forcibly bound within Revere Street and Marlborough Street parameters, to exclusive private schools, to certain class conceptions about himself. But something, perhaps the marital disharmony of the the household, gave the lie to these lessons; young Lowell started rebelling early.[76] One of the peculiar characteristics of the oppression of children is the double bind of a parent's insisting on a child's powerlessness ("I own you; I decided where you will go to school, etc."), and simultaneously insisting that the child assume adult emotional responsibilities.[77] In other words, the categories "child" and "adult" are defined and enforced by adults, who blur and alter these already arbitrary distinctions according to their own needs. Bobby Lowell, as a child in a world where being a "mama's boy" paradoxically meant husbanding and fathering his own needy and powerful mother, resisted this oppression though stubborn counterdefinition:

> "A penny for your thoughts, Schopenhauer," my mother would say. "I am thinking about pennies," I'd answer. "When *I* was a child I used to love telling Mamà everything I had done," Mother would say. "But you're not a child," I would answer. ("91 Revere Street," LS 20)

The boy's retort, in fact a non sequitur, attempts to establish difference and boundary in an experience of emotional claustrophobia. He throws his mother's seductive, mercantile, disguised plea for intimacy back in her face, by reading the request at face value. He may in fact have been thinking about pennies, but since this is not the kind of response Mother wants, she takes it, probably correctly, as a denial of access. He claims private space by denying her the right to use her now-defunct childhood as a bargaining chip—he rejects her attempt to tell him how to be a child. "I don't *want* to be the kind of child you were," he indicates to the reader through his brilliantly deft and distancing placement of the accent in her "Mamà," summing up his contempt for her social affectations. Lowell's perception, colored by scathing anger, is that she, in turn, has set herself up as a victim, anticipating rejection in calling her son after a philosopher noted for his misogyny. She has set him up as an adult male, herself the woman excluded from male philosophical discourse, and when the exclusion materializes, she punishes her son for being a child, that is, not the right *kind* of child, who would owe and gladly offer his mother access to his whole inner world.

In a later scene, caught between trying to obey both his naval superior, Admiral de Stahl, and his wife, Lowell's father has had to leave the house on Christmas Eve, as always, to sleep at the navy base. His mother, Lowell intimates, both resented this intrusion of the navy into her private life and relished the occasion it offered her for self-dramatization and for the chance to vent her frustration and contempt for her spineless husband:

> There was a gloating panic in her voice that showed she enjoyed the drama of talking to Admiral de Stahl. "Sir," she shrilled (on the telephone), "you have compelled my husband to leave me alone and defenseless on Christmas Eve!" She ran into my bedroom. She hugged me. She said, "Oh Bobby, it's such a comfort to have a man in the house." "I am not a man," I said. "I am a boy." ("91 Revere Street," LS 24)

There is no need to indulge the interpretive possibilities of Oedipal overkill here, except to point out the child's attempt to defend himself against invasion and inappropriate expectation; *he* is the one left alone and defenseless against the velocity of his mother's entrance into his "space." (Of course, Lowell writes as an adult; who knows whether he was really so eloquently self-protective at the time?) What may appear unfeeling and perverse on his part (doesn't every child dream of replacing one parent as the other's partner?) is an attempt to resist certain cultural expectations. Some of them are: you and I can gang up against father; women are defenseless, men are defenders; grown women need protection and defense more than male children—that is, men are to women as adults are to children—which leaves the male child in a double bind that cancels out any claim to identity, or any claim to protection and defense. The scene exemplifies the pressures on children to fulfill their parents' emotional needs while maintaining a façade of the opposite being done in a kind of doubly deceptive "Benito Cereno" scenario (Lowell adapted Melville's story for the stage). This is a subtle kind of slavery that partakes of the illusion of the Chain of Being—although children, as slaves, in fact support the master, although the "higher" elements of the Chain literally depend upon the "lower," the self-protective polemic of the system portrays women, children, slaves as "dependents" and the privileged man as the "provider." And boys, as Lowell attests, are under tremendous pressure to adapt their experience to this illusion. What could be more flattering and terrifying than this seductive invasion of one's bedroom, this appeal to oneself as savior? Despite the lack of overt violence, growing up like this is like growing up with a knife to one's throat.

Common psychoanalytic wisdom has it that every child *does* dream of replacing one parent as the other's partner. This theory, formulated by adults to interpret other adults' ambivalent feelings about their childhoods and their parents, is accepted by some of these adults as a fair analysis that names their early confusion. While it is important to acknowledge the possibility of gratification at being, momentarily, a preferred object of desire, and though modern psychoanalysis has done a great deal to acknowledge heretofore silenced rivalries and desires within the family and the participation of children in these dramas, one needs to beware of "blaming the victim" in child-adult relations. The seductive elements of incest may win out as adult memories over the sense of being terrorized and physically possessed, surrounded by the parent's body as Bobby Lowell is surrounded by his mother's. Both the terror and the gratification are submerged, forgotten and socially denied. According to Miller and Sherover-Marcuse, the submerged *pain* continues to control the survivor's life in adulthood; according to adherents of classical Freudian theory, the submerged *desire* governs the subsequent course of the subject's life.

Related to this complex of problems and controversies is the problem of language and its relation to infant or child sexuality/physicality. Individuation, or differentiation, has emerged as a central problematic for several contemporary literary and psychoanalytic theorists. Kristeva in particular posits a relationship between imaginative and energetic play with language—poetry—and the pre-Oedipal (and even pre-mirror) stage, in which the child experiences no identity separate from the mother. Traces of this stage break through the linear "logocentric" language use of Western patriarchal adulthood as instances of "poetic language." Kristeva, as Jacqueline Rose points out, acknowledges the horrific aspects of the undifferentiated state.[78] According to her theory of poetic language, the prose of "91 Revere Street" paradoxically represents the "thetic moment" of poetic language, in which the semiotic (presymbolic) breaks through into public discourse, bringing with it the anarchy of expression characteristic of presymbolism. Lowell fully acknowledges the horror of childhood while simultaneously profiting by the freedom its discourse embodies. (Even though the realm of the semiotic is, properly speaking, infancy and not all of childhood, the struggle to differentiate from Charlotte Lowell indicates Lowell as writing out of an experience of prolonged infancy, as it were.) Other French feminists — Luce Irigaray, for example — celebrate the presymbolic unproblematically as the ultimate unbounded harmony, a state ardently to be wished for. However, without Kristeva's caveats, this idyllic dream conceived by adult women overlooks the terrible claustrophobia and neglect infants can experience in undifferentiated relationships; Irigaray engages an almost oppressive lyricism in giving form to her praise of undifferentiation.[79] It is hard to know if children ever experience this blissful fancy, and the later longing for it and deification of what it could have been seems a retrogressive move — a little like, to use the Lowell example, mother enlisting child to gang up on phallogocentric, intrusive and fundamentally unnecessary father. This criticism does not serve Lowell, who is clearly struggling to burst out of his family, concretized in his mother's body. Problems of ego and self are not best resolved through retrogressive mystique. To touch again on nostalgia, you really can't go home again (nor would most of us want to); but you can create a new home in language. In the meantime, Lowell, who feels suffocated by female domination in his early life, continues to be torn between wanting to please (this part of the children's side of the equation is often overlooked by psychoanalysis) and wanting out; and the tortuous style characteristic of all work prior to "91 Revere Street" enacts this dual volition.

Assimilation and defiance — in spite of his attempts to ward off total absorption into his mother, Lowell does join her in his impatience and contempt for his emasculated father, who himself operates as a cut-off appendage to the family drama, a ridiculous and pitiable figure in decline. Given the pressures on the young Lowell, it is easy to predict a transition from childhood indignation to adult misogyny; Lowell, after all, is a grown man, a father himself, when he writes the scene. One of the dangers of unacknowledged and unredressed child oppression is that the adult subject will forever act unconsciously out of that feeling of victimization, even when the power dynamic is in fact very different. "She ran into my bedroom. She hugged me." "She" is the subject of all but the first and last sentences of the passage ("panic" and "I" fulfill that function in the other two sentences, respectively). The air is heavy with passivity and blame, as if the adult Lowell were still skulking resentfully on his bed, protesting his own innocence. The adult Lowell exhibits little overt sympathy for his mother, an intelligent and driven woman who believed too much in her social role to give creative expression to her intelligence, instead living her life begrudgingly and resentfully through the men in the family; but he leaves room for the reader to extrapolate from his text her frustration and sense of powerlessness. The stunning misogyny of the portrait is shot through with evidence for us to read it somewhat differently: as Lowell's own sympathetic identification with his mother's stunted and self-limiting life.

The poles of assimilation and defiance, Heaven and Hell, innocence and experience, that characterize adolescence, and on which we can look back with the pleasure/pain of nostalgia, work themselves permanently and horrifyingly into Lowell's life in the manic-depression of mental illness, and less dramatically into his work as an attempt to negotiate the controlled decorum of the old-world, patriarchal New Critics and his new Confessional mode. *Life Studies* and to a lesser extent *For the Union Dead* mark Lowell's poetic adolescence, in that he emerges semiautonomous and self-conscious from under the influence of both biological family and poetic family: he views his parents and ancestors with detached pathos that cuts them down to size, even as he finally acknowledges their crushing power over his psyche, and he declares independence from the New Critics and Agrarians with his new relaxed style and personal subject matter.

Revealing family secrets allows Lowell to break the formal rigidity that fueled hyperdramatic, manically religious earlier poems whose praise from New Critical quarters had brought him instant fame. "Colloquy in Black Rock," the Jonathan Edwards poems, and "The Quaker Graveyard in Nantucket" especially exemplify Lowell's early cryptic and overwrought style. "91 Revere Street" opens with

Lowell's public announcement of a Jewish ancestor, Major Mordecai Myers, a jibe at the sanitized reference to him as "M. Myers" in a cousin's "Biographical Sketches" (LS 11). Lowell goes beyond simply broadcasting this family secret—he identifies with and romanticizes his forefather, who, after a distinguished career in the military, "sponsored an enlightened law exempting Quakers from military service"; thus, the poet could imagine, this heroic man might have sanctioned Lowell's own defiant conscientious objector position in World War II. Mocking his own romantic illusions in the text, Lowell confesses that he was also yearningly certain that "Major Mordecai had lived in a more ritualistic, gaudy and animal world than twentieth century Boston." This reference to the Major's Jewishness demonstrates the extent to which Lowell starved for the mystique he projects onto Jews, the Mediterranean mystical ambience so lacking in his own family experience; his own earlier movement toward Catholicism had attempted to fill the sterile void of Boston Protestantism. At the same time, he hopes to discover family antecedents, still trying to construct a "legitimate" biological subfamily, an alternative undercurrent that would be the "hidden truth" to the overt coldness of his lived experience. Especially important is Myers's place in his father's family line, as Lowell attempts to counterbalance his mother's power with a dynamic and interesting forefather, and the stultifying Lowell/Winslow scenario with subcultural ethnic warmth. (Lowell did not explore the actual Jewish communities of Boston or New York; rather, he sought to undermine the family structure from within, reenacting his ambivalence about moving out of the family into a world of others.)[80]

Lowell's description of Myers's portrait, and the feelings and fantasies it elicited from him, constitute a modified instance of a technical convention of the modern lyric: that of Eliot's objective correlative, the projection outward of private emotions onto a presumably corresponding object, and the corollary introjection of these external objects. "Modified" here in that Mordecai's quality of Jewishness, rather than a bounded object, serves to externally anchor Lowell's desire for warmth and liveliness. The constant projection of inner experience onto what Marjorie Perloff has termed, in Lowell's words, the "unforgiveable landscape" of modern decay and detritus is mitigated in these confessional poems, especially, again, in "91 Revere

Street"; here, finally, Lowell implicitly acknowledges that his perception of the "earth choking its tears"[81] has its analogue in his own childhood asthma, dismissed by female relatives as "growing pains" (LS 41). This disease is increasingly understood in contemporary medical circles as internal crying. The mitigation is never complete; Lowell's externals are never freed from emotional coloring, and they continue to play an integral part in setting the psychological atmosphere of each poem. But the poet loosens the strict and repressive (imperialistic, even, and born of self-abnegation) insistence on objective correlative, not requiring natural objects, or anything outside the poet's psyche, to bear the entire burden of conveying emotional content. The attempt to "own" Mordecai's imagined "Jewish" qualities by placing these qualities within Lowell's own genealogy brings the correlative closer to its emotional referent. Furthermore, Lowell himself figures prominently in the passage as the child full of fantasies—Lowell *shows* the process of splitting off and projecting particular qualities onto an absent person/object, rather than presenting the correlative as a *fait accompli*. In this sense, the slightly pejorative term "confessional" can be understood as the poet's taking responsibility for his presence in the poem, for his agency in appropriating objects for self-representative purposes.

Again, the hoary Self raises its problematic unwieldy head. Confessional poetry has, like any other poetic genre, its conventions. Especially in the context of modern debates about voice and presence, the confession can be accorded no special status as truth-telling.[82] But with the heavy emphasis in the 1950s on psychotherapy as a way of "getting to" a "true self," rather than constructing one through narrative, the re-membering or invention of the past was seen as a liberating move, one designed to promote rather contradictory ideas: both an autonomous "healthy" ego and a successful social unit—that is, someone who is able to conform to social norms with a minimal degree of discomfort. The psychotherapeutic practices of the 1950s and early 1960s (including, for instance, prescription of addictive pharmaceuticals in combination with a talking cure, or, in a different vein, Merrill Moore's intimate relations with the Lowell family and his plan to collaborate with Mrs. Lowell on a biography of Lowell's early years)[83] seem fraught with fallacies, unprofessional conduct, and double binds impossible for the client to negotiate with any sense of empowerment. Contemporary psychoanalytic revisionists have refined and clarified the process: while one does not engage the process of verbal self-invention/exploration to posit a "true self," the trying out of various possibilities, the telling of family secrets, the acknowledgment of pain and the retrieval of memories does, inevitably, allow one to *see oneself differently*. As for the "trueness" of Miller's "true self," psychoanalytic narratives are powerful as long as their utterance, like Barfield's "poetic diction," effects a "felt change of consciousness" in the reader/listener, who here is also, and crucially, the speaker. Narrative's truth is contingent and provisional—"true" for as long as its undomesticated, defamiliarizing insights enable change. One does not, at best, "confess to" a fixed and monolithic set of experiences of which there is only one real interpretation. But this is not clear to the person confessing until those taboos have been broken and those memories retrieved and articulated. In other words, the "self" does not acquire transparency until one acknowledges and releases one's illusions, attachments and beliefs about that "self." Herein lies the value of Lowell's confessional poetry; this is why *Life Studies* indicates such a shift in his style and content. The style, especially, becomes more fluid and inclusive because he understands himself differently. I want to acknowledge the provisional nature of the subject "Robert Lowell" as the poet understands it in *Life Studies* and passing into *For the Union Dead*, and address the later ramifications of those revelations of oppressed childhood.

In a sweeping and flattering statement, Miller proclaims that "it is not the psychologists but the literary writers who are ahead of their time."[84] Lowell's writings accurately reflect the psychotherapeutic practices of his time, which tended toward the pharmaceutical and the Freudian, although he claimed to mistrust the "talking cure," submitting to it only because he had to, regarding visits to his therapist as "necessary chores."[85] Read against the grain of his intentions, however, his self-disclosures anticipate by several decades the findings of primarily feminist philosophers and therapists, who see the subtle cruelty of childrearing in the modern family as inevitably perpetrating both socially and personally destructive and self-destructive behavior—resulting in the obvious and endless family merry-go-round of physical and emotional violence and neglect.

Radical Nostalgia?

What then of the possible fertile alliance Sherover-Marcuse speaks of between the socially privileged and the world of others? What of the confirmation and corroboration of collective experience—the empathy—that indicates "authentic" (in Sartrean terms) experience? Did Lowell find or does his poetry enact, through acknowledging the pain of childhood, an empathetic participation in emancipatory activities? Lowell's politics and those of his poetry have been much discussed. An explicitly political poet, a self-appointed "witness to his age," he took well-publicized stands on a number of political issues throughout his life; in his "day" he was the leading national poet of the United States. Having served time in prison as a conscientious objector during World War II (his grounds for objection being the Allied bombing of Germany, and of Dresden in particular), he later opposed the Vietnam War in the March on the Pentagon, declined President Johnson's invitation to read at the White House, campaigned for Senator Eugene McCarthy on the latter's antiwar platform, and supported the student movement of the sixties. In each of these instances, he used his standing as an American aristocrat and premier national poet to draw attention to the position he took.

However, his poems show no sympathy for a structural critique of social injustice; as with his preoccupation with writers rather than writing, his interest in history lay in personalities—military or political leaders' integrity or lack thereof (and his "efforts to psychologize" the latter),[86] and the poignancy of the down-and-out in prisons and mental institutions. As Alan Williamson argues in *Pity the Monsters: The Political Vision of Robert Lowell*, Lowell's personal and "public" political poetry became increasingly interdependent.[87] Some of his best poems play with an identification with or alienation from his socially outcast "monsters": "Memories of West Street and Lepke," "Waking in the Blue," and the prose piece "Near the Unbalanced Aquarium" show the poet as one among the world's outcasts, one among the criminal and the insane. (During manic episodes, even such "monsters" as Hitler and Stalin took on a sympathetic glamor for Lowell.) But there is a bemusement in these pieces, as if Lowell were wondering, "What am I, a Boston Lowell, doing here? I feel kinship with these people because we are all alien from the respectable world; I feel alien from them because of my investment in the respectable world":

> I was a fire-breathing Catholic C.O.,
> and made my manic statement
> ... and then
> sat waiting sentence in the bull pen
> beside a Negro boy with curlicues
> of marijuana in his hair.
>
> ...
>
> Flabby, bald, lobotomized,
> [Lepke, the underworld czar] drifted in a sheepish calm,
> where no agonizing reappraisal
> jarred his concentration on the electric chair—
> hanging like an oasis in his air
> of lost connections. ...
>
> ("Memories of West Street and Lepke," LS 85)

Lowell's bemused irony and the gentle, self-conscious sense of noblesse oblige behind these desperate empathies differs from the self-consciousness of the South Boston girls and other writers from across the tracks—Walt Whitman, for example, or Etheridge Knight (compare "West Street," for instance, with Knight's "Hard Rock Returns to Prison from the Hospital for the Criminally Insane"). Divided against itself, Lowell's sense of inside/outside, participant/alien symmetrically complements these other writers' feelings of community/exclusion—but it has a different internal logic; their concerns were not his. One senses that in order to preserve the integrity of his psychic struggle, Lowell has to preserve "Otherness," like a sensitive and vulnerable version of the hypothetical newscasters covering the lives of Southie's poor. The creative and emotional catharsis Lowell gets from his acts of empathy *depend* upon structural inequity.

Lowell conducted his act of "consciousness-raising"—writing—in a community of writers presumably more interested in the craft and integrity of their art than the benefits of psychotherapy or social change. The prose piece "Near the Unbalanced Aquarium" offers a poignant, almost scathing instance of ineffectual "art therapy," in which Lowell competes with a fellow inmate of the Payne-Whitney Clinic in making imitations of Klee and Pollock—the use of ekphrasis barely wards off painful questions about the psychic utility of his preferred craft.[88] Lowell's writing did not take place in conditions designed to help loosen the tight grasp he tried to maintain on selfhood, on authorship and authority. His compulsive "desire to confess"[89] was not necessarily matched with a desire to let go of the secrets he was confessing—at least not to the extent of relinquishing to a collectivity the control and identity that self and secrets appear to offer. While Lowell could take pacificist, antiviolent positions in the public arena; and while his obsessive stranglehold on form, language, and personal information relaxed with the relatively colloquial syntax and open forms of *Life Studies* initiated by "Revere Street," he continued to suffer psychic and emotional inner violence which never entirely abated, and he continued to inflict psychic and physical violence on those close to him.

Without wishing to detract from Lowell's achievement, Robert von Hallberg has called him a quintessential liberal, unusual for postwar America in his insistence on the personal and his distaste for systematic social change; for von Hallberg, the weight of Lowell's political/historical opus demonstrates that "American liberalism has had . . . major imaginative embodiment in the last thirty-five years."[90] Given its consistency with notions of individuality and personal experience, Lowell's preferred but embattled genre, the lyric, could be called the exemplary liberal literary form. But further, the term "liberal," with its roots in *liber*, freedom, and its emphasis on tolerance rather than change, points toward Lowell's own need, once again projected onto the landscape of history and the political arena, to be free and tolerated rather than changed—his task, perhaps, was not to change himself or to effect change in others but simply to learn to find the world and himself tolerable. If a radical nostalgia impelled him outward, he was also, perforce, tremendously preoccupied with simply maintaining a clear sense of who "he" was—which maintenance, according to the desperate faith in self he had learned from the world of privilege and from self-defense against the chaos of mental illness, meant pushing others away, making sure he, and they, recognized their otherness. Lowell ripped away the sham nostalgia of the golden childhood, thus permitting himself the possibility of identification with others. But it remained an empathy based on shared pain and deprivation, an empathy tinged with a constant sense of superiority-run-aground, rather than an active building toward a new way of conceiving relations from which a new meaning of "Robert Lowell" could emerge.

4

Dirty Jokes and Angels
Jack Spicer and Robert Duncan
Writing the Gay Community

The clown of dignity sits in a tree.
The clown of games hangs there too.
Which is which and where they go —
The point is to make others see
That two men in a tree is clearly
The same thing as poetry.
                    Robin Blaser

Angel: Any homosexual male. Angel, to some, mends the crumpled
wings and pride of the denigrated fairy.
                    Bruce Rodgers

Introduction: Two Kings Between the Leaves

In 1855, Walt Whitman, an unknown journalist of working-class origin, answered Emerson's call for a national poet,[1] sending the latter a
copy of his self-published *Leaves of Grass*, the opening essay of which
quite clearly proposed Whitman himself as the poet laureate of the
United States, as both its spiritual avatar and its democratic representative.[2] Although controversy raged around *Leaves of Grass* throughout its many incarnations, much of this controversy stemming from
the homoerotic nature of the poetry and its sexual and emotional intensity, Whitman has to a large extent achieved his goal in being considered America's representative national poet. A century later, in
1955, Allen Ginsberg, the son of middle-class, leftist Jewish immigrants, wrote "Howl," and the following year skyrocketed to national
fame with the obscenity trials surrounding the poem, an explicitly

gay work whose long-line free-verse style and sweeping, oracular tone obviously owed much to Whitman.[3] Ginsberg's bearded public face underscored the self-consciousness with which he modeled himself on this "dear father, graybeard, lonely old courage-teacher."[4] In the decades that have followed, Ginsberg has been a spokesperson for nearly every major progressive movement in this country, persistently and flamboyantly civic-minded to the point that publicity for his readings routinely term him "the most well-known poet in America today."[5]

For Ginsberg as for other postwar gay poets who turned increasingly to Whitman as a pioneering forefather, same-sex eroticism, a severely marginalized set of desires and experiences, interacts dynamically and problematically with the civic imperative toward community; the necessarily centrifugal position of a stigmatized sexual orientation and the nationalistic, centripetal urge to establish and carry public weight cohabit these poets' consciousness. This is particularly observable in members of the San Francisco and Berkeley Renaissances, the poetic movements founded in the gay and Bohemian culture of those cities, nurturing and nurtured by its founders, among them Jack Spicer, Robert Duncan, and Ginsberg. The issues embedded in Whitman's conceptions of nationalism resurface in Jack Spicer's and Robert Duncan's relationships to various overlapping communities. What is their relationship, as poets, to the gay community as it appeared in the decades following World War II, during which time San Francisco became the "gay mecca"? What, in turn, was the relationship of this emergent but ostracized community, which they understood partly as a spiritual and cultural elite, to the mainstream that did not understand it? What is the role of eroticism in creating communities? Duncan and Spicer write as representatives for their community; simultaneously they are liminal figures bordering multiple worlds. Their poetic language comes to constitute the true domain of their sexual and political communities.

Whitman's certainty that he was America's national poet, and that America was the ultimate poem, crystallizes the explicit connection he made between nationalism and "adhesive" expression, and the close tie between his poetics of the body (indicated in his case by long lines of verse that emulate the natural rhythm of a man's breath) and same-sex desire—that is, between language and eroticism. These connections have come to form a kind of paradigmatic nexus of concerns for gay male American poets.[6] Jack Spicer, who never lived to see the flowering of gay liberation (he died of alcoholism in 1965), associated gay life in the 1950s and 1960s with acute alienation. His poetics espoused a theory of "outside," a denial of the personal far more extreme than Eliot's canonized objective correlative. Spicer went beyond advocating the displacement of emotion onto objects: he denied any relevance of the poet's emotions at all, insisting instead that the poet negate himself in the interest of automatic writing—in Spicer's case, dictation from "Mars."[7] Ironically, Spicer, critically and ambivalently concerned with the meaning of gay community, died a year before the first gay community center in the country was established, in his native San Francisco. Robert Duncan, until his death in early 1988, was a forerunner in the gay freedom movement who followed a steady trajectory of increased commitment to and acceptance of his marginal—hence powerful—identity.

I am not aiming for a neat dichotomy that treats Spicer's attitude as "bad," Duncan's as "good." As in Kaufman's case, the anguish of Spicer's marginality offers a demystifying tonic for outsider "wannabes" on a picaresque slumming jaunt. As he succumbed to the ravages of alcoholism, to the erotic pain and to the outsider's social death which were so integral to his aesthetic, Spicer's increasingly embittered and sparse lines reflect his ambivalence about membership in a cultural and social ghetto on the verge of breaking into political visibility. He lashes out—often very wittily—at other marginalized groups, at other gay poets, at the whole homosocial (but decidedly not out-gay) canon of modernist poets and poetry in which he is and is not a participant. Savaging, parodying, and paying homage to other poets in his Euro-American male tradition, Spicer's work is a campy compendium of obsessive barbs alluding to poetic greats, near-greats and self-designated greats-to-be (including his friend Robert Duncan). Thus, deploying camp as a "minority discourse" characterized by deterritorialized language, collectivity and inevitably political content, Spicer points toward his own affiliation with a tradition he simultaneously acknowledges as oppressive.

In equally edifying counterpoint, Duncan's ability to thrive in contradictory circumstances without self-pity or compromise offers a postmodern paradigm untainted with the elegiac cynicism of a failed modernism. Drawing heavily on the Romantics and the high modernists for his initial influences, Duncan eventually abandons the lyric's insistence on closure, in favor of open, aleatory forms; this turn resulted in some series that continued unfinished until his death: the "H.D. Book," whose chapters appeared in various magazines and which has never been published whole, and the "Structure of Rime" and "Passages" series. Implicit in Duncan's formal and thematic openness is a refusal of nostalgia, a gracious acceptance of the limits of the tradition by which Spicer, by contrast, felt so betrayed—and a polite refusal to be constrained by these limits. Both poets are affirmative and troubled, accepting and questioning, celebratory and impatient. Nevertheless, their works' differing treatment of similar themes mirrors some of the possibilities of gay consciousness from the 1940s through the 1960s, in a way that dramatizes both the tragic and exhilarating possibilities of life in a burgeoning culture that had tremendous vitality but as yet no political power or social visibility, and that shows the painful contradictions of occupying such an emergent position. The following two-part essay investigates these tensions and conjunctions, taking as its point of departure the problematic legacy of Platonism explored in the opening chapter.

Gay Platonism?

Robert K. Martin's *The Homosexual Tradition in American Poetry* identifies two strains of Platonism in gay male writing in America. The first strain focuses on Whitman's reading of Plato, which finds expression in "Scented Herbiage of My Breast" and "That Shadow My Likeness" among others, and which tends to center around an opposition between the real and the apparent.[8] Martin extrapolates from this example to show that gay writers speaking of and from their underground culture have developed codes through which to express the forbidden; in the course of this development, a gap has evolved between the immanence of false appearance, of feigned heterosexuality, and a "reality" of homoerotic desire. The gay "truth" is mediated by euphemism, oblique and ambiguous wording, or even downright alteration of meaning, such as the publication of female pronouns in place of the male ones written and deleted from original manuscripts. Thus readers must learn to read the text as if it concealed a truth more significant than that displayed on the text's surface. We learn to discern the "life of the spirit" which is "seen as greater than the life of the material body," which Whitman, quoted by

Martin, also calls the "mask of materials" and the "show of appearance, transcended only in death."[9] Martin convincingly cites the deliberately obfuscatory and self-protective changes Walt Whitman made in later editions of *Leaves of Grass*: changes in pronoun, use of code numbers in his journals to conceal his male lover's name, and other strategies of concealment.[10]

While the evidence is sound, and while it would be dishonest to remain silent about the pain of concealment that has marked many homoerotically inspired texts, overemphasis on the Platonic argument weighs gay literary criticism toward a victim-interpretation that threatens to replay naïvely the dichotomy of victim and oppressor, using a system of reading that privileges "interpretation." Gayness, according to such a Platonic schema, becomes the privileged, hidden truth/depth, feigned heterosexuality the debased appearance/surface. The victim, identified with the hidden/privileged, becomes the god who awaits interpretive understanding by a few or the maiden rescuable only by the brave hermeneut. The strategy of decoding focuses on the experience of the closet, on oppression as the primary informing aspect of gay life and culture. The battleground is staged for a war of liberation whose governing ethos is Nietzschean *ressentiment*, to be waged with the weapons of conventional exegesis.

The second strain of Platonism Martin discusses in his readings of Whitman and Crane, to which I would like to give a slightly different valence, is the notion that since love between two men cannot have a utilitarian (reproductive) outcome, this love facilitates, more than heterosexual union, the apprehension of "pure Beauty" untrammeled by material concerns. The ultimate union with this ideal happens through death. This idea echoes uneasily some of the unsavory aspects of straight canonical literature and criticism—in particular, that the most meaningful event in a person's (read Northern European man's) history is his confrontation with solitary death, sometimes aided by reflections on such tragic losses as the maturing of a woman or the passing of an imperial supremacy. More important, though, for this study, the idea of death as a "union with the absolute" can have a confining linear sense echoing the division of appearance and reality, complete with its value judgments: life is the pale artificial appearance, death the real thing, with no simultaneity or overlap between the two, only conflict.

On the contrary, much gay writing derives its power and delight from a fine sense of interplay *between* surface and depth, "appearance" and "reality," and even different states of consciousness and material being: life, death, and everything in between. For instance, Robert Duncan insists that etymologies do not supply a linear, two-dimensional history of the meanings of words but rather a multidimensional texture in which all meanings of all epochs live and interact any time a word is invoked. This interpretation rejects the idea of one meaning hidden behind another in hierarchic relationship, in favor of a concept of a rich and dynamic dappled reality. Like sunlight and shadow shifting through thick foliage, meanings constantly come forward and recede, elude us and become apprehensible.[11]

This concept resonates with contemporary theories of reading and interpretation: readers do not tease out the true meanings of a text hidden behind clues and cues and decoys. Instead, all the evidence is equally available and present, all the meaning on the surface; the active reader must attend to multiple possibilities of meaning. Admittedly, gay writing, like much other subcultural writing, employs a vernacular perhaps unfamiliar to nonmembers, which can limit these nonmembers' interpretative range. I sat through a class on Thom Gunn's "My Sad Captains" in which much metaphysical speculation obscured and silenced the poem's obvious sexual references; only when someone pointed out that the word "captain" has a very specific meaning in the gay male world (i.e., the dominant member of an s/m couple) did the members of the discussion acknowledge, despite their discomfort, the connection between a real physicality and community and the astral metaphysics they had initially chosen to foreground.[12] Gunn was not being coy or recondite; nothing was hidden—it was simply a matter of knowing one's vocabulary and not denying that interpretive possibility. But this is also simply part of learning to be a good reader and expanding the world of knowledge one brings to a text or to any experience; things don't seem hidden when you're trained to look for them. The reader's task is to *attend to all coexistent possibilities*, and to expand her or his consciousness to accomodate the widest range of coexistent possibilities.

Furthermore, at least in Duncan's and James Merrill's work, the spirit world, which includes but is not exclusively confined to the dead, and the material world coexist. Neither world is superior to the other—the denial of either, rather than the inability of the living to transcend the material realm, leads to a sense of pain and incompletion. The poet's job and privilege is to cross over, to be the shamanic point of contact whose "difference" allows access to those other realms. Myths of descent to the underworld, aleatory techniques and techniques of dictation, and occult games in which the poets contact spirits become prime subject matter and compositional methods for gay poets. Consciousness of death does not revolve around, or is not restricted to, loss, completion, finality, or even the transcendence of the immanent—it means the awareness of a multiplicity of worlds that approach and recede in a dance of constant change and transformation. James Merrill entitled his Ouija-inspired travelogue into different spheres *The Changing Light at Sandover*, not *Sunrise* or *Sunset at Sandover*, once again calling forth Duncan's organic image of dappled, polymorphous reality apprehended as light. Moreover, the syllables "over" in the titular place-name invoke the poem as a bridge between realms, a crossing over.[13]

Hart Crane's "The Bridge" (Crane, with Whitman, is the spiritual ancestor of gay American poets) likewise captures in its title the idea of crossing over, of the poet as bridge as well as celebrant of a nationalistic rite of passage in the bridge's conception and construction. Crane's national project in this poem is as explicit as Whitman's: the bridge is not only the Brooklyn Bridge and the poem not only a hymn to America in technological transition (another kind of passage from one world or era into another), but a railroad journey across the body of the nation itself. Just as Whitman's manly love would give physical expression to democracy, Crane embodies the country even as he holds it to be an Idea. (The crossing of vertical and lateral trajectories makes the poem dizzyingly complex and disorienting in its scope.)[14]

Whitman and Gay Democracy

Both Whitman and Duncan have used the image of a woven fabric whose pattern alternately highlights weft and warp: Duncan, in "At the Loom: Passages 2" and "Warp and Woof,"[15] to describe the creative process in the poet's use of language, Whitman in *Democratic Vistas*, to describe the relationship between "manly adhesiveness," by which he means homoerotic desire, and an ideal American democracy necessarily based on this desire.[16] Modern self-identified gay writers commonly take this as Whitman's gay manifesto:

> I confidently expect a time when there will be seen, running like a *half-hid warp* through all the myriad audible and visible worldly interests of America, threads of manly friendship, fond and loving, pure and sweet, strong and life-long, carried to degrees hitherto unknown … having the deepest relation to general politics. I say democracy infers such loving comradeship, as its most inevitable twin or counter part. (my emphasis)[17]

The image of half-hiddenness ("half-hid warp" is a redundancy), of the appearance and reappearance of a constant and sustaining factor in the social fabric of American democracy, plays upon and reverses the image of a love that must be conducted in the shadows; the supposedly "warped" love supplies the thread of continuity that runs straight through the text/ile of American history. It would not make sense to try to strip away the weft as if it obscured the "real truth" of the foundational warp; there would be no cloth left. Meaning is produced by the dissolution of differential value and distance between weft/surface/ appearance and warp/depth/meaning, not by "getting beyond" the one to grasp the other.[18] A fully embodied democracy would consist not only in the larger society's acceptance of this love, nor in the random scattering of sperm among whomever come who may (as is suggested in some of Whitman's poems)[19] but, in the context of the reading process, in the reader's role in the production of the text's meaning. In attending to and creating multiple possibilities of meaning out of the meeting of her or his own life experience with the text (the laying of weft through warp), the reader is weaver as much as the poet is.

Denied its specifically reproductive function, the role of sperm expands crucially in this context. A democratic and random scattering implies *dis*semination over *in*semination, broadening out an influence rather than delimiting it. Rather than a predictable, narrowing transformation from two to one (two lovers producing one child), which projects one life into the future in linear trajectory, the results of homosexual union, uncementable in offspring, are indeterminate and potentially limitless. These results often consist in shared knowledge, which is then further shared in widening concentric circles—at "seminaries," for example, single-sex institutions in which young men were trained and then scattered to carry the word, carrying with them an affectionate loyalty that impelled them outward rather than binding them in permanent stasis. Allen Ginsberg also speaks of the spiritual "Whispered Transmission" as part of the invisible poetic bond forged by gay intercourse.

> Neal Cassady slept with [Gavin Arthur] occasionally ... and Gavin Arthur had slept with Edward Carpenter, and Edward Carpenter had slept with Walt Whitman. So this is in a sense in the line of transmission ... that's an interesting thing to have as part of the mythology. Kerouac's heterosexual hero [Neal Cassady] who also slept with somebody who slept with somebody who slept with Whitman, and received the Whispered Transmission, capital W, capital T, of that love ... and I slept with (Cassady), so ... [20]

These men share a poetic, spiritual history, sperm as the essence of poetry. And since each of these men (including Cassady, the heterosexual hero) has probably slept with other men, each man is a point with contacts raying out all around him, intersecting with other men in invisible, concentric genealogies of morale–the connections are three-dimensionally lateral as well as two-dimensionally temporal (linear).[21] The problem with these physically ephemeral contacts is, of course, that their extent and effect often remains unknown. This type of erotic/poetic bonding takes a degree of faith difficult to sustain: How can one trust that one is "reaching" or "touching" anybody? And, in historical retrospect, how can a reader "know" if the touch is intended as erotic: Is (s)he or isn't (s)he "one of us" and what difference does it make; what is at stake in the question? A book is published to be read by anonymous readers, to have unpredictable effects on them; a series of affective encounters spreads in unbounded and often invisible expansion, diffused into nature ("look for me under your bootsoles") or into intangible spiritual realms (again, Merrill's *Sandover* suggests itself). In the paradigm of same-sex reproductive connections, people cannot be replicated, only touched or taught, in transitory encounters whose repercussions are paradoxically timeless.[22] From this point of view, homosexual versus heterosexual union can easily be cast into Victor Turner's two contrasting models for social organization, freewheeling "communitas," with its emphasis on intuitive, invisible cohesiveness ("It ... has an aspect of potentiality") and permeable boundaries vs. "structure" with its legalism and orderly visibility.[23] In Turner's somewhat romantic scheme, "communitas," not surprisingly, tends to occur in liminal situations—he even mentions the Beats and the hippies in his exposition, specifically naming Allen Ginsberg's "[eloquence] about the function of sexual freedom."[24] Ginsberg's remarks about the "Whispered Transmission" are doubtless based on a combination of known events and conjecture. However, this does not impair their import. The suggestion of past and future sexual possibilities enhances the mysticism and ultimate unknowability of same-sex bonding. Also, in terming the transmission "Whispered," a linguistic and oral form of intercourse, Ginsberg hints at an encompassing view of sexual activity: "sleeping with" does not necessarily mean engaging in sexual intercourse, though it means that too. Adrienne Rich's term "the lesbian continuum" captures this widening and complication of definition, as does Sedgwick's discussion of a "homosocial"/ homosexual continuum.[25]

Writing over a century ago, Whitman insists on difference and double consciousness. And this insistence takes the tone, not of the victim who must struggle to "act right" in each of his strictly separated worlds and who suffers under the superimposition of "appearance" over "reality," but of the celebrant of conjunctions within or across differences, of the interestingness of variegated textures promised by exploration of relationships "carried to degrees hitherto unknown."[26] A later incarnation of this celebratory double consciousness, Frank O'Hara's "Autobiographia Literaria," tranforms lonely marginality into centrality, shifting Lowellian despair into affirmation.

> When I was a child
> I played by myself in a
> corner of the schoolyard
> all alone.
>
> . . .
>
> If anyone was looking
> for me I hid behind a
> tree and cried out "I am
> an orphan."
>
> And here I am, the

center of all beauty!
writing these poems!
Imagine![27]

Whitman is above all a joyous witness to multiplicity and variation of all kinds, within the single fabric of the United States. His nationalism—his advocacy of "democracy"—lies precisely in his belief in coexisting differences within the United States. This concept of democracy, furthermore, necessarily includes all the various possibilities between two people—"democracy infers such loving comradeship, as its most inevitable twin or counterpart"—and goes further still, to the countless possibilities within each person: "I contain multitudes." Like the physical or social world, or like the world of a text with all of its material elements (phonemic and morphemic, etc.) and all its interpretive possibilities, each person has countless potentials; and the fulfillment of those *potentials* constitutes the person's *potency*, his "manliness." The idea of "inner democracy" acknowledges the possibility that the different roles assumed by marginal people—here, specifically, gay men—are not necessarily oppressive burdens but possibilities for freedom, and that the movement between roles or selves is not only a strategy for survival but an occasion for play and celebration. The margin becomes a frontier, sometimes explicitly associated with the American West.[28] When the legitimacy of the "twins"—manly love and democracy—is acknowledged, when gay men can finally come out, all people will be able, through erotically suffused friendship, to bring each other's potentials out into the open.

Conversely, these kinds of actualizing erotic relationships have to form a base on which such legitimacy can be built. The text itself—for example, the myriad puns in *Leaves of Grass* on the self and the body as the book held by the lover—becomes an erotic point of contact that furthers the project of adhesively realized democracy. The organic metaphors holding *Leaves of Grass* together, moreover, enrich the texture of book/body in process; manhood, like "nature," is a work in progress, constantly subject to re-vision. In an essay on "Leaves of Grass," Duncan follows Whitman's lead by using the word "interleafing" to refer self-reflexively to his thought process in writing the talk (FC, "Changing Perspectives in Reading Whitman," 165). A neologism based on the noun "interleaf" (a page, usually blank, bound between the other leaves of a book), the word stresses the potential for inscription, or the always ongoing process dependent on the blank space that guarantees a lack of completion. It captures, as well, the sense of organic collage that is Duncan's blueprint for processes of reality and of consciousness. Like the work the essay takes as its subject, it joins the image of a book with images of foliage and herbage.

The King's Two Bodies

Finally, before turning to a closer examination of Spicer's and Duncan's poetry, one more strand of the background warp needs to be brought forward and elucidated. These two "poet-kings" (to use their term that both acknowledges and completely rewrites Plato) studied medieval and renaissance history and literature at Berkeley under the late Ernst Kantorowicz, who had been a member of the "George-kreis," the small and elite circle that formed around the gay German poet Stefan George. Duncan, Spicer, and Robin Blaser formed their own "kreis" modeled on George's, and adopted his theory that the poet was a "priest-king whose duty was to guard and pass on the essence of the cultural heritage," not seeking a large public but "[addressing] himself to . . . disciples" and "[endowing] words with mystical properties."[29] Admittedly, the concept of a gay aestheticist elite seems worlds apart from Whitman's notions of a gay-inspired democratic nationalism, but the transition is somewhat problematically negotiated by Kantorowicz's analysis of the medieval concept of the king's two bodies, which warrants some explication here.[30]

This political and theological doctrine held the biological body of the ruler in complex and at times mystical relationship to his body politic, which was also his spiritual body. As it operated in medieval legal and political life, it was a versatile concept that could be multiply interpreted. The two bodies could be conceived of as separable (as in the case in which peasants had to pay a fee upon the natural death of the king even though his kingship was considered immortal; or in the case of the English Revolution, in which Parliament could invoke the spiritual king's leadership in taking up arms against Charles, the King's natural incarnation). On the other hand, the two kings could be conflated so that they were inseparable: the perfection of the spiritual king redeemed any possible failing of the natural king (thus the infallibility and hence political omnipotence even of child-kings, for example):

> He has not a Body natural distinct and divided by itself from the Office and Dignity royal, but a Body natural and a Body politic together indivisible; and these two bodies are incorporated in one Person, and make one Body and not divers, that is the Body corporate in the Body natural, *et e contra* the Body natural in the Body corporate.[31]

One of Kantorowicz's projects was to demystify any spiritual rationale for totalitarian national politics, and for the conflation of spiritual authority with the person of the leader, of which he, as a European Jew in exile, had had devastating personal experience in the 1930s and 1940s under the Third Reich. And yet the concept itself is powerfully seductive in some of its ramifications. Wildly divergent possibilities of interpretation indicate that it can be used either to undergird or to undermine the Platonic notion of the two realms of being. The second possibility, that of a head of state comprised of two inseparable physical and spiritual kinglinesses, has special significance here. This model, the image of two-worlds-in-one, and the acknowledgment of the physical not as a subordinate and separate reflection of a spiritual reality but as equal and inseparable from it, particularly appealed to the writers under discussion here.

It is not certain whether the members of the Berkeley circle were enthusiastic students of Kantorowicz primarily because he had belonged to the spiritual elite of the George-kreis, whether they were genuinely taken with the more mystical and integrative aspects of the king's two bodies, and whether they were wary, to the extent that Kantorowicz was, of the fascist dangers of this powerful concept. However, in a twentieth-century gay American literary circle, this model cannot help but resonate with Whitman's claim to national poethood and to his declaration of the primacy of homoerotic love in American political life. Whitman, the gay poet-king of democratic America, contains multitudes, his body electric constitutes the body politic of America through the physical and spiritual contact made in adhesive, manly, democratic (in the sense of random as well as comradely and egalitarian) love. However, it is important to note that Whitman is neither Hitler, though his youthful jingoism has not gone unnoticed by critics from the social margins, nor is he Plato, though we have seen Platonic vestiges in his and his heirs' words. Whitman's egalitarian conception of the body politic comprised of men linked in manly physical love is different from the fascist idea that the nation is reified in the body of its leader or in the bodies of its citizens. Whitman's nationalism was based on plurality; Hitler's on uniformity; Plato's, in *The Republic* at least, on exclusion.[32] And Crane's concept of bridging underscores the poet's role in embodying these connections. The gay poet himself is the meeting place of language and eroticism (since he utters words through his body), of otherworldly and this-worldly, of spirit and physical/material. One could say that, in this mediating position, the gay poet plays the liminal subject par excellence.

In spite of the dramatic shifts in the historical and social constitution of gay male identity since Whitman's time, and particularly since World War II, many of these themes continue to play themselves out in modern gay poetry. The work of Jack Spicer and Robert Duncan, friends and participants in the postwar gay/bohemian/Beat scene in San Francisco, reflect the gay poetic themes touched upon earlier: a multiplicity of worlds, the play of aleatory method and simultaneity of different realms (visible/invisible, worldly/otherworldly, etc.), a preoccupation with the body as spirit and with spirit as physical, an emphasis on process. The poems I will be examining were written before the Stonewall riot (which is commonly taken as the turning point in the politicization of gay culture), and capture the double valence of pre-Stonewall gay consciousness: alienation and unhappy expression of outsiderhood on the one hand, and on the other, tendencies toward affirmation, positive eroticism and the meaningful constitution of community. The poets thus bridge not only material and spiritual worlds, but two historical eras marked by different political climates and different attitudes toward homosexuality itself.

Spicer Agonistes: Ghosts, Angels, Fairies

So when I dreamed of Calamus, as I often did when I touched you or put my hand upon your hand, it was not as of a possible world, but as a lost paradise. A land my father Adam drove me out with the whip of shadow. In the last sense of the word—a fairy story. That is what I think about Calamus. That is what I think about your damned Calamus.

Jack Spicer

155

I prefer to attribute [poets' bitchiness] to love, that state that poets— ever so especially Jack Spicer—are wrapt up in their poems, so much so, that the (real?) manifestation of love is often, if not always, exceedingly strange to the uninvolved in its ultimate expression.
Richard Tagett

The postwar period through the 1960s marked a particular point in gay American history. Falling between World War II, in which there was an unprecedented attempt to exclude gay men systematically from induction into military service via a "psychiatric interview," and the Stonewall Inn riots of 1969, which marked the birth of militant gay liberation activism, these years witnessed the paradoxically related phenomena of increased systematic public persecution and the recognizable establishment of a self-identified gay community.[33] (In fact, despite public rhetoric that homosexuality was grounds for exemption from military service, the army became one crucial place of consolidation for a self-recognized gay community. In spite of the introduction of the psychiatric interview, it wasn't until after the war's demands for manpower died down that the military purges actually took place.) These two decades, furthermore, witnessed a swing in political atmosphere from the extreme conformity and conservatism of the 1950s to the relatively progressive 1960s, in which leftism was allowed into public discourse and a variety of choices of domestic style became publicly acceptable. The gay poet who lived through this transition found himself bridging historical epochs in which his own identity as a gay man took on different significance. Allen Ginsberg's explanation of the explicit sexuality in his poetry encapsulates this peculiar interdependency of freedom and censorship: his father also being a poet, Allen's conviction that he'd never be able to publish gave him the freedom to write whatever he wanted.[34] And in fact, his reading of "Howl" at San Francisco's Six Gallery in 1955 coupled with its publication the following year catapulted him and the entire Beat scene into national attention.

San Francisco, both a military and a bohemian center, and postwar grouping place for ex-soldiers, became one of the centers of the burgeoning gay cultural community. Simultaneously, it was becoming a focal point for poetic activity. Boisterous, celebratory poetry readings, meetings of poets' circles in bars and cafés as well as in private houses, the establishment of poetic networks, circles, and small presses, flowered in the San Francisco Renaissance. All of these aspects of San Francisco life have continued to evolve to the present date: the gay movement has grown to the degree that San Francisco is internationally known for it, and the poetry scene has continued to thrive and to mythologize itself, in spite of increasing hardship and the passing of national publicity. And both scenes continue to overlap in the figures of Judy Grahn, Thom Gunn, Paul Mariah, and others. (Ginsberg, the most famous of these poets, is now primarily associated with New York.) Although the relative confinement of public gay culture to the bar scene broke open after the Stonewall Inn riots, the social life of the period under discussion revolved predominantly around gay bars, which were vulnerable to police attacks at any moment, and in which physical contact between gay people was punishable by arrest. Many of these bars were subject to "gayola" pay-offs to local vice squads.

Jack Spicer's mature poetic life took place primarily in the bars of North Beach, in addition to his rented room in which the typewriter served as an ashtray and the only utensil was a glass permanently ambered by liquor.[35] While Bob Kaufman held court first at the Coexistence Bagel Shop and then at the Coffee Gallery, Spicer's bars were The Place and Gino & Carlo's. Certain figures, Spicer among them, were crossovers between the Beat bohemian scene and the gay scene:

> When he held forth at The Place, a popular North Beach rendezvous for writers, "the cast at the Spicer table ... really was something to rival 'Grand Hotel.'" Duncan, Spicer and Blaser formed a tight circle of mutual support and met almost daily for years. According to one younger poet under their tutelage, they "not only kept alive a public homosexual presence in their own work, but kept alive a tradition, teaching us about Rimbaud, Crane and Lorca. ... They carried into the contemporary culture the tradition of homosexual art and were sensitive to the work of European homosexual contemporaries. There was a conscious searching out, in fraternity, of homosexual writers. Thus, in my 'training' as a poet, homoerotic novels would be recommended to me. ... This was at a time when the English departments of the country told us that Walt Whitman *wasn't* gay." Because of their local stature, the three men helped to create "a social milieu in which it was possible to be gay."[36]

An ABD in linguistics from Berkeley (having resigned, like Kantorowicz, over the loyalty oath controversy), and co-initiator, with Duncan and

Blaser, of the "Berkeley Renaissance," Spicer identified as a gay poet so deeply that he would give his birthdate and place as "1946, Berkeley"—the year and place of his first encounter with these other poets and their establishment of a community.

His awareness of the gay community as a "minority group" with its own culture and history surfaces again and again in his work, tinged with both the bitterness and the pride that mark the emergence of a consciousness of one's social marginality. *After Lorca* and *Admonitions* are entirely comprised of poems and short prose pieces dedicated to (mostly male) friends, lovers, and members of the "circle"; in *Admonitions*, as the title suggests, the title of each poem is a direct address: "For Ebbe," "For Joe," "For Robert," "For Jack" (himself), and letters to Joe Dunn and Robin Blaser.

Spicer's letters, like Keats's, outline his poetics, and comprise the most explicit examples of his ideas of the indivisibility of the personal, the communal, the erotic, and the poetic. The first of the two letters from *Admonitions* just mentioned, to Joe Dunn, a former lover, addresses the question of "obscenity" in his poetry.

> In these poems the obscene (in word and content) is not used, as is common, for the sake of intensity, but rather as a kind of rhythm. . . . It is precisely because the obscenity is unnecessary that I use it, as I could have used any disturbances, as I could have used anything (remember the beat in jazz) which is regular and beside the point. (A, CB 55)[37]

The second, for Blaser, articulates his apprehension of and commitment to poetry as a process rather than a set of products:

> [Duncan claims] there is no such thing as good or bad poetry. There is—but not in relation to the single poem. There is really no single poem.
> That is why all my stuff from the past . . . looks foul to me. The poems belong nowhere. They are one night stands filled (the best of them) with their own emotions, but not pointing anywhere, as meaningless as sex in a Turkish bath. It was not my anger or my frustration that got in the way of my poetry but the fact that I viewed each anger and each frustration as unique—something to be converted into poetry as one would exchange foreign money. . . . Look at those other poems. Admire them if you like. They are beautiful but dumb.
> Poems should echo and re-echo against each other. . . . They cannot live alone any more than we can.

... Two inconsequential things combine together to become a
consequence. This is true of poems too. A poem is never to be
judged by itself alone. A poem is never by itself alone. (A, CB 61)

In both these letters, Spicer highlights and problematizes sexual language and imagery in a poetics, just as sexuality is highlighted and
necessarily problematized in a community defined by its sexual activity (highlighted and problematized, that is, both within the community and by onlookers and judges in the dominant culture).

Spicer speaks of poetry and of the gay community as well: sex provides the definition, the form, the rhythm of the community (as
rhythm gives a poem its form) although it is in some ways beside the
point, incidental to the real functioning and intent of community/
poetry. And, poignantly, while poems/people cannot live in isolation,
common forms of contact in the gay men's community—anonymous
encounters in parks, baths, bars, and bathrooms—strike Spicer as
empty, each incident "filled with its own emotions" but going nowhere, like a conventional collection of discrete poems. In "Last
Hokku," Spicer again reiterates his impatience with this self-involved
way of conceiving of both poems and personal life; the lines strike
particularly hard at "workshop poems," which make experience
static and reify it through conventionally "beautiful" language.

> I don't like dreams where a right sound
> Can put a minor emotion in amber.
>   (ONS, 84)

(Note the title of Spicer's posthumously collected early work, from
whence "Last Hokku" is taken: *One Night Stands*.) Poems, like people, should have a communal context *on their own terms*; a book
should be a community of poems. And human communities could be
dynamically based on and interdependent with these poem-
communities—the Berkeley circle, for example, and its later San
Francisco incarnation. But for a poet who signed letters "rex meo-
rum operum" and whose clique based itself on the elitist George coterie, Spicer's praxis concerning community could be quite radical:
believing poetry to be public domain and not the property of the isolated poet, he refused to copyright his books.

The cover of the *Collected Books* itself constitutes a neat bit of
intertextuality within this gay poetic community. Out of respect for
Spicer's concept of poem-communities, or serialism, Robin Blaser

chose to call his friend's posthumously collected works *The Collected Books of Jack Spicer*, rather than *The Collected Poems*. The illustration on the cover depicts, in recessed outline, the tarot card of the 4 of cups (hearts)—the same icon that underlies Blazer's poem "Cups," whose refrain is:

> . . . two men in a tree is clearly
> the same thing as poetry.[38]

In other words, gayness, poetry and community are of a piece, coextensive. Each element of this interweaving implies the others. Blaser's poem contains the characteristic embedded or explicit references to other gay poets; here the debt to Whitman is acknowledged:

> Amor entered disguised as grass. You both
> hoped your seed would fall among the roots
> of this tree and there grow up a second tree
> and guardian.
>
> WHAT IS THAT WRINKLES UNDER THE ROOT?
>
> SKIN, SEMEN, AND ARM AND FOOT.[39]

and here Spicer:

> There were two.
> Their posture
> taken out of the wall-
> paper (a ghost story)
> Jack talked. His
> determined privacy against
> my public face. The poem
> by dictation.[40]

Spicer's poems not only help to embody a gay community through language; they also document the gay subculture of the 1950s and 1960s as a minority group. As his books expanded conceptually to include his annotations of his own poems, poems that show the community as stigmatized also celebrate, ambiguously, details of the life:

> Away we go with no moon at all
> Actually we are going to hell.
> We pin our puns to our backs and cross in a car
> The intersection where lovers are.
> The wheel and the road turn into a stair

The pun at our backs is a yellow star.
We pinned our puns on the windshield like
We crossed each crossing in hell's despite.

A note meant to clarify this text reads:

"I like it better in L.A. because there're more men and they're
prettier," someone said in the Handlebar tonight. (HT, CB 119)

The multiple puns (moon, p/buns, cross, star/stair/stare) in this bleak
incantation, as well as the focus on p/buns as indices of difference,
point complicatedly toward a coextension of langue, physical/erotic
body parts, sacredness and cursedness. The well-developed gay vernacular with its elaborate wit, much of it word-playing or punning on
sexual imagery and/or reversals of stereotypical sex roles, is one of
the most salient features of gay culture, and like the yellow star
broadcasts itself as insignia of otherness. Again, the word "vernacular" suggests itself, connoting oppression through its etymological
origins in the Latin *verna*, a homeborn slave—the Other within the
state's boundaries.[41] The yellow star is also the "buns," or "moon,"
the flaunting of one's erotic and erogenous body parts through cos-
tume (tight, torn jeans or leather chaps) and physical mannerism,
which subject the wearer to the objectifying gaze, or "stare," of both
potential pick-up partners and judging members of the dominant
culture. The emphasis on "crossing" points not only to obvious religious notions of martyrdom and oppression, but to gay culture as a
"crossover" culture: "crossdressing," "gender-benders," crossing/
cruising between two worlds—"intersections where lovers are."
("Crossing" and "cruising" derive from the same etymological
root—the crux of movement and martyrdom.)

The act of love is a meeting of worlds; here, an intersection between hell and its opposite, heaven. The poem, drenched with the
loneliness of life on the borderline, is, of course, not an untroubled
affirmative presentation of a culture: the gay world is cruising to hell
in a handbasket—although the ambiguous ending with its odd phrasing taken from Blake, "in hell's despite," implies that it may keep
crossing back and forth across the borders in defiance of hell. The
rhythm of Spicer's poem echoes Blake's, which is part of the series
(the poem-community) of the *Songs of Experience*, and unlike other
poems in the series, has no complement in the *Songs of Innocence*:

Love seeketh not Itself to please,
Nor for itself hath any care;
But for another gives its ease,
And builds a Heaven in Hell's despair.

> So sang a little Clod of Clay
> Trodden with the cattles feet:
> But a Pebble of the brook,
> Warbled out these metres meet.

Love seeketh only Self to please,
To bind another to its delight;
Joys in anothers loss of ease,
And builds a Hell in Heavens despite.[42]

These opposite ways of understanding love articulate exactly the ambivalence Spicer evinced not only toward heterosexist culture, but toward his own sacred/damned community, with the self-seeking of its individual members vying with an acknowledged need for bonding and friendship if the community is to survive at all. The note also ambiguously holds the line between vapid bar talk and campily positive assertion of cultural values. L.A., of course, is Los Angeles, the city of angels: Heaven, or the Pebble's provocatively hellish rejoinder to the assertion of star-crossed love in the verse part of Spicer's poem. It is at least another reference to mixing worlds, since angels are crossover figures who inhabit both invisible and visible worlds, who have bodies only at will, and who mediate between Heaven and earth. The oppositions that Blake constructs—clod/pebble, selfless/selfish, as well as other/self, soft/hard, land/water, solid/permeable—become in Spicer's poem a dizzying series of metamorphoses: wheel and road become stair, round and straight become spiral, horizontal becomes vertical, front becomes back. And Blake's neat rhymes become skewed into off-rhyme: all/hell, stair/star, like/despite. Spicer's specifically homoeroticized revision of "The Clod and the Pebble" blows the cover off the Romantic canon's dissimulation or displacement of such homoerotic possibilities.

In stunning instances of "subaltern wit as a weapon,"[43] other poems' puns likewise advertise bawdy gay humor: "Concord Hymn" is glossed: " 'Conquered Him' is a poem by Emerson" (CB, HT, 120). And "Who Knew" turns Pound's most renowned imagist poem, "In a Station of the Metro," into an eerie masturbatory image that resonates with and highlights the loneliness of the original:

Ghosts drip
And then they leap
The boy sang and the singing that I heard:
Wet shadows on a stick.

(HT, CB 131)

The pain of the life emerges in "Several Years' Love":

They pushed their cocks in many places
And I'm not certain of their faces
Or which I kissed or which I didn't
Or which of both of them I hadn't.

(HT, CB 118)

The note reads: "The two loves are the pain The Poet had."

Spicer articulates most straightforwardly the tension between his need to assert the existence of a gay culture and to deny himself access to it in "The Unvert Manifesto and Other Papers Found in the Rare Book Room of the Boston Public Library in the Handwriting of Oliver Charming. By S.," an early series of documents that includes the antimanifesto "Unvert Manifesto." Clearly preoccupied with questions of sexual identity, this 1956 work constitutes part of Spicer's transition from more traditional lyric poetry to dictation (automatic writing), a distinct turning away from what he terms the "big lie of the personal" characteristic of the isolated poems he rejects in his letter to Blaser. The Manifesto reveals an effort to create an (anti) community in tension with an uneasiness about identity:

1. An unvert is neither an invert or an outvert, a pervert or a convert, an introvert or a retrovert. An unvert chooses to have no place to turn.
2. One should always masturbate on street corners.
   . . .
4. Sex should be a frightening experience like a dirty joke or an angel.
   . . .
6. An unvert must not be homosexual, heterosexual, bisexual or autosexual. He must be metasexual. . . . He must enjoy going to bed with his own tears.
   . . .
12. Jews and Negros are not allowed to be unverts. The Jew will never understand unversion and the Negro understands it too well.

(CB 341)

What comes out in the manifesto, so to speak, is a commitment to loneliness, even within the community for which the document could speak. (Think of Kaufman's poetic manifesto, "THE POET": "THE POET IS ALONE WITH / OTHERS LIKE HIMSELF.") Even within the community the "unvert" is isolated. "Three Marxist Essays," written seven years later, echoes the same idea.

> Homosexuality is essentially being alone. Which is a fight against the capitalist bosses who do not want us to be alone. Alone we are dangerous. Our dissatisfaction could ruin America. Our love could ruin the universe if we let it. (ONS 88)

This passage foreshadows the recognition of gay activism as a vital possibility in political life, but Spicer deconstructs traditional Marxism's emphasis on solidarity rather than solitude, emphasizing instead (like Genet) the revolutionary potential of the discomfort of isolation. And perhaps cruelest of all , even this isolation is public (as for Kaufman, whose POET is a public absence, a walking corpse): "One should always masturbate on street corners." The concept of "metasexuality"—crudely put, a preoccupation with sex not necessarily accompanied by sexual activity—again indicates a split between sexual activity as meaningful connection between two people or as a foundation for communal recognition, and sexuality as a charged but ultimately empty aura hovering over a fundamentally unsatisfying set of interactions.

Another section from the "Oliver Charming" series, "Excerpts from Oliver Charming's Diary," directly addresses Spicer's simultaneous discomfort and preoccupation with questions of culture and identity:

> "We homosexuals are the only minority group that completely lacks any vestige of a separate cultural heritage. We have no songs, no folklore, even our customs are borrowed from our upper-middleclass mothers," he [S.] said.
>
> "What about camping?" I [Oliver Charming] asked. "Isn't that a cultural pattern worthy at least of Ruth Benedict's cunt?"
>
> "What about camping?" he asked rhetorically. "A perpetual Jewish vaudeville joke—or at the very best, a minstrel show impeccably played by Negros in blackface."
>
> The trouble with S. is that he doesn't understand Martian . . .
> (CB 344)

The poet strains for a sense of community based on traditional ideas about culture; simultaneously, he cannot allow himself an uncritical acceptance of what he perceives as a problematic and undignified aspect of gay culture—especially problematic in that it might turn out to be the *only* strong cultural feature of the gay life. Here, though, as in the "Unvert Manifesto" 's twelfth guideline, he explicitly recognizes gay people as a political "minority group" and, as in "Car Song," draws the analogy, however dismissively, to Jews and Blacks. The lines of the "Unvert Manifesto" suggest that Spicer projects onto Blacks and Jews respectively the same mutually exclusive categories inhering in the Pebble and the Clod: Jews are materialistic and cannot understand the dissolution of norms; Blacks are all-expansive and boundariless, "in touch," at the deepest level, with everything that is "un." The poet, in the person of S., understands and resents the clown (with or without a breaking heart) persona that each of these groups has had to develop in response to oppression.[44] But Spicer does not use the analogy as an opportunity to unproblematically affirm a positive sense of gay identity, as one might assume from a perspective of the late 1960s and 1970s, when the "ethnicization" of gay culture and its alliance with other "target groups" became an important strategy in gay power politics.[45] Rather, Spicer's tone is one of uneasiness and scorn. One senses a jockeying for one-down on the hierarchy of the oppressed, a rivalry that comes out in bitterness and resentment.

Spicer makes and breaks connection to other "target groups" elsewhere as well, in uneasy recognition of analogy that leads to an attempt at distinction based on a more-oppressed-than-thou *ressentiment*. In "Answer to a Jew," Spicer asserts that:

When asked if I am of the Jew or Goyim,
When asked if I am an enemy of your people,
I would reply that I am of a somewhat older people:
The Gay, who are neither Jew nor Goyim,
Who were cut down in your Lord God Jehovah's first pogrom
Out at Sodom.
None of the nations ever protested about it
(We should never have nationalized angels) but show us
An angel again

Walking down Sodom St., wings folded,
And try us.

(ONS, 65)

"Manhattan" is more blatantly anti-Semitic:

The horror of this city. Stone piled on stone,
Dollar on dollar, cloud upon cloud!
The little Jewfaced children
Playing in the deep streets.

(ONS 65)

And in "Billy the Kid," the poet needs to hide from "Jew salesmen of amethyst pajamas"—Jewish exploiters of gay people (purple or amethyst being the "gay color").[46] The reference to "Negros in black-face" carries the implication of laughable, self-demeaning redundancy: the exaggerated and extravagant gestures and mannerisms of camp are the blackface assumed by men who love men. For someone uncomfortable with gay identity, this cultural pattern is frightening. But fright and horror have their positive significance as well—sex *should* be frightening, an angelic dirty joke.[47]

On the other hand, the poet as narrator Oliver Charming (itself a charmingly campy stage name) glosses the preceding dialogue with the observation that "S. doesn't understand Martian." "Martian" is Spicer's shorthand for poetically inspired language: he referred to his form of automatic writing as "taking dictation from Mars." Thus, S. doesn't understand or appreciate the poetry of camping, the divinely strange forms of language and self-presentation that result from alienation, the experience of "outside" from which the most authentic creative blessings flow.[48] Poetry, like sex, is a frightening series of angelic dirty jokes; as a form of camping, like "Negros in blackface," poetic language makes strange, defamiliarizes what we think we know. Although Spicer's image for the poet who takes dictation from the Martians is the modest and very twentieth-century radio transmitting whatever comes its way, it resonates with the more lofty (and possibly more pretentious) version of this phenomenon: the divinely possessed shaman who, because he mediates the spirit world, can transgress the rules of ordinary conduct. Though he may suffer acutely from the embarrassment of being "different" or finding himself doing "inappropriate" and clownish things, the gay man who camps publicly is no less a holy fool or an oracle.

Spicer, in fact, dissociated himself from the Beats partially because he considered their beatific and behavioral excesses to be vulgar and self-serving. For Spicer, Allen Ginsberg was too mired in his own personality, too much the clown, the gay camper, the public demagogue: in the last of his final series (the last poems he ever wrote, in fact), "Ten Poems for Downbeat," Spicer addresses Ginsberg bitterly:

> At least we both know how shitty the world is. You wearing a beard as a
> mask to disguise it. I wearing my tired smile. I don't see how you do it.
> One hundred thousand university students marching with you. Toward
> A necessity which is not love but is a name.
> King of the May . . . If [the police had] attacked
> The kind of love (not sex but love) you gave the one hundred thousand
> students I'd have been very glad. And loved the policemen . . .
>
> (BMV, CB 267)

On the other hand, Spicer himself loved to get others (including children) to use profanity in inappropriate situations (over the radio or in the classroom) or to read Apollinaire aloud in tough working-class bars. This could be seen as vulgar clowning, but without the publicly articulated ideology of "love" that Ginsberg used to justify himself, and without Ginsberg's constant emphasis on his own personality.[49] The exchange between Oliver Charming and S. ("Spicer"? "straight"? "square"?) exemplifies one of the tensions—concentration on victimization versus concentration on positive creativity—in "minority" theory. Again, Spicer here has split himself into two personae to work out his ambivalence (with "S.," in fact, writing Oliver Charming's diary), and significantly, in this instance at least the proponent of camping as cultural affirmation gets the last word.

Angels

Angelic dirty jokes: the oxymoron that captures Spicer's ambivalence is, at the same time, a beautifully telegraphic image of gay men's culture and in particular that of gay poets. The phrase bridges worlds, connecting the physical to the spiritual. The yoking together of angels—themselves points of contact between the spiritual and the material, eternity and temporality—and dirty jokes—instances of physicality mediated through "spirited" verbal wit—constitutes a point of contact, an intersection, between the spiritual and the physical. Gay men are angels and also "dirty jokes," ridiculous (but scary) in the eyes of the world, perhaps "beyond belief and beneath contempt"; but sharp and quick with language, their magical medium.[50] Two poetry anthologies published by Gay Sunshine Press, one of the better-known gay men's publishing companies, bring many of these tropes together in their titles: *Angels of the Lyre* and *Orgasms of Light*. The poems in these anthologies, as well as in *The Male Muse* and *Son of the Male Muse*, both published by the Crossing Press, consistently and explicitly combine angelic with sexual imagery and language.[51]

Bastard Angel, the title of the literary journal edited by gay Beat poet Harold Norse, and his *Memoirs of a Bastard Angel*[52] point to the same oxymoronic association of sexual or social illegitimacy with sanctity. This trope admittedly serves Beat as well as gay literature, and is another instance of crossover between two distinct but related subcultures; it perhaps finds its most well-known expression in the opening lines of the gay/Beat manifesto by Ginsberg:

> I saw the best minds of my generation destroyed by madness, starving hysterical naked,
> dragging themselves through the negro streets at dawn looking for an angry fix,
> angelheaded hipsters burning for the ancient heavenly connection . . . [53]

These three lines set forth the crucial Beat values: madness, nakedness, Blackness, anger, hipness, holiness, and more ambiguously gayness. Beat anthologies and critical works go under titles like *Genesis Angels: The Saga of Lew Welsh and the Beat Generation*, *Naked Angels*, and *Beat Angels*.[54] But I would argue that the Beat usage of the term has a somewhat different tone, more defiantly polemical, than the non-Beat gay usage. The Beats (including Ginsberg here—and this was part of Spicer's quarrel with him) seem to use angelic imagery more for the joy of high contrast, for oxymoronic shock value, than for any actual or sustained sense of otherworldliness. One anthology of contemporary San Francisco Bay area poetry includes the poetry of both ex-Beats and the current, possibly stronger, gay writing scene: its title, *Practicing Angels*, acknowledges and modifies both Beat and gay senses: the holiness of sustained and disciplined spiritual practice (a word more associated with Eastern than Western religious traditions); the sense of struggle (as in "practice makes perfect") implied in the slow and steady forging of a community and in the acknowledgment of the conscientious development of writerliness (as opposed to the brash spontaneity de rigueur in the Beat heyday). The sense of transcendent otherworldliness has been preserved, but with the implication of evolutionary process and pain: the cover photo shows a number of naked, winged men looking faintly Neanderthal, some stumbling, others stepping off these stumblers' backs into flight. The title and photo imply that the poets are (pre)humans practicing to be angels, and that simultaneously they are angels engaged in their spiritual practice, which is writing. Ascent is a group endeavor, accompanied by suffering: the dedication reads, in part, "To my brothers who are ill with AIDS." The epigraph for the collection of verbal artifacts, by gay writer Edmund White, enjoins respect for silence: "When company falls silent, the French say an angel is passing through." The publisher's name, however, Seismograph Press, echoes the old fire of apocalyptic defiance.[55]

The entry under "angel" in Bruce Rodgers's *The Queen's Vernacular: A Gay Lexicon* gives its meaning as "any homosexual male," and goes on to comment: "Angel, to some, mends the crumpled wings and pride of the denigrated fairy."[56] While the trope has strong currency in the gay community, its primary significance is not, I believe, compensatory. Rather, the word indicates an ethereal sense of belonging to multiple worlds, multiple planes of existence, of inhabiting space somewhere between the human and the divine. Another expression, to "have the beast for" someone, meaning to be sexually obsessed with him, conveys the same sense of plurality, only in the opposite, "downward" direction. Both effeminacy/ethereality and bestiality are implied in how the straight world views gay culture—hence the gay world, though often white and well-to-do, threatens the order imposed by the Great Chain of Being. Spicer jokes about this and about history and science, playing on the theory of evolution, in "A Postscript for Charles Olson":

> If nothing happens it is possible
> To make things happen.
> Human history shows this
> And an ape
> Is likely (presently) to be an angel.
> (A, CB 65)[57]

Enhanced by his familiarity with medieval angelology and his deep reading of Rilke, Spicer's use of angelic imagery is consistent with these meanings. In this context his preoccupation with angels can be understood as a recognition of a liminality based on physical and metaphysical in-between-ness, an intersection (where lovers are) based on whom one desires. Gay men, and especially gay poets, are conduits for other, spiritual worlds; they are angels. Why especially poets? Because language is the bridge between spirit and matter; it has its origins in the body and emerges as breath and sound, impalpable but transformative. The first four sections of Spicer's book *Language* are entitled "Thing Language," "Love Poems," "Intermissions," "Transformations": materiality, union, in-between periods, and changes are all intertwined through language, bodied forth in its "Morphemes," "Phonemes," and "Graphemes"—the final three sections. Substituting the word "language" for "this poem" in a note glossing "Awkward Bridge" (CB, HT 129), we can grasp one aspect of the poet/ linguist's project: "In language is a bridge between love and the idea of love. Tentative, rustling."[58]

In *The Heads of the Town Up to the Aether*, a book whose title underscores the ethereality and elitism of the gay poet (though it also alludes to drugs), the poem "Dillinger" raises the ambiguity of the angels' status in the eyes of the world.

> The human voices put the angels
> Pretty far away.
> (HT, CB 145)

And in "Drugs" he characteristically swipes at Ginsberg and simultaneously acknowledges his place in the gay world:

> But angel-talk howls
> At the edge of our beds
> And all of us now
> Are partners of hell.
> (HT, CB 139)

The note comments: "A definition of hell hovers over the whole poem. It is the first (and last) mention of angels." Clearly being an angel can feel like hell; or perhaps hell is the proper place for angels. For Spicer, moreover, contact with the spirit world, like sex, must be "frightening" to be authentic. Thus it is appropriate for angels "at the edge of our beds" to be associated with hell.[59]

Ghosts

Ghosts appear at least as frequently as angels in Spicer's work, and although ghosts, like angels and fairies, live between this world and other worlds, in the popular imagination ghosts are scarier and more unhappy, the Holy one notwithstanding. Caught between worlds and unable to find satisfaction in any of them, they represent unresolved souls who cannot come to rest in one life, desire that cannot be satisfied. Although ghosts do have a place in the more lighthearted aspect of gay men's culture, which has made Halloween so much its own that it is known as the "queens' Christmas," Spicer's ambivalence dwells on the sinister rather than the ludic aspects of the festival.[60] "All Hallows Eve" complains about the ephemerality of (a caricatured) love in the community of "fruits," a cynical *carpe diem*:

> Bring on the pumpkin colored wine.
> The ghosts of autumn ask our pardon—
> The withered flowers in the garden,
> The fruit that frosted on the vine.
>
> Each fickle life that testified
> The summer's quick magnificence
> Now masks its own significance
> And plays the spook to salve our pride.
>
> They wear bright costumes of the dead
> And posture in a clownish way
> The lover that we loved last May
> Now wears a gaping pumpkin head.
>
> . . .
>
> . . . every painted spook repeats
> The gestures of his burial.
>
> Come drink the wine and watch them play
> For there is nothing to be said.
> No exorcist can drive away
> The childish faces of the dead.
>
> (ONS 56)

Halloween is no playful game for Spicer. When not an occasion for lament about passing love/lust, it is a deadly serious calling-up of spirits. "A Prayer for Pvt. Graham Mackintosh on Halloween" shows

Spicer's complicated allegiance to the magic of the community he at times despises; he invokes the gay community's otherworldly powers in a curse on the military.

> Infernal warlocks dressed in pink
> And children wearing masks by night,
> Protect my friend from sundry harm
> And rest his body in your arms.
>
> Ghosts of eternal silences
> And pumpkin-faces wreathed in flame
> Consume the military flesh
> Of those who borrow young men's lives. . . .
> (ONS 61)

The most explicit and tersest conflictual expression of ghostliness is "Ghost Song":

> The in
>   ability to love
> The inability
>   to love
> In love . . .
>   (BM, CB 73)

The fifth line mitigates the sense of emptiness and lack of substance. But it also twists the phrase to bring into poignant relief the real suffering behind such inability—the pain of being both in love and unable to love, so that love becomes, rather than the process of poetic series or developing intimacy, a charged but isolated "run-in" with another. "The two loves are the pain The Poet had." However, *not* to love is not an option. The incantatory stammer of repetition invokes and insists on love. There's no way out but in to a closet of frustrated feeling. Being in is the opposite of being out, that is, out of the closet: self-identified and open about one's sexual preference. These five lines and their continued variation throughout the poem point to the double bind of the self-identified gay community at the time: the choice of love-object that identifies the community and gives it coherence is not only illegal but condemned by all institutional authorities: medical, religious, legal, and social. Having to hold in one's feelings and deny them expression cripples one's ability to love, since love is communication.

Spicer tends toward the sinister or the morbid: his affinity for "Martian" and other worlds can be attributed in part to an acute alienation from the immanent, the painful exigencies of being a gay poet during the McCarthy years. Duncan's phrase "autistic systems" describes Spicer's oeuvre even in its attempt to bridge realities; and Jim Herndon writes of Spicer's conviction that contact with the spirit world depended upon absolute, compulsive regularity of habit—the orderliness of the rules governing baseball, for example, chess, bridge, or one's own daily routine.[61] An obsession with syntax, which word derives etymologically from *syn*, "together," and *tassein*, "to arrange," indicates proper language use as a crucial realm of compulsive regularity: scrupulous attention to the rules of language permits access to the spirit world. According to Robert Duncan, Spicer was far more alienated than he: Spicer experienced his gayness as a necessary curse, like being a poet.[62] As for the Martian connection, Guido Cavalcanti, with whose poetry Spicer the medievalist was no doubt familiar, writes with similarly bitter irony of love coming not from Venus, goddess of beauty and harmony, but from Mars, the god of discord and war. For Spicer, who so closely linked love and poetry, this double alienation is apt: not only is love/poetry from the outer space of the 1950s, but it embodies conflict of epic and mythic proportions.[63] More generally, Spicer partakes of the gay tradition of bridging worlds, of revealing the connection of the physical to the spiritual, and of constituting, in his poetry, a gay community based on the work of gay forebears (Whitman, Lorca, Rimbaud, etc.) and a primarily gay readership comprised of his own friends and fellow poets.[64]

The prose of William Burroughs, godfather of gay punk, is, like Spicer's, tinged with seemingly negative overtones, even as it invokes a necessary and sustaining contact with other realms, as in the now-famous statement, "language is a virus from outer space"; his preoccupation with parapsychology, alteration of consciousness and mind control, and messages from beyond is tied up with specifically political and writerly concerns, namely freedom of speech, freedom of sexual expression, freedom of consciousness itself, and the simple issue of craft: How can these messages help me write better? For these writers, moreover, writing better means getting beyond the ego, the obsession with control that permeates "the big lie of the personal." Burroughs's cut-up collage techniques, Merrill's Ouija games and the Spicer-Duncan coterie's experiments with dictation are ways of trying to let other worlds in, to let them break through the dominant culture in our heads, the socially constructed ego's insistence on the linear rationality of *cogito ergo sum*.

Although Freud has been an important influence on several of these writers, they nevertheless tend not to refer to these other worlds simply as the "unconscious" or "subconscious." To do so would be once again to reduce the realm of creative resource to the single, atomized human individual—to conflate subjectivity with subjectivism, or the antidiscursive trope of the "lyrical I" with the individual. The scope of their apprehensions must be understood as greater than the single human mind, and the community they are trying to create is not simply a person-to-person bond. James Merrill, for example, writes out of an experience of playing the Ouija board with his lover David Jackson. The two men's hands move together in an aleatory game (which some, of course, would argue to be influenced by the wills, conscious or unconscious, of the participants). This union of two is already an unorthodox method of composition, undercutting the image of the solitary writer in the study or in nature. But it doesn't stop there: the two lovers spell out, letter by numinous letter, messages that come from far beyond their union as two individuals. Dead and imaginary people, old friends and famous writers, angels and other beings from other worlds participate in the game, which revolves around written language in its most unitary form—the incremental accumulation of letters. And the message goes far beyond the room where the lovers engage in their nightly occult ritual: Merrill is among the most respected and well known of contemporary poets, and through his publications in the most conventional literary magazines and by the most elite publishing houses, people who don't believe in spirits get to have contact with them. Though Merrill is considered far more formally conservative than the other writers examined in this chapter (he is never, for instance, classified as avant-garde, and has very little sympathy with the Beats or other members of the San Francisco Renaissance), he shares these metaphysical concerns and compositional techniques with them.[65] Burroughs's lecture "It Belongs to the Cucumbers: On the Subject of Raudive's Tape Voices" also suggests that phrases heard on factory-fresh blank tapes may be extraterrestrially generated messages, voices from the dead, or fragments of the listeners' or manufacturers' unconscious.[66]

Spicer's Self-Destruction

Paradoxically, Spicer's poetics, even as they leaned toward process, demanded that he become ever more ghostly and isolated:

> What I am . . . is by degrees a ghost.
> (HT, CB 182)

> Dear Lorca,
>   Loneliness is necessary for pure poetry. When someone intrudes into the poet's life (and any sudden personal contact, whether in the bed or in the heart, is an intrusion) he loses his balance for a moment, slips into being who he is, uses his poetry as one would use money or sympathy. The person who writes the poetry emerges, tentatively, like a hermit crab from a conch shell. The poet, for that instant, ceases to be a dead man.
> (AL, CB 48)

The process is one of self-negation rather than self-actualization. If poetry must eschew the "big lie of the personal," and if immature poets are wrong to confuse deep personal feeling with good poetry, the mature poet erases his self to make room for the poem, which comes to him through dictation. For Spicer, the notion of "process" in a body of poetry must be differentiated from the idea of process as self-exploration. "The emotion of a poem is not the emotion of people."[67] The poet should clear the airwaves so the Martians can transmit the proper message. The image that seizes most accurately on poetic process for Spicer is the car radio in Cocteau's film version of *Orphée*, which transmits broken poetic messages; the mature poet is the poet as transmitter, not source. The poet's self must die: as Spicer says to the dead Garcia Lorca, "That is how we dead men write to each other." (AL, CB 34) The empty poet becomes a (g)host body invaded by "alien and ghostlike language" as by a parasite.[68] The poem becomes a "collage of the real" (AL, CB 34), "thing language" unmediated by the poet's personality:

> the lemon [mentioned in a poem would be] a lemon that the reader could cut or squeeze or taste—a real lemon like a newspaper in a collage is a real newspaper. . . . How easy it is in erotic musings or in

the truer imagination of a dream to invent a beautiful boy. How difficult to take a boy in a blue bathing suit . . . and to make him visible in a poem . . . not as an image . . . but as something alive — caught forever in the structure of words. (AL, CB 33-34)[69]

The authenticity of a poem depends upon the self-annihilation of the poet: Spicer's last words, uttered to Robin Blaser in a fatal alcoholic coma, were: "My vocabulary did this to me. Your love will let you go on" (CB 326). At one level love and poetry are the same; at another, they are mutually and symmetrically exclusive. Coextensive, they also cancel each other out.

In an essay reminiscing on the Spicer-Duncan kreis, Richard Tagett speaks of Spicer's hard-line antipersonal poetics.

I prefer to attribute it to love, that state that poets — ever so especially Jack Spicer — are wrapt up in, in their poems, so much so, that the (real?) manifestation of love is often, if not always, exceedingly strange to the uninvolved in its ultimate expression.[70]

The double bind of Spicer's poetics is that in the name of love, they doom him to death — in his case not simply the ego death of Zen and Eastern philosophies, but, for one so self-consciously and problematically heir to Western thought, the death of the entire organism. Recent critics and champions of Spicer's work are quick to show the consonance between his aesthetic and contemporary "antimetaphysical" theories, linking his work to that of Derrida, among others.[71] However, the very "bitterness"[72] of his struggle against the personal puts his verse firmly in the modernist camp, as opposed to the postmodern; Spicer is, despite his would-be detachment, drenched in his own emotions of disillusionment. Wanting out is far different from being always already beyond. And what could love and its expression have meant anyway in the gay subculture from the 1940s through the early 1960s? Even for a poet such as Spicer, who had a consciously articulated allegiance to the gay literary tradition and a circle of peers, loneliness and isolation ruled as the significant features of his poetic and affective experience.

The sense of betrayal and abandonment that permeates his oeuvre indicates that he even felt estranged from the gay community and gay tradition; his work questions whether such things even existed, or whether he'd been lied to. Spicer's acknowledgement of the primary forebear of gay American literature is less than unequivocally complimentary; "Some Notes on Whitman for Allen Joyce" delineates his alienation from Whitman's optimistic vision of manly love.

> He was reaching for a world I can still remember. Sweet and painful. It is a world without magic and without god. . . . His love (oh, God, the loss) is different from my love.

> In his world roads go somewhere and you walk with someone whose hand you can hold. . . . In my world roads only go up and down and you are lucky if you can hold on to the road or even know that it is there.

> . . .

> Forgive me Walt Whitman, you whose fine mouth has sucked the cock of the heart of the country for fifty years. You did not ever understand cruelty. . . . Calamus cannot exist in the presence of cruelty. Not merely human cruelty, but the cruelty of shadows, the cruelty of spirits . . .

> So when I dreamed of Calamus, as I often did when I touched you or put my hand upon your hand, it was not as of a possible world, but as a lost paradise. A land my father Adam drove me out with the whip of shadow. In the last sense of the word—a fairy story. . . . That is what I think about your damned Calamus. (ONS 81-82)

One can point to Allen Ginsberg's long "marriage" with Peter Orlovsky, which began in 1955, to Robert Duncan's household with Jess Collins, established in 1951 and ending only with Duncan's death in 1988, and to Merrill's with David Jackson; and one could say, accurately, that everything is always possible, that it is not exclusively due to historical circumstances that Spicer's poetics revolve around the "distance between love and the expression of it." Spicer's aesthetic is, explicitly, that of "outside," as has been addressed in most Spicer criticism. Language comes from outside, and the poet in turn has to be outside to receive it—not only outside himself or outside the comforts of a domestic love relationship, but outside the dominant culture with its form of cruelty, its complacent and egocentric values. If "to be a homosexual is to be alone," how much more alone is the homosexual poet. The mediator, the channel for multiple energies and worlds, is beyond reach of human norms. In this way Spicer's version of gayness (or, as Ginsberg has it, "gaiety") becomes crucial to him—his outsiderhood and misery in some sense guarantee his authenticity as a poet. However, insofar as Spicer allowed himself the comfort of any identity and community, his network of gay poets afforded him the context he resented and craved. For all his ambivalence and unhappiness, the formulation of a gay identity and his loyalty and love for his gay poetic circle sustained Spicer as a poet and as a self-conscious member of an oppressed subculture, a "minority group."

Robert Duncan: Love and Language Evolving

Manhood is not something that's there but is only there the way we then make love. So our phrase making love is the same as making poems.

Robert Duncan

Confronting openly the discomfort of negotiating his sexuality in a hostile and frightened dominant culture, Robert Duncan also bridges disparate worlds. As early as 1944, at age twenty-six, he published a remarkable piece in Dwight McDonald's *Politics*. "The Homosexual in Society," which responds to an earlier *Partisan* article by James Agee on "the Negro pseudo-folk," calls for the "salvation" of yet another group through "the struggle of all humanity for freedom and individual integrity."[73] Duncan's piece, in which he explicitly adopts a political position, is a signal moment in gay cultural politics. It not only points toward the political oppression and silencing of gay men as a group, but warns that group itself against a reactive retreat into the cultural ghetto of an alienated superiority cult. It is in coming out, Duncan writes, coming out, that gay people can begin to dissolve the self-protective and simultaneously oppressive illusion of complete separateness. He calls for a bringing together of two worlds, gay and straight, which have been driven apart by the straight world's censure and then held apart by the gay world's self-protective insularity. As a result of this appeal for acceptance, Duncan's heretofore well-received poems were rejected by John Crowe Ransom at the *Kenyon Review*.[74] This dramatic break with the New Critical insistence on separateness (poetry from social context, gay from straight, good from bad poetry, for example) served as a milestone in the poet's continued willingness to bring different worlds together, and to do so with the rigorous lightness and egolessness that marks an Orphic mediator.[75]

Duncan's work forms a marked contrast to Spicer's. Spicer, his friend and fellow "poet-king," sought to purge his own ego with a vengeance that led to ever-increasing physical, emotional, and spiritual self-destruction; his spare, electrifying lines reflect this harsh brilliance like the naked filaments of struck lightning rods. The light of Robert Duncan's poetry, on the other hand, is diffuse and aerated, as well as being, at all times, more specifically politically programmatic — an astounding paradox for most students of contemporary poetics who tend to read lyricism and didacticism in almost exclusionary tension with each other. Rather than appealing to scary otherworldly creatures — ghosts, angels, Martians — Duncan chooses to see the otherworldly in everyday harmonious interaction with the here and now; the poet does not need to destroy himself to act the bridge. On the contrary, Duncan has always seen himself as already outside the norm, rather than having to empty himself out agonistically to make room for the Other. Not only were his adoptive parents theosophists who provided the young poet with a spiritual sensibility far different from Spicer's tyrannical Calvinist background, but early acceptance of his gayness was inextricable from a similar acceptance of the task of poet:

> Perhaps the sexual irregularity underlay and led to the poetic;
> neither as homosexual nor as poet could one take over readily the
> accepted paradigms and conventions of the Protestant ethic. (YC i)

The idea of love, and the poet's preoccupation with it, has comprised both subject matter and the structure from which the poetry emerges:

> In 1938, when I was nineteen, I had fallen in love and left college in
> my sophomore year, following my lover East. That first experience of
> a sexual relationship took over my life. I was moved by violent
> conflicts and yearnings, a need to be reassured in love that all but
> obscured any expression of loving. The opposites played in me: male
> and female, love and hate, tenderness and jealous anger, hope and
> fear. Here too [in addition to his experience in poetry] there had
> been the awakening of a rhythm, the imprint of a cadence at once
> physical and psychological, that could contain and project the
> components of an emerging homosexuality in an ardor that would
> prepare for the development of Eros and, eventually, for that
> domesticated or domesticating Love that governs the creation of a
> household and a lasting companionship. (YC i)

The book introduced by this paragraph is a collection of early poems (1939-1946) that was published in 1966; thus we have not only
the benefit of the poet's retrospective wisdom but also the knowledge that love and the relationship of sexuality to poetry has been an
ongoing concern for Duncan, even if the quality of the "love" and the
verse has changed. This early poetry is restrained by an incantational
formality that breaks open in later years—as if the young poet is trying to "figure" love "out," to call it into being (or out of the closet)
through formulas, chanting it in spite of its impossibility:

> How many miles to Love and back,
> Hobbyhorse Wise? askt Mr. Why.
>
> You can never get there.
> To where? To where?
>
> Hobbyhorse Poor, said Mr. Why:
> To Lack from Lack to Lack and back.
> ("King Haydn of Miami Beach," YC 42)
>
> My brother is black and wise to me.
> From the door to the bed I watch his eyes.
> My animal in his eyes I see.
>
> The mute intention we call love
> shakes like a forest of tall mute mothers
> shockt by the wiry sex of a child.
> My brother is tame and I am wild.
>
> . . .
>
> Never arrives from door to bed
> but stops in the dead,
> in the forest of eyes,
> The mute intention that we call mother.
> ("Mother Brother Door and Bed," YC 45)

The attempt to dope out what love is, to "be wise" to it, suspends it;
it can't ever culminate in contact. Love is mother, silent desire, surrounding and watching like Baudelaire's forest of symbols as the
speaker projects and introjects various qualities on his object of
desire/(br)Other (mon semblable, mon frère). "Others" are also our
closest relatives, our most taboo desires, ourselves. The sense of being "caught" by love itself in a forbidden act of homoerotic love with
a mirrored double/twin evokes a vertiginous sense of infinite re-

gress. In spite of the boundless energy and the adrenalin of shock, there is no resolution, just an endless dialectical dance of shifting and merging identity: bestiality and wisdom, darkness and light, wildness and tameness, which cannot reach synthesis within the poem's boundaries. Or rather, any synthesis occurs simply through the poem's presentation of fragments; although the two boys (if such there are) cannot come together, they are trapped in an electrifying tableau vivant which implicates them in each other for ever.

The twin is a demonic incubus as well as an angelic image of the king's two bodies: the spiritual joined to the biological, the two lovers joined in one hermaphroditic union, the self unified out of wild conflicts ("opposites played in me . . . ") — and also the demon of desire attaching itself, a look-alike parasite, to the consciousness of the speaker. The union of passion involves the hex/hoax trickery of transformation and also the pain of fading infatuation, or of dependent fixation.

> Your image is the daylight hoax
> on which my soul and body wrecks.
> The absence of your body is
> the drowning place, the deep abyss.
>
> *
>
> Unspeakable myself, king without a shell, remote,
> with my twin in the split-open chrysalis lies
> uncoiled in one image. The worm is laid bare.
> Incubus bone teeth and hair like an egg . . .
>
> . . .
>
> I
> and my twin, grown together, turnd, leapt
> and attempted to fly with one wing. . . .
>
> . . .
>
> I and my love break open the shell, cease,
> And cease to create our desire. . . .
> I and my twin in the chrysalis twist
> uncoiled in one image. . . .
> . . . the power of love
> is upside down. Time
> is an older father than *he* is.
> ("Random Lines: A Discourse on Love," YC 49-50)

Elsewhere the twin/lover image becomes a phallic Christ who

merges with the narrator in sexual Eucharist, a beloved Idea who does not necessarily relieve the loneliness of the young man becoming himself:

> Crowned by the quick of the body's thorn,
> His Christ has made me King of my world,
> voiced in its animal my angel, His light,
> my own. Glad Christ! Of whom partaking I
> am—as a universe is crucified in me—
> Christ-crosst upon the body of my world . . .
>
> I shall never, as Zeno knows well,
> arrive at my lover
> who waits before me . . .
> ("Treesbank Poems," YC 66-68)

Not a Christian, Duncan uses Christ as a joyous symbol of the bringing together of spirit and flesh, angel and animal: he is all human and all divine, as are the narrator and his lover, mirroring each other as they lie stretched, crucified, on each other's bodies. The death they suffer by crucifixion is the *petit mort* of orgasm and everyday sleep, "Our little Death from which we daily / do survive." The body's thorn, of course, is the penis which pricks. In their sexual joining, the two men, imaging each other, recreate the Passion without the traditional Christian guilt. The figure of Christ, like Spicer's angels and ghosts, represents an admixture of worldliness and otherworldliness at its cultural pinnacle: Christ himself is union personified, as is the gay poet. This becomes explicit in "The Truth and Life of Myth, " an essay from 1955, in which

> the Poet too, like the Son, in this myth of Love or Form, must go deep into the reality of His own Nature. In this mystery of the art, the Son's cry to the Father might be too the cry of the artist to the form he obeys. (FC 16)[76]

But the "Treesbank Poems," even in their celebration of union, are also somewhat closeted, kept in the shade. The poem's opening line, "I listen in the shade to one I love," sets forth the occasion for this rhapsodic meditation; aural rather than tactile contact initiates the "half-hidden" narrator's private reverie on passion and mortality. The poems follow a cyclical pattern of contact and meditation, con-

tact and meditation, which ultimately reconfirms the speaker's solitude even as, by the final lines, he has changed places with the lover
of the opening line, speaking to him half-hid in the shadows of sleep:

> . . . Now,
> watching over your loved form where it lies
> admitted to life's death-soundings, sleep,
> I toss alone. You have met other lovers there.
>
> . . .
> . . . You hunt
> among the shadows of your life that haunt
> sleep's depth and hear in every voice
> some reminder from the distant past,
> that ominous tone that tried to reach your ear
> even while I spoke to you of love.
>
> (YC 68)

Plato must be acknowledged as a subtext. However, although the
poem clearly plays on all our familiar opposites—distance and contact, spirit and body, solitude and community, and so on—Duncan
gives these opposites a different valence. Rather than the Platonic
idea of two unbridgeable levels of being, the Ideal and the Immanent; and rather than the Aristotelean modification thereof, which involves a graded hierarchy leading "up" to the Ideal and "down" to
the earthly; Duncan's poetry suggests that each person has all ranges
of being in him (here it is appropriate to speak in the male gender),
and that that range ("its animal my angel") is made immanent
through erotic contact with a br/Other *semblable*. The encounter
with the Other is an encounter with an aspect of oneself; but rather
than a solipsistic journey into the interior, this self-confrontation becomes the basis for union and community. As in "Mother Brother
Door and Bed," "properties" (that is, the qualities of each person)
are exchanged, ceasing to be property, and threatening all propriety;
the energy flickers from one to the other in shared excitement ("His
light, my own"); the lovers can change roles and identities and play
Christ-redeemer, Christ-human, and Christ-divine to each other. All
the different aspects of a psyche can thus come into consciousness
and active play. Although the dualistic structure is apparent even (or
especially) in the concept of erotic partnership, the two aspects of

the dualism derive their meaning from their simultaneity: the twins making love in the chrysalis form a new, third, relational element. The animal *is* the angel, "His light" *is* "my own." Consciousness itself is a shared activity. (Think, once again, of Merrill and Jackson playing the Ouija together; though the poems are published under Merrill's name, the partnership is not only crucial in the composing process but acknowledged in the poem.)

In these early poems erotic contact takes the form of charged, infatuated passion; and this belief in the power of passion is necessarily counterweighted with an anxiety about its frustration or, once appeased, its passing. In the later poems, written out of the stability of a "domesticated and domesticating" household which the poet established with the collagist Jess Collins for several decades, the rapture remains, but it is both less extreme and less tempered by the fear of closure. Though the language of the poems continues to be mystical and lofty, this development is reflected formally in the more open, looser shapes of the poems. Duncan now evinces a willingness to relax the tight, incantational, Eliotic control over line length, meter, consistency in tone and, in general, all the poetic boundaries that come into play in composition.

Both Spicer and Duncan came to write serial poems whose compositional development reflects an increasing belief in process, and in the poet/medium's ultimate lack of control over the meaning of the finished product. The poet constructs a world, open or closed, and that construction, like the improvised music that was finally being acknowledged as serious art at the time of this transition, surprises the poet and the poem itself. Spicer also has the obligatory Charlie Parker poem, "Song for Bird and Myself," in which he addresses Parker in a characteristic sexual pun:

> "And are we angels, Bird?"
>   "That's what we're trying to tell 'em, Jack
>   There aren't any angels except when
>   You and me blow 'em."
>
> (CB 346)

In a long discussion of the process and meaning of love and poetry, Duncan takes Plato to task on several counts, particularly for his lack of respect for the physical realm:

I think we're discovering a homosexual manhood in a more solid ground than was provided in the Greek world. In the Greek world they were thought of as a very special cult; Plato doesn't propose anything other than that. Higher thought; by being removed from women they were removed in their minds from triviality, and among trivialities were daily life, how you cook. . . . When Plato lists the goods he knows nothing of the goods of food and the bads of food. (GS 90-91)

Plato embodies the "superiority cult" against which the young Duncan had warned, over thirty years earlier, in "The Homosexual in Society." By positing an unbridgeable chasm between "them" and "us," women and men, food and ideas, Plato's philosophy has crippled the development of Western consciousness and relegated both thought and bodies to their respective ghettos. Duncan's domestic arrangements have continued to refuse these ghettos: explicitly drawing the analogy to Jews, he explains why he doesn't live in the Castro, San Francisco's gay neighborhood:

> Jess and I heave a great sigh of relief that we didn't take a place twelve years ago in the middle of the gay ghetto. . . . That's like would you like to check out on being Jewish by living in the Jewish ghetto. But remember they're not forced to live in this ghetto so it's not a ghetto like in Europe. We forget that the ghetto in Europe was a place where people were forced to live, consequently we've got a very different kind of Jewish experience . . . the freedom to be or not be in a synagogue for instance. (GS 92)

Plato's dichotomies, when pushed to their extreme, divide people into categories that inhibit their free range, their permission to exercise their faculties at large. Later in the same interview:

> I do not accept at all ideas as anything other than the flowers, the fluvia, odors and everything else of the world of material—the material world—(earlier in the interview I referred to) things, because things can be anything in Plato-land; it's materialism, utter materialism all the way through. And spirit is material, unless you think you're breathing anything other than material as you're breathing in and out. . . . And the whole material world is spiritual. . . . We fall in love with a man, really we're reaching toward the manhood we see possible in that person . . . manhood is not something that's there but is only there the way we then make love. So our phrase making love is the same as making poems. (GS 94)

Rather than the dangerous conflation Kantorowicz warned of in *The*

King's Two Bodies, this alternate reading of the coextension of spirit and matter points toward a holism that occurs through the process of constant becoming, a process based on contact and interaction, the exchange of energy of "Treesbank Poems" and "Mother Brother Door and Bed." It is closer to Whitman than to Hitler. Duncan in fact reverses the Platonic hierarchy; rather than the trickle-down theory of Idea replicated in inferior material objects, ideas are the epiphenomena of matter — not superfluous to it by any means, but ornamental emanations that enhance the whole of worldly being. Besides, in the very important statement that "manhood is not something that's there but is only there the way we then make love," Duncan stresses the idea of becoming, of process, in which meaning is created through interaction — as discussed earlier in the image of weaving and reading. Making poems, then, is as much in the reading and in the living as in the writing.

Bending the Bow, published in 1968, is perhaps Duncan's most sophisticated treatment of this complex of intermeshed forces: gay love, language, political life, the mystical aspects of the natural and the aesthetic world. The first and third poems of *Bending the Bow* are "Sonnet 4" and "5th Sonnet," though they are neither the fourth and fifth poems nor do they have fourteen lines. They are, however, love lyrics in the sonnet tradition; and the hint that they are a series that begins before the book does plunges us midstream into the process that becomes the book, the formal working out of ideas of love and language. "Sonnet 4" begins with language — the intimate and slightly archaic pronoun, in fact — as the sacred and secret exchange between lovers:

> He's given me his *thee* to keep
> secret, alone, in Love's name,
> for what sake I have only in faith.
> ("Sonnet 4," BB 3)[77]

The "5th Sonnet" extends the metaphor of love and language into dance, which through its rhythmic footwork and romantic union again associates lyric poetry with love. The word "dance" is derived from *danson*, to draw out or extend, which points not only to the linearity of poetic composition, the line made up of feet, the verse turning in time, but also to Duncan's idea of loving as bringing another out, drawing a man's best manhood out of his singularity into union. (Yeats's metaphor for poetic process leaps immediately to hand: How can we know the dancer from the dance?)

Two poems of the book, "Such is the Sickness of Many a Good Thing" and "Epilogos," concern the poet's difficulty in saying "I love you," even (especially) when most deeply in love, a frustration Duncan addresses in the first line of the Gay Sunshine interview:

> The shattering experience when I was in love is why couldn't I say "I love you" and saying was impossible for me. I was struck dumb because the depth of feeling was so fundamental that if you advanced to the level of speech, the network of things drawn into that fundamental point was so complex you couldn't speak from it. It was felt throughout the entire body and you could not find within it any actual confidence of loving. (GS 76)

It need scarcely be pointed out that whatever the poet may feel to be his personal difficulties, there is a historical reason why these words might lodge in a gay man's throat in the early sixties. It is hardly a safe utterance; the incriminating sentence becomes, as we have seen in Spicer's work, a central problematic in gay poetry.

This problematic of language and love is most ambitiously engaged, however, in the beginning of the "Passages" series, which has continued into Duncan's latest collections, *Groundwork I: Before the War* and *Groundwork II: In the Dark*, and in which form breaks open in a new way. The multifaceted title implies the architecture of the body, the throat as passage for speech, the passages of writing and speech itself, the process of transition that is life, and the possibility of passing to other lives or worlds and of their passing through us. It implies moreover an attention to organic form, in fact a concentration on it, because (in a synthetic move indicating his Whitmanesque legacy) the poet is convinced that the United States as a nation has come up against a boundary that hampers our further evolution. Our involvement in Vietnam is perhaps the crisis of this formal disaster:[78]

> We enter again and again the last days of our own history, for everywhere living productive forms in the evolution of forms fail, weaken, or grow monstrous, destroying the terms of their existence. ... Now, where other nations before us have floundered, we flounder. To defend a form that our very defense corrupts. We cannot rid ourselves of the form to which we now belong. And in this

drama of our own desperation we are drawn into a foreign
desperation.

... All my common animal being comes to the ox in his panic and,
driven by this speech, we imagine only man ... has, comes into a
speech words mean to come so deep that the amoeba is my brother
poet. ("Introduction: The War," BB i-ii)

Out of the catastrophic "unnaturalness" of America's course in the
world is born the necessity for a poetic rethinking, an organic recre-
ation of the world through poetry. In a sense almost conventionally
Dantesque in inspiration, our passage is forced through a birth canal
of harrowing proportions; anything is possible. The Chain of Being is
leveled when an amoeba is equal to a poet: the consequences are
apocalyptic, liberating and all-encompassing, and potentially devastating. "Polysemous—not only the nation but the soul and the poem
are involved in the event" (BB x).

In the apocalyptic vein, "The Fire: Passages 13" again touches
base with Whitman in a politically worked echo of the image of the
splitting twins, this time embedded in Whitman's own account,
drawn from "The Eighteenth Presidency," of growing tension between the antebellum Northern and Southern states. By implication,
North and South Vietnam, mind and body, and consciousness itself
are being sundered by fraternal discord. This long paragraph of Whitman, which comprises the central passage of Duncan's poem, demonstrates how the denial of adhesiveness can result in (inter)national
conflagration, concluding, "Their cherished secret scheme is to dissolve the union of These States ... (Whitman, 1856)." The rupture of
the union (Whitman does not say "nation," a singular indivisible, but
"These States," once again acknowledging the plurality and difference he elsewhere celebrates outright) would rupture the body
politic—a body not reified in the person of a ruler but rather given
meaning through the love that binds its citizens, its consensual (consensual) members. The Civil War is a war that pits brother against
brother, lover against lover, *semblable* against *semblable*. The independence declared in the city of brotherly love has been given the lie
by the bondage of slavery, and the war in turn would constitute the
catastrophic result of a union based on a lie. Even though the war is
an unnatural tragedy, it is the inevitable outcome of a union based on
hostility to manly love, just as the Vietnam War and the atomic age
mark the inevitable consequences of false American claims to free-

dom and democracy. Unconsummated love, or more specifically here love soured by social lies, by interdiction against the sentence "I love you," becomes a vertiginous panic before overwhelming evil; the suspended animation of "Mother Brother Door and Bed" is resolved in a roster of Famous Bad Rulers, a Kantorowiczian nightmare. Even the more benign among the powerful become suspect in this paranoia of warped love.

> Eisenhower's idiot grin, Nixon's
> black jaw, the sly glare in Goldwater's eye, or
> the look of Stevenson lying in the U.N. that our
> Nation save face •

> [Satan's] face multiplies from the time of Roosevelt, Stalin,
>   Churchill, Hitler, Mussolini; from the dream
>   of Oppenheimer, Fermi, Teller, Vannevar Bush,
>   brooding the nightmare formulae—to win the war!
>   (BB 43)[79]

This roster of figures with their fixation on Nationhood is the antithesis of the brotherly love through which a citizenry can actualize itself nonhierarchically. The sundering of the twins and the destruction of nature follows from the reified conception of Nationhood that would, for example, consider "saving face" a priority over truth, in a superimposition of the semblance of integrity (intactness) over a divided House. The incantational form of poetry, the magical sentence, is superseded by the "formula"—diminutive, inferior to "form"–for nuclear power, the sundering of the atomic unit.

Duncan frames the poem (the poem is also about painting) with two passages of single words, mostly conjuring images of the natural world, intimacy, and a play of "opposites," arranged to fill the entire width of the page. Here is the first:

jump	stone	hand	leaf	shadow	sun
day	plash	coin	light	downstream	fish
first	loosen	under	boat	harbor	circle
old	earth	bronze	dark	wall	waver
new	smell	purl	close	wet	green
now	rise	foot	warm	hold	cool

(BB 40)

The second is similarly laid out, with the same words, but their individual placement is rearranged. These passages are instances of a hierarchically arranged language in which every word has equal importance—they are not hammered out in linear sequence but can be read vertically, horizontally, left to right or right to left. Each word derives its significance from resonance with the words around it; each, suspended in a halo of white space, interacts across the spaces with other words to form images and sonic resonances. This suggests the exchange of energy between lovers in which manhood is "not something that's there but only in the way we then make love"; manhood/meaning is not an essential a priori presence, nor can it unfold in only one way, but it comes to the foreground, recedes, and changes, depending on how the reader plays with its possibilities. The "passage" from the first of these serenely dynamic word groups to the second forms the agitated body of the poem; it constitutes the in-between of the sundered whole, a universe of atomic, unitary words throbbing in relation to each other. The in-between is history, which Duncan documents through renaissance painting, Walt Whitman's pre-Civil War admonitions, and the invocation of the devils of World War II and the Eisenhower-McCarthy era.

In Duncan's Manichean worldview, however, "evil" is as integral a part of the world as "good"—and clearly the complexity of art and politics provide a hectic excitement, the tumultuous magnetic field across which the twin halves of Edenic language poetry resonate. The eruption of chaotic difference—in diction, sources, and subject matter—into a field of sameness, is simply a part of life, as much as is the everyday words of the poem's frame, even when that "difference" includes

> ... the daily news: the earthquakes, eruptions,
> flaming automobiles, enraged loves, wars against communism,
> heroin addicts, police raids, race riots ...

(BB 42)

The millenial thrust of this poem has a somewhat painfully conventional history in the Western aesthetic tradition; Duncan is, after all, self-consciously heir to that tradition. At the same time, the image of the sundered twins and its relation to the subversively healing possibilities of desire puts Duncan's project on the margins of this tradition. He has himself written of his simultaneous loyalty to and mistrust of conventional philosophic constructs.[80]

One of the (Orphic) puns that extends throughout *Bending the Bow* is furthered in the title of "Chords: Passages 14." The Preface has anticipated this anatomical and lyric flourish by joining Hermes, the "gay" messenger god, with Apollo, lover of Hyacinthus:

> Hermes, god of poets and thieves, lock-picker then [who "brings men out"], invented the bow and the lyre to confound Apollo, god of poetry. *"They do not apprehend how being at variance it agrees with itself,"* Heraklitus observes: *"there is a connexion working in both directions."* (BB iv)

The title poem, addressed to Denise Levertov, echoes these words of Heraklitus and adds: "And I would play Orpheus for you again, / Recall the arrow of song ... " (BB 7-8). "Chords: Passages 14" itself proclaims us finally in "Fairyland, The Shining Land" (BB 46-47). "Spelling: Passages 15" is likewise a familiar pun—the game is form, spelling letters (as in the Ouija) and incantation. First up for discussion is, of course, the letter X: evoking mystery, Christ, conflict, juncture, and mystical crossroads:

> Christos, Chronos, Chord are spelld with *chi*, **X**   not
> K   (*kappa*) . . .
>
> . . .
>
> **Xaire**, rejoice **Xaos**, the yawning abyss. **Xaracter**,
>   the mark engraved, the *intalgio* [*sic*] of a man.
>   Xaris, Xaritas   grace, favor.
>
> (BB 48-49)

By simply naming archaic words (which again, for Duncan, are not only of the past), he calls these qualities into being: chaos, caritas. The poem is intended for performance before a group, complete with blackboard, so that the sonic and visual effects are part of the incantational formula—the listeners participate in the rite until the room is alive with the energy of language. And the poem concludes with a cute, flirtatious address to a single lover/listener. A history-of-English lesson based on Otto Jespersen's *Language*:

She was a maid	•	*the maiden kween.*
It is made of silk	•	*a silken dress.*
The man is old	•	*in olden days.*
The gold is hid	•	*the hidden gold.*
The room is warm	•	*all nicen warm.*

Then Duncan puts a gay slant on Conan Doyle:

> "I wish your eyes would always flash like that, for
>   it looks so nice and manly."
> It looks so nicen manly.

(BB 50)

The spelling lesson has drawn out the manliness of the listener, called it into play; it can now be erotically engaged. However, it would not be fair to suggest that the poem invokes magic "only" to seduce. If an erotic encounter is a mystical event, as Duncan's opus seems to argue, intimate address can well be the key (the "lock-picker") to the final and most important mystery, which is love. Love is cute, familiar, everyday stuff; but a taboo form of love requires a carefully elaborated summons if it is to achieve the venerable status of the familiar. The lofty language and appeal to etymology in the earlier part of the poem lays the groundwork for co-loquialism, speaking together in everyday tones.

In a final footnote to this complex process of sexual/intellectual intimacy, Duncan found support for this idea in Alfred North Whitehead's *Process and Reality*, a book that inspired both him and Olson in different ways. In particular, Duncan was fascinated by one of Whitehead's formulations and wrote of it several times to Robin Blaser: the idea of a logical proposition not as a statement of facts but as a "lure of feeling" designed to engage and stimulate an interlocutor's emotional and intellectual participation.[81] "Spelling" equates logical with erotic "proposition": both pose an invitation to shared adventure. There are not even, strictly speaking, two different propositions at work here, or even two levels at which the one proposition operates: the poem's final proposition, or any decent poem at all, Duncan would argue, delivers indivisible erotic, emotional, spiritual, and intellectual pleasure.

"The Torso"

Perhaps Duncan's most successful mature love poem is the much-discussed and beautiful "The Torso: Passages 18," whose title is not only a body part but an ironic pun on the "twistedness" of male desire for another male body. It is one of the most intensely rapturous contemporary descriptions of a body seen through the eyes of love.

"Torso," which comes from the Latin *thyrsus*: "stalk, stem"; in turn from the Greek *thyrsos*: "stem, wand"; thus gives us two body parts for the price of one. In addition, the statuesque and vegetative overtones (evoking the calamus plant) connote both the idolatrous objectification and the sense of organic wholeness and harmony with the natural world that characterize initial love encounters. Judy Grahn points out that the *thyrsus* was a ceremonial object, a penis-shaped wand that was carried in Bacchanalian processions and used for sexual magic in rituals.[82]

The body of the poem follows the contours of the human body, down to the groin and then up again. Beginning with the head/ intellect, the poet posits a metaphor, that of the "red-flowering eucalyptus, / the madrone, the yew" with its myriad puns (you-call-lip-to-us, mother, you) and then interjects the nagging question (itself a "head trip") of "availability":[83] "Is he . . . " This is completed several lines later: " . . . *homosexual?*" The movement from the "treasure of his mouth" to the "root of the neck" issues into a mid-section comprised of a rewrite of the Song of Songs in gay male terms:

> *the clavicle*, for the neck is the stem of the great artery upward into his head that is beautiful

> At the rise of the pectoral muscles

> *the nipples*, for the breasts are like sleeping fountains of feeling in man, waiting above the beat of his heart, shielding the rise and fall of his breath, to be awakend

> At the axis of his mid hriff

> *the navel*, for in the pit of his stomach the chord from which first he was fed has its temple

> At the root of the groin

> *the pubic hair*, for the torso is the stem in which the man flowers forth and leads to the stamen of flesh in which his seed rises
>
> (BB 63-64)

This paean to the beloved's botanical/anatomical assets (an echo, also, of Whitman's celebratory catalogues) then moves back up into dialogue, in which, however, the beloved—or the speaker's own desire—speaks of falling, once again a downward trajectory. The

lines cut by caesuras of space are finally joined by the word "seeking" when the lover/twins clasp hands in direct allusion to Whitman
(bringing to mind again Duncan's and Whitman's peculiar pagan
Christologies):

you do not yet know   but through me
And I am with you everywhere.   In your falling
I have fallen from a high place.   I have raised myself
    from darkness in your   rising
        wherever you are
my hand in your hand   seeking   the locks, the keys . . .
(BB 64)

Part of what I have termed "rapturous" in this poem is the sense of
ethereality, the ether-reality à la Duncan: the "aerated" quality of the
words themselves and the way they look on the page, luminous,
surrounded by their auras of white space. The poem achieves an un-
hurried, calm lightness, in the sense of both weightlessness and lu-
minescence, remarkable in such an explicitly sexual poem, the more
so since it engages the language of gravity and darkness as well as
levity and brightness, and since it roots itself in organic metaphor.
The lover himself is Luciferian, light falling from a high place, but the
sense of menace one would assume in such an allusion is absent. It is
as if, for this theosophically raised boy, Christ and Lucifer amount to
the same thing: they are angels who, going down, make you rise.

Falling is a key concept for Duncan, who discusses the idea at
length in the Gay Sunshine interview. In a subversion of the typical
ascent to enlightenment, the fall is a fall *into* grace through a fall into
the confusion of (making) love, with the need to work out the meaning of that love over a lifetime. In "The Torso," falling initially means
falling in love; the torso/penis of the Other, with its statuary overtones, is erected as a fixed and lapidary love object. When this revered Other speaks, he intentionally descends from (falls off) his
pedestal, and simultaneously raises himself from darkness in sexual
erection ("your rising"). The trajectory of the speaker's falling in love
is crossed by his own sexual arousal, and by the trajectory of the beloved's gracious refusal of an unequal relationship. Rising and falling
are thus arranged in a chiasmus, an X of juncture between worlds of
meaning crossing each other in passage, in which sexuality dissolves

the vertical value system of rising-as-superior-to-falling. Gravity *is* levity, mapped out as follows:

Falling in love means elevating an Other
X
the Other's descent means erecting a penis,

in sexual and soul "commingling," with all the puns therein implied.

It is clear that in spite of the loaded language of the poem Duncan is not simply giving us the standard morality of idolatry and guilt in which the Luciferian upstart falls. According to traditional Judeo-Christian cues to the reader, where there is Lucifer, there ought to be hierarchy and an implied power struggle of epic proportions; Wordsworth duplicates the original Oedipal agony with Milton, and so on. "The Torso" provides the epic diction requisite for this type of reading. But this is not the first time that Duncan, who has read deeply in Milton, subverts the purpose of that glorious theological revolutionary in a way that would make the Puritan recoil. "VARIATIONS UPON PHRASES FROM MILTON'S *The Reason of Church Government*" opens with a phallic pun as its first word and continues the sensual homage:

Organized, as perfect as an army there
your body lies. It gleams upon the sweet
unorganized, the field of dark. It flashes
in the evening air perfection's battlements
as naked blade as unsheath'd self.

(YC 25)

In turning religious and political prose into highly wrought homoerotic poetry, Duncan preserves the spiritual impact of the literature he alludes to even as he deconstructs its thundering patriarchal puritanism. In "The Torso," Duncan counters the hubris of Milton (whose great undertaking was, after all, to justify God's ways to man) with humility:

What do you want of me?

I do not know, I said. I have fallen in love. He
has brought me into heights and depths my heart
would fear without him. . . .

(BB 64)

In these opening lines of dialogue, the speaker is willing not to know. Reversing cultural (and certainly Miltonic) masculinist norms characterized by first-strike certainty, this declaration of openness makes union possible; the manhood isn't "there," it's created in the willingness to forego certainty, to trust and to be led up and down.

But we find the greatest counter to Miltonic orthodoxy in the poem's most direct allusion: its evocation of the master of power writers and one of Duncan's gay literary forebears. Not only are Whitman and Crane implicated in this text,[84] but Christopher Marlowe supplies some of the most euphoric language of the poem (l. 4-6):

> *So thou wouldst smile, and take me in thine arms*
> *The sight of London to my exiled eyes*
> *Is as Elysium to my new-come soul*

as well as the final, restful resolution, the concluding: *"The King upon whose bosom let me lie."* Duncan takes both of these passages from the opening speech of *Edward the Second*.[85] Civil war ensues because the king will not repudiate his minion, who is, significantly for Duncan's play on vertical/sexual movement, repeatedly derided as an "upstart." Most upsetting to the nobles are Gaveston's relatively humble (and French) origins and the king's devotion, which blinds him to matters more befitting a head of state (territorial expansion and conquest, for example). When asked why he so loves Gaveston, the king responds: "Because he loves me more than all the world." Marlowe's play is an unrelieved tragedy of intolerance, in which the guise of concern for the state's welfare is unmasked as homophobia, deception, dishonesty, and lust for power. The social denial of "manly love" consequently unravels all relationships: the king's and Gaveston's, the internal machinations of the state, England's status among its neighboring nations, and finally, as Edward the Third condemns his mother and her lover for engineering the king's torture and death, the king's surviving family.

Although Duncan draws his verse from some of the most beautiful homoerotic love poetry in the language, Marlowe does not portray Edward or his lover as a model of virtue. If anything he presents the couple critically, an instance of rejection of the homosexual superiority cult against which the young Duncan had railed in *Politics*. Edward's attitude toward his role as head of state is cavalier and silly, and he is fully as capable of cruelty as his torturers. No one could read *Edward the Second* as a sentimental and naïve plea for gay men as more "loving," or "better," than the heterosexual population. On

the contrary, Duncan's use of Marlowe underscores the latter's vision
as truly beyond good and evil. Marlowe unravels the neat hierarchic
dichotomies implicit in those terms. And Duncan, by juxtaposing him
with Milton, follows suit. Nowhere is this invocation and dissolution
of opposites more evident than in the couplet that follows the opening Marlovian lines:

> If he be Truth
> I would dwell in the illusion of him

The collapse of surface and depth, of truth and illusion into art and
love, finally breaks the hold of the Platonic intimations over the
poem and over Duncan's opus in general. Clearly Plato's heir,
Duncan does not deny his influence, but engages and undoes this
primary tenet of Plato's binary metaphysics and its homophobic legacy in Western culture. In the final lines of the poem, Duncan both
acknowledges and dissolves, as does the process of love and of
"drawing out" another's manhood, the separation between speaking
subject and beloved object. In doing so, he makes a direct connection between self-realization through erotic community and his
choice to be gay.

> I am there.   Gathering me, you gather
>   yourSelf
>
> For my Other is not a woman but a man
> *the King upon whose bosom let me lie.*
>   (BB 65)

*. . . we fall in love with a man, really we're falling in love with the
manhood we see possible in that person. . . . and that manhood is not
something that's there but is only there the way we then make love. So
our phrase making love is the same as making poems.*

Orpheus: An Appendix

As every piece of writing on Spicer will affirm, to speak of Jack Spicer
is to speak of Orpheus. Supreme traveler between worlds, Orpheus
was, like the car radio, Spicer's model for lyric production. Not only
does Spicer's use of this device constitute an oblique reference to
Cocteau, and thus a participation in the "half-hid" encomium to
other gay writers that infuses much gay writing. (We know who our

ancestors are and we honor them, say all marginal writers.) The figure of Orpheus has come to represent the romantic, the rapturous,
the all-consuming spirit of poetry in the West. Significantly, his songs
appealed not only to his

> fellow-mortals, but wild beasts were softened by his strains, and
> gathering round him laid by their fierceness, and stood entranced
> with his lay. Nay, the very trees and rocks were sensible to the charm.
> The former crowded round him and the latter relaxed some of their
> hardness.[86]

In other words, his songs dissolve the rigid taxonomies of the Great
Chain of Being, leveling the whole structure, from human beings to
rocks. Lyric poetry becomes the great interrupter of "natural order"
(read "institutional discourse"); wild beasts, trees, rocks belie their
"natures" and act like people in response to this liminal form of utterance, whose salient feature is beauty. Orpheus's songs even
charmed the rulers of the underworld, where he descended to retrieve his consort. His poetry, then, mediates life and death, upper air
and underworld, because his lyric powers are so persuasive. In a moment of doubt in those powers he loses Eurydice again. And according to Ovid, Orpheus's reaction to Eurydice's death is not to shun
human company (as later versions would have it) but to introduce
man-boy love into Thrace. Thus Orpheus, mythic male counterpart to
historical Sappho, is the father of same-sex—man-boy—love as well
as the father of lyric poetry.[87]

There are also striking similarities between the Orpheus myth and
the biblical tale of Sodom and Gomorrah, which likewise entails an
interdiction against looking backwards during an escape from a fiery
and hellish place—fiery and hellish because in the popular understanding Jehovah destroyed it to punish homoerotic practices. Judy
Grahn's research has unearthed several slang expressions for gayness meaning to walk backwards.[88] And there are other versions of
descents into the underworld in which a man goes in search of a
lover or a comrade-in-arms: Gilgamesh, for example, distraught by
the death of his lover, the wild man Enkidu, argues and pleads his
way into the spirit world in order to question a spirit wise man "concerning the living and the dead."[89] One of the small Bay Area presses,
run by Robert Duncan, was named Enkidu Surrogate; it published

Duncan's own *Caesar's Gate*, a book of poems based on the *Inferno*, around the theme of a descent into the urban gay underworld; and Spicer's *Billy The Kid*, a dictated eulogy for a beautiful boy cast in the image of the (wild man) American Western outlaw-hero:

I

The radio told me about the death of Billy The Kid. . . . Let us fake out
a frontier—a poem somebody could hide in with a sheriff's posse
after him— . . . a poem with no hard corners, no houses to get lost in,
no underwebbing of customary magic, no New York Jew salesmen
of amethyst pajamas, only a place where Billy The Kid can hide when
he shoots people.

. . .

X

Billy The Kid
I love you
Billy The Kid
I back anything you say
And there was the desert
And the mouth of the river
Billy The Kid
(In spite of your death notices)
There is honey in the groin
Billy

(BK, CB 79-83)

Spicer used the Orpheus myth in a specifically gay context, inextricably linking gayness with lyric poetry.[90] In what he considered his juvenalia, that is, before the days of dictation that began roughly in 1956 with *After Lorca*, his two poems "Orpheus After Eurydice" and "Orpheus in Hell" speak directly of the figure of homoerotic Orpheus.

Then I, a singer and hunter, fished
In streams too deep for love . . .
Mella, mella peto
In medio flumine.
His flesh is honey and his bones are made
Of brown, brown sugar and he is a god.

. . .

> I, Orpheus, had raised a water god
> That wept a honey tear . . .
>
> (ONS 20)

Again, however, Spicer's pessimistic ambivalence surfaces. Robert Duncan writes, in the preface to Spicer's posthumously published early poems, that "it is part of the travesty of theatre that we find Eurydice out to be a young man (as in high poetry Maximin for Stefan George was a counterpart of Dante's Beatrice)" (ONS, xii). Thus, in the foregoing poem, Orpheus would "get" Eurydice and the only twist to the plot is gender. But this is not entirely so. "Mella petere in medio flumine" is an Ovidian proverb meaning a vain and futile attempt—to seek honey in the river. The refrain of futility, in spite of its sonic beauty, counterbalances and threatens to overwhelm the speaker's insistence on fulfillment. The poem, moreover, is as autoerotic as it is homoerotic. In "Billy The Kid," honey is at the groin. Here, Orpheus, going too deep for love, has "raised a water god," a phallic image who weeps a golden honey tear. If love is sweet, it is also impossible in the "human" realm. Perhaps Orpheus can accomplish the impossible: as Spicer says in "The Poet and Poetry—a Symposium" (the title echoing Plato's discourse on manly love):

> Orpheus was a singer. The proudest boast made about Orpheus was not that his poems were beautiful in and of themselves. There were no New Critics then. The proudest boast was that he, the singer with the songs, moved impossible audiences—trees, wild animals, the king of hell himself. (ONS 91-92)

Perhaps poetry can redeem "metasexuality" from self-pity; solitary masturbation can become a divine encounter:

> What have I gone to bed with all these years?
> What have I taken crying to my bed
> For love of me?
> Only the shadows of the sun and moon
> The dreaming groins, their creaking images.
> Only myself.
>   ("Imaginary Elegies I-VI," CB 337)

On the other hand, alienation and the impossibility of intimacy, in Spicer's world, are preconditions for poetry. In "Orpheus in Hell,"

hell is a bar with a "jukebox groaning of the damned," and Eurydice is the aggregation of dead presences who cannot be moved; rather, their voices seem to demand the poet's attention, reversing the poet's customary role from speaker to listener. In a final couple of lines foreshadowing Spicer's own turn toward dictation: "Later he would remember all those dead voices / And call them Eurydice." Eurydice is not a woman but an idea, an aural memory. Recall that at the time Spicer was writing, gay bars were illegal, as was any touching between men in places suspected as gay bars. Thus the alienation is not simply metaphysical; "metasexuality" was actually mandated by hostile law, and while they may have represented contact and solidarity for some, Spicer experienced the bars he lived in as hells of frustrated communication.[91]

Gertrude Stein's Doggerel "Yiddish" Women, Dogs, and Jews

Perhaps at this point I ought to say a little something about my vocabulary. My conversation, spoken and written, is usually flavored with the jargon of the hipster, the argot of the underworld, and Yiddish.

Lenny Bruce[1]

To become animal is to participate in movement, to stake out a path of escape in all its positivity, to cross a threshold, to reach a continuum of intensities that are valuable only in themselves, to find a world of pure intensities where all forms become undone, as do all the significations, signifiers, and signifieds, to the benefit of an unformed matter of deterritorialized flux, of nonsignifying signs.

Gilles Deleuze and Félix Guattari[2]

"Becoming-Animal" / Becoming Human

The second epigraph, from Deleuze and Guattari's *Kafka: Toward a Minor Literature*, sets forth a crucial if somewhat extravagant definition of their term "becoming-animal," a process which for them characterizes not only a typical and recurrent theme in Kafka's short stories but also Kafka's tortured and tortuous language use in general. Rendering the German language absurd is what they call a "burrowing" (underground) technique in which a Kafka-animal deconstructs and undermines from within the structures of an oppressor language and its corollary "major" literature. He does this in the service of the revolutionary establishment of a "minor" literature that, paradoxically, derives its authenticity by virtue of its non-establishability—minority discourse is "deterritorialized flux," a "continuum of pure intensities," a world in which form has no final resting place. His language, like the animal state imagined by Deleuze and Guattari, is always on the move, metamorphosing from nothing into nothing— or at least, nothing describable by recognizable, stable structure or meaning.

The following is a discussion of Gertrude Stein's work seen in the context of these issues. Like Kafka, she is Jewish, writing primarily in a country whose national language, not her native tongue, forces her into a polyglot position. This kind of multilinguality is typical not only for such self-exiled modernists as Pound in Italy, the Irishmen Joyce and Beckett and the African-American Wright, like Stein, in Paris; but also for the Others within the walls of the city. Speakers of Black English, Yiddish, the Nuyorican of New York's Puerto Rican community, which differs from other "Spanglishes," and of argots not accorded the dignity of literary status: "girl-talk," the "queen's vernacular," Bruce's (and Kaufman's) "hipster's jargon," the criminal argot Genet celebrates, snatches of immigrant languages that finally only have meaning within the family in their own peculiar and private evolution—all master, by necessity, a plurality of languages that reflects both cultural richesse and cultural dislocation. Unlike Kafka, Stein is a woman and a lesbian, and chooses the further deracination of writing in a country that is not her native land. If Kafka's modernist "minor" discourse is a deterritorialized "animal" language by virtue of its anarchistic potentials, one might imagine that that of his contemporary Gertrude Stein would also be. To approach the problematic of Stein's work as minority discourse, it is first necessary to explore the criteria by which the dominant culture *allows* minorities to have written discourses at all, and what such writing might look like. In Stein's case the writing of woman-as-Jew-as-animal becomes exemplary of modernism at its most "abstract" and, simultaneously, its most earthily vernacular—her peculiar position in language turns domestic girl-talk, pet-talk, Jew-talk into incantational Orphic collage.

To be sure, Deleuze and Guattari's provocative picture of revolutionary marginality, of "unmeaning" as language "becoming animal," is a figure; these two philosophers and literary theorists—indeed most human beings—cannot know nonhuman animal experience. Deleuze and Guattari do not intend the foregoing sentences as an empirical statement of how nonhuman sentient beings understand themselves or the world, any more than "The Metamorphosis" represents or attempts to represent an insect's life. The passage is a projection of what these collaborating authors—two white European male critics—believe to be "animal," and thus becomes, by a process of converse deduction, a window onto what "human" must mean for them, assuming, as I think we can, that the passage derives its passionate and almost lyrical conviction from an implicit disjunction between "animal" and "human." If "animal"—or even less specifically, "becoming-animal"—represents the ultimate in "deterritorialized," unstable, "unmeaning" intensities, then "human" must mean linear, territorial (nationalistic), rational, and so on—all the characteristics contemporary theorists have decried as "phallogocentric." "Human," in other words, means patriarchal, Western-metaphysical; it describes a particular ideology and power structure currently associated with the middle-class educated European white male.

Even though Deleuze and Guattari clearly intend to criticize what is "human" and to valorize as revolutionary what is "animal," they duplicate hierarchic assumptions implicit in the Great Chain of Being. The projection (and romanticizing) of anarchic characteristics onto nonhuman animals, and the yearning of the ostensibly privileged to appropriate these characteristics as emancipatory, tends to reinforce the perceived differences in potentially dangerous, essentializing ways. Women, people of color, gay people, and members of the working classes, for example, are all too aware of the dangers of this type of projection, however well-intended.[3] Unmanageability in both positive and negative guise becomes the realm of the "Other," a catchall term used to include and elide differences between all manner of "outsiders" while overstating, perhaps, the differences between one's own privileged positions and these glamorous "Others." By using animals, rather than women (as in Nietzsche's "Woman") or Blacks (as in Rimbaud's "mon livre nègre") as their figure for exuberant (self-)exclusion, Deleuze and Guattari have made explicit the bestialization of the outsider that underlies much of Western metaphysical, political, and medical discourse. This bestialization parallels and elides into the "feminization" of outsiders—Jews, people of color, working-class people, and others, and the reverse, as in John Lennon's classic and problematic observation that "woman is nigger of the world." Since the animal-rights movement currently constitutes a cutting edge of liberation activism in America (notably, the most active spokespeople for this movement tend to be women), this

kind of elision will be seen as increasingly unjust to animals themselves, not only (as it is seen now) as an insult to the marginalized
human who is being compared to nonhumans. Those of us who belong to groups traditionally and disparagingly compared to other
species may be extra sensitive to this danger. It is remarkable to a
woman reader, for example, that Mark Shell's provocative analysis
"Family Pet," examining pets as transitional objects, does not
mention that the status of family pets is similar to that of women and
children as the owned, quasi-human, quasi-alien property of a household. Shell's analysis of "Beauty and the Beast," which dwells on the
bestiality of the beast as representative of male sexual energy, overlooks the (for me) crucial point that it is Beauty whose body is bar-
tered as chattel by the father and the Beast (who owns a mansion,
gardens, and servants); Beauty, not the Beast, is the slave/woman/
child/pet. Furthermore, Shell offers the example of the Playboy
"bunny" in the same vein as "puppy love"—an asexual, nonthreaten-
ing, cuddly toy—when the Playboy bunny has long epitomized for
feminists the ultimate in sexual objectification; that is, the human is
rendered petlike in order that she may be sexually exploited.[4]

The compelling point in Deleuze and Guattari's formulations, and
those of others similarly preoccupied, remains the question of language and power(lessness). Human philosophers have distinguished
human from animal beings according to the major criteria of language use and reason. Since there can be no objective standards for
evaluating a truly human mastery over what these two skills are or
even mean, the terms of definition remain in the hands of those who
are politically powerful. Thus the status of children can be challenged ("infans" meaning "unspeaking"), and the nature of any
group's use of language or way of knowing things can be judged as
disqualifying them from the current understanding of what constitutes proper language use or display of the ability to reason.

What is the language of slaves, women, children, pets, and other
outsiders who break into the modernist arena? Is it "animal"
language—unintelligible because unintelligent; or unintelligible because supra-intelligent—beyond rationalism? Is it Kristeva's quasi-
mystical "semiotic realm" of the pre-Oedipal, pre-subject/object period of life—sibylline utterances that mediate the gods' intentions
through nonsense? Is it Houston A. Baker's "vernacular," the language of the homeborn slave, with its connotations both of popular

accessibility and specialized, in-group initiation—like the "jargon" of Kaufman, Bruce, and Frederick Douglass's fellow slaves? Any investigation of the intersection of "minority discourse" with modernism and postmodernism, especially when the "minor" writer is one as formidably influential as Stein, eventually leads to questions such as the ones outlined above. How is the language of those in between human and animal on the Great Chain of Being to be assessed or understood?

Doggerel

When being human means having access to certain rights, those whose humanity has historically been challenged need to demonstrate, in order to be granted those rights, certain skills designated as insignia of humanity. One of the telling features of the privileged denizens of the Chain—the "real" humans—was their facility with written language, their access to writing. As Henry Louis Gates has pointed out in his discussion of the case of Phillis Wheatley, this meant that "minority" writers (in this case a Black woman), had to demonstrate an ability to write in order to be taken seriously as human beings.[5] In the 1772 trial surrounding Phillis Wheatley's "authenticity" as an author, one of the points of controversy was the familiarity she demonstrated, through the allusions in her poetry, with Pope, Milton (both of whom she cited as influences), and classical mythology. The issue was considered important (threatening) enough to be judged by representative luminaries of the dominant culture, among them John Hancock, a future "founding father," and Massachusetts governor Thomas Hutchinson. What finally secured her credibility as the author of the poems, however, opened the door to other kinds of criticism. Her work, while original in the sense that she indeed wrote it, was "derivative" and hackneyed: Thomas Jefferson, for instance, said it scarcely merited the term "poetry."[6] The sense that she was an earnest, ingenuous counterfeit made her safe to the representatives of the Boston community who stamped their approval on her poems; and centuries later it was to inspire irritation and contempt on the part of some Black Art poets (Amiri Baraka among them) who saw the same qualities—lack of an "original voice," docility, triteness—as proof of an intimidated assimilationist spirit they did not want associated with Blackness.[7] Most recently, however, her work has undergone critical redemption due to the efforts of Black feminists and a later generation of Black critics.[8]

There is, of course, a double bind here: if one did write in imitation of white men, one was dismissed as "derivative"; if one's primary cultural expression was different from writing (dance, textile arts, or oral storytelling, for example), one was either not recognized at all, or derided as "flouting convention" in a way both childish and threatening (Isadora Duncan is a classic case of a woman derided as morally suspect because of the unconventionality and physicality of her art). This is especially poignant, it seems, in the case of women modernists. The characteristics praised in men such as Joyce and Pound for being "assaults on language," that is, on traditional language use, were not open to women. I still see Ph.D. oral examination booklists and syllabuses on "modernism" that omit Stein, Woolf, Hurston. Furthermore, men such as Pound, Eliot, and Joyce covered their flanks in this "assault" by their appeal to the authority of *older* patriarchal literary traditions: Pound's Provençal poets; Eliot's insistence, in "Tradition and Individual Talent," on claiming modernist writers as direct heirs to the Western literary tradition; and Joyce's engagement with the *Odyssey*. (Of course, some women did this as well: Hilda Doolittle's use of Greek mythological themes is a case in point. However, H. D. could be said to be reconstructing a buried matriarchal mythology more than borrowing from a patriarchal one.)

In other words, one of the ways of proving one's authenticity, as a member of a lower caste, is to sound trite and derivative—mass-cultural and mass-produced. The South Boston girls' poetry, for example, with its heavy rhymed couplets and its old-fashioned sense of what constitutes "poetry," could not be confused with the work of an MFA student in creative writing who is more likely to value the current conventions of "organic form" and "individual voice"; hence the Southie collection can be considered the authentic and unthreatening utterance of working-class teenagers. But its authenticity *as poetry* has been questioned, in the colleges and universities where I have presented it, precisely because its rhymes and stanzas do not attempt to simulate an unmediated cry of pain. It does not work hard enough at looking artless to be considered art by the keepers of the canon. The familiar terms of the high art / mass culture debates can be discerned as an undercurrent of this discussion; it is only one step from Andreas Huyssen's "feminization" to the "bestialization" of mass culture as "modernism's Other": the masses are seen as bestially slothful, domesticated by the drug and discipline of mass culture, but potentially anarchic when aroused by the wrong kind of mass culture—rock concerts and movies about gang violence, for example. When subculturals—Bob Kaufman, Robert Duncan, Gertrude Stein—storm the citadel of high art and take mass culture along, a fabulous hybrid poetry results, a bastard-child language born of doggerel and wild modernist abstractions.

"Doggerel," the favored term for derivative poetry, is "trivial, weakly constructed verse." The *Oxford English Dictionary*, always a suspect source because of its assumptions about what constitutes quotable literature, cites the first use of the term as occurring in Chaucer's *Canterbury Tales*; in the "Tale of Sir Thopas," one of his characters mocks his own verse as "rym doggerel."[9] *The Princeton Encyclopedia of Poetry and Poetics* offers an example of this "vice" contemptuously written by Samuel Johnson; canonical authors only use doggerel for "satirical or comical" ends. The *Princeton Encyclopedia* characterizes doggerel as "rough, poorly constructed verse characterized by monotonous rhyme and rhythm, cheap sentiment, triviality and lack of dignity," and cites Northrop Frye's speculation that it reflects an "unfinished creative process."[10] (Immediately this brings to mind the modernist penchant for process rather than product, and complicates any easy dichotomy between the beastly doggerel and the masterful modernist text.) Etymologically, *doggerel* stems from Italian "barrel stave," as in German "knuttelvers," or cudgel verse—rough-hewn poetry. It is also, by popular association, influenced by "dog," as in "dog latin"—fake or ungrammatical Latin. In each case there is a sense of cheap imitation, of high-art authenticity counterfeited by the clumsy "doggery"—the riffraff, the common people. "Bastard verse," says the *OED*, bastion of literary purity. What is "bastard"? Meaning "sham, inferior," the word is derived from "stable; barnyard animals." In other words, bad, overdetermined rhyme is etymologically associated with domestic animals. Through this association, it would seem to be a "women's" vice, via the "feminization of mass culture," and one might guess especially with owned women—chattel property—thus the authentication of Wheatley's authorship of specifically *un*startling, sentimental poetry. Most popular, "low-brow" fiction is currently written by women, and this phenomenon would appear to have a cultural tradition: as long ago as the previous century, Nathaniel Hawthorne bewailed the "damned mob of scribbling women" with whose "trash" the "public taste [was] occupied," and who, by association, made literary popularity in itself a shameful matter.[11] This mob's habit of using all three names especially annoyed him. (Their maiden and married names give them away as wives, in other words, inappropriate writers.) Samuel Johnson's remark about women preachers also comes to mind: like dogs walking on their hind legs, the remarkable thing is not that it's done well, but that it's done at all. The less well done it is, the more palatable.

Doggerel is characterized by formulaic or continued rhymes, clumsy meter, "cheap sentiment." There is something tremendously appealing about heavy rhyme: the unintentionally comical lines in the South Boston poetry: "The pot started to boil over / Someone had to let out Rover," or my favorite: "Now I'm in a home for unwed mothers / But why should you care you have all the others?" Some of the same effect can be found in Rastafarian poetry: "O terrible sin abortion! It is the worst of all / Eight letters spell the deadly sin, so is downfall ... "[12] I find the earnest desire to please, to display one's verbal acuity through this ornamentation, juxtaposed against the intensity of emotional outraged "message," powerfully moving. So must the general public: the 1989 movie *The Sea of Love* used rhyming personal ads as the mechanism that set in motion both a psychotic killer and a passion that redeems a couple of lost souls. Less profoundly compelling but poignant nonetheless is an example that appeared in the *Palo Alto Weekly*:

> I used to smoke, I still joke, I drink diet coke. I'm a double Y, I'm
> easy on the eye, I don't lie. I'm white, it'll be lust at first sight, think
> about it, tonight. ... I need a woman whose ears are long, whose
> back is straight and strong, who sometimes breaks out in song. Who
> wants to be a mother, who needs a faithful lover, who's not sleeping
> with another. Who's not overly fed, whose parents are still wed,
> who's good in, the kitchen. ... I was at large on Oahu when I was a
> lad. I'm a recycled husband, it's true and sad, but up to this date I'm
> not a dad. I've supported myself for twenty one years of my life, from
> slums far away still filled with strife. ... Gawd, I need a wife. ... [13]

One can almost see this doggerel wagging its tail with eagerness to delight and entertain. In the library section where I was directed by a computer search for "Doggerel" in book titles, I found *Doughboy Doggerel: Verse of the American Expeditionary Force 1918-1919, Cowboy Poetry: A Gathering, The Hobo's Hornbook, Betcha Ain't: Poems from Attica, Nuyorican Poetry.*[14] Would it be belaboring an obvious point to observe that ethnically and economically marginalized working people, whose often anonymous poetry appears in these anthologies, are typically considered to be writers of "bastard verse"? I have never heard the charge publicly leveled at Byron, but the most endearingly contrived couplet I can think of comes from *Don Juan*: "What men call gallantry, and gods adultery, / Is much more common where the climate's sultry."[15] Byron deconstructs the Romantic sublime and the notion of form as an organic extension of the poet's mental process with *Don Juan's* relentless stream of hilarious contortions.

As "bastard verse," doggerel cannot be proven to be descended from a line of clear heritage. It is itself a dangerous hybrid. The association of "bastard," with barnyard animals implies the "uncitationality" (un-pin-down-ability) of both women and of domesticated chattel. Women, slaves are bastard. Women write doggerel. Women, in contemporary misogynist slang, are "dogs" if they are found wanting in physical beauty, or "bitches" if their dispositions do not measure up. What exactly is a dog? Dog is god backwards, the Chain neatly and explicitly leveled ("level" being a palindrome whose reversal balances the chain: dog levels god) in a three-letter monosyllable, the central letter — o — a pivotal symbol in Western women's culture: the *Story of O* parodies women's sexual experience by asserting that we thrive on being nullified (zeroed); Monique Wittig punctuates *Les Guerrillères* with circles to reassert continuity, a dissolution of the teleology of "phallogocentric" linearity.[16] The canine deconstructs the canon. Dogs chase their own tails in play as a cliché for useless activity, as writing has been defined for women, even as writing would have proved their humanity. (In the nineteenth century, writing was determined to be hazardous to women's health, taking away the energy necessary for reproductive activities.) "A rose is a rose is a rose," in circular insignia above the bed of a lesbian couple, Gertrude Stein and Alice Toklas, blesses their non-reproductive — "useless" — sex play.

God-dog, goddamn, doggone! Anne Sexton adopted as her persona the "liberated female deity Ms. Dog" because it reversed and appropriated God for the newly resurgent feminist movement.[17] The model and model suburban housewife turned poet was the dog who dared be god, the woman who dared to write—who wrote to save her life, having heard a sonnet on TV at age twenty-eight after a nervous breakdown and deciding, "I could do that, maybe; I could try."[18] Elizabeth Bishop's "The Moose" explicitly reverses the Chain by offering the female moose/muse as epiphanic apparition, "high as a church, / homely as a house," inducing a "sweet sensation of joy" in the passengers of the bus the moose has stopped. En route to the divine encounter, three dogs herald the event: the maternal collie supervising a human leavetaking (l. 35); the prophetic single dog-bark accompanying the single red light that "swims through the dark" (l. 71); and the "dog / tucked in her shawl" that safeguards the home of the older couple, ensuring that "Now, it's all right now / even to fall asleep" (ll. 124-27). Here, both domestic and wild animals are protective goddesses, secretly governing human affairs and offering mystical sustenance.[19] We need hardly mention Marianne Moore's animal poems here, which render the described beasts abstract with her characteristically busy and difficult language; in a sense, Moore "deterritorializes" them, separates the name "swan" or "jerboa" or "snail" from our easy understanding of what these beings are.[20] The ubiquity of dogs—the poodles Basket I and II and Pepe the chihuahua—in Stein's later writings attest to their status as guardian spirits of experimental language. That a woman read and write continues to constitute an experiment in freedom and assimilation: Stein's *First Reader*, intended as a children's first experience with print, opens with "A dog said he was going to learn to read."[21] Likewise, the opening sentence of "Saving the Sentence" is "Qu'est-ce que c'est cette comédie d'un chien" (HW 13). What kind of joke is this, anyway, a woman creating language? A later piece in the same book also plays on language as a gendered domain: the appositive "Arthur a Grammar," reunderstood as the imperative "Author a grammar," shifts a description of patriarchal structure to a prescription for a woman (Stein herself, at least) to write her own grammar (HW 37).

In short, "doggerel" is poetry produced by "becoming-humans" en route to proving their full human status; it is in between human "poetry" and the animal "rhymes" or rhythms of everyday life and labor, a transitional genre. Closely related to oral culture, it probably has its origins in the same place as its now distant relative the lyric—in song. Certainly many of the hobo songs and much of the cowboy poetry we know comes to us with melody; think also of deeply moving rock lyrics whose effect flattens when we see only the lyrics on the album's inner sleeve. Some forms of "doggerel" still have their own attendant dance forms—breakdancing, for example, as movement accompanying rap music, a heavily rhymed form of poetry whose subject matter often joins sexual and verbal rhyming— "rapping"—prowess.

Rhyme and the trite phrase seem to be crucial factors in doggerel. Both of these fix things in memory and thus in time—their familiarity and hence success inevitably depends on the idea of time/narrative. Particularly, rhyme's delight hangs on the resolution of a temporal problem—two words separated temporally and spatially, whose aural kinship creates a relationship across time and space: literally, when this you hear/see, remember me. The earlier rhyme word creates memory and resolves the unfulfilled element of nostalgia. Rhyming words epitomize the paradox of difference within sameness, a concept central to all of Gertrude Stein's intellectual endeavors, from her early psychological studies of different types of temperament to her literary experiments in repetition and change.

Rhyme is a mnemonic device, like a "saying" that fixes a culture: "A stitch in time saves nine." "Early to bed and early to rise / makes a man healthy wealthy and wise." Ben Franklin's American epigrams and maxims capture the "hardworking decency" and perseverance Stein admired about the American middle class. Her own "talisman" sentences have much more to do with mental process and portraiture, but capture the culture of modernism through mass-cultural, middle-class domestic icons—the autograph book jingle, the family pet, the flower garden: "When this you see, remember me." "I am I because my little dog knows me." "A rose is a rose is a rose." In her work, these sentences and rhymes orient the reader amid a stream of private syllables. Rhyme is a public device, an ornament signifying public display. Obtrusive snatches of rhyme frame "Lifting Belly," for instance, in the same way "frozen frames" fix a film's endless succession of similar but slightly different frames, emerging out of and underscoring by their fixity the preceding frames' stream of movement:

Little love lifting
Little love light.
Little love heavy.
Lifting belly tight.
    (LB, YGS 51)

On a very simple-minded level, rhyme is language that calls attention to its own artistry—hence the embarrassment about rhyme in a period in which modernism has permeated popular culture with its prizing of "organic" form, and its relegation of rhyme either to the domain of overly conservative high-art poets—irascible conservatives such as Yvor Winters, who believed in the "orderliness" of rhyme as analogue to the orderliness of the moral universe;[22] or to the domain of the opposite end of the spectrum—writers of "doggerel," those poor benighted souls who believe that simply by rhyming words they are creating "art," the producers and consumers of mass-cultural greeting cards, song lyrics and advertisements. Rhyme is contrived: the Romantic-modernist dictum that poetry be an expression of spontaneity—of "spontaneous emotion" or perception—has led to a concept of poetry as "therapeutic" and that any statement of sentiment arranged with arbitrary line breaks constitutes a poem. To take just one example, a psychiatrist ("M.D."), a psychologist ("Ph.D.") and a poet collaborated to create the wildly popular ("2,000,000 COPIES IN PRINT") self-help book *How to Survive the Loss of a Love*; short, sentence-long poems on the right-hand page—in italics to call attention to their special status as poems—gloss and concretize the foregoing prosaic advice on "what to do with your Sundays," "how much pain to let yourself feel," "how to be good to yourself," and so on.[23] Across from chapter 14, "Surround Yourself with Things that Are Alive," is the following:

I'd have a nervous breakdown
only
I've been through
this too many
times to be
nervous.[24]

"Poetry" becomes a series of gentle, uplifting—"inspirational"—aperçus; rhyme would spoil the effect of unmediated thought. Rhyme belongs in the province of the vulgar or the overly refined—who are unconcerned with the primacy of "feelings."

"Yet Dish"

Richard Bridgman explicitly associates Stein's fondness for doggerel with her "domestic" period—the World War I years of forcibly circumscribed household activity on Mallorca during which she wrote much of *Bee Time Vine*.[25] The title *Bee Time Vine*, besides its nesting, honeyed and bucolic flavor, combines several familiar themes: "bovine," domestic animalism; "between," the in-between status of animal becoming human; and of course "time," the question of time and the human mind's construction of it through narrative, all of which are touched on implicitly in the composition of doggerel verse. In addition, doggerel is hybrid; to extend the agricultural implications of "vine," doggerel is a fruitful replenishing of language through combination and recombination. The other side of bastardry is hybrid vigor, the cross-pollination of "bee time vine." In one piece from *Bee Time Vine*, "Yet Dish," Stein explicitly alludes to a crossover language.

The cryptic "Yet Dish," which Richard Kostelanetz characterizes as a "skit" (YGS xi), is a collage of words and phrases from childhood woven asymmetrically by the governing linguistic metaphor, the mother's language, *mama loshen*, "Yid-Dish." The fracturing, rehearing of "Yiddish" as "yet dish" teases out the traditional association of Yiddish with the kitchen and domesticity sparked by the syllable "dish," the sense of confused time, time deferred, in the process of becoming, sparked by the syllable "yet." Stein treats the child's brain and aural mechanism as a *tabula rasa* typewriter transcribing phrases without differential emphasis or value ("Meal dread": Mildred in a heavy European accent—probably Mildred Aldrich, a close friend of Stein's Parisian household). What is Yiddish itself but a hybrid of:

XLVIII

Polish polish is it a hand, polish is it a hand or all . . .

XLIX

Rush in rush in slice.

L
Little gem in little gem in an. Extra.

LI
In the between egg in, in the between egg or on.
(YD, YGS 61)

Yiddish is a little Polish, a little "rush in"/Russian, a little "gem in"/
German—and as a crossover, immigrant language, Yiddish is by definition "in the between again." "Egg in" as "again" reverses and re-
capitulates the movement of puns in "yet dish" as "Yiddish": "egg in"
concretizes in a female symbolic round noun (egg) and a preposition
traditionally associated with women (*in*teriority, domesticity, the
"private" sphere) the strange temporality implicit in the word
"again." While "yet" implies deferment, a play of expectations in the
space between "now" and the future moment captured in the sus-
pension of "yet," "again" is cyclical, reassuring, constant, hypnotic: a
rose is a rose is a rose, again and again and again. Yiddish is in between again, a reassuring constant, a *lingua franca* in the change of
nationalities and national languages characterizing Jewish history,
mediating sacred language and that of the host(ile)/dominant gentile
culture. However, an in-between language is not only constant, but
infinitely flexible and changeable, adapting to and affecting subtly
the material conditions in which it finds itself, changing as if by
micromovements:

XLIV
Lean over not a coat low.
Lean over not a coat low by stand.
Lean over net. Lean over net a coat low hour stemmed
Lean over a coat low a great send. Lean over coat low extra extend.
(YD, YGS 60)

Language, which the poet Clark Coolidge has called "the thinnest
fabric or substance imaginable," is also the strongest and most elastic: it is a collagen.[26] This is especially true of a language invented on
the run, a language designed to serve in exile. Yiddish is a language
of movement, which binds to each other, with infinite permission for
change, the languages it travels through and connects. Even changes
in spelling, affecting changes in consciousness, are part of an unpredictable, unteleological progression:

XXIV
Meal dread so or bounce two sales. Meal dread so or bounce two sails
. . .

(YD, YGS 58)

or, in this famous passage from another work in which the lesbian
author gets to say "gay" over and over, invoking the principle of repetition that is one of the trademarks of Stein's earlier work:

> Helen Furr was living somewhere else then and telling some about
> being gay and she was gay then and she was living quite regularly
> then. She was regularly gay then. She was quite regular in being gay
> then. She remembered all the little ways of being gay. She used all
> the little ways of being gay. She was quite regularly gay. She told
> many then the ways of being gay, she taught very many then little
> ways they could use in being gay. She was living very well, she was
> gay then, she went on living then, she was regular in being gay, she
> always was living very well and was gay very well and was telling
> about little ways one could be learning to use in being gay, and later
> was telling them quite often, telling them again and again.
>   ("Miss Furr and Miss Skeene," SW 568)

The insistence on "regularity" belies the constant, slight alterations
that are micromovements in the continuum of the body of
language—language moves and changes infinitesimally and surprisingly *inside* the body cultural as well as the body physiobiological.
Language here is cinematic. Carolyn Copeland has commented on
Stein's filmicity: "Gertrude Stein spoke of the cinema technique and
how it is used to present one frame, slightly different from the next,
without exact repetition."[27] Language becomes a meditative dance;
the Heraklitean and electrical current in these endless, minutely
changing repetitions lies underneath the skin, in the charges between the words and the letters on the page, which can only be ap-
preciated when given full visual, auditory, oral, vibrational attention.
The animalism of "furr" and "skeene"/skin also evokes a multiplicity
of associations: the softness of pets and petting, the electrical and sexual charge of fur rubbing on fur, the rhyming regularity of animal
domesticity, the "naturalness" of a life at which the world looks
askance. "Skeene" is also, of course, a skein of yarn, a continuity, a
coil made from the fur or wool of animals who are shorn yearly without harm to them. Stein's piece is a skein of words, endlessly coiling.
The regularity of the replenishment of this natural resource, and of

the process of weaving the text/ile product (and the story is about "telling"), shows up the false distinction between the artist's fabrications and the beast's instinctual, sensuous functions.

The incantational effect of simple, concrete words repeated cumulatively opens up to different interpretational directions:

> XL
> Lock out sandy.
> Lock out sandy boot trees.
> Lock out sandy boot trees knit glass.
> Lock out sandy boot trees knit glass.
>
> (YD, YGS 60)

Each time a word is added, the parts of speech and the images accompanying the sounds change. "Lock out sandy" suggests locking a person or animal named Sandy out of a house or a room. Add "boot trees," and we get sandy boots or sandy boot trees. Add "knit glass" and "trees knit glass" — the image is of intricate winter icicles on bare trees — as well as, when "knit" is joined with the earlier syllable, "knit booties." Or, alternately, boot trees made of "knit glass," that is, glass sculpted to look braided or otherwise rhythmically enmeshed. Knit glass is a wonderful image for language — translucent or transparent patterns invisibly holding culture in shape from the inside.

The piece is not "about" Yiddish. It is written in English, and has no obviously apprehensible Yiddish phrases. Antirepresentational Steinians would rightfully say that even to suggest a "single meaning" or any meaning at all is reductive, an attempt to evade the much headier and more difficult project of talking about a text, about language, without talking about it as representational. Rather than suggesting a single meaning, in seeing "Yet Dish" as a field of possibilities, I'm teasing out, through the apprehension of a single pun, one thematic strand that gathers together implications of domesticity, exile and marginality, language play, and movement. Stein's text gives permission to hold multiple possibilities in question and to move in multiple directions, and this is also what the metaphor of Yiddish does; it speaks of a language that constantly generates new meanings and can neither be pinned down nor killed off.[28] As Deleuze and Guattari say of Kafka, who was also heavily influenced by Yiddish though he wrote in a dominant tongue,

What is complicated is Kafka's relation to Yiddish; he sees it less as a sort of linguistic territoriality for the Jews than as a nomadic movement of deterritorialization that reworks the German language.[29]

Of course, as Yiddishists are quick to point out, Yiddish is no more simply a "reworking" of German than Dutch is, or than French would be of Latin;[30] Deleuze and Guattari, in their attempt to valorize rootlessness as "deterritorialization," risk the charge of indulgence in a romantic, exoticizing form of anti-Semitism. But while the actual Yiddish language made its public appearance as a fixed and worthy literary venue just at the dawn of the high modernist age—the turn of the century—it has also operated metaphorically in the European imagination in precisely the way that Deleuze and Guattari outline it here. Paradoxically, as it becomes an internationally acclaimed literary language, written by men in the public sphere as opposed to simply being spoken in the private, women's domain, Yiddish also takes on the symbolic significance of an improvised language of exile characterized by the highly valorized modernist tenets of constant change and fragmentation. (Cynthia Ozick points out an additional irony: the highly self-conscious, minimalist artistry of Sholem Aleichem, who is largely responsible for this elevation of Yiddish into the modernist mainstream, has come to be misunderstood as simple-minded, transparent nostalgia—anathema to modernist sensibilities.)[31] In her use of Yiddish—again, not in her writing *about* or *in* Yiddish—in her invocation of Yiddish as a representative model of what happens when language cuts loose from the moorings of cultural and syntactical respectability or convention as a "mama loshen," Stein does not neutralize or "domesticate" (in the word's traditional sense) the subversive potential of a domestic language for a people with no official domicile. Rather, in its very domesticity, in its inherent status as domesticated, Yiddish is anarchic—a bastard, barnyard language of chattel animals: women, slaves—Jews. It is doggerel, "bastard German," the vernacular of European Jewry with all the etymological connotations of the term "vernacular" that Houston A. Baker has explored with reference to Black American culture—the language of the homeborn slave.[32] Sander Gilman (one of those who refers to Aleichem as simpleminded and pious—or, at least, comical and sentimental)[33] offers a sample of Christian-generated nonsensical "Jewish" poetry from sixteenth-century Germany:

> We poor Jews complain of the pain of hunger
> and must die, have no bread
> oime give compassio
> cullis mullis lassio
> Egypt was a good land
> wau wau wau wau wiriwau

and comments:

> The Jews' muddled German, mixed with bits of Italian, Latin and
> *dogg*erel (*wau* is the sound that German dogs make), illustrates the
> subhuman nature of the Jews' language, a language of marginality.
> But it also defuses any sense of anxiety about this marginality by
> turning this language into the language of the comic.[34]

The refrain is literally German dog-talk; Jews are dogs. Yiddish's elevation to a literary language, in fact a consciously revolutionary act
on the part of Sholem Aleichem and others, was characterized by an
even further deracination and declaration of antinationalistic independence: it abandoned its "pernicious" tendency toward etymological
correctness—that is, its allegiance to the host/oppressor languages it developed from. In the new literary movement, "words were used according to their precise Yiddish phonology and semantics, without
reference to—and sometimes in defiance of—their form and meaning in the stock languages."[35] Similarly, "Yet Dish," while using familiar words and syllables, declares independence from anything we
might know as literary, narrative English usage. It is a collage of other
languages, squeezed through a screen of English in a way that rends
and renders English collagistic, permeable, patterned, abstract, an
elastic membrane. (One could speculate that English functions as a
screen in the same way that screen-memories or screen-dreams
shield an adult from direct knowledge of primal trauma, which in this
case would be not Yiddish itself, but the brutality of anti-Semitism during the time when Yiddish was truly a living language—hence the
scorn and hatred many contemporary Jews have for Yiddish as the
"language of the ghetto.") Stein Yiddishizes English. She deconstructs or, in Deleuze and Guattari's terms, "deterritorializes" English
through her pre-Oedipal connection with a maternal language, both
"abstract" and "primal," that is itself an abstract collage of oppressor/
host languages.

The commonly spoken vernacular of European Jews since the

tenth century c.e., Yiddish, which means only "Jewish," has in fact only had an official, capitalized name and an acknowledged literary presence since the end of the nineteenth century, when it catapulted into cultural respectability. Prior to that time (which time corresponds to Stein's adolescence and early maturity), Yiddish was, in Cynthia Ozick's words, known by a

> term of opprobrium—*zhargón*. Gibberish; prattle; a subtongue; something less than a respectably cultivated language. Yiddish was "jargon" to the intellectuals despite its then eleven million speakers (before the Nazi decimation), despite the profusion of its press, its theatre, its secular educational systems, and its religious and political movements, and despite its long (though questionable) history of literary productivity.[36]

"Jargon," which we encountered in Bob Kaufman's project, once again takes on the double-edged connotations marking the controversies around Stein's work: it is both gibberish, the babble of animals, and a sophisticated code of ungraspable meaning, conveying esoteric knowledge of the chosen few—in Kaufman's case, the jazz hipster. Another hipster, a Jewish American verbal artist whose comedy was avowedly permeated with a Yiddish sensibility, comments on his relationship to abstraction and to the jazz world:

> The reports on me were now: "All Lenny Bruce seems concerned with is making the band laugh." That should have been my first hint of the direction in which I was going: abstraction. Musicians, jazz musicians especially, appreciate art forms that are *extensions* of realism, as opposed to realism in a representational form.[37]

Always on the run—from his inharmonious family, from the law, from himself—Bruce died in 1966 of what may have been an intentionally suicidal overdose of heroin.[38] Posthumously he became a cult figure of sorts, admired by a generation of alienated young Americans, perhaps representing (like Kafka and Kaufman) the self-destructive possibilities of Yiddishness, of lived "collagism," using Yiddish and his other in/subgroup languages as the "idiomatic fog that veils the user."[39] In Stein's case, several different "chosen few" minorities have claimed her as speaking for their esoteric communities: avant-garde modernists and more recently lesbian feminists have designated her the "mother of us all."[40] She has come to epitomize the spirit of brave experiment, both in her writing and in the

way she lived her affective life. In the same way that Yiddish impro-
vises its "jargon" in the realm of home and affection, the matter with
which Stein carried out her "abstract," nonrepresentational experiment in art and her "nonreproductive" experiment in domestic life is
not esoteric in the least: What could be more complacently democratic than everyday language and human affections in domestic
relationship? Like Kaufman, but more thoroughly because less po-
lemically, she "unmeans" English by turning the simplest and most
conversationally domestic syllables into literary and philosophical
discourse. The talisman sentence, "I am I because my little dog
knows me," for example, becomes a treatise on the difference between "entity" (movement, dedication to an unmediated apprehension of an object) and "identity" (a need to be fixed and recognized
and given meaning by an other), on the difference between "human
mind" and "human nature" (IP, WM 71-79). By foregrounding animal
recognition (intuition) over a rational process, moreover, the sentence revises and implicitly criticizes Descartes' *cogito ergo sum*, one
of the most devastating slogans of modern Western humanism.[41]
    A piece in English that takes Yiddish as its model? The cute "Yet
Dish" eludes comprehensive analysis, the salient feature of Stein's
work remaining what Marjorie Perloff calls its "indeterminacy."[42]
Possibilities proliferate, but one monolithic meaning can't be pinned
down. Is it "threatening"? I don't know. The critical establishment's
patronizing dismissals of Stein certainly suggest a degree of defensiveness, a self-constitutive response to a threat "from below."[43]
Stein's relation to this critical/literary mainstream is analogous to
Yiddish's relation to the national languages which comprise it and
which it replenishes, or even mass-cultural doggerel's relation to
high art's rigid fear of "ordinariness." Words like "shmooze,"
"kvetch," "shmageggie," and "schlepp" are appealing, fun to say, and
easily find their way into mainstream English. As Ozick points out, "it
is hard to be pretentious and elevated in Yiddish. . . . In its tenderer
mien, Yiddish is capable of a touching conversational intimacy with a
consoling and accessible God."[44] Yiddish, in other words, is "down
to earth," lower than either Hebrew or other national languages on the
linguistic chain of being. But Yiddish as a whole, discursive, linear
language barely exists, particularly after World War II. This fragmentation of a language through violence makes its surviving syllables
even more precious and more deconstructive than when Stein was

writing. As a diaspora language, Yiddish is now a quintessential de-constructive language, in that it has no unified cultural or geopoliti-cal referent. Its isolated words and inflections continue as haunting traces of what was already before the Holocaust a metalanguage. Sig-nificantly, Jacques Derrida, whose term "deconstruction" is, is a Sephardic Jew. The Sephardic equivalent of Yiddish—Judesmo or Ladino—is currently even more fragmented and evanescent than Yiddish. It is worth speculating about the relationship between Derrida's Jewishness, the status of Ladino, and his philosophy of the nonreferentiality of language. Just as Yiddish operates as a metaphor for Stein, who ostensibly writes in and about English, so Ladino or Judesmo could be seen as an underlying metaphor/model for Derrida's philosophy of language. The controversy that surrounds Derrida's theories involves people's unwillingness to accept the non-referentiality of comfortably established dominant languages. Just as Aimé Césaire has claimed that Hitler colonized Europe in a logical "eternal return" of Europe's colonization of Africa,[45] and just as Tadeusz Borowski found, after his release from Auschwitz, that the whole world is a concentration camp,[46] Derrida could be extrapolat-ing from a specific history of oppression. Unthreatening as long as it is left specific and localized, such an analysis becomes radically pow-erful and disturbing when more generally applied.

An elastic language, a language that slips through the cracks of other languages even as it bears the marks of the cultures and lan-guages it slips through, is a language that borrows and, in Deleuze and Guattari's terminology, burrows. Yiddish is an underground lan-guage, an animal language. Even the radical disjunction/conjunction between its spoken and written media points toward its status as "code"—the weird association of a homey (haimish), humorous, "household" language characterized by "coziness" and a sense of the diminutive with the high spiritual drama of Hebrew lettering creates a dizzying, defamiliarizing effect. The seemingly violent conjunction suggests two possibilities: either Yiddish is a "spoken" language and the lettering an "unnatural" superimposition—after all, it is the lan-guage of mothers (women were not permitted to learn Hebrew, though often the rabbi's wife would teach them clandestinely); or its aural accessibility and engaging warmth is deceptive—an alien threat rendering itself harmless and jovial and only assuming its true gran-deur in its transfixing written aspect. Or it is both animal and otherworldly, both domestic and transcendentally, passionately hieratic. Yiddish's power lies in its dissolution of a material/spiritual dichotomy. This is also the power of Stein's writing. (This is, of course, true to varying degrees of any language and any writer. But it is particularly true of as hybridized and fragmented a language as Yiddish and as "minor" a writer as Stein.) She fulfills the Williams-Creely dicta for the supremacy of the material in modernist poetry: "No ideas but in things," "No things but in words." What could be more grounded in the material than *Tender Buttons*, with its clitoral or nipplish title and its roster of "Objects," "Food," "Rooms"? And yet the "accusation" of abstraction, of nonreferentiality, of inaccessible intellectuality bordering on hocus-pocus has traditionally been associated with Stein. By its very colloquialism and overheardness, its collagism, even the most intimate, down-to-earth girl-talk of, for example, "Lifting Belly" or the intensely sexual "Sugar" from *Tender Buttons* has baffled readers of literature:

> A violent luck and a whole squeezing and even then quiet. Water is squeezing, water is almost squeezing on lard. Water, water is a mountain and it is selected and it is so practical that there is no use in money. . . .
>
> A question of sudden rises and more time than awfulness is so easy and shady. There is precisely that noise.
>
> A peck a small piece not privately overseen, not at all not a slice, not at all crestfallen and open, not at all mounting and chaining and evenly surpassing, all the bidding comes to tea.
>
> A separation is not tightly in worsted and sauce, it is so kept well and sectionally.
>
> . . . A little slight shadow and a solid fine furnace.
>
> The teasing is tender and trying and thoughtful. . . .
>
> Wet crossing and a likeness, any likeness, a likeness has blisters, it has that and teeth, it has the staggering blindly and a little green, any little green is ordinary . . .
>
> A blaze, a search in between, a cow, only any wet place, only this tune.
>
> Cut a gas jet uglier and then pierce pierce in between the next and negligence. Choose the rate to pay and pet pet very much. A collection of all around, a signal poison, a lack of languor and more hurts at ease . . .
>
> Cuddling comes in continuing a change.
>
> A piece of separate outstanding rushing is so blind with open delicacy.

A canoe is orderly. A period is solemn. A cow is accepted.
A nice old chain is widening, it is absent, it is laid by.

(TB, SW 485)

Toklas and Stein, "a little slight shadow and a solid fine furnace," are squeezing, teasing, blazing, and cuddling; they are tender and thoughtful and trying; they open delicately into wet crossings "in between" lardy, mountainous legs; they have cows (orgasms: "to have a cow" being children's argot for "to have a fit" or "to have a conniption"). The lovers "pierce pierce in between the next and negligence"/negligée and pet pet very much. Could the "nice old chain" be the outmoded Chain of Being, or the chain of linear referentiality, which the two women loosen and set aside? It's nice and it's old, and it's limited and not useful here. The firm but respectful tone of the last line echoes Stein's relation to the canonical civilization offered her by the Chain: she was completely unintimidated by it ("uncowed" would be an inappropriate term under the circumstances); she enjoyed aspects of it; she wrote what she wanted regardless of it. Writing the spoken English pillow talk of gay girls self-exiled in France, Stein again Yiddishizes English, making a cryptic, abstract, high-art text out of the intimate and the mundane. She makes English a burrowing language, a language always on the move, the overload of present participles (in "Miss Furr and Miss Skeene," for example) acknowledging process and change.

A digressive note on interpreting Stein, written in response to a seminar discussion on "Sugar": Stein works much better when collaboratively approached. Just as it is often hinted that Alice Toklas played an important role—beyond that of amanuensis—in creating Stein's work, so that the compositions, like Merrill's poems, are collaborations, so reading and having "ideas" about Stein's work is much more fun and productive when undertaken with one or more friends. In this light, a first academic project is perhaps the most inimical genre in which to try Stein. A solitary endeavor in which one's credentials rest on isolation and individual "originality," the individually generated book participates in the lonely, self-made "high-art" side of the high-culture/mass-culture continuum, and as such, suffers tremendous impoverishment.

In addition to tapping Yiddish's homey and domestic joys, Stein availed herself of the elevated Hebraic aspects of Jewish language as well. One Jungian critic has analyzed *Tender Buttons* as a meditative, circular process of prayer and self-creation.[47] Although prayer, meditation, and circularity are not the exclusive province of the Jewish religion, they have a place in the Jewish mystical tradition. But more than a direct influence of religious values or spiritual orientation, it would be in literary style *as philosophy* that Stein would affiliate herself with hieratic, ancient-world Jewishness. She does this explicitly in "Lecture 2: Narration" by proposing the Old Testament as a model for a new "American" prose/poetry characterized by a lack of "beginning and a middle and an ending" — characterized by, in other words, its radical attention to each moment and its radical inattention to causality, linearity, what afterwards came to be considered conventional narrative:

> In a kind of a way what has made the Old Testament such permanently good reading is that really in a way in the Old Testament writing there really was not any such thing there was not really any succession of anything and really in the Old Testament there is really no sentence existing and no paragraphing, think about this thing, think if you have not really been knowing this thing and then let us go on telling about what paragraphs and sentences have been what prose and poetry has been. So then in the Old Testament writing there is really no actual conclusion that anything is progressing that one thing is succeeding another thing, that anything in that sense in the sense of succeeding happening is a narrative of anything . . . [48]

Since "knowledge is not succession but an immediate existing,"[49] and since the Old Testament is characterized by lack of succession, the Old Testament stands as an exemplary antinarrative embodying "knowledge" and forcing one always to be present, fully aware. In offering a Hebrew text as a model for the American avant-garde, Stein echoes in theoretical terms the thematics of her earlier novel *The Making of Americans*, in which Jewish immigrants become representative models of middle-class America. (Stein in fact did try, in *The Making of Americans*, to undo this sense that "everything has meaning as beginning and middle and ending,"[50] and believed that "American writing," of which the *Making of Americans* was a prime example, could share this characteristic with the Old Testament.) She also, through addressing literary stylistics, plays upon the old historical theme of American immigrants as prodigals wandering in the wilderness — the close connection that European American immigrants from the 1600s onward have seen between their journey and that of the biblical Jews. Mary Dearborn's essay on *The Making of Americans* as an immigrant or "ethnic text" argues that the work prefigures a current mass-cultural genre: the dynastic family saga. Like the Old Testament, Stein's book explores the "notion of repetition" through its preoccupation with generations; generation rather than linear narration becomes the determinant of history.[51] I would add to Dearborn's speculations the possibility that generations also become an index of where one stands on the assimilation/differentiation continuum. And while, given her seeming reluctance to protect herself later during the German occupation of France, it may be farfetched to read Stein's lecture as a conscious attempt to educate the intelligentsia about its debt to an endangered people (the piece was written and delivered in 1935), it prefigures Erich Auerbach's similar observations about the Old Testament in the very conscious, though understated, project of *Mimesis*, written in Turkish exile for a world in which his culture was being actively and violently destroyed. For Auerbach in Turkey, for Stein in Paris, Czeslaw Milosz's observation rings true: "Language is the only homeland."[52]

Furthermore, Stein's oracular deconstruction of English— oracular, that is, in both its "oral" and "prophetic" (cryptically exhilarating) qualities—brings to mind Northrop Frye's essay on the development of "oracular poetry" in the "age of sensibility," and its debt to biblical Old Testament language.

> Oracular poetry in a long form tends to become a series of utterances, irregular in rhythm but strongly marked off one from the other. ... In Whitman, for instance ... the end of every line has a strong pause. ... Sometimes this oracular rhythm takes on at least a typographical resemblance to prose, as it does in Rimbaud's *Saison en Enfer*, or, more frequently, to a discontinuous blend of prose and verse in which the sentence, the paragraph and the line are much the same unit. The chief literary influence for this rhythm has always been the translated Bible.[53]

Frye associates this poetry with a "curiously intense awareness of the animal world," and offers Smart, Burns, and Cowper as examples— the latter two of whom are known for their verse's appropriation of popular rhyme forms, or doggerel.[54] To Frye's roster we might add the women poets mentioned earlier in this essay. A heavy line-concluding pause is further overdetermined not only when the end-words rhyme but additionally when these end-rhyme words coincide as parts of speech, effectively calling attention to phonetic (sonic) rather than syntactical significance; in other words, by foregrounding the signifier rather than the signified, these devices privilege the rhyming/aesthetic prowess of the poet over her or his ability to create linear meaning. Here is the necessary link between doggerel—typified by overuse of convention and cliché (heavy end-rhymes that foreground a poem's constructedness rather than its organicity), and avant-garde poetry—typified by the often ideologically motivated disengagement of signifier from signified and the privileging of the former.[55] Stein's language mixes fragments and sentences, ragtag snatches of doggerel in rhyming jingles, exclamations, and long unfolding prose sentences:

> Little places to sting.
> We used to play starspangled banner.
> Lifting belly is so near.
> Lifting belly is so dear.
> Lifting belly all around.
> Little belly makes a sound.
>
> (LB, YGS 14)

> Lifting belly is a language. It says island. . . . Lifting belly is a repetition.
>
> (LB 17)

> And so cold . . .
> Listen to me as yet I have no color. Red white and blue all out but you.
>
> (LB 18)

The "ensemble," to use one of Robert Duncan's words, is a crazy-quilt of anticonventional sexuality ("lifting belly" as an erotic act), semiotic self-referentiality ("Lifting belly is a language"), nationalism reduced to songs and counting-rhymes ("starspangled banner," "red white and blue all out but you"). Like Kaufman's "THE SUN IS A NEGRO," the almost childlike repetition becomes oracular through sonic meditation.

Any treatment of Stein's work as oracular must stress the "oral" to underscore its proximity and debt to everyday conversation and vernacular. If by terming Stein's poetry "oracular" we want to include the word's connotations of a transpersonal or otherworldly sensibility—a possibility for which I hope I have made a strong case—we must nonetheless bear in mind her own rejection of a "mystical" interpretation of her work, based on her belief that "mysticism" implied a pretension, a fuzzy imprecision and a lack of critical self-consciousness on the artist's part. "Yet Dish" swipes at Whitman's pretensions in that vein:

LII
Leaves of gas, leaves of get a towel louder.
(YD 61)

Difference

There is very little published about Stein as a Jew and what it may have meant in her writing. The index to Richard Bridgman's work, for example, enters "Judaism" under "Gertrude Stein: Opinions," as if one's conscious opinion of one's cultural and ethnic background reflected in total its influence on one.[56] He dismisses her Jewishness, as does Elizabeth Sprigge, by pointing out that she was not observant; both concede, however, that in her youth she had an "emotional tie to Judaism" and that she claimed, as do many contemporary Jews and ethnographers, that Judaism is a "race-feeling" rather than a religion. This affective connection, Bridgman states, became increasingly ambivalent, reflecting her ambivalent relationship with her overbearing, erratic, but religiously observant father, Daniel Stein.[57] In keeping with his general thesis that her abstraction was a self-protective code, Bridgman demonstrates Stein's gradual revision, in *The Making of Americans*, of "Jewish" to "German" to "middle-class" as emblematic of a gradual loss of interest in Jewishness and/or a turn to assimilation out of self-protectiveness. But recent attention to forms and expressions of ethnicity have suggested that one can, without much difficulty, retain a strong cultural identification with some aspects of a culture while rejecting others. This retention does not even need to a be a consciously intended affiliation. However, a line like "I do see how infidels talk. They talk with the language of dishes and daylight," from a significantly titled "Why Are There Whites to Console"[58] strongly indicates a conscious preoccupation with the relationship between Jewishness and language use: the particular way Jews use language (and especially how she as a Jew used language), the general problematics of a language not nationalistically affiliated, the meaning of a language in exile (which problem she consciously duplicates by being an English-speaking person in France), the relationship between a "Jewish" (Yiddish) use of language and a "women's" use of language through their mutual attention (as Stein represents it) to coziness and domesticity.

The phenomenon of "Yet Dish" allows for other associations as well. Stein embodied all of the golden triangle of European outsiderhood—as Hans Mayer delineates it in his *Outsiders*—of Jews, gay people, and women.[59] She was in addition a gay Jewish woman *writer* in the early part of this century, a pioneer in the American avant-garde before women could even vote in this country. Writing was like traveling in exile, stigmatized:

> You write a book and while you write it you are ashamed for
> everyone must think you are a silly or a crazy one and yet you write
> it and you are ashamed, you know you will be laughed at or pitied
> by everyone and you have a queer feeling and you are not very
> certain and you go on writing ... (MOA 485)

Bridgman quotes this passage in a rather limited discussion of Stein's sense of isolation as an eccentric, and in general, eccentrics' "[oppression] by American demands for conformity," which showed up, among other ways, in the "sameness of American girls." In this context, could "American" also suggest "heterosexual"? "Gentile"? just as elsewhere it seems to suggest "Jewish" or "of Jewish origin." Especially the use of the word "queer" in the above passage suggests a felt link between being a woman writer/intellectual and being gay. In the following passage, also offered by Bridgman simply as a defense of "eccentricity," the link between Jewishness and gayness seems almost explicit.

> It takes time to make queer people. ... Custom, passion, and a feel
> for mother earth are needed to breed vital singularity in any man,
> and alas, how poor we (Americans) are in all these three.

> Brother singulars, we are misplaced in a generation that knows not
> Joseph. We flee before the disapproval of our cousins, the courageous
> condescension of our friends who gallantly sometimes agree to walk
> the streets with us, from all them who never any way can understand
> why such ways and not the others are so dear to us, we fly to the

kindly comfort of an older world accustomed to take all manner of
strange forms into its bosom ... (MOA 21)

The interlapping of "queerness," Jewishness, creativity, womanliness
point toward a conscious apprehension, not only of "outsiderhood"
in general romanticized terms but in a specific apprehension of the
powerful Otherness of being a gay Jewish woman writer, "singular"
but in overlapping communities of fellow renegades.

The early novel *QED*, which Stein did not publish in her lifetime,
has been discussed as a psychological portrait of a lesbian love triangle, in which she fictionally embodies the early scholarly interest in
different psychological "types" that she developed under the men-
torship of William James at Harvard and Dr. Lewellys Barker at Johns
Hopkins.[60] The scientism of this title as well as the fatalism of the earlier one (Alice Toklas and Carl Van Vechten originally published it as
Things as They Are) ironically balances detached honesty with Stein's
early penchant for the positivism of the age; in the novel, Helen the
Anglo-American (based on May Bookstaver), Mabel whose "kinship
with decadent Italy was purely spiritual" (QED 71), and Adele
the Jewish type (Stein herself) are played off against each other in a
near "deadlock"(QED 133). The work seems as much a (self-)explo-
ration of "racialism" and "national character" as of a forbidden love
entanglement. In this way, Stein's work participates in the medico-
psychological scientific discourse of "character" that permeated
Western intellectual life (eugenics, Social Darwinism, anti-immigra-
tion), and that justified and contributed to the hegemony of the
Chain of Being through the consolidation of colonialist interests and
the privileging of the European white male.

James Mellow in particular suggests an influence on *QED* that
raises difficult questions about Stein's relationship to the scientiza-
tion of racial and gender difference and hierarchy.[61] This influence
was the book *Sex and Character*, written by Otto Weininger, an Aus-
trian Jewish philosopher and psychologist who converted to Christianity on the day he earned his Ph.D. in 1902.[62] Weininger, a notorious
"self-hating Jew," committed suicide when "confronted with the
problem of following his own [misogynist, anti-Semitic, male su-
premacist] philosophy."[63] Weininger was part of a general late nine-
teenth- and early twentieth-century movement toward the scientiza-

tion of mental processes, emotion, and character, a movement whose luminaries included William James, Freud, Darwin and, in her early medico-psychological career, Stein herself. Specific to Weininger, however, was the stark and explicit lack of self-acceptance evident in his relegation of Jews and women (and by extension, Jewish men feminized *as* women) to subhuman or abnormal status. The age was obsessed with the establishment of behavioral and existential norms; the middle class in particular proliferated and conflated images of abnormal Others—colonials, women, children, workers, homosexuals—in its attempt to establish its own legitimacy.[64]

Adele, the Jewish Stein character in *QED*, strongly affiliates with the middle class and its values of moderation and decency, despite her friends' protestations that she herself seems so bohemian, self-assertive, and foreign to the ideal image of the middle-class woman. In defending her love of the middle class, Adele gets carried away, then immediately alludes to her Jewishness, thus joining the two categories—Jewish and middle class—together:

> Good gracious! Here I am at it again. I never seem to know how to keep still, but both of you know already that I have the failing of my tribe. I believe in the sacred rites of conversation even when it is a monologue. (QED 57)

While defending the class that is busy consolidating its ranks against her as a Jew, Stein/Adele invokes her Jewishness in the context of what Weininger terms "faulty" Jewish language use, that is, a tendency toward free-association and illogic. And later she breaks up a fruitless display of politesse on the part of the other two women:

> Thereupon ensued between Helen and Mabel the inevitable and terminable offer and rejection of companionship that politeness demands and the elaborate discussion and explanation that always ensues when neither offer nor rejection are sincere. At last Adele broke in with an impatient "I always did thank God I wasn't born a woman," whereupon Mabel hastily bundled her wraps and disappeared down the companion-way. (QED 57-58)

This is not a straightforward passage either: in it, Adele/Stein both uses her Jewishness to curtail a display of useless gentile decorum bordering on the hypocritical, and participates in and exposes the misogynistic traditions of her own culture (she quotes an Orthodox Jewish morning prayer, the Baruch Ashakar blessing to be said on weekdays, which contains the line: "Thank God I wasn't born a woman"). The self-assertion masks itself in self-deprecation: Adele is, of course, a woman, and speaks here with a misogynist voice; she denies herself through the assertion. She cannot admit the real difference: her Jewishness at stake, she buries the issue in a passive-aggressive thrust at herself as well as at the other women. The concept of "womanliness" elides and encodes "gentile" with "genteel"; dismissing her gentile friends' excessive niceties, Adele invokes her Jewishness to say "Thank God I'm not one of *you*" (as Kaufman wrote "Thank God [that I am not white]"). Just as the Jewish man is not really a "man" to the extent that his socialization as a Jew feminizes him by the standards of a dominant gentile culture, a Jewish *woman* "wasn't born a woman" to the extent that her socialization as a *Jewish* woman masculinizes her—"disappears" her femininity—in the eyes of the non-Jewish majority. The exchange foreshadows, with self-incriminating irony, contemporary debates in which subaltern feminists call white middle-class feminists to task for using the term "women" to mean white middle-class feminists. The key to understanding the complexity of Adele/Stein's assertion/denial is to acknowledge difference located in the intersection of gender *and* "race," not just in one or the other.

The influence of Weininger specifically and the concerns he embodied generally—evident in Stein's preoccupation with gender types, dependency/ independence, national or racial character, "genius" in relation to gender, classifiable personality types—can possibly be understood as a rewriting of those concerns, or at least of the pessimistic and self-damning conclusions Weininger reached. The revisions, in *Making of Americans*, of "Jewish" to "German" to "middle class," rather than suggesting only a self-distancing from one's origins, also indicates an affiliation with certain homey, familial, and stable values as "Jewish" *and* middle class rather than seeing the middle class as a norm that excludes Jews and Jewishness—there was, after all, a sizeable German-Jewish American middle class, to which Stein and her family of origin belonged. The domesticity of Yiddish (which Stein, as a German Jew who probably did not grow up in a Yiddish-language environment, invokes strictly for symbolic purposes) and of the role of Jewish women, the emphasis on "decency" and the social concern Gertrude Stein associates with Jewishness in her early Radcliffe themes[65] may be her characteristically idiosyncratic appropriation of what was originally an inimical and self-rejecting condemnation of her "type." On the other hand, it is possible that the assimilated Jew's obsession with systems of character, physical type, mental processes, and so on reflects an attempt to control, by intellectual mastery, a system of exclusion. The anxiety of "passing" generates a search for systemic order in which one can find one's place; as Sartre has eloquently observed of the "inauthentic" Jew, "he absorbs all knowledge with an avidity which is not to be confused with disinterested curiosity. He hopes to become a 'man,' nothing but a man, a man like all other men. . . . He cultivates himself in order to destroy the Jew in himself."[66] My father, for example, who passed as gentile to the extent that he was able to in his adult professional life, was a medical anthropologist who traveled the world measuring the body parts of dark-skinned people and running studies on "Harvard men" that attempted to correlate body build and "race" with temperament, intellect, and personality. Weininger's books (as well as Schopenhauer's, whose misogyny Weininger emulated), as well as other early classics of what was to become sociobiology after my father's death (including turn-of-the century gems on phrenology and the works of his abusive mentors William Sheldon and Ernest Hooton), lined the bookcases in his study along with those of Maimonides and Spinoza. He was secretly plagued by what it could possibly mean to be a "man" in the hostile dominant culture of Protestant and Irish Catholic Boston, a culture that deemed his bookishness, his verbal acumen and sensitivity, his passion for Western culture unmanly even as it rewarded his achievements. Stein's early literary experiments with African-American language and culture (*Three Lives*) constitute a similar though possibly more recuperable ethnographic movement to study (the otherness of) oneself by attending to the otherness of another Other.[67]

Sander Gilman has suggested that "the linkage between misogyny and anti-Semitism during the latter half of the nineteenth century" stemmed from the fact that "both Jews and women were becoming more visible on the horizon of European consciousness through their articulated demands for emancipation."[68] Against this backdrop Weininger deployed his self-lacerating backlash. Some of his theories of women's language eerily foreshadow, in condemning terms, what French feminists have appropriated as antipatriarchal virtues:

Women do not think logically. Rather they "think" by association. "The logical axioms are the foundation of all formation of mental conceptions, and women are devoid of these. . . . This want of definiteness in the ideas of women is the source of that 'sensitiveness' which gives the widest scope to vague associations and allows the most radically different things to be grouped together."[69]

Jews (and by Jews, Weininger, Sartre, and Gilman appear to mean Jewish men) have much the same relation to language as women, only Jews have no "center" to their language or their worldview, as do women, whose proper center is "man." "The Jew is thus a degenerate woman!" Gilman comments disgustedly on Weininger. Weininger stipulates that "Jewishness" and "femaleness" are not necessarily essential to Jews and women; they are characteristics anyone can have, though all Jews and all women have those characteristics. This notion, reminiscent of contemporary ideas about "*écriture feminine*," according to which one does not have to be a biological woman to write as a woman, also prefigures Lenny Bruce's recuperative and nonessentialist conception of "Jew" and "goy":

I'm Jewish. Count Basie's Jewish. Ray Charles is Jewish. Eddie Cantor's goyish. The B'nai Brith is goyish. The Hadassah is Jewish. Marine Corps—heavy goyish, dangerous.
Kool-Aid is goyish. All Drake's Cakes are goyish. Pumpernickel is Jewish and, as you know, white bread is very goyish. Instant potatoes—goyish. Black cherry soda's very Jewish. Macaroons are very Jewish. . . . Trailer parks are so goyish that Jews won't go near them.
Balls are goyish. Titties are Jewish. Mouths are Jewish. All Italians are Jewish. Greeks are goyish. Eugene O'Neill—Jewish. Dylan Thomas—Jewish. Steve Allen is goyish, though. It's the hair. He combs his hair in the boys' room with that soap all the time.[70]

Bruce opposes Weininger by prizing the characteristics scorned by the latter; he also challenges Gilman by accepting the metaphoricity of Jewishness, and by affirming rather than recoiling from the feminization of Jewishness. Bruce's inversion of Weininger's hierarchy, in privileging "Jewishness" over "goyishness," insists on difference and classification even while it deconstructs this difference. The Jew/woman parallel remains ("The B'nai Brith is goyish. The Hadassah is Jewish. . . . Balls are goyish. Titties are Jewish"), but occupies a position implicitly superior (more "soulful") than that of goy/man. While

Stein's Adele is not presented as overtly "superior" to the other fictional women, the focus on her as a tremendously sympathetic protagonist, the only woman to whose point of view the reader is privy, indicates that Stein (though she uses "woman" as metaphoric for "Jew") likewise privileges the Jew in *QED*. Having steeped herself in psychological experimentation both in her prewriting professional career and in reflecting honestly on her lived experience, she approaches the anxiety-producing subject of "difference" with engaged clinical enthusiasm rather than dread.

The prizing of and deconstruction of difference empowers marginal writers in the modernist tradition.[71] In cutting the ground out from under the geopolitical, literary, semantic territory on which the drama of difference and exclusion/inclusion is played, Stein unmeans and unmaps—deterritorializes—the language of difference and exclusion/inclusion. The metaphor of "Yiddish" serves as her burrowing tool as she moves (and "moving is existing")[72] through and under conventional languages and conventional narrative strategies, drawing from them scraps and fragments from which to make a different kind of homeland in language (an animal shelter?). "Make it new," the high modernist said, through abstract, antirepresentational rendering. The vernacular is always new.

Afterword: Closer than Close

When I wrote to Susan Johnson asking permission to use her poetry in my book, I enclosed a copy of an article in which I had already done so (using only her first initial, since I'd been unable to locate her earlier). She wrote back that she'd read the article three times over and could I explain the passage on "teenage culture . . . (as) self-parodic and simultaneously tremendously moving, (necessitating the) removal into hyperreality of self-dramatization (etc)." I feel permanently cured of Jamesonisms. She also enclosed two new poems inspired by parts of the essay. One, she wrote, was "the result of an experience I had meeting a girl I hadn't seen in years (a student at City Roots) also part of it came from a section in your article: 'who didn't have a thing in the world except his youth and strength, both of which were dwindling before his very eyes.' " The other was a response to Burroughs's dictum drawing the parallel between warm-blooded creatures' need to dream and humans' need for art. Here they are, in that order, first her response to the chance encounter with an old friend and to the patronizing characterization of Southie as a young ruffian:

Image

A haunting image through broken glass.

Huge brown eyes in a sunken face.
shadowed eyes, distant gaze.

Well of anger served well in youth,
destroyed the day it was in vain.

How long? Ten years ago.
Strength to burn.

shadowed eyes, distant gaze.
destroyed the day it was in vain.

And second the response to Burroughs:

Dreams die on the Inside.
As I sit in the body of middle age,
I think back to a youth that fades.

Time wanders, seasons past.

Now I rage at the time thats past.

"Why did you steal the best of me
those dreams I held so close to me"

Truths voice will not be still and
it rages back from deep within.

Your wrong you know, "I didn't kill
you long ago." Im just the Brick
that holds the age of your own
Bitterness and Rage.

Don't you know

Dreams don't die from age or time,
Dreams die on the inside.

Susan is currently unemployed, living with her grandmother. She writes every day, inspired most recently, like many of my nonacademic friends, by Natalie Goldberg's Zen-based exercises;[1] inspired by May Sarton and Scott Fitzgerald, her current favorite writers; inspired by her own ability to theorize and poeticize her life. She is amused by professors she studies with occasionally in night-school community college literature courses: "They've never worked," she says, laughing. "Here I was, holding two jobs and showing up at night for my two hours of fun, and they've never been out of school."

The two poems reflect the struggle with the dichotomies—youth/ age, potential/poverty—that would militate against her self-realization. She is aging in the same straitened circumstances in which she came into the world, watching friends worn down by increasing poverty and lack of opportunity, feeling the anger and dreams that used to "burn" turn into implosive dead weight because time, youth, vigor are ebbing. But, "truths voice" tells her, dreams die on the inside. Not "age or time" but the internalized despair of unexpressed anger and creativity—unexpressed because unacknowledged and unsupported in an environment of poverty—has thwarted the dreams of youth. Externalized and aesthetically cast, these dreams, anger and creativity would be transformed, circulate, participate in the world of meaning and currency, exchange and communication. The exchange between us enabled that externalization. She had continued to write since our contact in 1981; nonetheless, my sharing the piece I wrote on her poetry reinspired her to imagine a narrative of her life based on her ongoing creative activity, on her identity as a writer as well as a woman growing older. The two poems I received from her and the accompanying explanations of what it was in my piece that sparked her poems comprise only one filament of the web of sustaining poetic activity to which both of us owe our lives. The particularity of Susan's and my experience, the "micro-ness" of the micropractice of two women reconnecting through poetry in no way diminishes its broader significance. On the contrary, the import of this exchange as local enhances its possibilities; the social, geopolitical and psychic traces located in fly-by-night anecdotes (historemes), textual fragments or other semio-bytes honor a stylistic specificity, creating ever more intimate "un/meanings" that challenge the crude doxa of discourse.[2]

So why should anyone read this? What does this arguably too nonlinear compendium of essays on American (post)modernist poets, which proceeds more nearly by the "logic of metaphor" than by any other, add to anyone's understanding of contemporary poetics in American culture?[3] Its primary intent—or my primary intent for it—has been to add pleasure, the transgressive element in post-Platonic modern life. I do not mean this in the facile sense of the "easy listening" that flavors much writing on poetry; or even in the pleasure of "hard listening" that flavors much cultural theory. The intensity of the interstices where poetic consciousness lives, the ineluctability of the dark end of the street, offers a quality of pleasure that is other and more sustaining than the *frisson* afforded by a glimpse of the exotic or the reassuring complacency of a domesticating celebration of "diversity." Marginal imagining loses itself in a self-feeding desire that is anything but reassuring. The work presented here affords a kind of pleasure occasioned by but far exceeding the aesthetic—an unmanageable surplus of cognitive, apperceptive, and kinetic human energy that approaches the Dickinsonian decapitation (poetry as capital punishment), or Hart Crane's frenzy to find the "single, new *word*, never before spoken and impossible actually to enunciate" that his words were always fluttering on the brink of.[4]

The fear of having the top of one's head taken off, of losing oneself in the *ekstasis* of the Word is the fear of being separated from human concerns: "If I really go into poetry, give myself over to the dark end of the street, enter the realm of antidiscourse, I'll disappear." Pleasure, it sometimes seems, is the antithesis of community and defies its logic, just as the sublime defies the aesthetic or *jouissance* transgresses the phallic law of the symbolic order. All the reassuring fatalism of the "always already recuperables" does not assuage the fear of our subjective annihilation in the face of the unmanageability of pleasure, that pleasure which, were one to sustain the consciousness to record it during its forays on perception, would be understood to be thoroughly soaked in *un*conscionable shame. This is the complex Eve Sedgwick writes about so hypersmartly in "A Poem is Being Written," or that Jean Genet indicates as some unnameably powerful vulnerability that "for want of other words—I shall call poetry."

What the poets of this study have attempted is to stay conscious in exile, which means living/writing at the limits of experience, inviting the consciousness of the unbearable shame of social outsiderhood into the forefront of their imaginative work. The stuttering specificity of their poetic language names that shame as glory and that fear as pleasure: the bop of Kaufman's devolving-animal "wago wailo wailo," Spicer's "in/ability to love/in/love," the "little rush in little rush in slice" of Stein's nomadic "Yet Dish" and the "torched mind" of Cheryl's tortured orthography recording the inventions of Charlotte's "tortured mind." Their poetic language enacts for us the metamorphosis promised by Frederick Douglass' famous chiasmus: "You have seen how a man was made a slave; you shall see how a slave was made a man." As in James Carr's ballad, the "sin" the lovers know to be "wrong" resolves in the end-rhyme "strong."

Is this a tale of triumph and redemption? Not in any facile sense, though the fact of Susan's—not to mention my own—survival to this date is no inconsiderable feat attributable to poetic activity. The adjectival end-rhyme "strong" in James Carr's powerful soul song refers to "our love," which of course remains beyond the pale of decorum *because* of its strength. Its power reinscribes its transgressiveness. The majority of these writers did not write their way into biographical or textual health, respectability, or even harmonious relation with their non-respectability. From biographical evidence, only Stein and Duncan could be said to "resolve" their outsider status in peaceful domestic situations untroubled by economic hardship; their work, however, continues to occupy nonrespectable places in a shadow-canon, a kind of scary, indeterminate halo of experimentalism that surrounds the "real" canon like an aura that waxes and wanes with the literary weather, highlighting and simultaneously cluing us in to the illusory nature of the central canon. The dark end of the street remains a shifting, discomfiting terrain; an alternative to the Chain, to be sure, but fraught with yearning, anguish and pleasure pitched to a degree that alters the quotidian meaning of those words. The battlefield of antidiscourse is strewn with the riddled bodies of the dead; the war is not won by those who walk away alive. It's not won at all.

Fragmentation and constant reinvention—of self and of language, of the self as constituted through language—are the touchstones of this project. The intact autonomy of the unitary "lyric I" and the duplicity of the binarisms that have held that isolated "I" in place cede to the brokenness of multiplicity, the fluidity of a diffuse consciousness necessary to survive the increasing hardships of marginality. Economically and politically, the picture is more frighteningly grim that it was when most of these writers were active. Impoverishment, homelessness and infant mortality, particularly among "minorities," have reached proportions in the contemporary United States that completely confound our claims to global primacy in technological and ideological sophistication and in economic wellbeing. In a way that is probably being felt with some immediacy by readers of this book, the breakdown in academic disciplinarity that we may celebrate in our progressive study groups and conferences has triggered a crackdown on our less material freedoms—the intellectual honesty we try to honor—as well as on our livelihoods and the well-being of our families. These are the real causes for shame; not the pleasures and horrors of poetic activity but the casual nonchalance with which the casualties of these struggles are cast aside by terrified and defensive empires of meaning. Reinvention is not simply a Pollyannaish concept made trendy by intellectual dillettantes; it's what has to happen when one is up against the wall, when all known methods, resources, and language are no longer intelligible. The grimaces and cries of crack-addicted infants and the halting honesties uttered by Persons With AIDS in the privacy of their own hospice-sponsored support groups may constitute the "real" avant-gardes of postliterary contemporary poetry, the front lines of undreamed-of expression.

But that is another project.

Nonetheless, even in this context, it is possible to speak of continuity, persistence, survival—plodding words that contrast, perhaps, with the high-pitched urgency of "pleasure," "shame," "glory," "fear," and with the textual discontinuity, fragmentation and vanguard audacity I have obviously valued in the foregoing essays. But these low-profile, tenacious Latinates *do* resonate with a guerrilla consciousness that marks the poetic strategies I've outlined, and with the ideas of commitment, passion, and subversion that have inadequately framed these unframeable textual events. The ubiquitous energy of language travels the streets sometimes covertly and unobtrusively as well as flamboyantly, forming a translucent kinetic web that feeds and sustains the isolated and the fragmented. Bob Kaufman paces the streets of North Beach, trailing ashes from the glowing end of a cigarette as constantly lit as the flaming cenotaph of the unknown soldier, disappearing and reappearing in the interplay between shadow and streetlight that marks his beat.[5] This is the continued presence of poetry in modern life. "If darkness induces reverie and is the medium of a diffuse eroticism, nighttime remains for many poets . . . the moment of quiescence necessary to the dawning of new awareness."[6] Intimacy and invasion: it is my hope that the nocturnal texts and lives explored here have marauded the reader's empathetic faculties, have broken-and-entered them in the quiet of darkness, have left behind spores of the possibilities of new consciousnesses and new communities.

Notes

Pre-Monitions: Definitions, Explanations, Acknowledgments

1. See, for example, Terry Cooney, *The Rise of the New York Intellectuals*: Partisan Review *and Its Circle* (Madison: University of Wisconsin Press, 1986); Keith Tuma, "Contemporary American Poetry and the Pseudo Avant-Garde," *Chicago Review* 36: 3-4, pp. 43-50; Richard Kostelanetz, "What Is Avant-Garde?" *The Avant-Garde Tradition in Literature*, ed. Richard Kostelanetz (Buffalo: Prometheus, 1982), pp. 3-6.

2. Kostelanetz, "Avant-Garde," p. 3.

3. Charles Russell, *Poets, Prophets, and Revolutionaries: The Literary Avant-Garde from Rimbaud to Postmodernism* (New York: Oxford University Press, 1985).

4. Peter Bürger, *Theory of the Avant-Garde*, trans. Michael Shaw (Minneapolis: University of Minnesota Press, 1984.

5. Philippe Sollers, *Writing and the Experience of Limits*, trans. Philip Bernard with David Hayman (New York: Columbia University Press, 1983), p. 6.

6. Diane Wood Middlebrook, *Anne Sexton: A Biography* (Boston: Houghton Mifflin, 1991), pp. 50, 64.

7. David Henderson, author's notes, April 1986.

8. See, for example, Barbara Harlow's *Resistance Literature* (New York: Methuen, 1987), which treats very consciously, politically emancipationist literature by politically engaged writers of Central and South America, Africa, and the Middle East.

9. Louis A. Renza, *"A White Heron" and the Question of Minor Literature* (Madison: University of Wisconsin Press, 1984).

10. Gilles Deleuze and Félix Guattari, *Kafka: Toward a Minor Literature*, trans. Dana Polan (Minneapolis: University of Minnesota Press, 1986).

11. Judy Grahn, *The Highest Apple: Sappho and the Lesbian Poetic Tradition* (San Francisco: Spinsters Ink, 1985), p. xvi.

12. Janice Perlman's *The Myth of Marginality* (Berkeley: University of California Press, 1976) is a detailed presentation of this argument; although her subject matter is the slum dwellers of Brazil, her review of socioeconomic marginality theories and their origins in psychology is pertinent to North American studies as well, and can even be to some extent transposed into literary terms.

13. H. Bruce Franklin, *Prison Literature: The Victim as Criminal and Artist* (Westport, Conn.: Lawrence Hill, 1982), pp. xxiii-xxiv.

14. Grahn, *Highest Apple*.

15. Bob Kaufman, "Abomunist Manifesto," *Solitudes Crowded with Loneliness* (New York: New Directions, 1965), p. 80.

16. Julia Kristeva, *Revolution in Poetic Language*, trans. Margaret Waller (New York: Columbia University Press, 1984).

17. Jack Spicer, "Dear Robin," *The Collected Books of Jack Spicer*, ed. Robin Blaser, *Admonitions* (Santa Barbara: Black Sparrow Press, 1975), p. 61.

18. Clark Coolidge, "Arrangement," *Talking Poetics from Naropa Institute*, vol. I, ed. Anne Waldman and Marilyn Webb (Boulder: Shambala, 1978), p. 152.

19. See, for example, Marianne DeKoven, *A Different Voice: The Experimental Writings of Gertrude Stein* (Madison: University of Wisconsin Press, 1983); Judy Grahn, *Highest Apple*; Mary Dearborn, *Pocahontas' Daughters* (London: Oxford University Press, 1986); Rebecca Mark, introduction to Gertrude Stein's *Lifting Belly* (Tallahassee, Flor.: Naiad Press, 1989); and Lisa Ruddick, *Reading Gertrude Stein: Body, Text, Gnosis* (Ithaca: Cornell University Press, 1990).

20. Duncan paraphrased by Spicer, "Dear Robin," *Collected Books*, p. 61.

1. Introductions and Interdictions

1. Dave Marsh, *The Heart of Rock and Soul* (New York: Plume, 1989), p. 268.

2. Jacques Derrida, "Implications: Interview with Henri Ronse," trans. Alan Bass, *Positions* (Chicago: University of Chicago Press, 1981), p. 12.

3. On the term and concept of "defamiliarization," see, for example, Boris Tomashevsky, "Thematics," esp. pp. 78-92, in *The Russian Formalists*, ed. L. T. Lemon and M. J. Reis (Lincoln: University of Nebraska Press, 1965), pp. 61-95.

4. The term "thick description" comes from Clifford Geertz's description of his ethnographic method in "Thick Description: Toward an Interpretive Theory of Culture," in *The Interpretation of Cultures* (New York: Basic Books, 1973).

5. Jean Genet, *The Thief's Journal*, trans. Bernard Frechtman (New York: Grove Press, 1964), p. 53.

6. Plato, *The Republic*, Book 10, trans. Desmond Lee (Harmondsworth, England: Penguin, 1953), pp. 421-29. See also *Ion*.

7. Ibid., and Trinh T. Minh-ha, "Introduction," *Discourse: A Journal for Theoretical Studies in Media and Culture* 2:2 (Spring-Summer 1989), pp. 5-17.

8. W. E. B. Du Bois, "Of Our Spiritual Strivings," *The Souls of Black Folk* (New York: Signet, 1969), p. 45.

9. Ibid., p. 43.

10. James Clifford, "Introduction: The Pure Products Go Crazy," *The Predicament of Culture: Twentieth-Century Ethnography, Literature, and Art* (Cambridge, Mass.: Harvard University Press, 1988), pp. 1-17.

11. Gayatri Chakravorty Spivak, "Three Women's Texts and a Critique of Imperialism," *"Race," Writing and Difference*, ed. Henry Louis Gates, Jr. (Chicago: University of Chicago Press, 1985), p. 262.

12. See, for example, Hans Robert Jauss, "E. *La douceur du foyer*. Lyric Poetry of the Year 1857 as a Model for the Communication of Social Norms," *Aesthetic Experience*

and Literary Hermeneutics, trans. Michael Shaw (Minneapolis: University of Minnesota Press, 1982), pp. 263-93.

13. Robert von Hallberg, *American Poetry and Culture, 1945-1980* (Cambridge, Mass.: Harvard University, 1985).

14. This apt phrase was supplied by Wahneema Lubiano, M/MLA, November 1989, Minneapolis.

15. Jean Genet, *The Thief's Journal*, p. 205: "Saintliness means turning pain to good account."

16. Owen Barfield, *Poetic Diction* (Middletown, Conn.: Wesleyan University Press, 1973), p. 48.

17. Henry Louis Gates, Jr., "Writing 'Race' and the Difference It Makes," *"Race," Writing, and Difference*, p. 5.

18. Arthur Lovejoy, *The Great Chain of Being* (Cambridge, Mass.: Harvard University Press, 1936), p. 326.

19. See Plato, *Republic*, Book 10.

20. For a summary of these ideas, see Lovejoy, *Great Chain*, pp. 55-58.

21. Aristotle, *Poetics*, trans. Lane Cooper (Boston: Ginn and Company, 1913), p. 93.

22. Friedrich Nietzsche, *A Genealogy of Morals, Basic Writings of Nietzsche*, trans. Walter Kaufmann (New York: Random House, 1968), "First Essay, Section 5," p. 466.

23. Nietzsche, *Genealogy*, "First Essay, Section 5," p. 465.

24. Gerald Else, *Aristotle's Poetics: The Argument* (Cambridge, Mass.: Harvard University Press, 1957), p. 75, cited by Kaufmann; Nietzsche, *Genealogy*, p. 465n.

25. Nietzsche, *Genealogy*, pp. 461-62.

26. Page Dubois, *Centaurs and Amazons: Women and the Prehistory of the Great Chain of Being* (Ann Arbor: University of Michigan Press, 1982).

27. Dubois, *Centaurs*, p. 1.

28. Ibid., p. 138.

29. Sappho, *Poems*, trans. Mary Barnard (Berkeley: University of California Press, 1958), p. 41.

30. Aristotle, *Poetics*, p. 93.

31. Plato, *Republic*, p. 438.

32. Karlheinz Stierle, "Identité du Discours et Transgression Lyrique," *Poétique* 32 (November 1977), trans. Jean-Paul Colin, pp. 422-41.

33. Ibid., p. 431.

34. Plato, *Republic*, p. 437.

35. Ibid., p. 437.

36. For a somewhat different feminist reading of Sappho's lyrics, see Jack Winkler, "Garden of Nymphs: Public and Private in Sappho's Lyrics," *Women's Studies* 8 (1981), pp. 65-91.

37. Eric Gans, "Naissance du Moi Lyrique: du Féminin au Masculin," *Poétique* 46 (April 1981), pp. 129-39.

38. Some of the ethnopoetic scholars concerned with these problems are Jerome Rothenberg, Diane Rothenberg, and Dennis Tedlock. See, for example, Rothenberg and Rothenberg, eds., *Symposium of the Whole: A Range of Discourse Toward an Ethnopoetics* (Berkeley: University of California Press, 1983); Tedlock, *The Spoken Word and the Work of Interpretation* (Philadelphia: University of Pennsylvania Press, 1983), and "Beyond Logocentrism: Trace and Voice among the Quiché Maya," *boundary 2* 8:

2 (1979), pp. 321-33; or the journal *Alcheringa*, which Tedlock and Jerome Rothenberg edited.

39. Judy Grahn, Interview. *Aurora* (Spring 1983), p. 1.

40. In connection with this, see Hans Mayers's *Outsiders*, trans. Denis M. Sweet (Cambridge, Mass.: MIT Press, 1982), which explores the subjective "monsterhood" experienced by nontraditional women, Jews, and gay men in Europe and its literary tradition.

41. Judy Lucero, "I Speak in an Illusion," *De Colores: Journal of Emerging Raza Philosophies* 1:1 (Winter 1973), p. 76.

42. Trinh Minh-ha, "Introduction," pp. 5-6.

43. Allan Megill, *Prophets of Extremity* (Berkeley: University of California Press, 1985), p. 18.

44. For an analysis of the aphorism and an analogy between aphorisms and lyric poetry, see J. P. Stern's *Lichtenberg: A Doctrine of Scattered Occasions* (Bloomington: University of Indiana Press, 1959), pp. 112-20, 198-208; for Nietzsche on tempo: *Beyond Good and Evil, Basic Writings*, Sections 27, 27n, p. 229; 28, 28n, pp. 230-31; p. 246, 246n, p. 372.

45. A second and equally provocative reason for mentioning modern philosophers' chafing against the confines of a system based on dualism and gradation is the problematic association of some of these thinkers—specifically Nietzsche and Heidegger— with modern fascism, whether through conscious affiliation or through posthumous (mis)representation by others. This seems to be one possible consequence of an "antihumanism" that simultaneously can't break out of its own humanistic/oppressive referents, such that any critique of humanism is either experienced by the writer himself or interpreted by others as "nihilistic." Erich Heller, for example, in *The Disinherited Mind* (New York: Meridian, 1959), which title itself has melancholy implications of a humanistic legacy lost or no longer tenable in the modern world, speaks pessimistically of modern European man's inevitable doom, Europe's spiritual bankruptcy, and Nietzsche's "strategy of despair" (p. 116; three of the eight essays in the book treat Nietzsche) as a way of accommodating the inevitable "eclipse of traditional values" which will leave "modern European man, this pampered child of the optimistically rational eighteenth century ... astray in a wilderness without path or guidance" (p. 171). (There are many who would greet such an eclipse with strategies of celebration.) Heller, though sensitive to the problems brought about by the schismatic nature of traditional humanism, interprets this "strategy of despair" in language that reproduces the tensions responsible for this despair. He points toward "spiritual conquest" as the only way Nietzsche can "defeat" a "historic inevitability" (p. 117). Doom on the one hand and conquest on the other set up a hierarchic dichotomy of "active/passive," or "winner/loser" that reproduces the system, replete with resonances of its global political consequences, that Nietzsche is trying to overturn.

Similarly, a recent handbook on twentieth-century culture—*Twentieth-Century Culture: A Biographical Companion*, ed. Allan Bullock and R. B. Woodings (New York: Harper and Row, 1983)—characterizes Heidegger, who demonstrated Nietzsche's participation in the system even as he tried to "overturn" it, and who saw himself more successfully engaged in the same task of tearing the seemingly all-inclusive fabric of Western metaphysics, as having a "gloomy picture of man's place in nature" and summarizes his work in terms absolutely conforming to the famous "man/nature" split: "*Dasein* ... is what differentiates men from the inert material surroundings within which they find they have been arbitrarily "thrown"; it is a condition characterized by anxious awareness of the future, and as containing both the necessity of choice and death, the cessation of being" (p. 315). Even the contemporary poststructuralist critical investigation into the arbitrariness of hierarchic dualisms has been termed, sometimes pejoratively, "deconstruction," and attributed with destructive intentions or results: reducing everything to meaninglessness, purposive obscurantism, sterility, and so forth. One work on all four philosophers—Nietzsche, Heidegger, Foucault, and Derrida—characterizes them as "crisis thinkers"(Megill, *Prophets*, inside cover).

It would be reductive to claim that these criticisms or even the sympathetic interpretations of scholars like Heller are wrong, and that they simply misconstrue or overlook the intentions, the actual meaning, or the revolutionary potential of these kinds of counterhegemonic philosophy. It is, unfortunately, impossible to definitively refute the fascists' interpretation of Nietzsche, even though it is possible to offer alternate, coherent, and certainly more palatable readings, and even though there is no question but that he would have been horrified to see this particular use of his work. (Heidegger, on the other hand, was explicitly enthusiastic about Hitler's leadership in Germany's imperialist endeavors.) And poststructuralists' insistence on separating signifier from a narrow correspondence with a one-and-only signified can easily lead to a sense that physical events and agency cannot be of primary importance since they can never be spoken about unambiguously—such that, for example, genocide can be spoken of as a "final solution," or, more recently, as a series of "disappearances."

The two reasons for looking at attempts to undermine or overturn the system from within—the stylistic poeticity of these attempts, and their unemancipatory aspects—combine in an uncomfortable problematic. What are the limitations and possibilities of challenges to a system coming from those whose interests are ostensibly served by that system? This question becomes most relevant in an examination of poetry by straight white upwardly mobile men, though it is also worth acknowledging in a review of attempted philosophical mutinies. Clearly, in this work on the liberatory possibilities of poetry, a pattern of co-optation has emerged in the foregoing paragraphs that must be acknowledged, from seemingly milder transgressions (the reproduction of the conceptual forms these privileged philosophers or poets struggle against), to a more sinister connection, by virtue of its valorization of nonreferential uses of language and the doors that open to mystification, between poetic discourse and fascism (Americans are reminded of Ezra Pound, one of our most acknowledged innovators, whose poetry has deeply inspired and influenced anti-Fascists such as Allen Ginsberg and Ernesto Cardenal). Plato's banishment of poets from the ideal republic ruled by philosopher-kings of rational discourse makes a certain amount of melancholy sense in this context; since we have established him as the philosopher who crystallized the antithesis between these two forms of discourse, it is not surprising that the heirs of a tradition based on this split would view or experience as "uncivilizing" any gesture toward dissolving the opposition. While this work does not pretend to philosophical expertise, these questions inform it. The anarchic and subjective potential of poetry in modern life can begin to suggest some of the reasons for its misappropriation and also its inherently subversive—in a liberatory sense—possibilities.

46. Walter Benjamin, "On Some Motifs in Baudelaire," *Illuminations*, trans. Harry Zohn (New York: Schocken, 1974), pp. 155ff.

47. Gilles Deleuze and Félix Guattari, *Kafka: Toward a Minor Literature*, trans. Dana Polan (Minneapolis: University of Minnesota Press, 1986), pp. 16-17.

48. Ibid., p. 17.

49. Jacques Rancière, "Ronds de fumée: Les poètes ouvriers dans la France de Louis-Philippe," *Revue des Sciences Humaines* 61:190 (April-June 1983), pp. 31-47.

50. Bob Kaufman, "All Hallows, Jack O'Lantern Weather, North of Time," *The Ancient Rain: Poems 1956-1978* (New York: New Directions, 1981), p. 48.

51. Deleuze and Guattari, *Kafka*, p. 17.

52. Du Bois, *Souls*, p. 46.

53. Ibid., p. 52.

54. Ibid., p. 45.

55. Sheila Rowbotham, *Woman's Consciousness, Man's World* (Harmondsworth, England: Penguin, 1973); Frantz Fanon, *Black Skin, White Masks*, trans. Charles Lam Markmann (New York: Grove Press, 1967).

2. "Unmeaning Jargon" / Uncanonized Beatitude: Bob Kaufman, Poet

1. The phrase "prince of street poets" appears in the eulogy "Tribute to a Street Poet," *People's Tribune* 13:6 (March 7, 1986), p. 7.

2. The biographical details included here were drawn from Raymond Foye's editor's preface to Kaufman's *The Ancient Rain: Poems 1956-1978*, pp. ix-x, and the blurb on the back of that book; *Dictionary of Literary Biography*, vol. 41, 1978 ed., s.v. "Bob Kaufman," by Jon Woodson; ibid., vol. 16, s.v. "Bob Kaufman," by A. D. Winans; and *Contemporary Poets*, s.v. "Bob Kaufman" (New York: St. Martin's Press, 1981). For eulogies, see Steve Abbott's "Hidden Master of the Beats," *Poetry Flash* 155 (February 1986), pp. 1ff; George Tsongas, "Local Color: The Passing of a Beat Boulevardier," *Bay Guardian*, February 1986, pp. 5ff; "Legendary Beat Poet Bob Kaufman Dies (The 'Black American Rimbaud')" *San Francisco Chronicle*, January 13, 1986, p. 7; Christopher Hitchens, "American Notes," *Times Literary Supplement*, March 7, 1986, p. 246; and the "Tribute to a Street Poet" cited above. Alix Geluardi told me the joke among his North Beach friends, February 1986, author's notes; George Kaufman, the poet's older brother, supplied the alternate genealogy in an interview on David Henderson's "Tribute to Bob Kaufman," KPFA Radio, April 26, 1986, and in an interview he granted me in January of 1991; likewise Marlene Blackwell, October 1990. See also David Henderson's "Bob Kaufman: Poet of North Beach," in *KPFA Folio*, April 1986, p. 1. The poet's widow, Eileen Kaufman, however, stands by the version of Kaufman's origins made famous in the legend. "Bob Kaufman" in Hayden Carruth's anthology *The Voice That Is Great Within Us* (New York: Bantam, 1970), pp. 538-40, furnishes a typical example of the biographical sketches in anthologies. For some of the wilder pieces of misinformation about Kaufman, see Alan Lomax and Raoul Abdul's *3000 Years of Black Poetry* (Greenwich, Conn.: Fawcett, 1970), p. 247, which gives the poet's date and place of birth as "around 1935 in San Francisco"; and Gerald Nicosia's biography of Jack Kerouac, *Memory Babe* (New York: Grove Press, 1983), p. 525, which characterizes Kaufman as a "Jewish . . . Haitian steeped in Christianity and voodoo."

3. Quoted by A. James Arnold, *Modernism and Negritude: The Poetry and Poetics of Aimé Césaire* (Cambridge, Mass.: Harvard University Press, 1981), p. 55.

4. Some of these eulogies are collected in *Would You Wear My Eyes? A Tribute to Bob Kaufman*, ed. Bob Kaufman Collective (San Francisco: The Bob Kaufman Collective, 1988).

5. Barbara Christian, "What Ever Happened to Bob Kaufman?" *Black World* 21:12, (September 1972), pp. 20-29.

6. Charles Nilon, "Bob Kaufman, Black Speech, and Charlie Parker," unpublished manuscript delivered as a talk at the America Culture Association / Popular Culture Association Conference, Montreal, March 1987.

7. Foye quotes Kaufman in *The Ancient Rain*, p. ix. Although I don't want to over-emphasize the connection, the reference to Nietzsche is not haphazard; Aimé Césaire and Federico García Lorca, both of whose influences permeate Kaufman's work, found aspects of Nietzsche's work deeply inspiring. Nietzsche, like the later surrealists and Negritude poets whom Kaufman emulated, was centrally concerned with antirational-ism as a challenge to traditional Western metaphysics. See Clayton Eshleman and An-nette Smith's translators' introduction to *The Collected Poetry of Aimé Césaire* (Berke-ley: University of California Press, 1983), p. 3; Arnold, *Modernism and Negritude*, pp. 54-55; and García Lorca, "The Duende: Theory and Divertissement," *The Poet in New York*, trans. Ben Belitt (New York: Grove Press, 1955), p. 155.

The information about Kaufman's grandmother comes from Steve Abbott's "Hidden Master of the Beats." This detail, too, may be apocryphal, or partially true. The trope of an older woman—the storyteller—who transmits ancestral wisdom, sometimes along with dominant cultural values, as well as Kaufman's legendary Martiniquan heritage, echoes the life of Césaire, whose paternal grandmother, a "pronouncedly African phys-ical type [who] exercised considerable moral authority and was a kind of spiritual ad-visor to the people around her," taught Césaire to read and write by age four (see Arnold, *Modernism and Negritude*, p. 4). In Kaufman's case, the conflated figures of the ex-slave grandmother and the schoolteacher mother work together to provide this double-edged education for the poet. This trope may be what Stephen Henderson re-fers to as a "mascon" for African-American culture: that is, a trope characteristic of that culture. "Mascon" abbreviates "mass concentration," indicating a saturation with cul-tural significance. See Henderson, "The Form of Things Unknown," *Understanding the New Black Poetry* (New York: William Morrow, 1972), pp. 3-69.

8. Jean Genet, *The Thief's Journal*, p. 205.

9. On the demography of the Beats, their voluntary poverty and active spurning of artistic recognition, see the first chapter of John Arthur Maynard's *Venice West: The Beat Generation in Southern California* (New Brunswick: Rutgers University Press, 1991).

10. Kimberly Benston, "I Yam What I Am: The Topos of (Un)Naming in Afro-Amer-ican Literature," *Black Literature and Literary Theory*, ed. Henry Louis Gates, Jr. (New York: Methuen, 1984), pp. 151-74.

11. Emile Snyder, "Aimé Césaire: The Reclaiming of the Land," *Exile and Tradition*, ed. Rowland Smith (New York: Africana, 1976), pp. 33-34.

12. For a brilliant synopsis on the significance of naming and unnaming in marginal art production, see the first and last paragraphs of James Brown's autobiography. The book takes us from: "I wasn't supposed to be James. I wasn't supposed to be Brown. And I wasn't supposed to be alive," an incisive summary of the predicament of the Other who isn't supposed to *be* at all, and yet without whom the socius cannot func-tion, to "there's JAMES BROWN the myth and James Brown the man. The people own JAMES BROWN . . . the minute I say 'I'm JAMES BROWN' and believe it, then it will be the end of James Brown. I'm James Brown," an equally eloquent representation of the necessity and performative power of Du Bois's "double consciousness." James Brown

with Bruce Tucker, *James Brown, the Godfather of Soul* (New York: Thunder's Mouth Press, 1986, 1990), pp. 1, 267.

13. Christian, "Whatever Happened," p. 27. Christian argues that the "Abomunist Manifesto" is a "blueprint for a revolutionary way of life." "Abomunist Manifesto, by Bomkauf," *Solitudes Crowded with Loneliness* (New York: New Directions, 1965), p. 75. Henceforth all references to Kaufman's poems will appear in the text with the following code: SCL, *Solitudes Crowded with Loneliness*; GS, *Golden Sardine* (San Francisco: City Lights, 1967); and AR, *Ancient Rain: Poems 1956-1978*.

14. Quoted by Arnold Rampersad in *The Life of Langston Hughes*, vol. 1 (New York: Oxford University Press, 1986), p. 64.

15. Aimé Césaire and René Dépestre, "Interview with Aimé Césaire," *Discourse on Colonialism*, trans. Joan Pinkham (New York: Monthly Review Press, 1972), p. 29.

16. Ishmael Reed, ed., *Yardbird Reader* (Berkeley: Yardbird Publishing Cooperative, 1972), vol. 1, p. i.

17. Bob Kaufman, *Does the Secret Mind Whisper?* (San Francisco: City Lights, 1960); for a discussion and examples of work songs, see H. Bruce Franklin, *Prison Literature in America* (New York: Oxford University Press: 1978), pp. 82-126, and see especially pp. 116, 117, 164-65. W. E. B. Du Bois, "Of the Sorrow Songs," *Souls*, pp. 264-76; Frederick Douglass, *Narrative of the Life of Frederick Douglass, an American Slave* (Harmondsworth, England: Penguin, 1982), pp. 57-58; and Julia Kristeva, *Revolution in Poetic Language*, trans. Margaret Waller (New York: Columbia University Press, 1984), p. 155. James Brown, "Say It Loud—I'm Black and I'm Proud," *21 Golden Years*, Poly-Gram Records, 1977. For more on the jargon and language play of imitated jazz hipsters, see Neil Leonard, "The Jazzman's Verbal Usage," *Black American Literature Forum* 20: 1-2 (1986), pp. 151-60.

18. Chessman's case was notable for its role in the death-penalty controversy; not only were the crimes of which he was accused not nearly as severe as those of others who got reprieves or lesser sentences, but there was evidence of his innocence, as well as substantially questionable conduct on the part of the State of California's judicial system. See Chessman's autobiography, *Cell 2455 Death Row* (New York: Prentice-Hall, 1954); and Milton Machlin and William Reid Woodfield, *Ninth Life* (New York: G.P. Putnam's Sons, 1961).

19. This segment of the "Manifesto" brings to mind, and was probably influenced by, the comedian Lord Buckley's routine "The Naz," with its hip-talking treatment of Jesus: "But, I'm gonna put a Cat on you, who was the Sweetest, Grooviest, Strongest, Wailinist, Swinginest, Jumpinest most far out Cat that ever Stomped on this Sweet Green Sphere, and they called this here Cat, THE NAZ, that was the Cat's name. . . . Now the Naz was the kind of a Cat that came on so cool and so wild and so groovy and so *WITH IT*, that when he laid it *down WHAM!* It stayed there!" Richard Lord Buckley, "The Naz," *Hiparama of the Classics* (San Francisco: City Lights, 1960), pp. 14-17.

20. It should be clear that I do not intend the term "self-mythologizing" as derogatory. On the contrary, the inherent sense of drama in the narrative construction of a life like Kaufman's is of ritual necessity. As I have said, dramas like these serve an aesthetic and social function in the literary community.

Clifford Geertz, in *Islam Observed* (New Haven: Yale University Press, 1968), pp. 28-29 and 87, discusses the power of a public figure's withdrawal and contemplation. More important (from a cultural and communal point of view) than the function they serve in the individual's spiritual development, these periods of withdrawal become the focal point of myths that shape not only spiritual but political aspects of a community. Geertz dramatizes this point through the figure of Sukarno, the charismatic demagogue who first led the Indonesian struggle for freedom from the Dutch and then became Indonesia's first president, and who, despite his extremely public and colorful career, had, and mythologized, a period of contemplative isolation that he credits as providing the foundation of his political convictions. Many artists have had periods of silence or have stopped producing "art" altogether, including Genet, Rimbaud, Melville, Miles Davis, Thelonius Monk, and Tillie Olsen, whose *Silences* (New York: Delta, 1978) addresses the "downside"—poverty, overwork, lack of social validation, gender conditioning—of periods of silence.

I heard the story of the French TV crew from Paul Landry in April 1986.

21. The phrase "making an aesthetic choice based on exigency" was supplied by Wahneema Lubiano in the course of a discussion about this subject. For details on shamanic illness, see Joan Halifax, *Shamanic Voices* (New York: E.P. Dutton, 1979), pp. 3ff.

22. For an early taste of the controversy around (mis)appropriation of the term "shaman," see Gerald Hobson, "The Rise of the White Shaman as a New Version of Cultural Imperialism," *Y'bird*, 1:1 (1978), pp. 85-95. This issue has become even more pointed in recent years with the popular success of the books of Lynn Andrews, a non-Native who writes ambiguously fictionalized spiritual autobiographies.

23. David Henderson, July 1990, author's notes.

24. Lynne Wildey, letter to the *Berkeley Monthly*, May 1986, p. 5.

25. Kush, April 1986, author's notes.

26. David Henderson, July 1990, author's notes.

27. Susan Willis's discussion of mutilation and freedom in the literature of slavery appears in "Eruptions of Funk: Historicizing Toni Morrison," *Black Literature*, pp. 276-77 and 283n. Baraka on drug addiction: *Blues People* (New York: William Morris, 1963), pp. 201-2. For a fuller analysis of the zombi myth, the coextension of life and death, and its socioeconomic significance in New World-African belief systems, see Maximilien Laroche's "The Myth of the Zombie" in *Exile and Tradition*, pp. 44-61.

28. Langston Hughes, "Wise Men," *The Messenger*, June 1927, p. 11.

29. The simultaneity of grave and womb, in which the poet-shaman, stripped of "personal" identity, finds him- or herself in a transitional, almost larval state that is both prehuman and posthumous, is characteristic of what Victor Turner calls a "liminal" stage. The term comes from the Latin *limen*, or threshold, and refers to stages in rites of passage from youth to adulthood. The youths undergo such an in-between period to shed the known of childhood for the will-be-known of adulthood—they dwell in the unknown for a while, albeit a highly ritualized unknown. More generally, the word "liminal" could be used to characterize anybody or any condition that is "between two worlds," i.e., Kaufman himself, and most of the writers in this study. I would argue, also, that lyric poetry is a liminal genre, since it mediates the world of polar opposites; better yet, these opposites dissolve in poetry, and certainly in the "Poetic state" Kaufman lived in. See Turner, "Betwixt and Between," *The Forest of Symbols* (Ithaca: Cornell University Press, 1967), pp. 93-111.

30. St. John of the Cross, *Poems*, trans. Roy Campbell (New York: Pantheon, 1951); *Poems*, trans. E. Allison Peers (London: Burns, Oates, 1961). E. A. Peers is the major translator of St. John, whose translations were also published by New York Catholic houses Sheed and Ward and Image Books. St. John, *Poems*, trans. John Frederick Nims, (New York: Grove Press, 1959; and New Directions, 1967). Finally, St. John was fully

integrated into the secular literary mainstream when Penguin Books reprinted the Campbell translations in 1960.

31. Tales of Kaufman's impromptu recitations of Williams, Yeats, Eliot, Hughes, Lorca and other canonical modernists are plentiful among his surviving North Beach milieu; the phrase "eidetic memory" is another epithet associated with his name. Al Young alerted me to the Tennessee Williams connection through an anecdote of his only meeting with Kaufman: the latter burst into Young's apartment reciting poetry at a furious pace, challenged Young to identify the poet, and then slapped his back pocket emphatically to indicate Williams's then-new volume, announcing in rejoinder to Young's profession of ignorance: "That's my man Williams!" Williams, *In the Winter of Cities: Collected Poems of Tennessee Williams* (New York: New Directions, 1964), pp. 11ff.: "The marvelous children / cut their pure ice capers / north of time . . . I have seen them earlier than morning across the hall . . . I have seen their pencil-mark distinctions . . . I have seen them / never less than azure-eyed and earnest." In part II of the same poem occurs a passage that, according to Alix Geluardi, Kaufman in his declining years would call out from the screen door of his home in Fairfax: "O Mother of Blue Mountain boys / Come to the screen door, calling, *Come home! Come home!*"

32. The collapse of time and space implied in a title like "North of Time," and the related phenomenon of synesthesia, are two aspects of surrealism integrally connected to Kaufman's predicament. For a European Jewish analysis of synesthesia as an attempt to heal an imaginative consciousness fragmented under industrial capitalism, see Walter Benjamin, "On Some Motifs in Baudelaire," pp. 181ff. For discussions of African surrealism and of the Caribbean as natural home of the surreal, see Léopold Sédar Senghor, *Prose and Poetry*, trans. John Reed and Clive Wake (London: Oxford University Press, 1965), pp. 84-85; and André Breton's introduction to the first French edition of Césaire's *Cahier d'un Retour au Pays Natal*.

33. The issue of shock treatments is complex. Electroshock treatments were a common form of psychotherapy in the fifties and early sixties. Although the term "elective" must be understood as highly qualified, given doctor-patient relations in those years (and particularly male doctor-female patient relations), several well-known poets underwent elective shock treatment: Robert Lowell, for example, and Sylvia Plath (both confessional poets); and many others (Sexton, Roethke, Snodgrass, Berryman) were hospitalized for extreme emotional and mental disorders. Kaufman's shock treatments, however, differed significantly in that they were not only not elective in any sense, but their administration was explicitly punitive. They were not intended as treatment for diagnosed psychic disorders but, in the context of his color and social class, functioned as consequences of the social and racial transgression of being "uppity" and confrontational.

Along with a positively engaged fascination with psychoanalysis and self-exploration, the era features a body of predominantly antagonistic—antipsychiatric—literature concerning mental insitutions, including Plath's novel *The Bell Jar* (1966), Kesey's *One Flew Over the Cuckoo's Nest* (1962), and Allen Ginsberg's *Howl* (1955), the last of which became, along with Kaufman's broadsides, the closest thing to a Beat "manifesto."

34. Elaine Scarry, *The Body in Pain: The Making and Unmaking of the World* (London: Oxford University Press, 1985).

35. Henry Louis Gates's analysis of the use of race as an index of difference is developed in his "Editor's Introduction: Writing 'Race' and the Difference It Makes,"

'Race,' Writing, and Difference, p. 5. The Lorca translation offered here is Stephen Spender's and J. L. Gili's, from *The Selected Poems of Federico Garcia Lorca*, ed. Francisco Garcia Lorca and Donald Allen (New York: New Directions, 1955), p. 64. Alix Geluardi told me about the trip to Kesey's, describing it as a "very green, happy, family time" for Kaufman (author's notes, February 1986).

36. Robert Duncan, *Caesar's Gate* (Calif.: Sand Dollar, 1972), p. xxxv. Judy Grahn also mentions the significance of green in gay culture, relating it to pre-Celtic, tribal societies in the British Isles (fairies), who suffered persecution and extinction because of their pagan worship (*Another Mother Tongue: Gay Words, Gay Worlds* [Boston: Beacon Press, 1984], p. 18). Although Kaufman was not gay, many of his major influences were or may have been (Lorca, Whitman, Rimbaud, Eliot, Crane), and he shares with gay culture the particular shaman-outlaw sensibility under discussion here.

37. Césaire, Edward Brathwaite and Alejo Carpentier all use green in connection with magical events, transformations, or identification with nature. See especially Carpentier's *The Kingdom of This World*, trans. Harriet de Onis (New York: Alfred Knopf, 1957); and Eshleman and Smith's discussion of Césaire's use of African myths and his "vegetal" identification in *The Collected Poetry*, p. 11, and especially "Les pur sang" / "The Thoroughbreds" ("I grow like a plant / remorseless and unwarped ... / pure and confident as a plant"), pp. 90-103; and Brathwaite's *The Arrivants: A New World Trilogy* (London: Oxford University Press, 1973): the color green comes up consistently, but the most striking resemblance to Kaufman's use of it comes in the final lines of "Tom" (p. 16):

> not green alone
> not Africa alone
> not dark alone
> not fear
> alone
> but Cortez
> and Drake
> Magellan
> and that Ferdinand
> the sailor
> who pierced the salt seas to this land.

The quotes describing *Second April*, whose title is taken from Edna St. Vincent Millay, come from the blurb on the back of the broadside (San Francisco: City Lights, 1959). The Galvez Greens, George Kaufman told me, was a park in New Orleans where amateur baseball players, particularly African-Americans who were prohibited from professional participation in the game, would come together to play (author's notes, January 1991).

38. St. John's Jewish parents were forced to convert under the terrors of the Inquisition. According to legend, Crispus Attucks was the first African-American—the first American at all—martyred in the American Revolutionary cause at the Boston Massacre, and has come to be known as the first African-American hero. However, Hiller B. Zobel's evidence argues that Attucks, though he claimed to be a Barbadian by the name of Michael Johnson, was posthumously declared to be Crispus Attucks, a Black American, or a Native American member of the Natick people from Framingham with or without African ancestry. He was "variously described as a black and an Indian."

This ambiguity may have arisen from Attucks's own use of an alias, but also from the use of epithets referring to Attucks as a "stout molattoe," a "South Sea Islander" or as yelling like an Indian. James Clifford's research on the Wampanoag Indians reveals that in eighteenth-century Mashpee, Massachusetts, a town that was and continues to be characterized by a large Native American presence, the local term "South Sea Indian" initially referred to a Native American from South Massachusetts Bay (not from the Caribbean); furthermore, due to a relatively high rate of Indian/African-descent intermarriage and an admixture of Cape Verde islanders, nonwhite people in Massachusetts were known simply as "colored," and the term "South Sea Islander" or "Indian" could have referred to anyone of any "colored" mixture, including African-Americans, of whom 14 were recorded in the 1776 Mashpee census. The population of that small part of Upper Cape Cod shares with that of Louisiana, Kaufman's birthplace, the cultural and ethnic heterogeneity that at once underscores the play of multicultural difference and undermines attempts to essentialize "racial" *categories* of difference. I have come across several informal references to Kaufman's Native ancestry. See Hiller B. Zobel's *The Boston Massacre* (New York: Norton, 1970), pp. 191, 214, 350; and James Clifford, "Identity in Mashpee," *The Predicament of Culture*, esp. pp. 294-300. During a discussion on the point of Attucks's origins, Father Alberto Huerta, Kaufman's Spanish translator, suggested that both Kaufman and Attucks become, through the indeterminacy of their ancestry, "archetypes of resistance" for people of color in the West.

39. Lorca, "Los Negros," trans. Ben Belitt, pp.16-29; "El Rey de Harlem," the poem from which the last two lines of "Oregon" are drawn, pp. 18-25.

40. Dante Alighieri, *Paradiso*, trans. John Sinclair (New York: Oxford University Press, 1939). The deconstructive significance of the white pearl on the white forehead (iii: 10-16) has been pointed out by John Freccero (author's notes, March 1982).

41. The sun has another special significance for Kaufman; the Louis from whom the poet's home state took its colonial name was the "Sun King"; elsewhere Kaufman explicitly acknowledges the connection, punning on the new Louis (Armstrong) to whom the French king's legacy is bequeathed ("Like Father, Like Sun," AR 35).

42. For an interpretation of antebellum African-American use of religious language as encoded references to escape to freedom in the North and struggles against slavery, see Franklin, *Prison Literature*, pp. 87-94. See also Paul Lawrence Dunbar's poem "An Ante-bellum Sermon" in *The Black Poets*, ed. Dudley Randall (New York: Bantam, 1971), p. 44. The less sophisticated interpretation, that the slaves turned to the "master's religion" for the only solace available in these conditions of hardship, is something I recall from grammar and high school history classes. It also seems to me to underlie some of the irritation and mistrust of religion-as-opiate that was expressed during the time of militant activism in the sixties and seventies. For citations on sea shanties and Black American work songs, see Franklin, pp. 95-96. His source is Janos Marothy's *Music and the Bourgeois; Music and the Proletarian* (Budapest: Akademiai Kiado, 1974).

43. George Kaufman, interview, January 1991. Though George Kaufman belonged to the more conservative, AFL-affiliated union, he was "amazed" by and admired his younger brother's powerful oratorical efforts on behalf of the NMU (author's notes, January 1991).

44. For a discussion of *The Life of Olaudah Equiano, or Gustavus Vassa, the African. Written by Himself* (1789), see Houston A. Baker's *Blues, Ideology, and Afro-American Literature: A Vernacular Theory* (Chicago: University of Chicago Press, 1984), pp. 31-

55. Kaufman's role in smuggling Jews out of Europe into Palestine during his merchant marine days is mentioned by his brother in David Henderson's KPFA radio program. It is not clear exactly how long Kaufman worked in the merchant marine: although legend puts it at twenty years, this is unlikely, at least for active sea duty. Had he joined at thirteen, he would have been thirty-three when he quit, which would have been in 1959; and by 1959 he was already an active participant in the San Francisco Beat scene. Had he joined at the age of eighteen, as his brother claims, he would have been thirty-eight and the year 1964, which is clearly impossible. Frederick Douglass's reverie on Chesapeake Bay (pp. 106-7) is extremely complex, and in this context I am limiting its full significance. See p. 124 for details about his first escape attempt, and pp. 130ff. for details about the caulking and shipbuilding job. Langston Hughes, *The Big Sea: An Autobiography* (New York: Thunder's Mouth Press, [1940], 1986), pp. 3-4.

The list of contemporary African-American texts that treat the Middle Passage is perhaps endless; one example may suffice here. Paule Marshall's novel *Praise Song for the Widow* (New York: G.P. Putnam's Sons, 1983), in which a Caribbean holiday whose ritual involves sailing from one island to another becomes, for the seasick protagonist, both a rebirth and a replaying of the voyage in the slave ship: "She was alone in the deck house. That much she was certain of. Yet she had the impression ... of other bodies lying crowded with her in the hot, airless dark. A multitude it felt like lay packed around her in the filth and stench of themselves, just as she was. Their moans, rising and falling with each rise and plunge of the schooner, enlarged upon the one filling her head. Their suffering—the depth of it, the weight of it in the cramped space—made hers of no consequence" (p. 209).

The term "Middle Passage" itself is of nautical origin, describing the route across the middle of the Atlantic, as distinguished from the north and south passages: having heard the term only in relation to African-American history, I had always assumed it to mean the transitional shift—the limbo period—between being free Africans and enslaved three-fifths-of-Americans.

45. Bruce Nelson, *Workers on the Waterfront: Seamen, Longshoremen, and Unionism in the 1930s* (Urbana: University of Illinois Press, 1988), p. 20. Nelson, pp. 12, 20, cites Elmo Paul Hohman, *History of American Merchant Seamen* (Camden, Conn.: Shoe String Press, 1956), pp. 28-29; and U.S. Congress, House Committee on Merchant Marine and Fisheries, *Hearing on Bills Relating to the Rights and Duties of Seamen*, 54th Cong., 1st sess., 1896 (Washington, D.C.: Government Printing Office, 1896), pp. 38, 45.

46. Zobel, *Boston Massacre*, pp. 350, 292.

47. Bernard Raskin, *On a True Course: A History of the National Maritime Union, AFL-CIO* (New York: National Maritime Union, 1967).

48. Chandler Brossard, *Who Walk in Darkness* ("the suppressed original version!") (New York: Harper and Row, 1952); or the altered version (New York: New Directions, 1952). The fact that there are two versions of the book, as well as the menacing ambiguity of its content, points toward the anxiety around race even in the supposedly hippest of circles.

49. Hughes, "Long Trip," *Selected Poems of Langston Hughes* (New York: Alfred Knopf, 1959), p. 52.

50. Walt Whitman, "Sea Drift," *The Collected Writings of Walt Whitman*, ed. Gay Wilson Allen and Sculley Bradley, vol. 4, *Leaves of Grass* (New York: New York University Press, 1965), pp. 246-63; (Harmondsworth, England: Penguin, 1986), pp. 275-91. Henry

Louis Gates, Jr., remarked upon the black and white antecedents of African-American texts in a workshop on Zora Neale Hurston's *Their Eyes Were Watching God* in February 1986 at Stanford University.

51. "Hart Crane," *The Norton Anthology of American Literature, vol. II*, ed. Gott - man et al. (New York: Norton, 1979), p. 1350.

52. Hart Crane, "At Melville's Tomb" *The Complete Poems and Selected Letters of Hart Crane*, ed. Brom Weber (New York: Liveright Publishing, 1933), p. 34.

53. See Crane's "Voyages," *Complete Poems*, p. 36. Reviewing *Closing Time Till Dawn* (San Francisco: The Bob Kaufman Collective, 1986), Kaufman's posthumously published collaboration with Janice Blue, Tom Clark explicitly proposes Crane as Kaufman's main literary forebear: "Kaufman survived to the age of 61 [actually 60], well beyond the span of many self-consuming poet-visionaries—including Hart Crane, the poet whose work Kaufman's probably has most in common with. Kaufman's poems resemble Crane's in their rhetorical locutions, their leaps between elliptical, daring images, and (to use Crane's own phrases) their 'emotional dynamics' and reliance on a 'logic of metaphor.' Kaufman's best poems, though, have something extra—a quality of gentleness and compassion, a radiating of hope and light that relieves the brokenness of experience. In these 'metaphysical designs of want and care,' as Kaufman once called his poems, things often seem to be hovering at the brink of some ecstatic transformation—a transfiguration of the personal realm into eternal dimensions" (Tom Clark's "A Hipster Poet's Nocturnal Muse," *San Francisco Chronicle Book Review*, August 3, 1986, p. 3).

54. John Milton, "Lycidas," *Complete Poems and Major Prose*, ed. Merritt Hughes (Indianapolis: Bobbs-Merrill, 1975), p. 125, l. 173.

55. See, for example, Michael Moon, "Desublimating the Male Sublime: Autoerotics, Anal Erotics, and Corporal Violence in Melville and William Burroughs," paper presented in December 1989 at MLA, Washington, D.C.; and Thomas Yingling, *Hart Crane and the Homosexual Text* (Chicago: University of Chicago Press, 1990), p. 63.

56. Yingling, *Hart Crane*, p. 78.

57. Crane, "Voyages II," l. 22, *Complete Poems*, p. 35.

58. Crane, "Black Tambourine," *Complete Poems*, p. 4; *The Letters of Hart Crane, 1916-1932*, ed. Brom Weber (Berkeley: University of California Press, 1965), p. 77.

59. Kaufman's survival of four shipwrecks is mentioned by A. D. Winans's biographical sketch in *Dictionary of Literary Biography*, vol. 16, p. 275.

60. See Du Bois, *Souls*; Stephen Henderson, *New Black Poetry*; Hughes, *Selected Poems*; LeRoi Jones/Amiri Baraka, *Blues People*; Ntozake Shange, "takin' a solo / a poetic possibility / a poetic imperative," *Nappy Edges* (New York: St. Martin's Press, 1978), pp. 2-12; Baker, *Blues*. This list is only partial, and could be infinitely expanded.

61. Jones/Baraka, *Blues People*, pp. 188-89. For a detailed comparison of Charlie Parker's music and Kaufman's poetry, see Charles Nilon.

62. Baraka, *The Autobiography: LeRoi Jones/Amiri Baraka* (New York: Freundlich Books, 1984), pp. 58-60.

63. Nathaniel Mackey on *Tribute to Bob Kaufman*, KPFA Radio, April 1991.

64. John Birks Gillespie with Al Fraser, *To Be or Not to Bop: Memoirs of Dizzy Gillespie* (New York: Da Capo, 1979), p. 281.

65. Miles Davis with Quincy Troupe, *Miles: The Autobiography* (New York: Simon and Schuster, 1990), p. 7.

66. One could further postulate on the "masculinism" of these ejaculations. Joel Fineman, using as his sources Roman Jakobson, Morris Halle, and Freud, has written of "b," "p," and "d" words that indicate a paternal orientation ("papa" etc.) and the "m" and "n" words that indicate a maternal affiliation. Both the "b, p, d" sounds and the "m, n" sounds are among the earliest, if not the earliest, acquired in childhood. One connection he does not make is, by extension, that of fatherhood to elimination or "below the waist" activities (poo-poo, doo-doo, piss, petting), and motherhood to oral functions (nursing, mammaries, mmm, yummy, nay-nays, necking). Does this mean that "Sha-na-na" and the classic cartoon opera singer's "mimimi" indicate certain pseudo-doowoppers and tenors are maternally fixated? This is altogether too silly for serious subjects like bebop. What could it mean here? It's a stretch, but in such a con-text, the deployment of infantile references to elimination and sexual release in a highly intellectual and aesthetic structure indicates a consummate tricksterism. See Joel Fineman, "The Structure of Allegorical Desire," *Allegory and Representation*, ed. Stephen J. Greenblatt (Baltimore: Johns Hopkins University Press, 1981), pp. 26-60, esp. pp. 54-55, 34n and 39n.

67. Ruth Finnegan's argument for the drum as a verbal rather than musical instru-ment is in "Drum Language and Literature," *Oral Literature in Africa* (London: Clar-endon, 1970), pp. 481-99.

68. Hughes, *Selected Poems*, p. 87.

69. See Paul Oliver, *Savannah Syncopators: African Retentions in the Blues* (New York: Stein and Day, 1970), pp. 43-52.

70. Ibid., pp. 47-48.

71. Ibid., p. 49.

72. Davis with Troupe, *Miles*, p. 397.

73. Kofi Awoonor, *The Breast of the Earth: A Survey of the History, Culture and Lit-erature of Africa South of the Sahara* (Garden City, N.Y.: Anchor Press, 1975), pp. 115-25.

3. The Child Who Writes / The Child Who Died

1. Jean-Paul Sartre, *Saint Genet*, trans. Bernard Frechtman (New York: George Bra-ziller, 1963), p. 9.

2. Andreas Huyssen, "Mass Culture as Woman: Modernism's Other," in *Studies in Entertainment: Critical Approaches to Mass Culture*, ed. Tania Modleski (Bloomington: Indiana University Press, 1986), pp. 188-207.

3. Judy Grahn, interview, *Aurora* (Spring 1983), p. 1.

4. I would like to acknowledge the assistance, encouragement and inspiration of Barbara Machtinger, who was my colleague and "boss" at City Roots; Renato Rosaldo, in whose seminar I initially realized that I was "allowed to" write about texts that moved me and in which I had a personal stake; and particularly Cheryl Mellen, Char-lotte Osborne, and Susan Johnson, whose writing in the face of adversity sustained me for many years, and who have given me permission to share their work.

5. Official document entitled "Memorial to Boston," quoted in John J. Toomey and Edward Rankin, *History of South Boston* (Boston, 1901), pp. 153-54.

6. George V. Higgins, *Style Versus Substance: Boston, Kevin White and the Politics of Illusion* (New York: Macmillan, 1984), pp. 43-44.

7. For more information on the South Boston busing crisis and on the relation of South Boston to other ethnic groups in Boston, see Higgins; J. Anthony Lukas, *Common Ground* (New York: Alfred Knopf, 1986), especially the "McGoff" sections; Ione Malloy, *Southie Won't Go* (Urbana: University of Illinois Press, 1986); Alan Lupo, *Liberty's Chosen Home: The Politics of Violence in Boston* (Boston: Beacon Press, 1988); and James Jennings and Mel King, *From Access to Power: Black Politics in Boston* (Cambridge, Mass.: Schenkman, 1986).

8. See, for example, "South Boston and Ethnic Identity," presented at the American Sociological Association, 1982, p. 10. The title page was missing from the manuscript copy I was given. Much of the information presented here about South Boston is drawn from this article.

9. Ibid., p. 10.

10. Charlotte Osborne, letter to author, December 26, 1991: "Valiums, Quaaludes, and angel dust were never part of my life."

11. Ibid.

12. Dick Hebdige, *Subculture: The Meaning of Style* (London: Methuen, 1979); Paul E. Willis, *Profane Culture* (London: Routledge and Kegan Paul, 1978); Stuart Hall, Tony Jefferson et al., *Resistance Through Rituals* (London: Hutchinson, 1976); Mike Brake, *Comparative Youth Culture* (London: Routledge and Kegan Paul, 1985); Geoff Mungham and Geoff Pearson, eds., *Working Class Youth Culture* (London: Routledge and Kegan Paul, 1976). These works, for the most part, mention but do not redress satisfactorily the lack of writing on young women. Angela McRobbie's work is a welcome exception—her essay on fan clubs and girl's culture appears in Hall and Jefferson, and she has edited with Mica Nava *Gender and Generation* (London: Routledge and Kegan Paul, 1987). For another look at young working-class women artists, see the interview with graffiti artists Lady Pink and Lady Heart: Nancy Guevara, "Graffiti Talk: Words, Walls and Women," *Tabloid: a Review of Mass Culture and Everyday Life* 9 (Winter 1985), pp. 20-24.

13. Charlotte Osborne's letter.

14. Ibid. Charlotte writes that her brother has since obtained his adoption papers and they had a joyful reunion after twenty-seven years of separation. Included in this update is the information that she is now (1991) thirty years old, happily married, and since September 1991 the mother of a beautiful baby girl named Miriah. She teaches ceramics to adults and children, but more importantly, she writes, "I teach my daughter what love is."

15.

A ~~forched~~ Tortured mind
AN Adult mind tRApped in a body years yonger
A peace of soul & mind FoR which I Hunger
Being toRN ApaRt by A FAmily I can't please
When will this toRmented mind be at Ease

Needed By MANY, Loved by ~~note~~ note
The weight I bare is more then a ton
A tourched mind that wants to be free
Alway wondering if others can see
~~can see~~

For Around my friends I try to hide
Those haunting words "I wish I died"
But to die by my own hand would Be a sin
And there's always the thought of what
Could of been

I act as if I'm happy to be me
Only because I don't want people to see
That I've been this way for quite
A while
A torched mind behind a smile

By
Charlotte

16. Willis, *Profane Culture*, p. 3.

17. Paraphrased from a lecture on film script writing, Naropa Institute, July 1977. The same notion appears frequently in Burroughs's interviews and essays.

18. John Berger, *Ways of Seeing* (London: The British Broadcasting Corporation, 1972), pp. 45ff.

19. Tania Modleski, *Loving With a Vengeance: Mass-Produced Fantasies for Women* (London: Methuen, 1985), p. 55.

20. Fredric Jameson, "Baudelaire as Modernist and Postmodernist," *Lyric Poetry: Beyond New Criticism*, ed. Chaviva Hosek and Patricia Parker (Ithaca: Cornell University Press, 1985), pp. 255-56.

21. For a comprehensive overview of the development of the term "youth culture," see Graham Murdock and Robin McCron, "Youth and Class: The Career of a Confusion," in Mungham and Pearson, pp. 10-26. Murdock and McCron are especially careful to expose the fallacy that "youth culture" is a cross-class phenomenon, and that the term "youth culture" has itself been used to obscure class differences. What is most often referred to as "youth culture," they argue, is actually working-class youth culture as defined by the market economy. This is because as members of the wage-earning work force, the working-class youth, especially in the relative economic expansion after World War II, became mass-market consumers, and the products geared toward them became metonymic emblems of "youth" and its values. The relevance here of their critique of the notion of a classless "youth culture" lies in the ease with which

"youth" as an idea can be manipulated to represent any number of threatening or con-soling ideas of rebellion, grace, physicality, intensity.

22. Ken Auletta, "Reporter at Large: The Underclass," *The New Yorker*, November 16, 1981, pp. 63ff; Janet Cooke, "Jimmy's World," *Washington Post*, September 28, 1980, p. A1; Stephen Crane, *Maggie: A Girl of the Streets* (New York: Norton, 1979).

23. This interpretation of a "community of place" was offered by George Lipsitz.

24. Susan Stewart, *On Longing* (Baltimore: Johns Hopkins University Press, 1985), p. 146-47.

25. Jameson, "Baudelaire," p. 255.

26. Jean-François Lyotard, trans. Régis Durand, "Appendix: Answering the Question: What Is Postmodernism?" in *The Postmodern Condition: A Report on Knowledge* (Min-neapolis: University of Minnesota Press, 1985), pp. 77-79.

27. Jameson, "Baudelaire," p. 261.

28. As in other forms of the marginalization of youth, which will be further dis-cussed in the section of this chapter that treats Robert Lowell, this "continued youth" imposed by the middle class on the poor is ambiguous. The reverse is also true; the middle class expects the poor to "parent" them just as adults expect their children, or men expect women, to parent them by serving their needs, by undergoing sacrifices for the middle class's benefit, by enduring what they themselves could not. Theirs is the power of definition, so their actual economic and social dependency on the poor can be masked as its opposite, as in the rhetoric surrounding the "welfare state" con-cept. I thank Mary Wood for bringing this point to my attention.

29. Jameson, "Baudelaire," p. 262.

30. Susan Sontag, "Notes on Camp," *Against Interpretation and Other Essays* (New York: Farrar, Strauss and Giroux, 1966), pp. 279-92.

31. Richard Louv, *America II* (Los Angeles: Jeremy Tarcher, 1980), pp. 5-6.

32. Renato Rosaldo, "Imperialist Nostalgia," *Culture and Truth* (Boston: Beacon Press, 1989), pp. 68-87.

33. Janice Doane and Devon Hodges, *Nostalgia and Sexual Difference: The Resis-tance to Contemporary Feminism* (London: Methuen, 1987).

34. Hougan, *Decadence: Radical Nostalgia, Narcissism and Decline in the Seventies* (New York: William Morrow, 1975), pp. 194-95.

35. See Susan Stewart, *On Longing* (Baltimore: Johns Hopkins University Press, 1985), pp. 145-50, for a discussion of the symbolic value of tourist art.

36. Audre Lorde, *The Black Unicorn: Poems* (New York: Norton, 1978). Even a poem with as different a perspective on the pan-African predicament as Countee Cullen's "Heritage" looks on Africa as a dream-puzzle; what must it or can it mean to twentieth-century Black Americans? Cullen evokes exotic images ("spicy grove, cinnamon tree / What is Africa to me?") to question them and acknowledge the ambiguity of his felt connection—not to assert these images as truth.

37. Cynthia Ozick, *The Pagan Rabbi and Other Stories* (New York: Dutton, 1983), and Maxine Hong Kingston, *The Woman Warrior* (New York: Alfred Knopf, 1976). For more on recreating ethnicity, see Michael Fischer's "Ethnicity and the Postmodern Arts of Memory," in *Writing Culture: The Poetics and Politics of Ethnography*, ed. James Clif-ford and George E. Marcus (Berkeley: University of California Press, 1986), pp. 194-233.

38. Audre Lorde, "The Master's Tools Will Never Dismantle the Master's House," *This Bridge Called My Back: Writings by Radical Women of Color*, ed. Cherie Moraga and Gloria Anzaldúa (Boston: Persephone Press, 1981), pp. 98-101. For an exposition

of neo-Freudian concepts of the Phallus's representation of socio-discursive authority, see Jacques Lacan, *Feminine Sexuality*, trans. Jacqueline Rose (New York: Norton, 1982).

39. Not much has been written specifically about the relation of the resurgence of the lyric's popularity to the rise of industrial capitalism. Anne Williams claims that the rise of the lyric paralleled the rise of the novel in *Prophetic Strain: The Greater Lyric in the Eighteenth Century* (Chicago: University of Chicago Press, 1984), p. 38. For an analysis of the development of the novel in relation to the rise of industrial capitalism and the creed of individualism, see Ian Watt, *The Rise of the Novel* (Berkeley: University of California Press, 1957).

40. William Wordsworth, "Ode: Intimations of Immortality from Recollections of Early Childhood," *The Poetical Works of William Wordsworth*, vol. 4, ed. E. de Selincourt and Helen Darishire (Oxford: Clarendon Press, 1947), pp. 282-83.

41. That poetry critical of the cruelty of child labor can be read as a lie—as a denial of the truth and the perpetration of a myth of bliss—points to the complicated debates surrounding the role of poetry in society. Some theorists have argued that poetry acts as almost a photographic negative of contemporaneous social, historical, economic events—that is, in the progress of industrial capitalism. The two—poetry and society—are interdependent but symmetrically opposed: complementary, perhaps. See Theodor Adorno, "The Lyric in Society," *Telos* 20 (1974), pp. 56-71; and Benjamin, "On Some Motifs in Baudelaire."

42. Eve Kosofsky Sedgwick, "A Poem Is Being Written," *Representations* 17 (Winter 1987), pp. 110-43.

43. Philippe Ariès. *Centuries of Childhood: A Social History of Family Life*, trans. Robert Baldick (London: Cape, 1962).

44. Alice Miller, *For Your Own Good: Hidden Cruelty in Child-Rearing and the Roots of Violence*, trans. Hildegarde and Hunter Hannum (New York: Farrar, Straus and Giroux, 1983), p. 283.

45. Ibid., p. 284.

46. Ricky Sherover-Marcuse, "Toward a Perspective on Unlearning Racism: 12 Working Assumptions," #7.

47. Sherover-Marcuse, "Liberation Theory: Part I. Axioms and Working Assumptions about the Perpetuation of Social Oppression," p. 2, axiom 13.

48. Sherover-Marcuse, "Toward a Perspective," #12.

49. Sartre, *Saint Genet*; and *The Family Idiot*, trans. Carol Cosman (Chicago: University of Chicago Press, 1981).

50. Countee Cullen, "Incident," *Color* (New York: Harper and Brothers, 1925), p. 15.

51. Miller, Sherover-Marcuse, Sartre, Althusser all occupy relatively privileged social positions (except that the former two are women and Sherover-Marcuse is Jewish, a significant distinction to be made within contemporary "whiteness") as bourgeois intellectuals and professionals. In my urgency to establish a place for children in the roster of out-castes am I perversely blind to the inequities of race and class? Am I indulging in a disingenuous "me-too-ism"—after all, I fit the formulaic and sketchy description I just applied to my informing theorists—designed to place me in the company of Kaufman, Osborne, Genet? In writing about Lowell it is perhaps tautological to invoke the names and ideas of those who share his social position, his concerns with his individual psychopathology, his sense of the tremendous spiritual and emotional

impoverishment of worldly privilege and the psychic battering that conditioned him to conceal personal shame and inadequacy behind social standing. However, I think not. Recent African-American art and theory coming from the economic as well as ethnic/racial margin is as much concerned with the early lessons of childhood as these older, European models. Michele Wallace's introduction to the new edition of her *Black Macho and the Myth of the Superwoman* (New York: Verso, 1990), pp. xvii-xxx-viii, bell hooks's most recent musings on the Black family (public lecture, Walker Art Center, Minneapolis, 1991), David Mura's writings about pornography as a "male grief" (Minneapolis: Milkweed Editions, 1987), and the spate of films coming from young African-American men—particularly *Straight Out of Brooklyn* and *Boyz N the Hood*—as well as Richard Pryor's solo work through *Jojo Dancer*, combine an awareness of social trauma with a sensitivity to the trauma of childhood interpellation. The exquisitely painful honesty of much of this work moves it beyond the self-dramatizing confines of a confessional mode and into the realm of social urgency in a way that Robert Lowell's work, for all its empathetic accessibility, did not achieve.

52. Julia Kristeva, *Revolution in Poetic Language*, trans. Margaret Waller (New York: Columbia University Press, 1984).

53. Miller specifically mentions the memory of a strong love of and identification with nature as a characteristic of a sensitive and abused / neglected child (*The Drama of the Gifted Child* [New York: Basic Books, 1981]). This observation has tremendous possibilities for rereading Wordsworth, Roethke, and the German Romantics—the latter especially because Miller's evidence for "poisonous" or abusive pedagogy is drawn primarily from German child-rearing manuals of the last three centuries.

54. Jochen Schulte-Sasse, "Foreword," Peter Bürger, *Theory of the Avant-Garde*, trans. Michael Shaw (Minneapolis: University of Minnesota Press, 1984), p. xxviii.

55. Sedgwick, "A Poem Is Being Written."

56. Stewart, *On Longing*, pp. xi-xii.

57. "Abnormal reticence": W. R. Johnson, *The Idea of Lyric: Lyric Modes in Ancient and Modern Poems* (Berkeley: University of California Press, 1982), p. 1.

58. In a lecture on gay poetic history given at Naropa Institute in July 1980, Harold Norse, a gay North Beach Beat poet, has explicitly connected the "objective correlative" with Eliot's need to keep his homoerotic feelings in the closet. Denying himself direct expression of his love for Jean Verdenal, Eliot built his poetics around displacement and the substitution of objects for expression of feeling. This very poignant and provocative hypothesis implies that the whole of academically legitimated poetics of twentieth-century America is founded on the pain of gay emotional self-denial. See chapter 4, "Dirty Jokes and Angels: Jack Spicer and Robert Duncan Writing the Gay Community," note 7.

59. For example, Richard Poirier: "Robert Lowell is, by something like a critical consensus, the greatest American poet of the mid-century, probably the greatest poet writing in English" ("Our Truest Historian," *New York Herald Tribune Weekly Book Review*, Oct. 11, 1964, p. 1); Stanley Kunitz: "[Lowell is] . . . the most celebrated poet in English of his generation . . . " ("Talk with Robert Lowell," *New York Times Book Review*, Oct. 11, 1964, pp. 34-49). Some of the university press books will be cited in this essay: Cornell's by Marjorie Perloff; Yale's by Allan Williamson; Princeton's by Steven Gould Axelrod; Harvard's by Vereen Bell (*Robert Lowell: Nihilist as Hero*, 1983).

60. The term "confessional" was coined by M. L. Rosenthal in a review of *Life Studies* which became a book on "them"—the confessional poets, that is, not the *Life Stud-*

ies. See Diane Wood Middlebrook, *Anne Sexton: A Biography* (Boston: Houghton-Mifflin, 1991), p. 112. For descriptions of Lowell's famous workshops, see Middlebrook, especially chapter 5, "Mentors: 1958-1959," pp. 93-115.

61. Robert Lowell, *Life Studies,* and *Imitations,* and *For the Union Dead* (New York: Farrar, Straus and Giroux, 1959, 1961, and 1964 respectively). Henceforth Lowell's work will be cited in the text as follows: LS: *Life Studies*; I: *Imitations*; FUD: *For the Union Dead.*

62. Ian Hamilton, *Robert Lowell: A Biography* (New York: Random House, 1983), pp. 234-35.

63. Ibid., p. 239.

64. Perloff, *The Poetic Art of Robert Lowell* (Ithaca: Cornell University Press, 1973), p. xi.

65. Ibid., p. 99.

66. Ibid.

67. For an explanation of the term "homosocial," see Eve Kosofsky Sedgwick, *Between Men: English Literature and Male Homosocial Desire* (New York: Columbia University Press, 1985), pp. 1-5.

68. See Perloff, "The Limits of Imitation: Robert Lowell's Rimbaud," *Robert Lowell,* pp. 59-75, for a thorough discussion of "Nostalgia" and of other critics' responses to it as autobiography. She argues for a nonbiographical reading of the poem, in which "elle" is the river, and "lui" is the sun. See also the biographies of Rimbaud published in the fifties and sixties, which are enraptured with Rimbaud's painful childhood, in particular Enid Starkie's *Arthur Rimbaud* (New York: New Directions, 1961) and Elisabeth Hanson's *My Poor Arthur* (New York: Henry Holt, 1959). One might speculate on women biographers' attraction to Rimbaud and the primacy they place on his relationship with his overbearing and tyrannical mother.

69. Arthur Rimbaud, "Le Bateau Ivre," *Oeuvres Complètes* (Paris: Editions Gallimard, 1963), pp. 66-69.

70. *Imitations,* xi.

71. Perloff, *Robert Lowell,* p. 13.

72. Hamilton, *Robert Lowell,* quoting a letter from Merrill Moore to Lowell's father, p. 65, also Lowell to Ransom, p. 57. On Tate's involvement in Lowell's bouts with psychiatric and police confinement, concluding in his complaint to Mrs. Lowell about being a substitute parent, pp. 156-60.

73. Ibid., p. 67.

74. Lowell, National Book Award acceptance speech, March 23, 1960, quoted by Hamilton, *Robert Lowell,* p. 277.

75. See Hamilton, *Robert Lowell,* p. 237, for Tate's letter to Lowell: "*All* the poems about your family, including the one about you and Elizabeth, are definitely *bad.* I do not think you ought to publish them. . . . Quite bluntly, these details, presented in *causerie* and at random, are of interest only to you. They are, of course, of great interest to me because I am one of your oldest friends. But they have no public or literary interest" (The italics are Tate's). Tate subsequently changed his mind, after the poems' publication. See Hamilton, pp. 268-73, for other critical responses, both American and British, including warm praise from William Carlos Williams and A. Alvarez, and mixed reviews, from the cautious to the vicious, from M. L. Rosenthal in *The Nation,* F. W. Dupee in *Partisan Review,* Joseph Bennett for the *Hudson Review,* and Thom Gunn in the *Yale Review,* etc.

76. Miller stresses that most children repress their negative memories of childhood; remembering and speaking about it to a sympathetic interlocutor can literally save a person's life. Though Lowell does not seem to have had a confidant as a child, he was unusually aware of his own feelings; perhaps this is what saved him from the suicide that overtook so many of his contemporaries: Plath, Sexton, Berryman, et al. One could also argue that Lowell's confessions came too late, and his self-destructive compulsions were tantamount to suicide; Lowell certainly had no greater claim to mental health than his peers, and the severity of his mental and emotional illness may indicate that simple utterance—confession—is not enough. Miller, *For Your Own Good*, p. 284.

77. See, for example, Louise Eichenbaum and Susie Orbach, *Understanding Women: Feminist Psychotherapy* (Harmondsworth, England: Penguin, 1983), p. 38. While this work focuses exclusively on women's upbringings and self-denial in the interest of others, this paradigm could be expanded and accomodated to apply to boys and men. It is a psychotherapeutic truism, especially initiated by the currently popular concept of the "adult child."

78. Jacqueline Rose, "Julia Kristeva—Take Two," *Sexuality in the Field of Vision* (London: Verso, 1986), pp. 141-64.

79. Luce Irigaray, "When Our Lips Speak Together," trans. Carolyn Burke, *Signs* 6:1 (Autumn 1980), pp. 69-79.

80. Lowell's attitude toward actual Jews was awkward, embarrassed and ambivalently well-intentioned. In spite of his indignation about the Jews' treatment in Europe and the Soviet Union, his shaky friendship with Delmore Schwartz (which broke decisively after Lowell's liaison with Schwartz's ex-wife, Gertrude Buckman) foundered after a dinner at Lowell's parents', during which Schwartz was constantly reminded of his Jewishness (Hamilton, *Robert Lowell*, p. 110). Lowell also remarked to Jean Stafford, his then wife, "I would never have a Jew as a close friend." C. David Heymann, *American Aristocracy: The Lives and Times of James Russell, Amy and Robert Lowell* (New York: Dodd, Mead, 1980), pp. 362-63.

81. Lowell quoted by Perloff, *Robert Lowell*, pp. 3-4.

82. Robert von Hallberg, *American Poetry and Culture, 1945-1980*, p. 93. See also Perloff's discussion of "The Confessional Mode: Romanticism and Realism," pp. 80-99, and Heymann, *American Aristocracy*, pp. 396-408.

83. Hamilton, *Robert Lowell*, p. 200.

84. Miller, p. 278.

85. Hamilton, *Robert Lowell*, p. 287.

86. von Hallberg, *American Poetry*, p. 173.

87. Alan Williamson, *Pity the Monsters: The Political Vision of Robert Lowell* (New Haven: Yale University Press, 1974).

88. Robert Lowell, "Near the Unbalanced Aquarium," *Collected Prose* (New York: Farrar, Straus and Giroux, 1987), pp. 358-59.

89. Heymann, *American Aristocracy*, p. 363.

90. von Hallberg, *American Poetry*, p. 174.

4. Dirty Jokes and Angels: Jack Spicer and Robert Duncan Writing the Gay Community

1. Ralph Waldo Emerson, "The Poet," *Selected Essays*, ed. Larzer Ziff (Harmondsworth: Penguin, 1982), pp. 259-84.

2. Walt Whitman, "Preface 1855—Leaves of Grass, First Edition," in *The Collected Writings of Walt Whitman*, Vol. 4, *Leaves of Grass: Comprehensive Readers' Edition*, Gay Wilson Allen and Sculley Bradley (New York: New York University Press, 1965), pp. 709-29.

3. Allen Ginsberg, "Howl," *Howl* (San Francisco: City Lights, 1956), pp. 9-22.

4. Ginsberg, "A Supermarket in California," *Howl*, p. 24.

5. San Jose Poetry Center flyer, May, 1988.

6. Gertrude Stein plays an analogous role in lesbian American literary history, drawing together themes of national identity (*The Making of Americans*), language and same-sex desire (*Lifting Belly* and *Tender Buttons*), the constitution of identity and community through erotic partnership (*The Autobiography of Alice B. Toklas*).

7. See the reference to Harold Norse's lecture on gay poetic history given at the Naropa Institute in July, 1980, cited in note 53 to chapter 3. See also Robert K. Martin, *The Homosexual Tradition in American Poetry* (Austin: University of Texas Press, 1979), p. xx.

8. Martin, *Homosexual Tradition*, pp. 61-63 and 85; Walt Whitman, "Scented Herbiage of My Breast," "That Shadow My Likeness," *The Collected Poems*, ed. Francis Murphy, *Calamus* (Harmondsworth, England: Penguin, 1975), pp. 146 and 167, respectively.

9. Martin, *Homosexual Tradition*, p. 61.

10. Ibid., pp. 1-8. See also Ed Cohen's "Writing Gone Wilde: Homoerotic Desire in the Closet of Representation," *PMLA* (October 1987), pp. 801-13, for a demonstration of how an ostensibly "straight" text both conceals and offers a homoerotic subversion of "normative standards of male same-sex behavior" (*PMLA*, p. 760).

11. Robert Duncan explained his theory of etymology in a lecture at Stanford University, May 1984. Duncan is literally second-sighted, following an accident in his third year which left him permanently cross-eyed, seeing everything double—that is, always seeing two separate and overlapping images where the normal-sighted person would see only one; this difference in vision lends authority to his claims that the physical is inextricably interwoven with the spiritual. For a detailed account of Duncan's physical eyesight and its relation to his aesthetic vision, see Ekbert Faas's *Young Robert Duncan: Portrait of the Poet as Homosexual in Society* (Santa Barbara: Black Sparrow Press, 1983), pp. 18-20.

12. Thom Gunn, "My Sad Captains," *Moly* and *My Sad Captains* (New York: Farrar, Straus and Giroux, 1973), p. 91.

13. James Merrill, *The Changing Light at Sandover* (Boston: Atheneum Press, 1982).

14. Hart Crane, "The Bridge," *The Complete Poems and Selected Letters of Hart Crane*, ed. Brom Weber (Garden City, N.Y.: Anchor Books, 1966), pp. 45-117.

15. Robert Duncan, "At the Loom: Passages 2," *Bending the Bow* (New York: New Directions, 1968), pp. 11-13; "Warp and Woof: Notes from a Talk," *Talking Poetics from Naropa Institute*, vol. 1, ed. Anne Waldman and Marilyn Webb (Boulder: Shambhala, 1978), pp. 1-10. Henceforth, works by Duncan will be cited in the text, abbreviated as follows: YC, *The Years as Catches* (San Francisco: Oyez, 1966); BB, *Bending the Bow*

(New York: New Directions, 1968); FC, *Fictive Certainties* (New York: New Directions, 1985); OF, *The Opening of the Field* (New York: Grove Press, 1960); CG, *Caesar's Gate* (San Francisco: Sand Dollar, 1972); RB, *Roots and Branches* (New York: New Directions, 1964); GS, interview in *Gay Sunshine Interviews Volume II*, ed. Winston Leyland (San Francisco: Gay Sunshine Press, 1975), interview conducted by Steve Abbott and Aaron Shurin, pp. 77-94.

16. Michael Lynch, in an article on the phrenological origins of the notion of "adhesiveness," demonstrates that the word originally referred to friendly affection or nationalistic sentiment, but that Whitman appropriated it to designate same-sex, manly eroticism. This connection illuminates the poet's assertion of the inseparability of private homoerotic feeling and public citizenly relationships (" 'Here is Adhesiveness': From Friendship to Homosexuality," *Victorian Studies* 29:1 [Autumn 1985], pp. 67-96).

17. Walt Whitman, *Democratic Vistas*, in *Complete Prose Works* (Boston, 1898). This particular passage served as Ginsberg's epigraph to *The Fall of America: Poems of These States, 1965-1971* (San Francisco: City Lights Books, 1973), which he dedicated to Whitman. The choice of epigraph, dedication, and Ginsberg's own title suggest that for Ginsberg in 1971, the power structure of America would have to fall in order for Whitman's "democratic vistas" to be fully realized. It also serves as the epigraph to Martin's book.

Many key figures discussed in this study see the recognition of their experience of marginality and its acceptance into American public life to be integral to the political well-being of the nation as a whole, as well as to the health of the group they speak for. Not only does Whitman make this claim about manly friendship in "Democratic Vistas," but W. E. B. Du Bois, in *The Souls of Black Folk*, refers to the "problem of the color line" as the crucial issue facing twentieth-century America (p. xi); and Adrienne Rich's apocalyptically titled "When We Dead Awaken: Writing as Re-vision" (Rich, *On Lies, Secrets and Silence: Selected Prose 1966-1978* [New York: Norton, 1979], pp. 33-49) makes the same claim for gender relations. As Ricky Sherover-Marcuse has pointed out, it is all too painfully obvious to the target group in any given form of oppression how barren are the lives of those who cannot accept them as equal; thus the argument is that recognition of the humanity of the target group would heal the entirety of the wounded society.

18. See, again, Faas's pages (notably page 20) on Duncan's eyesight in relation to the most often employed stylistic device in his critical writings: the phrase "back of . . ." to indicate a transition to a deeper exegesis of a given passage. The image conjured by this phrase is of layered texture contributing to overall substance, rather than a hierarchic implication that what is "back of" is truer than what is "up front."

19. Martin, *Homosexual Tradition*, pp. 23 and 37.

20. Allen Ginsberg, *Gay Sunshine Interview* (Bolinas: Grey Fox Press, 1973), p. 16. Ginsberg's gay "begat" series, in that it is a "Whispered Transmission," holds the fine tension between esoteric elitism and the notion of democracy. Though he became an icon of New Age democracy during the Free Speech and Flower Power movements, and though his personal appearance for many years emulated Whitman's almost parodic rugged populist look, Ginsberg speaks touchingly to the desire to believe in a secret society of gay *confrères* who share privileged knowledge.

21. Some of the same shimmering ephemerality and "half-hid" bonds of mystico-literary affection inform Michel Foucault's eulogy for Jean Hyppolite, "The Discourse on Language," in which the happy, dreamy, polymorphous current of words connect-

ing the lecturer to his dead mentor underlies and undermines the rigidly defined world of institutional discourse. Alluding to Rimbaud's "Bateau Ivre," he says: "Inclination speaks out: 'I don't want to enter the risky world of discourse; I want nothing to do with it insofar as it is decisive and final; I would like to feel it all around me, calm and transparent, profound, infinitely open, with others responding to my expectations, and truth emerging, one by one. All I want is to allow myself to be borne along, within it, and by it, a happy wreck.' Institutions reply: ' . . . we're here to show you discourse is within the established order of things . . . and if it should happen to have a certain power, then it is we, and we alone, who give it that power.' " Foucault goes on to identify systems of exclusion in modern institutional discourse, and follows Whitman in his concerns: "The areas where this web [of prohibitions] is most tightly woven today, where the danger spots are most numerous, are those dealing with politics and sexuality . . . speech is not merely the medium which manifests — or dissembles — desire; it is also the object of desire." Foucault emphasizes the difficulties of negotiating this intermeshing of politics, sexuality, and utterance; the elite participants in the sea of words are also silenced. Unutterability is both privileged secret bond and prohibited liaison, ineffable and taboo. Philosophers who create and underwrite institutional discourse are also its most vulnerable victims. "The Discourse on Language," *The Archaeology of Knowledge & The Discourse on Language*, trans. A. M. Sheridan Smith (New York: Pantheon, 1972), pp. 215-37.

22. It is interesting to consider the effects the AIDS epidemic has had and will have on this philosophy of connectedness. Initially, the finding that promiscuous sex increased one's chances of contracting AIDS prompted a turn away from multiple partners to an ideal of monogamy; now, the emphasis has once more shifted back to the possibility of multiple partnership — using "safe sex" techniques — rather than exclusive monogamy.

23. Victor Turner, *The Ritual Process* (Ithaca: Cornell University Press, 1969), p. 127.

24. Ibid., p. 113. For Turner's entire argument, see chapter 3 of this work, "Liminality and Communitas," pp. 94-130.

25. Rich, "It Is the Lesbian Within Us," *On Lies, Secrets and Silence*, pp. 199-202; Sedgwick, *Between Men* (New York: Columbia University Press, 1985).

26. Again, in "The Discourse on Language," Foucault addresses the "opposition of true and false as a . . . system of exclusion . . . in a state of constant flux, supported by a system of institutions imposing and manipulating them, acting . . . [not] without an element . . . of violence?" (p. 217). In other words, Foucault points to the historical exigencies informing the division of truth and falsity: given that these are historical, and not immutable, constructs, why not play with them, investigate, use up, and transgress the roles available to one's subculture? Why not give "appearance" its due as well as "reality"? Gay culture has developed the fine talent for playing in the space between the two: What is parodic? What is "authentic"? Foucault, though his talk stresses the difficulties — the impossibilities — inherent in ever-compromising and ever-emancipatory speech, plays dazzlingly with the very impossibilities he articulates. A renegade son of the philosophic tradition, he plays along Plato's faultline dividing history and poetry. (Is this gay philosophy: "I contradict myself? very well then, I contradict myself"?)

27. Frank O'Hara, "Autobiographia Literaria," *The Selected Poems of Frank O'Hara*, ed. Donald Allen (New York: Random House, 1974), p. 3.

28. Besides Whitman and Crane, whose concern with American expansionism pervades *Leaves of Grass* and *The Bridge* respectively, see Jack Spicer's *Billy The Kid*, a homoerotic fanatasy of Billy in the Old West, and William Burroughs's *The Place of Dead Roads* (New York: Holt, Rinehart and Winston, 1983), a satirical saga of the West complete with a gay outlaw gang named the Wild Fruits.

29. "Stefan George," *Twentieth-Century Culture*, ed. Bullock and Woodings, pp. 264-65.

30. For more on Stefan George and the larger issue of nationalism and the body, see George L. Mosse, *Nationalism and Sexuality* (New York: H. Fertig, 1985), pp. 49, 58-61.

31. Ernst Kantorowicz quoting Edmund Plowden in *The King's Two Bodies: A Study in Medieval Political Theology* (Princeton: Princeton University Press, 1957), p. 9.

32. We can see the Hitlerian model resurfacing in the national obsession with ex-President Reagan's colon in conjunction with his own statements that Nicaragua is a "cancer of communism" threatening the whole of the Americas: little did Che Guevara know how accurate would be the metaphor that those of us "living in the United States live in the belly of the beast." Also, and perhaps more clearly, the current national rage to retrieve MIAs from Vietnamese soil constitutes an example of the way an embattled nation concretizes the notion of the body politic: until the physical remains of these soliders are returned, America is not "whole." However, there are emblems of Nazism that find their way into some aspects of gay male culture, especially the s/m culture. As in the case of camping or drag queen culture, there is always some controversy over whether these symbols are parodic or unreflectingly imitative; likewise in the prose of Jean Genet, for example, it is never unambiguously clear whether his fascination with and adulation of Nazism is to be taken at face value or is subtly critical.

33. For extended treatment of the development of San Francisco as a gay community, and of the formation of gay culture in the 1950s and 1960s, see John D'Emilio, *Sexual Politics, Sexual Communities: The Making of a Homosexual Minority in the United States 1940-1970* (Chicago: University of Chicago Press, 1983); and Jonathon Katz, *Gay American History* (New York: Thomas Y. Crowell, 1976).

34. This personal anecdote resurfaces as a line in "Cosmopolitan Greetings," a recent poem of one-line aphorisms, mostly on the subject of censorship and subjectivity, addressed to Eastern Europeans: "If you don't show anyone, you can write anything."

35. For vividly depressing descriptions of Spicer's room, see Lew Ellingham's "The Broadway Tunnel" and Richard Tagett's "Mono/graphic Letter—Jack Spicer & Proximities" in *Manroot: The Jack Spicer Issue* 10 (Fall 1974-Winter 1975), pp. 46 and 161, respectively.

36. John D'Emilio, quoting first J. F. Goodwin and then Stan Persky in *Sexual Politics, Sexual Communities*, p. 180. D'Emilio offers convincing evidence of the points of contact between Beat and Gay culture, acknowledging the former in helping to legitimize the latter. Stan Persky, Robin Blaser's lover during some of the Renaissance years, is now an editor of the Canadian gay periodical *Body Politic*, and of *Flaunting It!*, a collection of *Body Politic* writings.

37. In the following section, references to Spicer's work will be given in the text. CB stands for *The Collected Books Of Jack Spicer* (Santa Barbara: Black Sparrow Press, 1975). Within that collection, AL is *After Lorca*, A is *Admonitions*, BM is *A Book of Music*, BK is *Billy The Kid*, HT is *Heads of the Town Up to the Aether*, L is *Language*, BMV

is *Book of Magazine Verse*. ONS is *One Night Stand and Other Poems* (Bolinas: Grey Fox, 1980).

38. Robin Blaser, *Cups* (San Francisco: Four Seasons Foundation, 1968), Part 1.

39. Ibid., Part 10.

40. Ibid., Part 1.

41. Baker, *Blues*, p. xii.

42. William Blake, "The Clod and the Pebble," *Songs of Innocence and of Experience*, in *The Poetry and Prose of William Blake*, ed. David V. Erdman with commentary by Harold Bloom (Garden City: Doubleday, 1965), p. 19, plate 32. Geoffrey Keynes, editor of *Songs of Innocence and of Experience* (New York: Orion Press, 1967), furnishes an example of typical commentary that focuses on the sharp contrast between the malleable Clod's unselfishness and the hard Pebble's "materialism."

43. The phrase is Renato Rosaldo's. See his *Culture and Truth* (Boston: Beacon, 1988), pp. 190ff.

44. See, for example, in the African-American tradition, Langston Hughes's Pierrot poems, and the accusations Zora Neale Hurston had to sustain from her own colleagues that she was "cuttin' de monkey for white folks," to Smokey Robinson's "Tears of a Clown" and "The Tracks of My Tears." It can also be discerned in the subject matter informing much of the Jewish comic tradition, as in the following joke:

In March 1940, in a Jewish refugee center in Paris, the person in charge asks the first refugee:

"Where would you like to go?"
"London," she answers.
"And you?" he asks the second.
"Sweden."
"And you?" of the third.
"New Zealand."
"New Zealand! Why so far?"
"Far from what?"

45. Gay activists' uses of positive analogies between gay and other oppressed American cultures has been discussed by John D'Emilio in *Sexual Politics*, pp. 233ff., and by Barbara Ehrenreich, *The Hearts of Men* (Garden City: Anchor Press, 1983), pp. 128-30. The phrase "ethnicization of homosexuality" is hers.

46. See Judy Grahn, *Another Mother Tongue: Gay Words, Gay Worlds* (Boston: Beacon Press, 1984), pp. 3-19.

47. Robert Martin mentions the crying-clown trope in gay culture in connection with Hart Crane: "Crane lived daily with the societal oppression of homosexuality, and his poetry reflects the ways in which he internalized that oppression. For him the recognition of his homosexuality meant a recognition of himself as an outsider, what he repeatedly portrayed as a tragic clown of love" (Martin, *Homosexual Tradition*, p. xviii).

48. See Robin Blaser's essay, "The Practice of Outside" (CB 271-329) for a full exploration of the meaning of this term in Spicer's poetics.

49. See James Herndon's and Robin Blaser's reminiscences in *The Collected Books*, pp. 351, 375-76. Much of Spicer's negativity and resentment can be attributed to inevitable disintegration of personality in the advanced stages of alcoholism, but the arenas in which this resentment plays itself out are significant. Also, since alcoholism has

reached epidemic proportions among gay people in the United States (one out of three is the common lore), the issue is not unrelated.

50. "Beyond belief and beneath contempt"—Robert Duncan, "Changing Perspectives in Reading Whitman," FC, p. 179. He is discussing faith, necessary for poetry as for theology, in the context of Whitman's interest in George Fox, founder of the Quakers, "Society of Friends," a name that resonates well with Whitman's "adhesive" ambitions.

51. Winston Leyland, ed., *Angels of the Lyre* (San Francisco: Gay Sunshine/ Panjandrum Press, 1975); Leyland, ed., *Orgasms of Light* (San Francisco: Gay Sunshine Press, 1977); Ian Young, *The Male Muse* (Trumansburg, N.Y.: Crossing Press, 1973); *Son of the Male Muse* (Trumansburg, N.Y.: Crossing Press, 1983).

52. Harold Norse, *Memoirs of a Bastard Angel* (New York: William Morrow, 1989).

53. Allen Ginsberg, "Howl," *Howl*, p. 9.

54. Aram Saroyan, *Genesis Angels: The Saga of Lew Welsh and the Beat Generation* (New York: William Morris, 1979); John Tytell, *Naked Angels* (New York: McGraw-Hill, 1976); Arthur Knight and Kit Knight, eds., *Beat Angels* (Unspeakable Visions of the Individual, 1972).

55. Michale Mayo, ed., *Practicing Angels: A Contemporary Anthology of San Francisco Bay Area Poetry* (San Francisco: Seismograph Press, 1986). The book includes such Beat names as Lawrence Ferlinghetti, Gregory Corso, and Bob Kaufman, as well as Judy Grahn, Steve Abbott, Paul Mariah, Harold Norse, and others.

56. Bruce Rodgers, *The Queen's Vernacular: A Gay Lexicon* (San Francisco: Straight Arrow, 1972).

57. See also, in the tradition of ape-angel tropes, James Merrill: in a 500-page treatise on the shadowy and angelic spirit world, he recounts a trip to see a friend's chimpanzees. He links the two explicitly:

> . . . that whole
> Fantastic monkey business of the soul
> Between lives, gathered to its patron's breast . . .
> (*Sandover*, pp. 18-19)

And see Nietzsche's similar jokes about "natural history," undoing and undermining neat culturally constructed categories of animal, human, and angelic perfection: "The Perfect Woman.—The perfect woman is a higher type of humanity than the perfect man, and also something much rarer. The natural history of animals furnishes grounds in support of this theory." *Human, All-Too-Human*, trans. Helen Zimmern (Edinburgh: T.N. Foulis, 1910), aphorism #377. Both of them approach their subjects through an animal/human dichotomy, but what Nietzsche does with man/woman, Spicer does with gay/hetero.

58. Larry Oakner has pointed to Spicer's intertextual allusion in this poem, which is, of course, Hart Crane's *The Bridge*, a similar attempt to explore the "poetic problem of distance between poet and poem or the experience" ("Jack Spicer: The Poet as Radio," *Manroot*, p. 9).

59. The motorcycle gang Hell's Angels, while not an avowedly gay group, share many symbols and styles with the gay men's leather community. Again, with postmodern indeterminacy, the gay community uses these emblems of machismo playfully, for satiric purposes, and/or out of a desire to embody a particular image of manhood.

60. See Bruce Rodgers, *Queen's Vernacular*.

61. Robert Duncan, "autistic systems," ONS, p. ix. For Jack Spicer's obsession with routine, see James Herndon, *Everything As Expected* (San Francisco, 1973), section 3.

62. Duncan, ONS, p. xiv.

63. John Freccero pointed out to me Guido Cavalcanti's "Donna Me Pregha" with its sardonic Martian reference. As Duncan counterbalances his friend Spicer's disillusionment with his affirmative love poetry, so Dante, Duncan's major influence, counters his friend Cavalcanti's bitterness in the *Commedia*, which trilogy constitutes the ultimate affirmation of heterosexual love. See Charles Singleton's commentary in Dante Alighieri's *Inferno* (Princeton: Princeton University Press, 1970), x: 69; and in *Commentary*, p. 154.

64. An obvious objection to this thesis would be to point to some of Duncan's and Spicer's acknowledged literary influences—Yeats, Rilke, Blake—who use aleatory or occult compositional methods or participate in unorthodox spiritual beliefs and efforts to join the physical and spiritual realms, and who are, according to all evidence, heterosexual. My contention is not that only out gay writers are concerned with the occult, or with spiritism, or with eroticism as a form of spiritual expression; but rather that these are characteristic preoccupations for gay male poets, to the point that some gay writers have themselves complained about the "high spiritual tone which so much gay erotic poetry takes," in one case welcoming, by contrast, Rimbaud and Verlaine's "good dirty fun." (An odd comment on that painful relationship.) J. Murat and W. Gunn's translators' introduction to Arthur Rimbaud and Paul Verlaine's *A Lover's Cock* (San Francisco: Gay Sunshine Press, 1979), p. 8.

One might also point to such writers as Frank O'Hara, who declares his allegiance to the here-and-now, to "personism," to the ephemera of names and places and urban events, and who would react with embarrassment in the face of lofty spirituality. I would argue that, like Ntozake Shange's poetry, O'Hara's seemingly random musings on city life, train schedules and catalogues of books, friends, and works of art are about energy. The exuberance with which his verse sweeps along, and the interplay of everyday events, entertainment-news, and his own consciousness as a recording surface, point beyond themselves to a joie de vivre that has to do with aleatory play and an openness of spirit, which has resonance with the collagistic poetics of the other writers more carefully studied here.

65. At a colloquium given at Stanford University in 1984, Merrill was asked what he thought of Robert Duncan's work and if he felt his own had any affinity with it. He said that people are always asking him that question and he didn't know why. He had no response—as far as he is concerned, there is no connection between their two oeuvres at all.

66. William S. Burroughs, "It Belongs to the Cucumbers: On the Subject of Raudive's Tape Voices," *Talking Poetics from Naropa Institute*, Vol. 1, ed. Anne Waldman and Marilyn Webb (Boulder: Shambhala, 1978), pp. 63-81.

67. Spicer quoted by Tagett, *Manroot*, p. 160.

68. Michael Davidson, "Jack Spicer," *Dictionary of Literary Biography*, vol. 16, p. 511.

69. The idea of subcultural style as "collage" has been explored by Hal Foster in "Readings in Cultural Resistance," *Recodings* (Port Townsend, Wash.: Bay Press, 1985), p. 170.

70. Tagett, *Manroot*, p. 161.

71. W. V. Spanos, "Jack Spicer's Poetry of Absence: An Introduction," *boundary 2: Jack Spicer* 6:1 (Fall 1977), pp. 1-2; and Colin Christopher Stuart and John Scoggan, "The Orientation of the Parasols: Saussure, Derrida, and Spicer," pp. 191-257 of the same volume.

72. Stuart and Scoggan, "Orientation," p. 193.

73. Robert Duncan, "The Homosexual in Society," *Politics*, (August 1944), pp. 209-11.

74. See Faas, *Young Robert Duncan*, pp. 151-54.

75. One difficulty people have commonly had with Duncan and his work is the sense of "staginess," or stylized self-presentation. Ekbert Faas takes this multiple role playing as the central problematic of Duncan's early life, titling the chronologically arranged chapters after different roles: "Husband and Gigolo," "The Homosexual in Society," "The Shaman Poet," "From Symmes to Duncan," etc. To explain this self-consciousness and self-reflexive preoccupation with mask in Duncan's life and work, Faas turns to aesthetic theories other than the Western Romantic notion of spontaneous unselfconscious act of empathy, quoting Sanskrit aestheticians and Brecht on Chinese art. However, it also seems clear that this sense of watching an audience watching one is a direct consequence of being in a precariously marginal situation, reflecting the double consciousness I addressed in the introductory chapter of this study. In Duncan's case, while it was acceptable, as a teenager and young adult, to clown around and "camp," any false—or rather true—move involving actual sexual contact could send one to jail. Again, this aesthetic balances with astonishing and admirable delicacy between victimage and empowerment, dissolving, as it does so, that very division. (See Faas, *Young Robert Duncan*, p. 81.)

76. Robert K. Martin writes about Whitman's use of the figure of Christ as well: "Whitman often compared himself to Christ. (This comparison is felt by many to be blasphemous and a sign of arrogance on the part of Whitman. It must be remembered that Whitman was not a Christian and that his reference therefore cannnot be blasphemous. Whitman compares himself not to a divinity but to a moral teacher) . . . It is quite possible . . . that Whitman was aware of the theory that Christianity had in fact begun as a homosexual cult, with the relationship between Jesus and St. John, the Beloved disciple, as the paradigm. . . . The New Jerusalem of brotherly love was to be located in America, founded, likewise, by Whitman" (Martin, *Homosexual Tradition*, p. 42). While there is some similarity to Duncan's use of the Christ figure, I would argue that Duncan is specifically interested in Christ's divinity and simultaneous humanity, as a paradigm for the possibilities of union in gay physical love. Duncan is less interested in moral teaching on a large scale, but certainly believes that to fall in love is to "bring out" someone's manliness into the world, where it can be an active (moral and aesthetic) force. In the "nature sermon" he delivered several years before "Treesbank Poems" were written, he claims that "I hold Christ above all men, yet I am not a Christian. If I have a veneration for Christ I have the same for Vanzetti. . . . Most of us have not been inside a church for a long time . . . yet . . . there are times when we come together in bed that we make a meeting place together" (quoted by Faas, *Young Robert Duncan*, p. 84). However, in "The Truth and Life of Myth," Duncan vehemently denounces well-meaning humanists who deny the spirit and mystery of Christianity or any other theology in favor of a merely ethical interpretation of the Bible (FC, p. 15).

77. John Granger, in unpublished work from University of California, San Diego, has discussed the centrality of pronouns and their mystery as a characteristic of gay

writing. While I am not concerned with a wholesale application of theory here, I do want to mention this idea as worthy of pursuit. Also, Jean Genet, in what must be the most concretized situation of a gay writer in the prison-house of language, writes from Fontevrault Prison of the "soufflement," the erotic whisperings of gay lovers who construct a discourse of mingled breath, kisses and a personal argot peculiar to the relationship, as life-breath itself, wrested from and defying the tomb of incarceration. While Genet's incarceration is, of course, literal, it must also be recognized that any kind of intimate expression of the "love that dare not speak its name" is resistance to social silencing. This is almost too obvious for words, but it must be said, at least in a footnote. See Genet's *Miracle of the Rose*, trans. Bernard Frechtman (New York: Grove Press, 1966), p. 232.

78. Speaking of "formal disasters" and their human consequences, Jack Spicer wrote that Troy lost the Trojan war because of inadequate sentence structure and because Trojans had "no idea of true or false syntax" ("Transformations II," *Language*, CB, p. 233).

79. Some would argue that Duncan is at his most pretentious and least effective in these sweeping, epic political denunciations. Cary Nelson, though, in *Our Last First Poets*, offers a sympathetic and convincing analysis of the crisis in poetic language brought about by the Vietnam war: faced with the horror, not only of physical torment, but of a national psychic dishonesty that paralyzed conventional modes of lyrical expression, poets such as Levertov, Duncan, Bly, and Merwin had to discover a language adequate in its acknowledged inadequacy. For several of these writers, their political poetry has marked a change in their literary reputations, not necesssarily for the better. See "Whitman in Vietnam," *Our Last First Poets* (Urbana: University of Illinois Press, 1981), pp. 1-29.

80. See "The Self in Postmodern Poetry," FC, pp. 226, 231. Duncan here discusses the construct of the "self," his mistrust of his own deeply held belief in it, and his mistrust of this mistrust as simply an alternate, equally rigid credo.

81. See, for example, Duncan's letter to Robin Blaser dated June 4, 1957, in *Ironwood 22, Robert Duncan: A Special Issue* 11:2 (Fall 1983), pp. 102-3.

82. Judy Grahn, *Another Mother Tongue: Gay Words, Gay Worlds* (Boston: Beacon Press, 1984), pp. 97, 207. It is also interesting that in Ovid's account of the killing of Orpheus, the female Bacchantes misuse their "leaf-decked thyrsi, made for a different purpose," as missile weapons instead of ritual symbols of procreation. Ovid, *Metamorphoses*, trans. Mary Innes (Harmondsworth: Penguin, 1955), pp. 246-47.

83. Cary Nelson discusses this poem at length in "Form and Dissolution in Robert Duncan's Aesthetic," *Our Last First Poets*, pp. 130-36; and points out the issue of availability specifically on pp. 132-33. Joseph Conte mentions Duncan's gay use of the traditional *blason*, a poetic form in which every part of a woman's body must be complimented. (*Unending Design: The Forms of Postmodern Poetry* [Ithaca, N.Y.: Cornell University Press, 1991], p. 66). See also Robert Martin's reading of the poem in *Homosexual Tradition*, pp. 173-74.

84. Martin, *Homosexual Tradition*, p. 173.

85. See Christopher Marlowe, *Edward the Second*, in *Marlowe*, ed. Havelock Ellis (New York: Hill and Wang, 1956), p. 269.

86. Thomas Bulfinch, *Bulfinch's Mythology* (New York: Random House), pp. 150-53.

87. Ovid, *Metamorphoses*, p. 227.

88. Grahn, *Another Mother Tongue*, p. 106.

89. N. K. Sandars, trans., *The Epic of Gilgamesh* (Harmondsworth, England: Penguin, 1960), p. 98.

90. It is possible that these resonances of detail and content across cultures and across eras may point to an underlying, earlier, gay version of the descent and its connection to poetry; but it is not necessary to establish or to believe this in order to grant that modern gay poets have appropriated certain aspects of the myth.

For example, the same-sex aspect of such a myth would imply that one is descending in order to contact the unknown spirit part of one's own being. Certainly in Judy Grahn's poem "Descent to the Butch of the Realm," a seduction by Ereshkigal, the Sumerian Queen of the Underworld, of Inana, Queen of the Sky or upper world, is not only the seduction of one woman by another, but a tale of creative death, the stripping away of personality, the appeal of the core, unbounded, harrowing creativity (spirit) of a person's psyche–i.e., in Freudian terms, the id or the unconscious appealing to the ego and superego to descend into its depths. "My name is Naked of Expectations." Only when one descends to this realm can real poetry come to life. The downwardness of such apotheosis, again, undermines the Great Chain's, and other symbolism of Western metaphysics', predilection for ascent as the privileged direction of fulfillment. "Descent to the Butch of the Realm," a frightening, angelic dirty joke, dissolves the artificial distance between the loftiness of angels and the earthiness of explicit sexual reference. Grahn, "Descent to the Butch of the Realm," *Zyzzyva* 1:4 (Winter 1985), pp. 40-46.

91. See, again, John D'Emilio, *Sexual Politics*, on this point. Ekbert Faas also mentions, in *Young Robert Duncan*, the realities of illegal sexual expression: Duncan's friend, the poet Sanders Russell, served a prison sentence for homosexuality (pp. 195-96); and Duncan's first "serious" relationship dissolved in part because of the suffocating pressures of closet life (pp. 63-65).

5. Gertrude Stein's Doggerel "Yiddish": Women, Dogs, and Jews

1. Lenny Bruce, *How to Talk Dirty and Influence People* (Chicago: Playboy Press, 1972), p. 6.

2. Gilles Deleuze and Félix Guattari, *Kafka: Toward a Minor Literature*, trans. Dana Polan (Minneapolis: University of Minnesota Press, 1986), p. 13.

3. For a variety of voices responding to Deleuze and Guattari's text along these lines, see *Cultural Critique: The Nature and Context of Minority Discourse* 6, 7 (Spring 1987).

4. Mark Shell, "The Family Pet," *Representations* 15 (Summer 1986), pp. 121-53.

5. Henry Louis Gates, Jr., "Writing Race and the Difference It Makes," *Critical Inquiry* 12:1 (Autumn 1985), pp. 1-20; and "Phillis Wheatley and the Nature of the Negro," *Critical Essays on Phillis Wheatley*, William H. Robinson, ed. (Boston: G. K. Hall, 1982), pp. 215-33.

6. Thomas Jefferson, "[On the unacceptability of blacks in white America]," *Phillis Wheatley*, ed. Robinson, pp. 42-43.

7. LeRoi Jones/Amiri Baraka, "On the Myth of a Negro Literature," *Home* (New York: William Morrow, 1966), pp. 105-6. Baraka later gave a fuller explanation/recantation of his position in this essay: "I think it is true that Melville and Joyce are certainly better than Phyllis [*sic*] Wheatley or Charles Chesnutt, that's accurate enough—but the analysis was not clear. So at times it looks as though I'm just putting

down black literature, when in reality I was trying to make a very exact *class* analysis of this middle-class black literature was weak, why black music was strong. Then I definitely didn't make a class analysis of Melville and Joyce to show their weak and strong points. . . . [This was a function of my] not having read enough." Kimberly Benston, "Amiri Baraka: An Interview," *boundary 2* 6:2 (Winter 1978), p. 304.

8. See, for example, Alice Walker, "In Search of Our Mothers' Gardens," *In Search of Our Mothers' Gardens* (New York: Harcourt Brace Jovanovich, 1983), pp. 231-43; and the later essays in Robinson's book *Critical Essays on Phillis Wheatley.*

9. Geoffrey Chaucer, *Canterbury Tales*, in *The Works of Geoffrey Chaucer*, 2d ed., ed. F. N. Robinson (Boston: Houghton Mifflin, 1857), fragment 7, l. 925.

10. *The Princeton Encyclopedia of Poetry and Poetics*, 1974 ed. S.v. "Doggerel," by Lucy B. Palache.

11. Nathaniel Hawthorne, quoted by James R. Mellow, *Nathaniel Hawthorne in His Times* (Boston: Houghton Mifflin, 1980), p. 456.

12. See Leonard E. Barrett, "Appendix: A Selection of Rastafarian Poetry," *The Rastafarians: Sounds of Cultural Dissonance* (Boston: Beacon Press, 1977), pp. 229-37.

13. *Palo Alto Weekly*, January 20, 1988, p. 41.

14. Alfred E. Cornebise, ed., *Doughboy Doggerel* (Athens: Ohio University Press, 1985); Hal Cannon, ed., *Cowboy Poetry: A Gathering* (Salt Lake City: G. M. Smith, 1985); George Milburn, ed., *The Hobo's Hornbook: A Repertory for a Gutter Jongleur* (New York: Ives Washburn, 1930); Celes Tisdale, ed., *Betcha Ain't: Poems from Attica* (Detroit: Broadside Press, 1974); Miguel Algarin and Miguel Pinero, eds., *Nuyorican Poetry: An Anthology of Puerto Rican Words and Feelings* (New York: William Morrow, 1975).

15. George Gordon, Lord Byron, *Don Juan*, in *Poetical Works*, ed. Frederick Page (Oxford: Oxford University Press, 1970), I: 63.

16. Pauline Réage, *The Story of O*, trans. Sabine d'Estrée (New York: Grove Press, 1965); and Monique Wittig, *Les Guerrillères*, trans. David Le Vay (New York: Viking, 1971).

17. Maxine Kumin, Introduction, in Anne Sexton, *The Complete Poems* (Boston: Houghton Mifflin, 1981), p. xxx.

18. Barbara Kevles, "Anne Sexton: The Art of Poetry," *Anne Sexton: The Artist and Her Critics*, ed. J. D. McClatchy (Bloomington: University of Indiana Press, 1978), p. 4.

19. Elizabeth Bishop, "The Moose," *The Complete Poems, 1927-1979* (New York: Farrar, Straus, and Giroux, 1983), pp. 169-73.

20. Marianne Moore, *The Complete Poems* (Harmondsworth: Penguin, 1986).

21. Gertrude Stein, *The Gertrude Stein First Reader and Three Plays* (Boston: Houghton Mifflin, 1948), p. 7. Henceforth works by Stein will be noted in the text by the following code: FR is *First Reader*; HW is *How to Write* (New York: Dover, 1975); LB is "Lifting Belly," in *The Yale Gertrude Stein*; YD is "Yet Dish" in *The Yale Gertrude Stein*; MOA is *The Making of Americans* (New York: Harcourt, Brace, 1934); QED is *QED*, in *Fernhurst, Q.E.D. and Other Early Writings* (New York: Liveright, 1974), pp. 51-133; IP is "Identity a Poem" in *What Are Masterpieces*; WAM is *What Are Masterpieces* (New York: Pitman, 1940); YGS is *The Yale Gertrude Stein*, ed. Richard Kostelanetz (New Haven: Yale University Press, 1980); AFM is *As Fine as Melanctha* (New Haven: Yale University Press, 1954); TB is *Tender Buttons*, in *Selected Writings of Gertrude Stein*; SW is *Selected Writings of Gertrude Stein*, ed. Carl Van Vechten (New York: Vintage, 1962).

22. For a brief and typical contemporary casting of Winters's career, see Hayden Carruth, "Yvor Winters," *The Voice That Is Great Within Us*, p. 226.

23. Melba Colgrove, Harold H. Bloomfield, and Peter McWilliams, *How to Survive the Loss of a Love* (New York: Bantam Books, 1976). Peter McWilliams is the poet.

24. Ibid., p. 45. The recently revised edition (Los Angeles: Prelude Press, 1991) lists this chapter as chapter 22, and the layout of the corresponding poem (and all of them) has been changed from left-justified to centered:

> *I'd have a nervous breakdown*
> *only*
> *I've been through*
> *this too many*
> *times to be*
> *nervous.*

(p. 63)

One could speculate that since the book's purpose is to heal its readers, a "centered" poem will suggest and help manifest a centered subject.

25. Richard Bridgman, *Gertrude Stein in Pieces* (New York: Oxford University Press, 1970), p. 158.

26. Clark Coolidge, lecture, Naropa Institute, July 1977.

27. Carolyn Faunce Copeland, *Language and Time and Gertrude Stein* (Iowa City: University of Iowa Press, 1975), p. 85.

28. See Joshua A. Fishman, "The Lively Life of a Dead Language (Or, 'Everyone Knows that Yiddish Died Long Ago')," *The Language of Inequality*, ed. Nessa Wolfson and Joan Manes (New York: Mouton, 1985), pp. 207-22.

29. Deleuze and Guattari, *Kafka*, p. 25.

30. Cynthia Ozick, "A Critic at Large: Sholem Aleichem's Revolution," *The New Yorker*, March 28, 1988, p. 99.

31. Ozick, "A Critic," especially pp. 103-5.

32. Houston A. Baker, *Blues*, p. xii.

33. Sander L. Gilman, *Jewish Self-Hatred: Anti-Semitism and the Hidden Language of the Jews* (Baltimore: Johns Hopkins University Press, 1986), p. 342.

34. Ibid., p. 76.

35. *Princeton Encyclopedia of Poetry and Poetics*, 1974 ed., s.v. "Yiddish Poetry," by Uriel Weinreich.

36. Ozick, "Critic at Large," p. 99.

37. Bruce, *How to Talk Dirty*, p. 46.

38. Albert Goldman (from the journalism of Lawrence Schiller), *Ladies and Gentlemen, Lenny Bruce!!* (New York: Random House, 1974), pp. 558-61.

39. Bruce, *The (Almost) Unpublished Lenny Bruce* (Philadelphia: Running Press, 1984), p. 63. Here, "user" means not only user of language, but smoker of marijuana, and the idiomatic fog is the aromatic haze of dope smoke. The idea of specialized language as a mind-altering substance complicates and enhances the possibility of critical work on Bruce as a "semanticist," a key term in his defense at his many obscenity trials.

40. See, for example, Kostelanetz's introduction to the *Yale Gertrude Stein*, pp. xiii-xxxi; and Judy Grahn, "Writing from a House of Women," *The Highest Apple*, pp. 62-70.

41. This possibility was suggested by Stacey Vallas.

42. Marjorie Perloff, "Poetry as Word-System: The Art of Gertrude Stein," *The Poetics*

of Indeterminacy: Rimbaud to Cage (Princeton: Princeton University Press, 1981), pp. 67-108.

43. For a nice distillation of these opinions, see the epigraphs opening Neil Schmitz's "The Gaiety of Gertrude Stein," *Of Huck and Alice: Humorous Writing in American Literature* (Minneapolis: University of Minnesota Press, 1983), p. 160. He quotes B. L. Reid as calling Stein a "vulgar genius," which epithet unintentionally hails her as a genius of the vernacular.

44. Ozick, "Critic at Large," p. 99.

45. Césaire, *Discourse on Colonialism*, pp. 14-15.

46. Jan Kott, "Introduction," trans. Michael Kandel; Tadeusz Borowski, *This Way for the Gas, Ladies and Gentlemen*, trans. Barbara Vedder (Harmondsworth, England: Penguin, 1976), p. 25.

47. Allegra Stewart, *Gertrude Stein and the Present* (Cambridge, Mass.: Harvard University Press, 1967), p. 72.

48. Stein, "Lecture 2: Narration," *The Poetics of the New American Poetry*, ed. Donald Allen (New York: Grove Press, 1973), p. 106.

49. "Lecture 2," p. 107.

50. "Lecture 2," p. 111.

51. Mary Dearborn, *"The Making of Americans* as an Ethnic Text," *Pocahontas's Daughters* (New York: Oxford University Press, 1986), pp. 159-88.

52. Used as an epigraph by Irena Klepfisz for her poem "Fradel Schtok," *The Tribe of Dina: A Jewish Women's Anthology*, ed. Irena Klepfisz and Melanie Kaye/Kantrowitz (Boston: Beacon Press, 1989), p. 160.

53. Northrop Frye, "Toward Defining an Age of Sensibility," *Poets of Sensibility and the Sublime*, ed. Harold Bloom (New York: Chelsea House, 1986), p. 15.

54. Ibid., p. 16.

55. See Anthony Easthope, *Poetry as Discourse* (New York: Methuen, 1983), pp. 90-91. For a related discussion of these structural concerns and their import in mass and folk-cultural poetry, specifically African-American oral rhymes that treat rhyming and "signifying" thematically, see Henry Gates, *The Signifying Monkey* (New York: Oxford University Press, 1988), pp. 62-63. For an elegant discussion of the fallacies of considering the binarism of cliché/experiment to be the genesis and informing trope of the twentieth-century avant-garde, see Jochen Schulte-Sasse's foreword to Peter Bürger's *Theory of the Avant-Garde.*

56. Bridgman, *Gertrude Stein*, p. 407.

57. Ibid., p. 161; Elizabeth Sprigge, *Gertrude Stein: Her Life and Work* (New York: Harper and Brothers, 1957), p. 10; Fred Rosenbaum, *Free to Choose: The Making of a Jewish Community in the American West (The Jews of Oakland, California)* (Berkeley: The Judah L. Magnes Memorial Museum, 1976), p. 16.

58. Gertrude Stein, "Why Are There Whites to Console," *As Fine as Melanctha* (New Haven: Yale University Press, 1954), pp. 198-218.

59. Hans Mayer, *Outsiders: A Study in Life and Letters*, trans. Denis M. Sweet (Cambridge, Mass.: MIT Press, 1982).

60. Bridgman, *Gertrude Stein*, pp. 22-39.

61. James Mellow, *Charmed Circle: Gertrude Stein and Company* (New York: Avon, 1974), pp. 151-52.

62. Otto Weininger, *Sex and Character* (New York: G. P. Putnam's Sons, 1906).

63. *Encyclopedia Judaica*, 1971 ed. S. v. "Otto Weininger."

64. See especially Ed Cohen's *Talk on the Wilde Side: Toward a Genealogy of the Discourse on Male Sexuality,* (New York: Routledge, 1992).

65. Bridgman, *Gertrude Stein,* 160-61.

66. Jean-Paul Sartre, *Anti-Semite and Jew,* trans. George Becker (New York: Schocken Books: 1948), pp. 97-98.

67. See Renato Rosaldo's sensitive account of this phenomenon in the introduction to *Ilongot Headhunting 1883-1974* (Stanford: Stanford University Press, 1980). Rosaldo traces the identification/objectification with/of an Other in the career of anthropologist William Jones, and by extension in his own career, which, since the publication of *Ilongot Headhunting,* has turned more directly toward issues of Rosaldo's insider/outsider status as a Chicano anthropologist; see *Culture and Truth* (Boston: Beacon Press, 1988).

68. Gilman, p. 244.

69. Gilman quoting Weininger, pp. 244-45.

70. Lenny Bruce quoted by Arthur Naiman under the heading "goy," *Every Goy's Guide to Common Jewish Expressions* (New York: Ballantine, 1981), p. 49. The variation on this in Bruce's autobiography runs as follows: "To me, if you live in New York or any other big city, you are Jewish. It doesn't matter even if you're Catholic; if you live in New York you're Jewish. If you live in Butte, Montana, you're going to be goyish even if you're Jewish.

"Evaporated milk is goyish even if the Jews invented it. Chocolate is Jewish and fudge is goyish. . . .

"Negroes are all Jews. Italians are all Jews. Irishmen who have rejected their religion are Jews. Mouths are very Jewish. And bosoms. Baton-twirling is very goyish" (Bruce, *How to Talk Dirty,* p. 6).

71. For a detailed discussion of the confluence of feminism and experimental writing in Stein, see Marianne DeKoven, *A Different Voice: Gertrude Stein's Experimental Writing* (Madison: University of Wisconsin Press, 1983).

72. Stein, "Portraits and Repetition" *Lectures in America* (New Haven: Yale University Press, 1954), p. 165.

6. Afterword: Closer than Close

1. Natalie Goldberg, *Writing Down the Bones* (Boulder, Colo.: Shambalah, 1986).

2. The term "historeme" for "anecdote" is Joel Fineman's; author's notes, 1988.

3. The "logic of metaphor," Hart Crane, "General Aims and Theories," *The Complete Poems and Selected Letters and Prose,* ed. Brom Weber (Garden City, N.Y.: Anchor Books, 1966), p. 221.

4. Ibid.

5. The image of Kaufman and his cigarette owes its origins to Andrei Codrescu's radio obituary for Kaufman, "All Things Considered," January 1986.

6. Trinh T. Minh-ha, "Yellow Sprouts," *When the Moon Waxes Red: Representation, Gender and Cultural Politics* (New York: Routledge, 1991), p. 1.

Bibliography

Abbott, Steve. "Hidden Master of the Beats." *Poetry Flash* 155, 1986, p. 1.

ACTS 6: A Book of Correspondences for Jack Spicer. Edited by David Levi-Strauss and Benjamin Hollander. San Francisco: ACTS, 1987.

Adorno, Theodor. "The Lyric in Society." *Telos* 20, 1974, pp. 56-71.

Ahearn, Edward J. *Rimbaud: Visions and Habitations.* Berkeley: University of California Press, 1983.

Algarin, Miguel, and Miguel Pinero. *Nuyorican Poetry: An Anthology of Puerto Rican Words and Feelings.* New York: William Morrow, 1975.

Alighieri, Dante. *Inferno.* Translated and edited by Charles S. Singleton. Princeton: Princeton University Press, 1970.

_____. *Paradiso.* Translated by John Sinclair. New York: Oxford University Press, 1939.

Allen, Donald. *The Poetics of the New American Poetry.* New York: Grove Press, 1973.

Ariès, Philippe. *Centuries of Childhood: A Social History of Family Life.* Translated by Robert Baldick. London: Cape, 1962.

Aristotle. *Poetics.* Translated by Lane Cooper. Boston: Ginn and Company, 1913.

Arnold, A. James. *Modernism and Negritude: The Poetry and Poetics of Aimé Césaire.* Cambridge, Mass.: Harvard University Press, 1981.

Auerbach, Erich. *Mimesis: The Representation of Reality in Western Literature.* Translated by Willard R. Trask. Princeton: Princeton University Press, 1953.

Auletta, Ken. "Reporter at Large: The Underclass." *The New Yorker.* (November 16, 1981), pp. 63ff.

Awoonor, Kofi. *The Breast of the Earth: A Survey of the History, Culture and Literature of Africa South of the Sahara.* Garden City: Anchor Press, 1975.

Axelrod, Steven Gould. *Robert Lowell: Life and Art.* Princeton: Princeton University Press, 1978.

Baker, Houston. *Blues, Ideology, and Afro-American Literature.* Chicago: University of Chicago Press, 1984.

Baraka, Amiri (LeRoi Jones). *The Autobiography.* New York: Freundlich Books, 1984.

_____. *Blues People.* New York: William Morrow, 1962.

_____. *Home.* New York: William Morrow, 1966.

Barfield, Owen. *Poetic Diction: A Study in Meaning.* Middletown, Conn.: Wesleyan University Press, 1973.

Bibliography

Barrett, Leonard E. *The Rastafarians: Sounds of Cultural Dissonance*. Boston: Beacon Press, 1977.

Beatitude 29. Edited by Neeli Cherkovski. San Francisco: Beatitude, 1980.

Beatitude 33. Edited by Jeffrey Grossman. San Francisco: Beatitude, 1985.

Bell, Vereen. *Robert Lowell: Nihilist as Hero*. Cambridge, Mass.: Harvard University Press, 1983.

Benjamin, Walter. *Illuminations*. Translated by Harry Zohn. New York: Schocken Books, 1969.

Benston, Kimberly. "Amiri Baraka: An Interview." *boundary 2* 6:2 (Supplement on Amiri Baraka) (Winter 1977), pp. 303-16.

————. "I Yam What I Am: The Topos of (Un)Naming in Afro-American Literature." *Black Literature and Literary Theory*. Edited by Henry Louis Gates, Jr. London: Methuen, 1984, pp. 151-74.

Berger, John. *Ways of Seeing*. London: The British Broadcasting Corporation, 1972.

Bertolff, Robert J., and Ian W. Reid. *Robert Duncan: Scales of the Marvelous*. New York: New Directions, 1979.

Bishop, Elizabeth. *The Complete Poems, 1927-1979*. New York: Farrar, Straus and Giroux, 1983.

Blake, William. *Songs of Innocence and of Experience*. Edited by Geoffrey Keynes. New York: Orion Press, 1967.

Blaser, Robin. *Cups*. San Francisco: Four Seasons Foundation, 1968.

Bob Kaufman Collective, ed. *Would You Wear My Eyes? A Tribute to Bob Kaufman*. San Francisco: The Bob Kaufman Collective, 1988.

Borowski, Tadeusz. *This Way for the Gas, Ladies and Gentlemen*. Translated by Barbara Vedder. Harmondsworth: Penguin, 1976.

boundary 2: Supplement on Amiri Baraka. 6:2 (Winter 1978).

boundary 2: Robert Duncan. 8:2 (Winter 1980).

boundary 2: Jack Spicer. 6:1 (Fall 1977).

Brake, Mike. *Comparative Youth Culture*. London: Routledge and Kegan Paul, 1985.

Brathwaite, Edward K. *The Arrivants: A New World Trilogy*. London: Oxford University Press, 1973.

Bridgman, Richard. *Gertrude Stein in Pieces*. New York: Oxford University Press, 1970.

Brinnin, John Malcolm. *The Third Rose: Gertrude Stein and Her World*. Boston: Little, Brown, 1959.

Brossard, Chandler. *Who Walk in Darkness*. New York: New Directions, 1952.

————. *Who Walk in Darkness (The Suppressed Original Version)*. New York: Harper and Rowe, 1952.

Brown, James with Bruce Tucker. *James Brown, The Godfather of Soul*. New York: Thunder's Mouth Press, 1986, 1990.

Bruce, Honey (with Dana Benenson). *Honey: The Life and Loves of Lenny's Shady Lady*. Chicago: Playboy Press, 1976.

Bruce, Lenny. *How to Talk Dirty and Influence People*. Chicago: Playboy Press, 1972.

————. *The (Almost) Unpublished Lenny Bruce*. Philadelphia: Running Press, 1984.

Buckley, Richard (Lord Buckley). *Hiparama of the Classics*. San Francisco: City Lights Books, 1960.

Bullock, Alan, and R. B. Woodings. *Twentieth-Century Culture: A Biographical Companion*. New York: Harper and Row, 1983.

Bibliography

Bürger, Peter. *Theory of the Avant-Garde*. Translated by Michael Shaw. Foreword, Jochen Schulte-Sasse. Minneapolis: University of Minnesota, 1984.

Burroughs, William S. "It Belongs to the Cucumbers: On the Subject of Raudive's Tapes." *Talking Poetics from Naropa Institute*, Volume I. Edited by Anne Waldman and Marilyn Webb. Boulder: Shambhala, 1978, pp. 63-81.

_____. *The Place of Dead Roads*. New York: Holt, Rinehart and Winston, 1983.

Byron, Lord (George Gordon). *Don Juan*. In *Poetical Works*. Edited by Frederick Page. Oxford: Oxford University Press, 1970.

Camus, Albert. *The Stranger*. Translated by Stuart Gilbert. New York: Vintage, 1946.

Cannon, Hal, ed. *Cowboy Poetry: A Gathering*. Salt Lake City: G. M. Smith, 1985.

Carpentier, Alejo. *The Kingdom of This World*. Translated by Harriet de Onis. New York: Alfred Knopf, 1957.

Carruth, Hayden, ed. *The Voice That Is Great Within Us*. New York: Bantam, 1970.

Césaire, Aimé. *Collected Poetry*. Translated by Clayton Eshleman and Annette Smith. Berkeley: University of California Press, 1983.

_____. *Discourse On Colonialism*. Translated by Joan Pinkham. New York: Monthly Review Press, 1972.

Chaucer, Geoffrey. *The Canterbury Tales*. In *The Works of Geoffrey Chaucer*, 2d ed. Edited by F. N. Robinson. Boston: Houghton Mifflin, 1957.

Chessman, Caryl. *Cell 2455 Death Row*. New York: Prentice-Hall, 1954.

Christian, Barbara. "Whatever Happened to Bob Kaufman?" *Black World* 21:12 (September 1972), pp. 20-29.

Clark, Tom. "A Hipster Poet's Nocturnal Muse." Review of Bob Kaufman and Janice Blue's *Closing Time Til Dawn. San Francisco Chronicle Book Review* (August 3, 1986).

Clay, Mel. *Jazz-Jails and God: Bob Kaufman, an Impressionistic Biography*. San Francisco: Androgyne Press, 1986.

Clifford, James. *The Predicament of Culture*. Cambridge, Mass.: Harvard University Press, 1988.

Cohen, Ed. *Talk on the Wilde Side: Towards the Genealogy of a Discourse on Male Sexuality*. New York: Routledge, 1992.

_____. "Writing Gone Wilde: Homoerotic Desire in the Closet of Representation." *PMLA* (October 1987), pp. 801-13.

Colgrove, Melba, Harold H. Bloomfield, and Peter McWilliams. *How to Survive the Loss of a Love*. New York: Bantam Books, 1976.

Conte, Joseph. *Unending Design: The Forms of Postmodern Poetry*. Ithaca, N.Y.: Cornell University Press, 1991.

Contemporary Poets, 1981 ed. S.v. "Bob Kaufman." New York: St. Martin's Press.

Cooke, Janet, "Jimmy's World," *The Washington Post* (September 28, 1980), p. A1.

Coolidge, Clark. "Arrangement." *Talking Poetics from Naropa Institute*, Vol. 1. Edited by Anne Waldman and Marilyn Webb. Boulder: Shambhala, 1978, pp. 143-169.

Cooney, Terry. *The Rise of the New York Intellectuals: Partisan Review and Its Circle*. Madison: University of Wisconsin Press, 1986.

Copeland, Carolyn Faunce. *Language and Time and Gertrude Stein*. Iowa City: University of Iowa Press, 1975.

Cornebise, Alfred E. *Doughboy Doggerel: Verse of the American Expeditionary Force 1918-1919*. Athens, Ohio: University of Ohio Press, 1985.

Bibliography

Crane, Hart. *Complete Poems and Selected Letters and Prose*. Edited by Brom Weber. Garden City: Anchor Books, 1966.

———. *Letters of Hart Crane, 1916-1932*. Edited by Brom Weber. Berkeley: University of California Press, 1965.

Crane, Stephen. *Maggie: A Girl of the Streets*. New York: Norton, 1979.

Cullen, Countee. *Color*. New York: Harper and Brothers, 1925.

Cultural Critique 6, 7: *The Nature and Context of Minority Discourse* (Winter 1986-87; Spring 1987).

Dauwer, Leo P. *I Remember Southie*. Boston: The Christopher Publishing House, 1975.

Davis, David Brion. *The Problem of Slavery in Western Culture*. Ithaca: Cornell University Press, 1966.

Davis, Miles, with Quincy Troupe. *Miles: The Autobiography*. New York: Simon and Schuster, 1990.

Dearborn, Mary V., *Pocahontas's Daughters*. New York: Oxford University Press, 1986.

DeKoven, Marianne. *A Different Voice: Gertrude Stein's Experimental Writing*. Madison: University of Wisconsin Press, 1983.

Deleuze, Gilles, and Félix Guattari. *Kafka: Toward a Minor Literature*. Translated by Dana Polan. Minneapolis: University of Minnesota Press, 1986.

D'Emilio, John. *Sexual Politics, Sexual Communities: The Making of a Homosexual Minority in the United States, 1940-1970*. Chicago: University of Chicago Press, 1983.

Doane, Janice, and Devon Hodges. *Nostalgia and Sexual Difference: The Resistance to Contemporary Feminism*. London: Methuen, 1987.

Dictionary of Literary Biography, Vol. 16, 1978 ed. S.v. "Bob Kaufman," by A. D. Winans.

———, Vol. 41, 1978 ed. S.v. "Bob Kaufman," by Jon Woodson.

Douglass, Frederick. *Narrative of the Life of Frederick Douglass, an American Slave*. Edited by Houston A. Baker. Harmondsworth: Penguin, 1982.

Dubois, Page. *Centaurs and Amazons: Women and the Prehistory of the Great Chain of Being*. Ann Arbor: University of Michigan Press, 1982.

Du Bois, W. E. B. *The Souls of Black Folk*. New York: Signet Classics, 1969.

Duncan, Robert. *Fictive Certainties*. New York: New Directions, 1985.

———. "The Homosexual in Society," *Politics* 1:7 (August 1944), pp. 209-11.

———. *Caesar's Gate*. California: Sand Dollar, 1972.

———. *Bending the Bow*. New York: New Directions, 1968.

———. *Groundwork I: Before the War*. New York: New Directions, 1984.

———. *Groundwork II: In the Dark*. New York: New Directions, 1987.

———. "Warp and Woof: Notes from a Talk." *Talking Poetics from Naropa Institute*, Vol. 1. Edited by Anne Waldman and Marilyn Webb. Boulder: Shambhala, 1978, pp. 1-10.

———. *The Years as Catches*. Berkeley: Oyez, 1966.

Ehrenreich, Barbara. *The Hearts of Men*. Garden City: Anchor Books, 1983.

Eichenbaum, Louise, and Orbach, Susie. *Understanding Women: Feminist Psychotherapy*. Harmondsworth, England: Penguin, 1983.

Else, Gerald. *Aristotle's Poetics: The Argument*. Cambridge, Mass.: Harvard University Press, 1957.

Encyclopedia Judaica, 1971 ed. S.v. "Otto Weininger."

Faas, Ekbert. *Young Robert Duncan: Portrait of the Poet as Homosexual in Society*. Santa Barbara: Black Sparrow Press, 1983.

Bibliography

Fanon, Frantz. *Black Skin, White Masks*. Translated by Charles Lam Markmann. New York: Grove Press, 1967.

Fineman, Joel. "The Structure of Allegorical Desire." *Allegory and Representation*. Edited by Stephen J. Greenblatt. Baltimore: Johns Hopkins University Press, 1981, pp. 26-60.

Finnegan, Ruth. *Oral Literature in Africa*. London: Clarendon Books, 1970.

Fischer, Michael, "Ethnicity and the Post-Modern Arts of Memory," *Writing Culture: The Poetics and Politics of Ethnography*. Edited by James Clifford and George Marcus. Berkeley: University of California Press, 1986.

Fishman, Joshua A. "The Lively Life of a Dead Language (or 'Everyone Knows that Yiddish Died Long Ago')." *The Language of Inequality*. Edited by Nessa Wolfson and Joan Manes. New York: Mouton, 1985, pp. 207-22.

Foster, Hal. *Recodings: Art, Spectacle, Cultural Politics*. Port Townsend, Wash.: Bay Press, 1985.

Foucault, Michel. "Discourse on Language." *The Archaeology of Knowledge*. Translated by Rupert Swyer. New York: Pantheon, 1972, pp. 215-37.

_____. *The History of Sexuality: Volume I*. Translated by Robert Hurley. New York: Pantheon, 1978.

Foye, Raymond. "Private Sadness / Notes on the Poetry of Bob Kaufman," *Beatitude 29* (1980), pp. 71-83.

Franklin, H. Bruce. *Prison Literature in America: The Victim as Criminal and Artist*. Westport, Conn.: Lawrence Hill, 1978.

Frye, Northrop. "Toward Defining an Age of Sensibility." *Poets of Sensibility and the Sublime*. Edited by Harold Bloom. New York: Chelsea House, 1986, pp. 11-18.

Gans, Eric. "Naissance du Moi Lyrique: du Féminin au Masculin." *Poétique* 46 (April 1981), pp. 129-39.

Gates, Henry Louis, Jr., ed. *Black Literature and Literary Theory*. New York: Methuen, 1984.

_____. *The Signifying Monkey*. New York: Oxford University Press, 1988.

_____. "Writing Race and the Difference it Makes," *Critical Inquiry* 12:1 (Autumn 1985); also published as *"Race," Writing and Difference*. Chicago: University of Chicago Press, 1986, pp. 1-20.

Geertz, Clifford. *The Interpretation of Cultures*. New York: Basic Books, 1973.

_____. *Islam Observed*. New Haven: Yale University Press, 1968.

Genet, Jean. *Miracle of the Rose*. Translated by Bernard Frechtman. New York: Grove Press, 1966.

_____. *The Thief's Journal*. Translated by Bernard Frechtman. New York: Grove Press, 1964.

Gillespie, Dizzy with Al Fraser. *To Be or Not to Bop: Memoirs of Dizzy Gillespie*. New York: Da Capo, 1979.

Gilman, Sander L. *Jewish Self-Hatred: Anti-Semitism and the Hidden Language of the Jews*. Baltimore: Johns Hopkins University Press, 1986.

Ginsberg, Allen. *Howl and Other Poems*. San Francisco: City Lights, 1956.

_____. The Fall of America. San Francisco: City Lights, 1966.

_____. *Gay Sunshine Interview*. Bolinas: Grey Fox, 1973.

Goldman, Albert (based on the journalism of Lawrence Schiller). *Ladies and Gentlemen, Lenny Bruce!!* New York: Random House, 1974.

Bibliography

Grahn, Judy. *Another Mother Tongue: Gay Words, Gay Worlds*. Boston: Beacon Press, 1984.

———. "Descent to the Bitch of the Realm." *Zyzzyva* 1:4 (Winter 1985), pp. 40-46.

———. *The Highest Apple: Sappho and the Lesbian Tradition in Poetry*. San Francisco: Spinsters Ink, 1985.

———. "Interview." *Aurora*. (Spring 1983), p. 1.

Guevara, Nancy. "Graffiti Talk: Words, Walls and Women." *Tabloid: A Review of Mass Culture and Everyday Life* 9 (Winter 1985), pp. 20-24.

Gunn, Thom. *Moly* and *My Sad Captains*. New York: Farrar, Straus and Giroux, 1973.

Halifax, Joan. *Shamanic Voices*. New York: E. P. Dutton, 1979.

Hall, Stuart, and Tony Jefferson. *Resistance Through Rituals*. London: Hutchinson, 1976.

Hamilton, Ian. *Robert Lowell: A Biography*. New York: Random House, 1982.

Hanson, Elizabeth. *My Poor Arthur*. New York: Henry Holt, 1959.

Harlow, Barbara. *Resistance Literature*. New York: Methuen, 1987.

Hebdige, Dick. *Subculture: The Meaning of Style*. London: Methuen, 1979.

Heller, Erich. *The Disinherited Mind*. New York: Meridian Books, 1959.

Henderson, David. "Bob Kaufman: Poet of North Beach," *KPFA Folio* (April 1986), p. 1.

———. "Tribute to Bob Kaufman." KPFA Radio, April 26, 1986.

Henderson, Stephen. *Understanding the New Black Poetry*. New York: William Morrow, 1972.

Herndon, James. *Everything as Expected*. San Francisco, 1973.

Heymann, C. David. *American Aristocracy: The Lives and Times of James Russell, Amy, and Robert Lowell*. New York: Dodd, Mead, 1980.

Higgins, George V. *Style Versus Substance: Kevin White and the Politics of Illusion*. New York: Macmillan, 1984.

Hitchens, Christopher. "American Notes." *Times Literary Supplement*, March 7, 1986, p. 246.

Hougan, James. *Decadence: Radical Nostalgia, Narcissism and Decline in the Seventies*. New York: William Morrow, 1975.

Hosek, Chaviva, and Patricia Parker. *Lyric Poetry: Beyond New Criticism*. Ithaca: Cornell University Press, 1985.

Hughes, Langston. *The Big Sea*. New York: Thunder's Mouth Press, 1940, 1986.

———. *Selected Poems of Langston Hughes*. New York: Alfred A. Knopf, 1959.

———. "Wise Men." *The Messenger* (June 1927), p. 11.

Huyssen, Andreas. "Mass Culture as Woman: Modernism's Other," *Studies in Entertainment: Critical Approaches to Mass Culture*. Edited by Tania Modleski. Bloomington: Indiana University Press, 1986, pp. 188-207.

Irigaray, Luce. "When Our Lips Speak Together." Translated by Carolyn Burke. *Signs* 6:1 (Autumn 1980), pp. 69-79.

Ironwood 22: Robert Duncan: A Special Issue 11:2 (Fall 1983).

Ironwood 28: Jack Spicer and Emily Dickinson: Listening for the Invisible 14:2 (Fall 1986).

Jameson, Fredric. "Baudelaire as Modernist and Postmodernist." *Lyric Poetry: Beyond New Criticism*. Edited by Chaviva Hosek and Patricia Parker. Ithaca: Cornell University Press, 1985.

Jauss, Hans Robert. *Aesthetic Experience and Literary Hermeneutics*. Translated from the German by Michael Shaw. Minneapolis: University of Minnesota Press, 1982.

Bibliography

Jennings, James, and Mel King. *From Access to Power: Black Politics in Boston*. Cambridge, Mass.: Schenkman Books, 1986.

John of the Cross, Saint. *Poems*. Translated by John Frederick Nims. New York: Grove Press, 1959.

_____. *Poems*. Translated by Roy Campbell. Baltimore: Penguin, 1960.

Johnson, W. R. *The Idea of Lyric: Lyric Modes in Ancient and Modern Poems*. Berkeley: University of California Press, 1982.

Jonas, Stephen. *2 for Jack Spicer*. South San Francisco: ManRoot Books, 1974.

Kantorowicz, Ernst. *The King's Two Bodies*. Princeton: Princeton University Press, 1957.

Katz, Jonathan. *Gay American History*. New York: Thomas Y. Crowell, 1976.

Kaufman, Bob. *The Ancient Rain: Poems 1956-1978*. New York: New Directions, 1981.

_____. *Does the Secret Mind Whisper?* San Francisco: City Lights, 1960.

_____. *Golden Sardine*. San Francisco: City Lights, 1967.

_____. *Second April*. San Francisco: City Lights, 1959.

_____. *Solitudes Crowded with Loneliness*. New York: New Directions, 1965.

_____. *Three Authors: Burroughs, Pélieu, Kaufman*. Translated by Claude Pélieu. *Solitudes*. Paris: L'Herne, 1969.

Kaufman, Bob, and Janice Blue. *Closing Time Til Dawn*. San Francisco: The Bob Kaufman Collective, 1986.

Kaufman, Eileen. San Francisco, California. Interview, July, 1986.

Kaufman, George. Berkeley, California. Interview, January, 1991.

Kesey, Ken. *One Flew Over the Cuckoo's Nest*. New York: Viking, 1962.

Kevles, Barbara. "The Art of Poetry: Anne Sexton." *Anne Sexton: The Artist and Her Critics*. Edited by J. D. McClatchy. Bloomington: Indiana University Press, 1978, pp. 1-9.

Kingston, Maxine Hong. *The Woman Warrior*. New York: Alfred Knopf, 1976.

Klepfisz, Irena. "Fradel Schtok." *The Tribe of Dina: A Jewish Women's Anthology*. Edited by Irena Klepfisz and Melanie Kaye/Kantorowitz. Boston: Beacon Press, 1989, p. 160.

_____ and Kaye/Kantorowitz, Melanie. *The Tribe of Dina: A Jewish Women's Anthology*. Boston: Beacon Press, 1989.

Knight, Arthur, and Kit Knight. *Beat Angels*. San Francisco: Unspeakable Visions of the Individual, 1972.

Kofsky, Frank. *Lenny Bruce: The Comedian as Social Critic and Secular Moralist*. New York: Monad Press, 1974.

Kostelanetz, Richard, ed. *The Avant-Garde Tradition in Literature*. Buffalo, N.Y.: Prometheus Books, 1982.

Kristeva, Julia. *Revolution in Poetic Language*. Translated by Margaret Waller. New York: Columbia University Press, 1984.

Kunitz, Stanley. "Talk With Robert Lowell." *New York Herald Tribune Weekly Book Review*. October 11, 1964, pp. 34-49.

Lacan, Jacques. *Feminine Sexuality*. Translated by Jacqueline Rose. London: Verso, 1982.

Lacoue-Labarthe, Philippe and Jean-Luc Nancy, eds. *Le Retrait du Politique*. Paris: Editions Galilée, 1983.

Laroche, Maximilien. "The Myth of the Zombi." *Exile and Tradition*. Edited by Roland Smith. New York: Africana, 1976, pp. 44-61.

"Legendary Beat Poet Bob Kaufman Dies (The 'Black American Rimbaud')." *San Francisco Chronicle* (January 13, 1986), p. 7.

Bibliography

Leonard, Neil. "The Jazzman's Verbal Usage." *Black American Literature Forum* 20:1, 2 (1986), pp. 151-60.

Levi-Strauss, David, and Benjamin Hollander, eds. *A Book of Correspondences of Jack Spicer*, see *ACTS* 6.

Leyland, Michael, ed. *Gay Sunshine Interviews, Vol. II*. San Francisco: Gay Sunshine Press, 1982.

―――, ed. *Angels of the Lyre: A Gay Poetry Anthology*. San Francisco: Panjandrum Press/Gay Sunshine Press, 1975.

―――, ed. *Orgasms of Light*. San Francisco: Gay Sunshine Press, 1977.

Lomax, Alan, and Raoul Abdul. *3000 Years of Black Poetry*. Greenwich, Conn.: Fawcett Books, 1970.

Lorca, Federico Garcia. *The Poet in New York*. Translated by Ben Belitt. New York: Grove Press, 1955.

―――. *Selected Poems*. Edited by Donald Allen and Francisco Garcia Lorca. Translated by Stephen Spender and J. L. Gili. New York: New Directions, 1955.

Lorde, Audre. *The Black Unicorn: Poems*. New York: Norton, 1978.

―――. "The Master's Tools Will Never Dismantle the Master's House." *This Bridge Called My Back: Radical Writings by Women of Color*. Edited by Cherie Moraga and Gloria Anzaldúa. Watertown, Mass.: Persephone Press, 1981, pp. 98-101.

Louv, Richard. *America II*. Los Angeles: Jeremy Tarcher, 1980.

Lovejoy, Arthur O. *The Great Chain of Being: A Study of the History of an Idea*. Cambridge, Mass.: Harvard University Press, 1936.

Lowell, Robert. *Collected Prose*. New York: Farrar, Straus and Giroux, 1986.

―――. *Imitations*. New York: Farrar, Straus and Giroux, 1961.

―――. *Life Studies and For the Union Dead*. New York: Farrar, Straus and Giroux, 1964.

Lucas, J. Anthony. *Common Ground*. New York: Alfred Knopf, 1986.

Lucero, Judy. "I Live in an Illusion." *De Colores: A Journal of Emerging Raza Philosophies* 1:1 (Winter 1973), p. 76.

Lupo, Alan. *Liberty's Chosen Home: The Politics of Violence in Boston*. Boston: Beacon Press, 1988.

Lynch, Michael. " 'Here is Adhesiveness': From Friendship to Homosexuality," *Victorian Studies* 29:1 (Autumn 1985), pp. 67-96.

Lyotard, Jean-François. *The Postmodern Condition: A Report on Knowledge*. Translated by Geoff Bennington and Brian Massumi. Minneapolis: University of Minnesota Press, 1984.

Machlin, Milton and William Woodfield. *Ninth Life*. New York: G. P. Putnam's Sons, 1961.

Major, Clarence. *The New Black Poetry*. New York: International Publishers, 1969.

Malloy, Ione. *Southie Won't Go*. Urbana: University of Illinois Press, 1986.

Mariah, Paul, ed. *ManRoot: The Jack Spicer Issue* 10 (Fall 1974-Winter 1975).

Marlowe, Christopher. *Edward the Second*. In *Marlowe*. Edited by Havelock Ellis. New York: Hill and Wang, 1956.

Marothy, Janos. *Music and the Bourgeois; Music and the Proletarian*. Budapest: Academiai Kiado, 1974.

Marshall, Paule. *Praisesong for the Widow*. New York: G. P. Putnam's Sons, 1983.

Martin, Robert K. *The Homosexual Tradition in American Poetry*. Austin: University of Texas Press, 1979.

Bibliography

Mayer, Hans. *Outsiders: A Study in Life and Letters*. Translated by Denis M. Sweet. Cambridge, Mass.: The MIT Press, 1982.

Maynard, John Arthur. *Venice West: The Beat Generation in Southern California*. New Brunswick: Rutgers University Press, 1991.

Mayo, Michael, ed. *Practicing Angels: A Contemporary Anthology of San Francisco Bay Area Poetry*. San Francisco: Seismograph Publications, 1986.

McClatchy, J. D. *Anne Sexton: The Artist and Her Critics*. Bloomington: Indiana University Press, 1978.

McRobbie, Angela and Micah Nava. *Gender and Generation*. London: Routledge and Kegan Paul, 1987.

Megill, Allan. *Prophets of Extremity: Nietzsche, Heidegger, Foucault, Derrida*. Berkeley: University of California Press, 1985.

Mellow, James R. *Charmed Circle: Gertude Stein and Company*. New York: Holt, Rinehart and Winston, 1974.

_____. *Nathaniel Hawthorne in His Times*. Boston: Houghton Mifflin, 1980.

Merrill, James. *The Changing Light at Sandover*. Boston: Atheneum, 1983.

Milburn, George, ed. *The Hobo's Hornbook: A Repertory for a Gutter Jongleur*. New York: Ives Washburn, 1930.

Miller, Alice. *Prisoners of Childhood (The Drama of the Gifted Child)*. Translated by Ruth Ward. New York: Basic Books, 1981.

_____. *For Your Own Good: Hidden Cruelty in Child-Rearing and the Roots of Violence*. Translated by Hildegard and Hunter Hannum. New York: Farrar, Straus and Giroux, 1984.

Milton, John. *Complete Poems and Major Prose*. Edited by Merritt Hughes. Indianapolis: Bobbs-Merrill, 1975.

Modleski, Tania. *Loving With a Vengeance: Mass-Produced Fantasies for Women*. New York: Methuen, 1982.

_____, ed. *Studies in Entertainment: Critical Approaches to Mass Culture*. Bloomington: Indiana University Press, 1986.

Moon, Michael. "Desublimating the Male Sublime: Autoerotics, Anal Erotics, and Corporal Violence in Melville and William Burroughs." Paper presented in December 1989 at MLA, Washington, D.C.

Moore, Marianne. *The Complete Poems*. Harmondsworth, England: Penguin, 1986.

Moraga, Cherie, and Anzaldúa, Gloria. *This Bridge Called My Back: Writings by Radical Women of Color*. Watertown, Mass.: Persephone Press, 1981.

Mosse, George L. *Nationalism and Sexuality*. New York: H. Fertig, 1985.

Mungham, Geoff, and Geoff Pearson. *Working Class Youth Culture*. Routledge and Kegan Paul, 1976.

Mura, David. *Pornography: A Male Grief*. Minneapolis: Milkweed Editions, 1987.

Naiman, Arthur. *Every Goy's Guide to Common Jewish Expressions*. New York: Ballantine Books, 1981.

Nelson, Bruce. *Workers on the Waterfront*. Urbana: University of Illinois Press, 1988.

Nelson, Cary. *Our Last First Poets*. Urbana: University of Illinois Press, 1981.

Nicosia, Gerald. *Memory Babe*. New York: Grove Press, 1983.

Nietzsche, Friedrich. *The Basic Writings of Nietzsche*. Translated and edited by Walter Kaufmann. New York: Random House, 1968.

_____. *Human, All-Too-Human*. Translated by Helen Zimmern. Edinburgh: T. N. Foulis, 1910.

Bibliography

Nilon, Charles. "Bob Kaufman, Black Speech, and Charlie Parker," unpublished manuscript, American Popular Culture Association, 1987.

Norse, Harold, *Memoirs of a Bastard Angel*. New York: William Morrow, 1989.

O'Hara, Frank. *The Selected Poems*. Edited by Donald Allen. New York: Random House, 1974.

Olsen, Tillie. *Silences*. New York: Delta, 1978.

Ozick, Cynthia. "A Critic at Large: Sholem Aleichem's Revolution." *The New Yorker* (March 28, 1988), pp. 99-108.

_____. *The Pagan Rabbi and Other Stories*. New York: E.P. Dutton, 1983.

Palo Alto Weekly. January 20, 1988.

Perlman, Janice. *The Myth of Marginality*. Berkeley: University of California Press, 1976.

Perloff, Marjorie. *The Poetic Art of Robert Lowell*. Ithaca: Cornell University Press, 1973.

_____. *The Poetics of Indeterminacy: Rimbaud to Cage*. Princeton: Princeton University Press, 1981.

Plath, Sylvia. *The Bell Jar*. London: Faber, 1966.

Plato. *The Republic*. Translated by Desmond Lee. Harmondsworth, England: Penguin, 1953.

Poirier, Richard. "Our Truest Historian." *New York Herald Tribune Weekly Book Review* (October 11, 1964), p. 1.

Princeton Encyclopedia of Poetry and Poetics. Edited by Alex Preminger. Princeton: Princeton University Press, 1974.

Rampersad, Arnold. *The Life of Langston Hughes*, Vol. I. New York: Oxford University Press, 1986.

Randall, Dudley, ed. *The Black Poets*. New York: Bantam, 1971.

Rancière, Jacques. "La réprésentation de l'ouvrier ou la classe impossible." *Le retrait du politique*. Edited by Philippe Lacoue-Labarthe and Jean-Luc Nancy. Paris: Editions Galilée, 1983, pp. 89-111.

_____. "Ronds de fumée: (Les poètes ouvriers dans la France de Louis-Philippe)." *Revue des Sciences Humaines* 61:190 (April-June 1983), pp. 31-47.

Raskin, Bernard. *On a True Course: The Story of the National Maritime Union of America, AFL-CIO*. New York: National Maritime Union of America, 1967.

Réage, Pauline. *The Story of O*. Translated by Sabine d'Estrée. New York: Grove Press, 1965.

Reed, Ishmael, ed. *Yardbird Reader* 1:1 (1972).

Renza, Louis A. *"A White Heron" and the Question of Minor Literature*. Madison: University of Wisconsin Press, 1984.

Rich, Adrienne. *On Lies, Secrets and Silence: Selected Prose 1966-1978*. New York: Norton, 1979.

Rigney, Francis J., and L. Douglas Smith. *The Real Bohemia*. New York: Basic Books, 1961.

Rimbaud, Arthur. *Poésies*. Paris: Librairies Générales Françaises, 1972.

Rimbaud, Arthur and Paul Verlaine. *A Lover's Cock*. Translated by J. Murat and W. Gunn. San Francisco: Gay Sunshine Press, 1979.

Robinson, William H., ed. *Critical Essays on Phillis Wheatley*. Boston: G. K. Hall, 1982.

Rodgers, Bruce. *The Queen's Vernacular: A Gay Lexicon*. San Francisco: Straight Arrow, 1972.

Rosaldo, Renato. *Culture and Truth*. Boston: Beacon Press, 1988.

_____. *Ilongot Headhunting 1883-1974*. Stanford: Stanford University Press, 1980.

Rose, Jacqueline. *Sexuality in the Field of Vision*. London: Verso, 1986.

Rosenbaum, Fred. *Free to Choose: The Making of a Jewish Community in the American West (The Jews of Oakland, California)*. Berkeley: Judah L. Magnes Memorial Museum, 1976.

Rothenberg, Diane, and Jerome Rothenberg. *Symposium of the Whole: A Range of Discourse Toward an Ethnopoetics*. Berkeley: University of California Press, 1981.

Rowbotham, Sheila. *Woman's Consciousness, Man's World*. Harmondsworth, England: Penguin, 1973.

Russell, Charles. *Poets, Prophets and Revolutionaries: The Literary Avant-Garde from Rimbaud Through Postmodernism*. New York: Oxford University Press, 1985.

Salas, Floyd, ed. *Stories and Poems from Close to Home*. Berkeley: Ortalda, 1986.

Salinger, J. D. *The Catcher in the Rye*. Boston: Little, Brown, 1951.

Sappho. *Sappho: A New Translation*. Translated by Mary Barnard. Berkeley: University of California Press, 1958.

Saroyan, Aram. *Genesis Angels: The Saga of Lew Welsh and the Beat Generation*. New York: William Morris, 1979.

Sartre, Jean-Paul. *Anti-Semite and Jew*. Translated by George J. Becker. New York: Schocken Books, 1948.

_____. *The Family Idiot*. Translated by Carol Cosman. Chicago: University of Chicago Press, 1987.

_____. *Saint Genet*. Translated by Bernard Frechtman. New York: George Braziller, 1963.

Scarry, Elaine. *The Body in Pain*. London: Oxford University Press, 1985.

Schmitz, Neil. *Of Huck and Alice*. Minneapolis: University of Minnesota Press, 1983.

Sedgwick, Eve Kosofsky. *Between Men: English Literature and Male Homosocial Desire*. New York: Columbia University Press, 1985.

_____. *The Epistemology of the Closet*. New York: Routledge, 1991.

_____. "A Poem Is Being Written," *Representations* 17 (Winter 1987), pp. 110-43.

Senghor, Léopold Sédar. *Prose and Poetry*. Translated by John Reed and Clive Wake. London: Oxford University Press, 1965.

Sexton, Anne. *The Complete Poems*. Boston: Houghton Mifflin, 1981.

Seymour, Tony. *No Gods to Guide, No Herds to Follow: Bob Kaufman's "Street-Bop-Zen!!"* San Francisco: Tony Seymour, 1986.

Shange, Ntozake. *Nappy Edges*. New York: St. Martin's Press, 1978.

Shell, Marc. "The Family Pet," *Representations* 15 (Summer 1986), pp. 121-53.

Shelley, Percy Bysshe. *Shelley's Prose and Poetry*. Edited by Donald H. Reiman and Sharon B. Powers. New York: Norton, 1977.

Sherover-Marcuse, Ricky. "Liberation Theory: Part I. Axioms and Working Assumptions about the Perpetuation of Social Oppression," photocopied worksheet.

_____. "Toward a Perspective on Unlearning Racism: 12 Working Assumptions," photocopied worksheet.

Smith, Rowland, ed. *Exile and Tradition*. New York: Africana, 1976.

Snyder, Emil. "Aimé Césaire: The Reclaiming of the Land." *Exile and Tradition*. Edited by Rowland Smith. New York: Africana, 1976, pp. 31-43.

Sollers, Philippe. *Writing and the Experience of Limits*. Translated by Philip Bernard with David Hayman. New York: Columbia University Press, 1983.

Bibliography

Sontag, Susan. "Notes on Camp." *Against Interpretation and Other Essays.* New York: Farrar, Straus and Giroux, 1966, pp. 275-92.

"South Boston and Ethnic Identity." Unpublished talk, American Sociological Association, 1980.

Spanos, W. V. "Jack Spicer's Poetics of Absence: An Introduction." *boundary 2: Jack Spicer* 6:1 (Fall 1977), pp. 1-2.

Spicer, Jack. *The Collected Books.* Santa Barbara: Black Sparrow Press, 1975.

_____. *One Night Stand & Other Poems.* Bolinas: Grey Fox Press, 1980.

Spicer, Jack, and Robert Duncan. *An Ode and Arcadia.* Berkeley: Ark Press, 1974.

Sprigge, Elizabeth. *Gertrude Stein: Her Life and Work.* New York: Harper and Brothers, 1957.

Starer, Jacqueline. *Les écrivains beats et le voyage.* Paris: Didier, 1977.

Starkie, Enid. *Arthur Rimbaud.* New York: New Directions, 1961.

Stein, Gertrude. *As Fine as Melanctha.* New Haven: Yale University Press, 1954.

_____. *Fernhurst, Q.E.D. and Other Early Writings.* New York: Liveright, 1971.

_____. *The Gertrude Stein First Reader and Three Plays.* Boston: Houghton Mifflin Company, 1948.

_____. *How To Write.* New York: Dover Publications, 1975.

_____. "Identity a Poem." *What Are Masterpieces.* New York: Pitman, 1940.

_____. "Lecture 2: Narration," *The Poetics of the New American Poetry.* Edited by Donald Allen. New York: Grove Press, 1973.

_____. *The Making of Americans.* New York: Harcourt Brace, 1934.

_____. *Selected Writings of Gertrude Stein.* Edited by Carl Van Vechten. New York: Random House, 1962.

_____. *The Yale Gertrude Stein.* Edited by Richard Kostelanetz. New Haven: Yale University Press, 1980.

Stern, J. P. *Lichtenberg: A Doctrine of Scattered Occasions.* Bloomington: Indiana University Press, 1959.

Stewart, Allegra. *Gertrude Stein and the Present.* Cambridge, Mass.: Harvard University Press, 1967.

Stewart, Susan. *On Longing.* Baltimore: The Johns Hopkins University Press, 1985.

Stierle, Karlheinz. "Identité du discours et transgression lyrique." Translated by Jean-Paul Colin. *Poétique* 32 (November 1977), pp. 422-41.

Stuart, Colin Christopher, and John Scoggan. "The Orientation of the Parasols." *boundary 2: Jack Spicer* 6:1 (Fall 1977), pp. 191-257.

Tedlock, Dennis. "Beyond Logocentrism: Trace and Voice Among the Quiché Maya," *boundary 2* 8:1 (Fall 1979), pp. 321-33.

_____. *The Spoken Word and the Work of Interpretation.* Philadelphia: University of Pennsylvania Press, 1983.

Tisdale, Celes, ed. *Betcha Ain't: Poems from Attica.* Detroit: Broadside Press, 1974.

Tomashevsky, Boris. "Thematics." *Russian Formalist Criticism.* Edited by L. T. Lemon and M. J. Reis. Lincoln: University of Nebraska Press, 1965, pp. 61-95.

Toomey, John J., and Edward Rankin. *History of South Boston.* Boston: 1901.

"Tribute to a Street Poet." *People's Tribune* 13:6 (March 7, 1986), p. 7.

Trinh T. Minh-ha. "Introduction." *Discourse: A Journal for Theoretical Studies in Media and Culture.* 2:1 (Spring-Summer 1989), pp. 5-17.

_____. *When the Moon Waxes Red: Representation, Gender and Cultural Politics.* New York: Routledge, 1991.

Bibliography

Tsongas, George. "Local Color: The Passing of a Beat Boulevardier." *Bay Area Guardian* (February 1986), pp. 5ff.

Tuma, Keith. "Contemporary American Poetry and the Pseudo Avant-Garde." *Chicago Review* 36:3-4 (Summer 1990), pp. 43-50.

Turner, Victor. *The Forest of Symbols*. Ithaca: Cornell University Press, 1967.

_____. *The Ritual Process: Structure and Anti-Structure*. Ithaca: Cornell University Press, 1969.

Tytell, John. *Naked Angels*. New York: McGraw Hill, 1976.

Victorian Studies 29:1 (Autumn 1985).

Von Hallberg, Robert. *American Poetry and Culture, 1945-1980*. Cambridge, Mass.: Harvard University Press, 1985.

Waldman, Anne, and Webb, Marilyn, eds. *Talking Poetics from Naropa Institute*, Vol. 1. Boulder: Shambhala, 1978.

Walker, Alice. *In Search of Our Mothers' Gardens*. New York: Harcourt Brace Jovanovich, 1983.

Wallace, Michelle. *Black Macho and the Myth of the Superwoman*. New York: Verso, 1990.

Watt, Ian P. *The Rise of the Novel*. Berkeley: University of California Press, 1957.

Weininger, Otto. *Sex and Character*. New York: G. P. Putnam's Sons, 1906.

Whitman, Walt. *Democratic Vistas*. In *Complete Prose*. Boston: 1898.

_____. *Leaves of Grass*. In *The Complete Poems*. Edited by Francis Murphy. Harmondsworth, England: Penguin, 1986.

Wieners, John. *Selected Poems*. Santa Barbara: Black Sparrow Press, 1986.

Wildey, Lynne. "Letter to the Editor: Another Side of Bob Kaufman." *The Berkeley Monthly* (May 1986), p. 5.

Williams, Anne. *Prophetic Strain: The Greater Lyric in the Eighteenth Century*. Chicago: University of Chicago Press, 1984.

Williams, Tennessee. *In the Winter of Cities: Collected Poems*. New York: New Directions, 1964.

Williamson, Alan. *Pity the Monsters: The Political Vision of Robert Lowell*. New Haven: Yale University Press, 1974.

Willis, Paul. *Profane Culture*. London: Routledge and Kegan Paul, 1978.

Willis, Susan. "Eruptions of Funk: Historicizing Toni Morrison." *Black Literature and Literary Theory*. Edited by Henry Louis Gates, Jr. London: Methuen, 1984, pp. 263-83.

Winans, A. D. "The Beat Goes On." *Second Coming* 14:1 (1986), pp. 5-9.

Winkler, Jack. "Garden of Nymphs: Public and Private in Sappho's Lyrics." *Women's Studies* 8 (1981) pp. 65-91.

Wittig, Monique. *Les Guerrillères*. Translated by David Le Vay. New York: Viking, 1971.

Wolfson, Nessa, and Joan Manes. *The Language of Inequality*. New York: Mouton, 1985.

Yingling, Thomas. *Hart Crane and the Homosexual Text*. Chicago: University of Chicago Press, 1990.

Young, Ian. *The Male Muse*. Trumansburg, N.Y.: The Crossing Press, 1973.

_____. *Son of the Male Muse*. Trumansburg, N.Y.: The Crossing Press, 1983.

Zobel, Hiller B. *The Boston Massacre*. New York: Norton, 1970.

Zyzzyva 1:4 (Winter, 1985).

Index

Compiled by Frieda Knobloch

Index

Index

Confessional school, 117, 119, 122
Cooder, Ry, 1
Coolidge, Clark, 215
Cortez, Jayne, 69
countermemory, 5
Cowley, Malcolm, 66
Crane, Hart, 8, 146, 148, 157, 239; and Duncan, 196; and Kaufman, 46, 56-57, 63, 65-68, 75; and Spicer, 199
Crane, Stephen, 106, 107
Creely, Robert, 24, 100, 121, 223
Crossing Press, the, 168
Cullen, Countee, 40, 119

Dante Alighieri, 57, 188, 199, 200
"Dark End of the Street, The," 1-2, 3-4
Dark End of the Street, The, 2-4, 5
Darwin, Charles, 231
Davis, Bette, 64
Davis, Miles, 69, 70, 71, 75
Dearborn, Mary, 226
death, 146-47; interchangeable with life, 44-48
deconstruction, 222
defamiliarization, vii, xvii, 5, 166, 222
Deleuze, Gilles, and Félix Guattari, xiii, 12, 26, 29, 30, 202-5, 217-18, 219, 222
Democratic Vistas (Whitman), 148-49
Derrida, Jacques, 2, 24, 25, 37, 176, 222
Descartes, René, 221
deterritorialization, vii, 5-6, 27, 144, 202, 204, 219
Dickinson, Emily, 100, 108
discontinuity, ix-x, xiv, 24
discourse: dominant, 9; philosophical, 22. *See also* poetry, as antidiscursive
doggerel, 206-12, 214, 218, 221, 226, 227
domesticity, 215, 216, 221, 229, 232
Don Juan (Byron), 210
Doolittle, Hilda (H.D.), 207
Douglass, Frederick, 40, 58-59, 63, 64, 206, 239
Doyle, Arthur Conan, 192
drum, West African, 68, 71-73
Dubois, Page, 16-18, 25
Du Bois, W. E. B., 8, 30, 31, 40, 68
Duke, David, 93
Duncan, Isadora, 207

Duncan, Robert, xv, xviii, 5-7, 32, 54-55, 143, 177, 189-99, 208, 227, 240; and Robin Blaser, 153, 192; and Hart Crane, 196; and Jess Collins, 177, 184; and Allen Ginsberg, 143; and Ernst Kantorowicz, 153-54; and Christopher Marlowe, 196-97; and Jack Spicer, 143-45, 153, 157-58, 173, 174, 176, 179, 182, 184, 187, 200; and Walt Whitman, 148, 152-53, 187, 188, 190, 194, 196
Duncan, Robert, works cited: *Bending the Bow,* 186, 191; *Caesar's Gate,* 199; "Changing Perspectives in Reading Whitman," 152; "Chords: Passages 14," 191; "Epilogos," 187; "Fairyland, the Shining Land," 191; "The Fire: Passages 13," 188; Gay Sunshine interview, 184-85, 187, 194; *Groundwork I: Before the War,* 187; *Groundwork II: In the Dark,* 187; "The H.D. Book," 145; "The Homosexual in Society," 178; "Introduction: The War," 188-89; "King Haydn of Miami Beach," 180; "Mother Brother Door and Bed," 180, 183, 186, 189; "Passages" series, 145, 187; "Random Lines: A Discourse on Love," 181; "Sonnet 4," 186; "5th Sonnet," 186; "Spelling: Passages 15," 191; "Structure of Rime," 145; "Such is the Sickness of Many a Good Thing," 187; "The Torso: Passages 18," 192-95; "Treesbank Poems," 182, 186
Dunn, Joe, 158

écriture féminine, 234
Edward the Second (Marlowe), 196-97
Eliot, T. S., 8, 48, 49, 121, 136, 144, 184
Else, Gerald, 15
Emerson, Ralph Waldo, 119, 130, 142
Enkidu Surrogate, 198
Equiano, Olaudah, 58
eroticism, ix-x, 150, 155; and language, 143, 161
essentialism, 124, 204; psychic, 117; strategic, 112
ethnicity, 12, 117, 228
ethnopoetics, 21
exile, 7, 19, 29; language in, 215, 218, 229

Index

existentialism, 36, 63

family, the, 114, 115, 117, 138
fascism, 154-55
feminism, French, 134, 233-34
feminist philosophers and therapists, 138
feminization: of outsiders, 204, 207; of poetry, 7
Fischer, Michael, 12
Flaubert, Gustav, 25, 34, 119, 124
Fleurs du Mal, Les (Baudelaire), 25
Foucault, Michel, 18, 24, 25, 78, 117
fragmentation, 22, 75, 240
Franklin, Aretha, 1
Franklin, Benjamin, 212
Franklin, H. Bruce, xiii
Freud, Sigmund, 115-16, 119, 231
Freudianism, 117
Frye, Northrop, 208, 226

Gandhi, 111
Gandhi, Mohandas, 42
Gans, Eric, 21
Garvey, Marcus, 59
Gates, Henry Louis, Jr., 12, 54, 64, 112, 206
gay activism, 144, 156, 164
gay community, 143, 155, 156, 168; and Duncan, 183, 186, 197; and Spicer, 144, 158-65, 172-78
gay community in San Francisco, 156-57
gay cultural crossover with Beats, 156-57, 163
gay culture/scene, 6, 66, 146, 155, 156, 199; coming/being out, 178; and Jewish ghetto experience, 185; and Spicer, 158, 160-65, 167-70, 171, 176, 178
gay history, 156-57, 158
gayness/gay identity, 160, 164-65, 177-78, 179
gay people, 170, 204, 229
gay poetic tradition, 143-44, 145-46, 150-51, 173; and Duncan, 145, 196; and Spicer, 145, 173, 176
gay poets, 167, 170, 178
gay presses, 168
gay punk, 173

gay vernacular, 147, 161, 169. *See also* angels
gaze, the, 103
Geertz, Clifford, 32
Genesis Angels: The Saga of Lew Welsh and the Beat Generation (Saroyan), 168
gender, 11, 12, 117, 230, 232
Genet, Jean, 4, 7, 11, 37, 42, 77, 79, 107, 119, 203, 239
Genealogy of Morals, On the (Nietzsche), 14
George, Stefan, 153, 200
George-kreis/coterie, 153, 154, 159
ghosts, 171-72, 175, 179, 182
Gillespie, Dizzy, 69, 70
Gilman, Sander, 218-19, 233, 234
Gino and Carlo's, 157
Ginsberg, Allen, 8, 60, 122, 130, 142-43, 150-51, 156, 168, 177. *See also* Spicer, Jack
graffiti writers, 96
Grahn, Judy, xiii, 22, 157, 193, 198
Great Chain of Being, The (Lovejoy), 14
Great Chain of Being, the, xii, xiv, 8, 12-16, 56-58, 118, 133, 169, 188, 198, 204, 206, 224
griots, West African, 68; and Kaufman, 73-76
Guattari, Félix. *See* Deleuze, Gilles
Guerrillères, Les (Wittig), 210
Gunn, Thom, 147, 157

Hallberg, Robert Von, 9-10, 141
Hawkes, John, viii
Hawthorne, Nathaniel, 209
Heart's Needle, The (Snodgrass), 123
Heidegger, Martin, 24
Henderson, David, 35
Henderson, Stephen, 68
Hermes, 191
Herndon, Jim, 173
hierarchy, xiv, 13-16, 100, 183, 186
Higginson, Thomas, 100
high culture, 105; as masculinized, 77, 79; and mass culture, 8, 207

Index

Nietzsche, Friedrich, 14-15, 24, 37, 146, 204
Nilon, Charles, 36
Nin, Anaïs, xvii
Norse, Harold, 168
nostalgia, 106, 110-15, 120, 218; and Duncan, 145; and Lowell, 122, 134-35, 141; radical, 111, 113, 120, 139, 141; and South Boston Poets, 122
Novalis, 113
novel, the, 121

objective correlative, 104-5, 136, 137, 144
obscenity, 142, 158
Odyssey, The, 110, 113, 207
O'Hara, Frank, 151
Oliver, Paul, 74
Olson, Charles, 8, 169
On Longing (Stewart), 108
Opffer, Emil, 65, 66
oppression, xi-xii, 6, 8, 22, 40, 49, 56, 146, 178; categories of, 11-12
Orgasms of Light (Leyland), 168
Orlovsky, Peter, 177
Orphée, 175
Orpheus, 75, 197-201
Osborne, Charlotte. *See* South Boston Poets
Other, the, 8, 9, 93, 179, 194, 204; as dangerous, 16; homeborn slave as, 161
Others, 28, 60, 79, 180, 203; as contraband underminers, 9-10, 203; as outsiders, 21, 204
outsiderhood. *See* marginality; marginalization
Outsiders (Mayer), 229
Oxford English Dictionary, The, 208
Ozick, Cynthia, 112, 218, 220, 221

Paradiso (Dante), 57
Parker, Charlie, 69, 70, 184
Partisan Review, viii, 178
Passage to India, A, 111
Payne-Whitney Clinic, the, 140
Peer, E. Allison, 48
people of color, xii, 60, 204
Perloff, Marjorie, 124, 128, 136, 221
Phallus, the, 113

philosophy, Eastern, 176
philosophy, Western, 8, 12-17, 37, 185, 190, 204, 221; and poetry, 7, 10, 17-23, 37. *See also* Great Chain of Being, the
Pity the Monsters: The Political Vision of Robert Lowell (Williamson), 139
place, 6
Place, The, 157
Plath, Sylvia, 122
Plato, 7, 8, 12-13, 14, 16, 145, 153, 154, 155; and Duncan, 183-86, 197; and Spicer, 200
pleasure, 192, 238-39
Poe, Edgar Allan, 43
Poems (St. John of the Cross), 48
poems: communities of, 158-60, 161
Poet in New York, The (Lorca), 56
poet, the: as medium, 74, 155, 166, 173, 175, 178, 184, 198; as shaman, 42, 44-45, 148, 166
Poetics (Aristotle), 14, 15
poetics, antipersonal, 158-63, 173-76
poetry: as antidiscursive, vii, 22, 103; as communal/public, 22, 48, 97; as public domain, 159; and ritual, 16, 21, 44, 68, 97-98, 191; and sexuality, 180; as way of life, xvi, 33, 44
Poets, Prophets and Revolutionaries: The Literary Avant-Garde from Rimbaud through Postmodernism (Russell), viii-ix
Politics, 7, 178, 196
polyvocality, xvi
postmodernism, 9, 105, 107, 108-9, 110, 122, 176, 206
postmodern poetry, 16, 25, 104. *See also* language poetry; language poets
Pound, Ezra, viii, 8, 162, 207
Practicing Angels (Mayo), 168
primitivism, 8
prison literature, xiii, 26
privilege, 113, 119
Process and Reality (Whitehead), 192
Proust, Marcel, 25, 34
psychoanalysis, 115, 134, 137-38
psychology, popular, 115, 117

Index

Index

Maria Damon is assistant professor of English at the University of Minnesota.